BATMAN CHRONICLES

VOLUME THREE

BATMAN CREATED BY BOB KANE

ALL STORIES WRITTEN BY BILL FINGER. ALL COVERS AND STORIES PENCILED BY BOB KANE
AND INKED BY JERRY ROBINSON AND GEORGE ROUSSOS, UNLESS OTHERWISE NOTED.

* THESE STORIES WERE ORIGINALLY UNTITLED. THEY ARE TITLED HERE FOR YOUR CONVENIENCE.

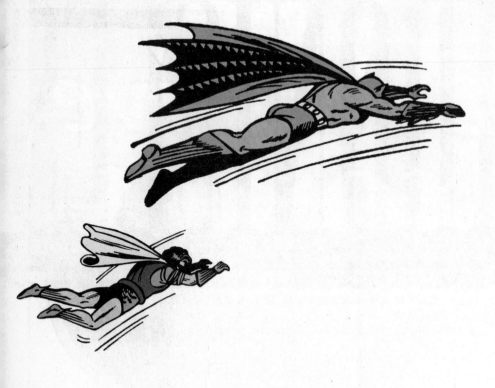

Dan DiDio SENIOR VP-EXECUTIVE EDITOR ☆ Whitney Ellsworth EDITOR-ORIGINAL SERIES ☆ Bob Joy EDITOR-COLLECTED EDITION
Robbin Brosterman SENIOR ART DIRECTOR ☆ Paul Levitz PRESIDENT & PUBLISHER ☆ Georg Brewer VP-DESIGN & DC DIRECT CREATIVE
Richard Bruning SENIOR VP-CREATIVE DIRECTOR ☆ Patrick Caldon EXECUTIVE VP-FINANCE & OPERATIONS ☆ Chris Caramalis VP-FINANCE
John Cunningham VP-MARKETING ☆ Terri Cunningham VP-MANAGING EDITOR ☆ Alison Gill VP-MANUFACTURING
Hank Kanalz VP-GENERAL MANAGER, WILDSTORM ☆ Jim Lee EDITORIAL DIRECTOR-WILDSTORM ☆ Paula Lowitt SENIOR VP-BUSINESS & LEGAL AFFAIRS
MaryEllen McLaughlin VP-ADVERTISING & CUSTOM PUBLISHING ☆ John Nee VP-BUSINESS DEVELOPMENT
Gregory Noveck SENIOR VP-CREATIVE AFFAIRS ☆ Sue Pohja VP-BOOK TRADE SALES ☆ Cheryl Rubin SENIOR VP-BRAND MANAGEMENT
Jeff Trojan VP-BUSINESS DEVELOPMENT, DC DIRECT ☆ Bob Wayne VP-SALES

Cover art by Bob Kane.

THE BATMAN CHRONICLES VOLUME 3. Published by DC Comics. Cover and compilation copyright ©2007 DC Comics.
Originally published in single magazine form in BATMAN 4-5, DETECTIVE COMICS 46-50, and WORLD'S BEST COMICS 1.
Copyright 1940-1941 DC Comics. All Rights Reserved. All characters, their distinctive likenesses and related elements featured in this
publication are trademarks of DC Comics. The stories, characters and incidents featured in this publication are entirely fictional. DC Comics does
not read or accept unsolicited submissions of ideas, stories or artwork.

DC Comics, 1700 Broadway, New York, NY 10019

A Warner Bros. Entertainment Company
Printed in Canada. First Printing.
ISBN: 1-4012-1347-2
ISBN 13: 978-1-4012-1347-3

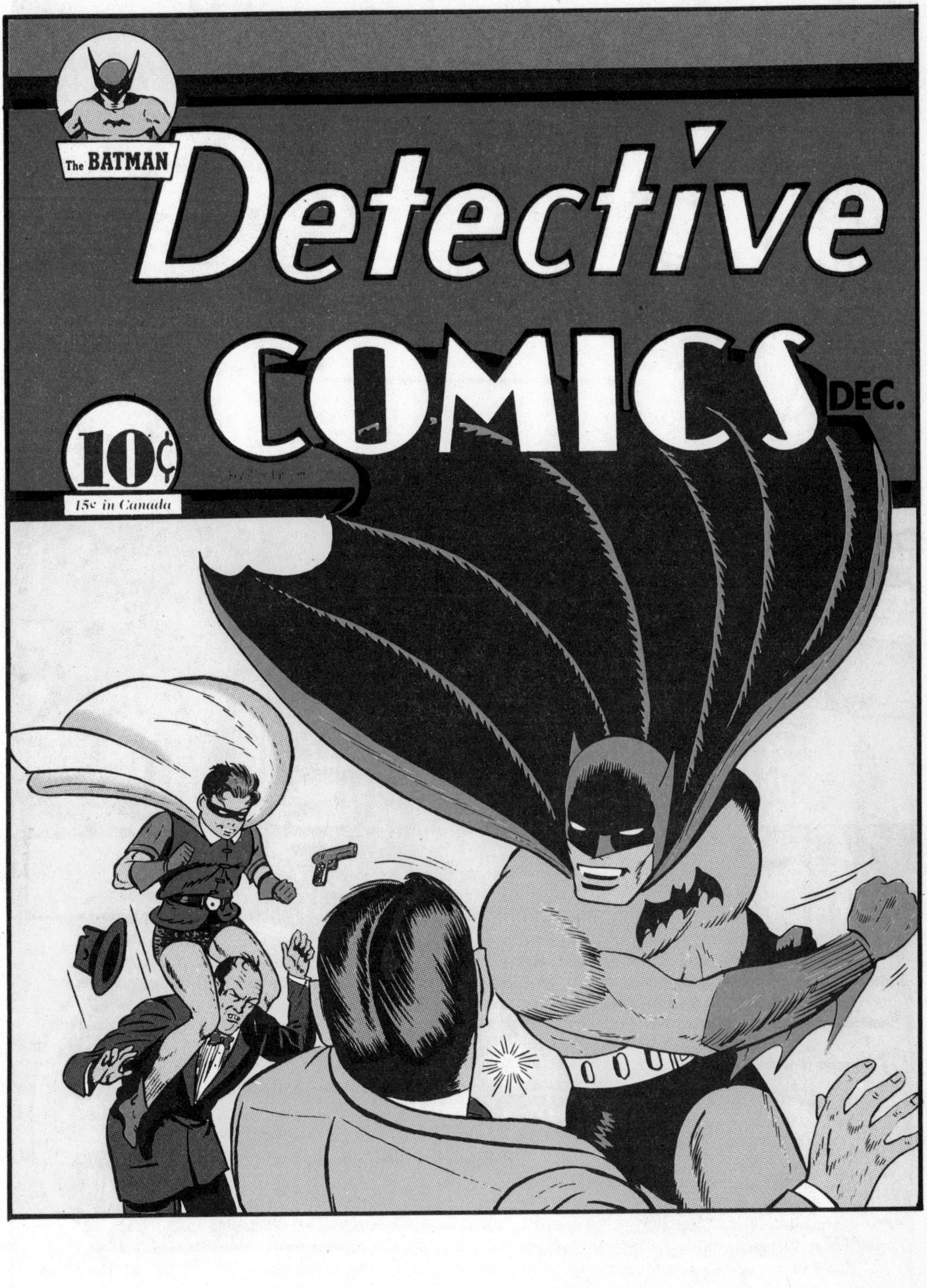
The BATMAN
Detective
COMICS
DEC.
10¢
15¢ in Canada

BAT MAN

WITH *Robin* —THE BOY WONDER—

BY BOB KANE

ONCE AGAIN CRIME REARS ITS UGLY HEAD TO PREY UPON SOCIETY..... AND ONCE AGAIN EMERGES THAT SUPER-FOE OF CRIME — THE **BATMAN!** GARBED IN THE HUES OF NIGHT ITSELF, HE HOVERS ABOVE THE HORDES OF EVIL LIKE IMPENDING DOOM..... AND ALWAYS AT HIS SIDE, LIKE A STRONG RIGHT ARM, IS GRINNING, RECKLESS **ROBIN**, THE BOY WONDER, WHO IS SOMETHING OF A CRIME-BUSTER IN HIS OWN RIGHT!

FLETCHER SILVER CO.

AS THE THIEVES BEGIN TO LOOT A WAREHOUSE, SUDDENLY A BAT-CLOAKED SHAPE SWINGS OVER THEIR HEADS...

...TO PLUMMET DOWN LIGHTLY ATOP THE WAREHOUSE STEPS!

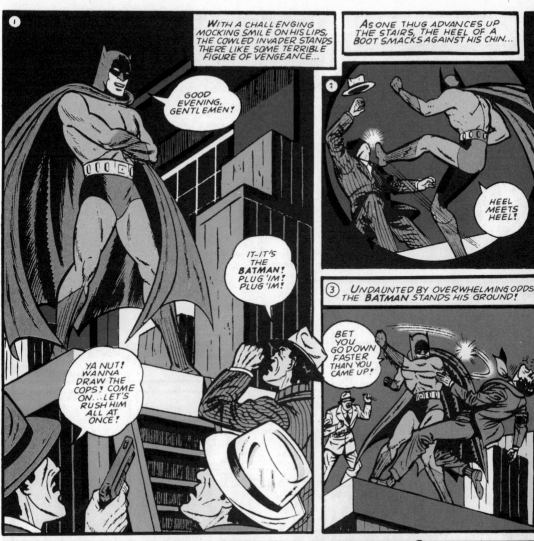

WITH A CHALLENGING MOCKING SMILE ON HIS LIPS, THE COWLED INVADER STANDS THERE LIKE SOME TERRIBLE FIGURE OF VENGEANCE...

GOOD EVENING, GENTLEMEN!

AS ONE THUG ADVANCES UP THE STAIRS, THE HEEL OF A BOOT SMACKS AGAINST HIS CHIN...

HEEL MEETS HEEL!

IT-IT'S THE BATMAN! PLUG 'IM! PLUG 'IM!

YA NUT! WANNA DRAW THE COPS! COME ON...LET'S RUSH HIM ALL AT ONCE!

③ UNDAUNTED BY OVERWHELMING ODDS, THE BATMAN STANDS HIS GROUND!

BET YOU GO DOWN FASTER THAN YOU CAME UP!

④ THE CRACK OF A BOARD WARNS THE BATMAN OF DANGER AND.....

CUTE LITTLE CUT-UP, AREN'T YOU?

⑤ PICKING THE MAN UP AS IF HE WERE A CHILD.....

⑥ ...HE HURLS HIM AT THE ONCOMING HOODLUMS!

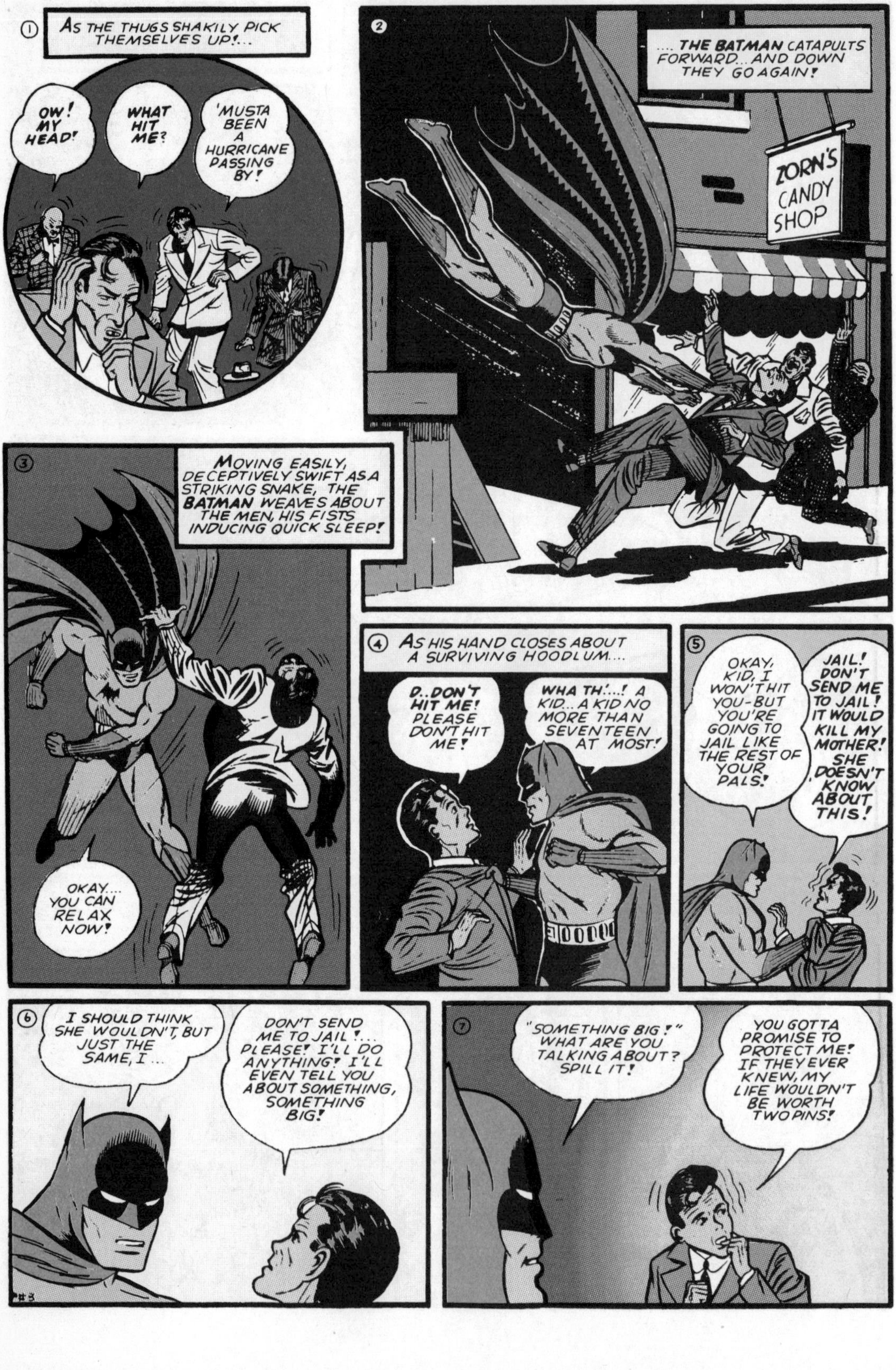
AS THE THUGS SHAKILY PICK THEMSELVES UP!...
OW! MY HEAD!
WHAT HIT ME?
'MUSTA BEEN A HURRICANE PASSING BY!
.... THE BATMAN CATAPULTS FORWARD... AND DOWN THEY GO AGAIN!
ZORN'S CANDY SHOP
MOVING EASILY, DECEPTIVELY SWIFT AS A STRIKING SNAKE, THE BATMAN WEAVES ABOUT THE MEN, HIS FISTS INDUCING QUICK SLEEP!
OKAY.... YOU CAN RELAX NOW!
AS HIS HAND CLOSES ABOUT A SURVIVING HOODLUM....
D..DON'T HIT ME! PLEASE DON'T HIT ME!
WHA TH'...! A KID... A KID NO MORE THAN SEVENTEEN AT MOST!
OKAY, KID, I WON'T HIT YOU-BUT YOU'RE GOING TO JAIL LIKE THE REST OF YOUR PALS!
JAIL! DON'T SEND ME TO JAIL! IT WOULD KILL MY MOTHER! SHE DOESN'T KNOW ABOUT THIS!
I SHOULD THINK SHE WOULDN'T, BUT JUST THE SAME, I ...
DON'T SEND ME TO JAIL!... PLEASE! I'LL DO ANYTHING! I'LL EVEN TELL YOU ABOUT SOMETHING, SOMETHING BIG!
"SOMETHING BIG!" WHAT ARE YOU TALKING ABOUT? SPILL IT!
YOU GOTTA PROMISE TO PROTECT ME! IF THEY EVER KNEW, MY LIFE WOULDN'T BE WORTH TWO PINS!

THESE MEN CAN'T HEAR A THING! THEY'RE BLISSFULLY UNCONSCIOUS OF EVERYTHING! TALK!

WELL.... CARSTAIRS, THE RACKETEER, IS PLANNING SOMETHING, CAUSE HE GOT A BIG GANG TOGETHER LAST NIGHT!... HE SAYS WE'RE GONNA BE MILLIONAIRES IF WE STRING ALONG WITH HIM!

HE SAYS THE PEOPLE AND THE COPS WON'T PUT UP ANY FIGHT WHEN WE DO OUR JOBS! HE'S WORKING WITH SOME PROFESSOR THAT PLANNED THE WHOLE THING!

ALL OF US GOT A VIAL OF THESE PILLS. THEY'RE SUPPOSED TO MAKE US IMMUNE TO THE PROFESSOR'S STUFF IF WE SWALLOW ONE!

IN THAT CASE, I'LL TAKE A FEW PILLS WITH ME. THEY MIGHT COME IN HANDY AT THE RIGHT MOMENT! NOW... WHEN IS THE NEXT MEETING OF CARSTAIRS' MEN?

ER SILVER CO.

WE'RE SUPPOSED TO GO TO ONE TONIGHT!.... BUT IT LOOKS LIKE THESE GUYS WON'T BE ABLE TO GO.... IF YOU'RE GONNA TURN 'EM IN!

BOTH YOU AND THESE MEN WILL GO! IT WILL BE WORTH IT IF I CAN FIND OUT A WAY TO COMBAT THE PROFESSOR'S MENACE TO THE PEOPLE.

YOU'RE GOING TO THAT MEETING TONIGHT! I'LL MEET YOU HERE TOMORROW NIGHT AT TWELVE SHARP! YOU'RE TO TELL ME ALL THAT WENT ON! UNDERSTAND?

(GULP!) OKAY, IF YOU SAY SO!

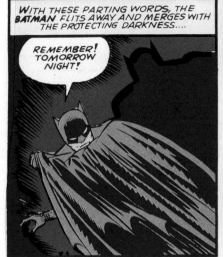

WITH THESE PARTING WORDS, THE BATMAN FLITS AWAY AND MERGES WITH THE PROTECTING DARKNESS....

REMEMBER! TOMORROW NIGHT!

GONE! ...IT'S... IT'S AS IF HE DISAPPEARED IN THE SHADOWS-- LIKE-LIKE A GHOST!

SOMETIME LATER THE HOODLUMS AWAKEN, AND RISE ON SHAK'Y LEGS.....

GOSH! ME JAW FEELS AS IF IT'S BROKE!

THE BATMAN! HE AIN'T HERE! WADAYA SUPPOSE HAPPENED?

IT'S A BREAK FER US, ANYWAY! C'MON, LET'S GET GOIN' T' THAT MEETIN'! ---BUT QUICK!

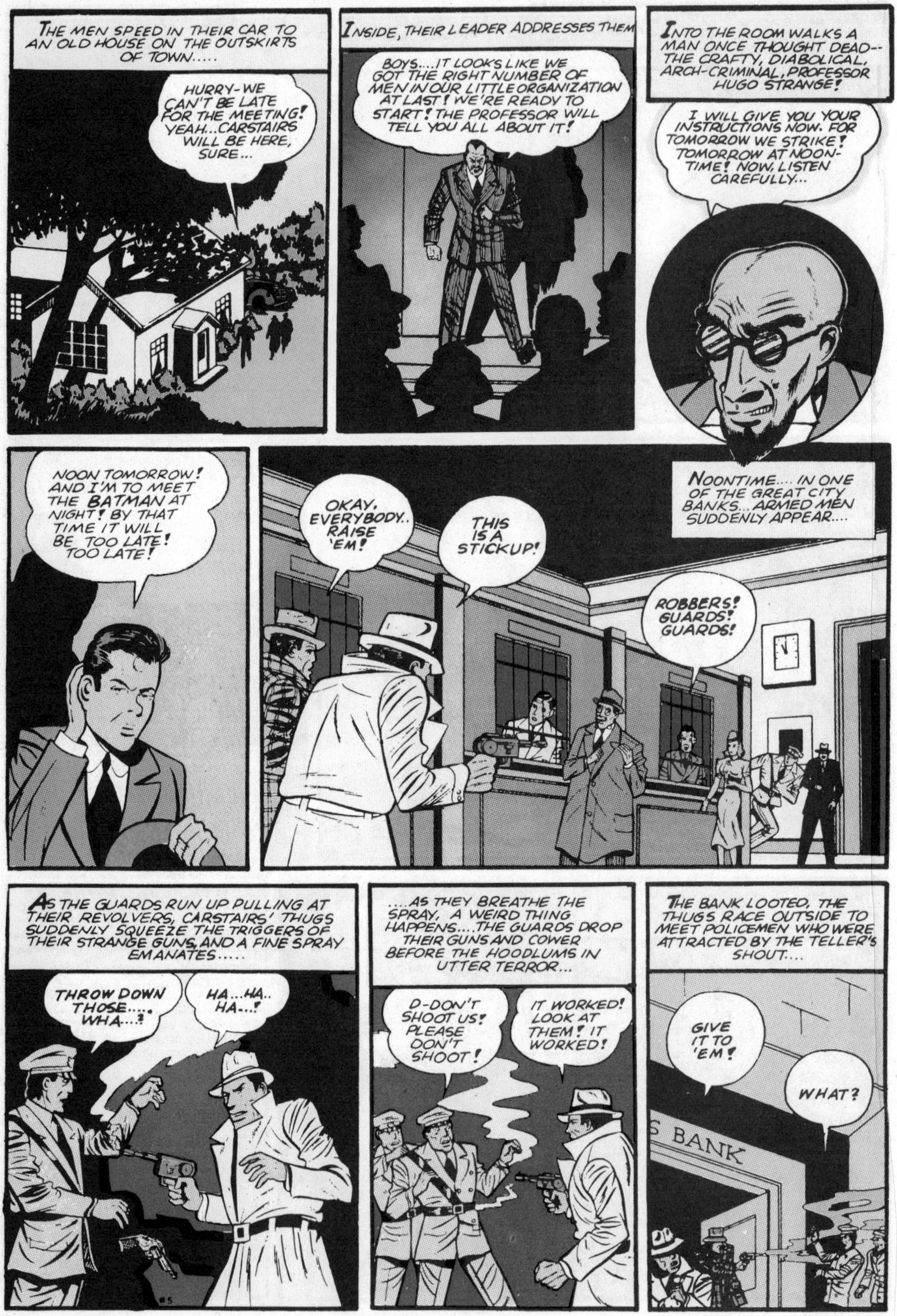
THE MEN SPEED IN THEIR CAR TO AN OLD HOUSE ON THE OUTSKIRTS OF TOWN.....
HURRY-WE CAN'T BE LATE FOR THE MEETING! YEAH...CARSTAIRS WILL BE HERE, SURE...
INSIDE, THEIR LEADER ADDRESSES THEM
BOYS....IT LOOKS LIKE WE GOT THE RIGHT NUMBER OF MEN IN OUR LITTLE ORGANIZATION AT LAST! WE'RE READY TO START! THE PROFESSOR WILL TELL YOU ALL ABOUT IT!
INTO THE ROOM WALKS A MAN ONCE THOUGHT DEAD-- THE CRAFTY, DIABOLICAL, ARCH-CRIMINAL, PROFESSOR HUGO STRANGE!
I WILL GIVE YOU YOUR INSTRUCTIONS NOW. FOR TOMORROW WE STRIKE! TOMORROW AT NOON-TIME! NOW, LISTEN CAREFULLY...
NOON TOMORROW! AND I'M TO MEET THE BATMAN AT NIGHT! BY THAT TIME IT WILL BE TOO LATE! TOO LATE!
NOONTIME.... IN ONE OF THE GREAT CITY BANKS... ARMED MEN SUDDENLY APPEAR....
OKAY, EVERYBODY.. RAISE 'EM!
THIS IS A STICKUP!
ROBBERS! GUARDS! GUARDS!
AS THE GUARDS RUN UP PULLING AT THEIR REVOLVERS, CARSTAIRS' THUGS SUDDENLY SQUEEZE THE TRIGGERS OF THEIR STRANGE GUNS, AND A FINE SPRAY EMANATES.....
THROW DOWN THOSE..... WHA...?
HA...HA.. HA...!
.....AS THEY BREATHE THE SPRAY, A WEIRD THING HAPPENS....THE GUARDS DROP THEIR GUNS AND COWER BEFORE THE HOODLUMS IN UTTER TERROR...
D-DON'T SHOOT US! PLEASE DON'T SHOOT!
IT WORKED! LOOK AT THEM! IT WORKED!
THE BANK LOOTED, THE THUGS RACE OUTSIDE TO MEET POLICEMEN WHO WERE ATTRACTED BY THE TELLER'S SHOUT....
GIVE IT TO 'EM!
WHAT?
S BANK

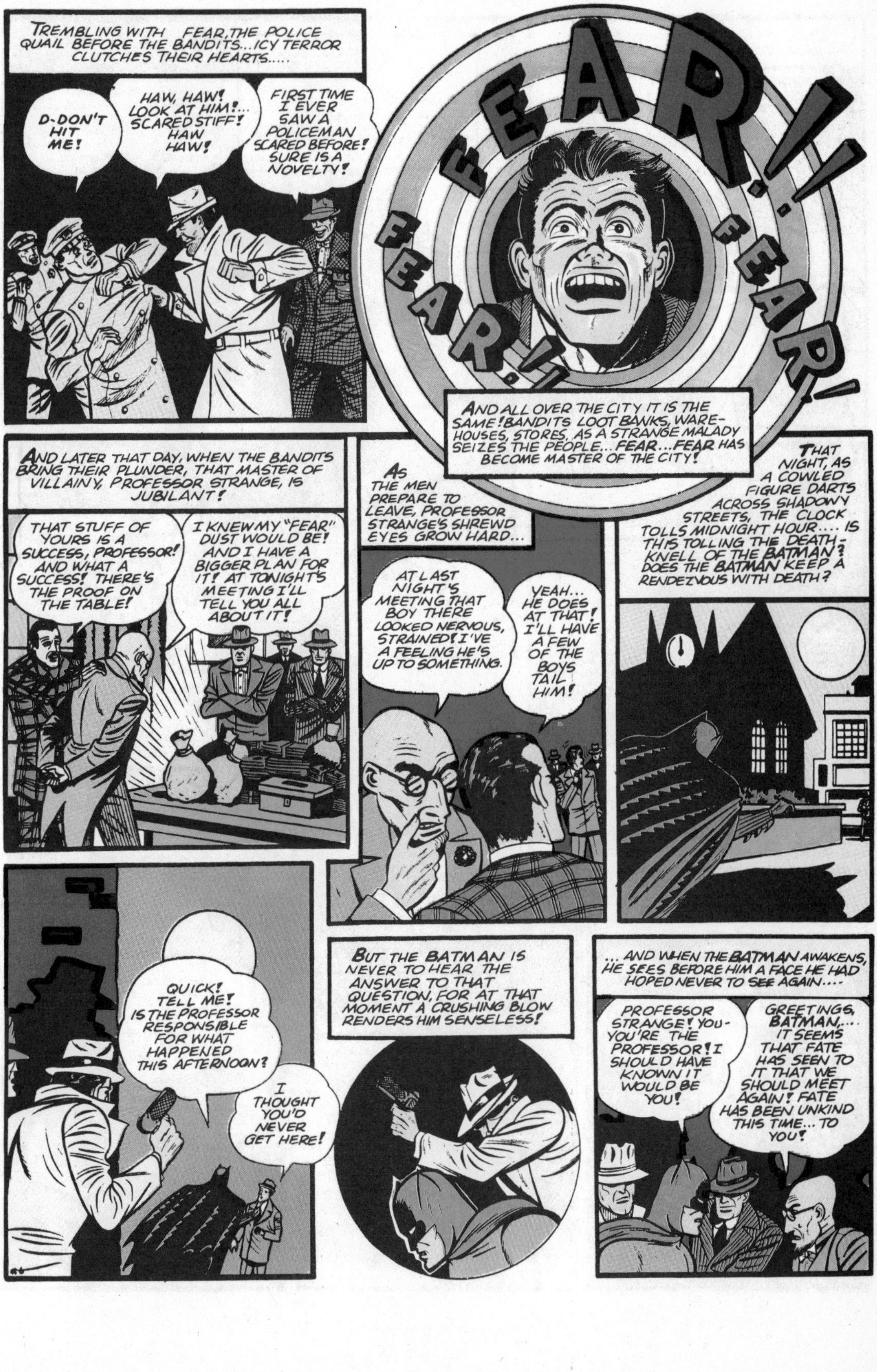
TREMBLING WITH FEAR, THE POLICE QUAIL BEFORE THE BANDITS... ICY TERROR CLUTCHES THEIR HEARTS.....
D-DON'T HIT ME!
HAW, HAW! LOOK AT HIM!... SCARED STIFF! HAW HAW!
FIRST TIME I EVER SAW A POLICEMAN SCARED BEFORE! SURE IS A NOVELTY!
FEAR!! FEAR! FEAR!!
AND ALL OVER THE CITY IT IS THE SAME! BANDITS LOOT BANKS, WAREHOUSES, STORES, AS A STRANGE MALADY SEIZES THE PEOPLE... FEAR... FEAR HAS BECOME MASTER OF THE CITY!
AND LATER THAT DAY, WHEN THE BANDITS BRING THEIR PLUNDER, THAT MASTER OF VILLAINY, PROFESSOR STRANGE, IS JUBILANT!
THAT STUFF OF YOURS IS A SUCCESS, PROFESSOR! AND WHAT A SUCCESS! THERE'S THE PROOF ON THE TABLE!
I KNEW MY "FEAR" DUST WOULD BE! AND I HAVE A BIGGER PLAN FOR IT! AT TONIGHT'S MEETING I'LL TELL YOU ALL ABOUT IT!
AS THE MEN PREPARE TO LEAVE, PROFESSOR STRANGE'S SHREWD EYES GROW HARD...
AT LAST NIGHT'S MEETING THAT BOY THERE LOOKED NERVOUS, STRAINED! I'VE A FEELING HE'S UP TO SOMETHING.
YEAH... HE DOES AT THAT! I'LL HAVE A FEW OF THE BOYS TAIL HIM!
THAT NIGHT, AS A COWLED FIGURE DARTS ACROSS SHADOWY STREETS, THE CLOCK TOLLS MIDNIGHT HOUR.... IS THIS TOLLING THE DEATH-KNELL OF THE BATMAN? DOES THE BATMAN KEEP A RENDEZVOUS WITH DEATH?
QUICK! TELL ME! IS THE PROFESSOR RESPONSIBLE FOR WHAT HAPPENED THIS AFTERNOON?
I THOUGHT YOU'D NEVER GET HERE!
BUT THE BATMAN IS NEVER TO HEAR THE ANSWER TO THAT QUESTION, FOR AT THAT MOMENT A CRUSHING BLOW RENDERS HIM SENSELESS!
... AND WHEN THE BATMAN AWAKENS, HE SEES BEFORE HIM A FACE HE HAD HOPED NEVER TO SEE AGAIN....
PROFESSOR STRANGE! YOU-YOU'RE THE PROFESSOR! I SHOULD HAVE KNOWN IT WOULD BE YOU!
GREETINGS, BATMAN,... IT SEEMS THAT FATE HAS SEEN TO IT THAT WE SHOULD MEET AGAIN! FATE HAS BEEN UNKIND THIS TIME... TO YOU!

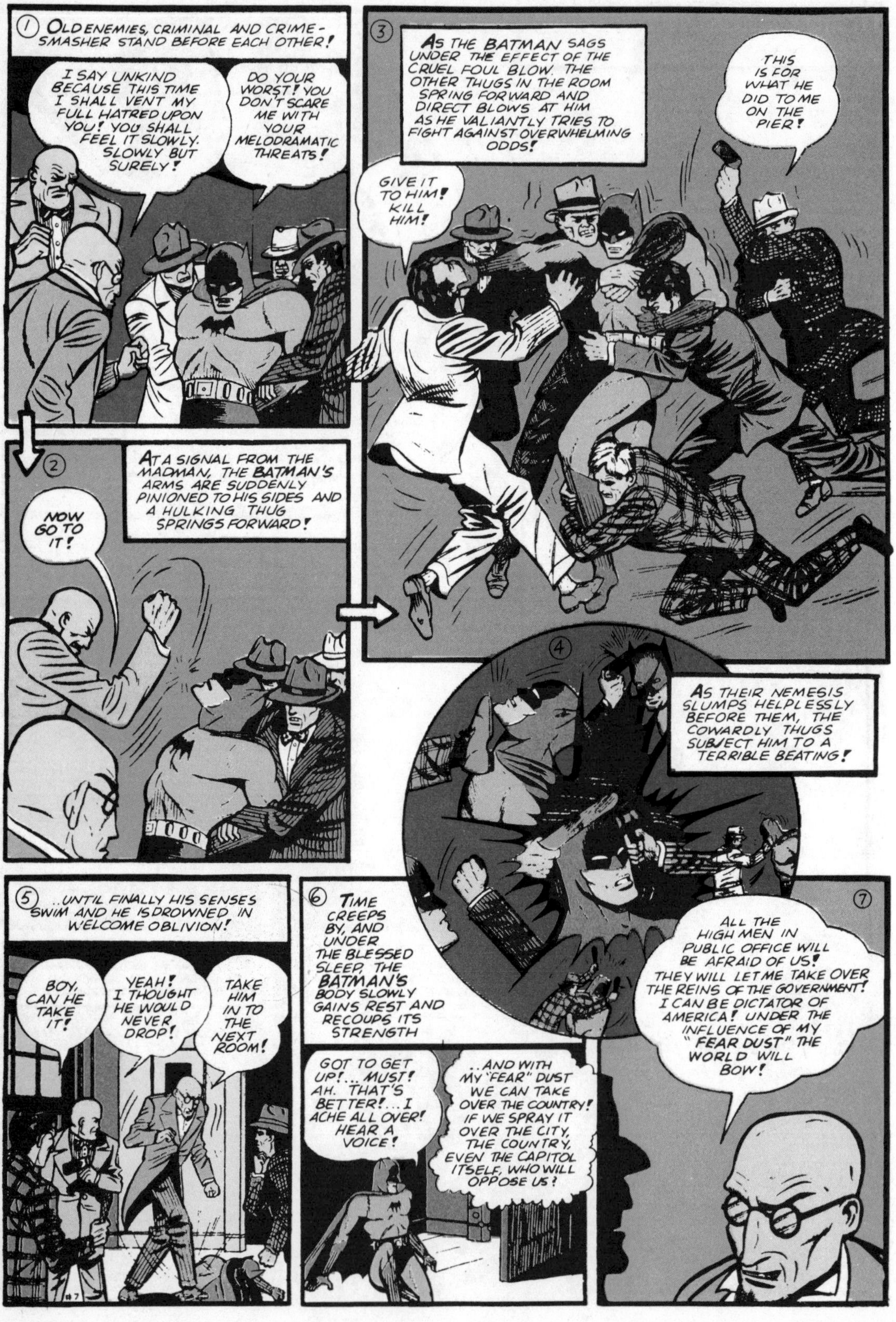
1
OLD ENEMIES, CRIMINAL AND CRIME-SMASHER STAND BEFORE EACH OTHER!
I SAY UNKIND BECAUSE THIS TIME I SHALL VENT MY FULL HATRED UPON YOU! YOU SHALL FEEL IT SLOWLY. SLOWLY BUT SURELY!
DO YOUR WORST! YOU DON'T SCARE ME WITH YOUR MELODRAMATIC THREATS!
2
AT A SIGNAL FROM THE MADMAN, THE BATMAN'S ARMS ARE SUDDENLY PINIONED TO HIS SIDES AND A HULKING THUG SPRINGS FORWARD!
NOW GO TO IT!
3
AS THE BATMAN SAGS UNDER THE EFFECT OF THE CRUEL FOUL BLOW, THE OTHER THUGS IN THE ROOM SPRING FORWARD AND DIRECT BLOWS AT HIM AS HE VALIANTLY TRIES TO FIGHT AGAINST OVERWHELMING ODDS!
GIVE IT TO HIM! KILL HIM!
THIS IS FOR WHAT HE DID TO ME ON THE PIER!
4
AS THEIR NEMESIS SLUMPS HELPLESSLY BEFORE THEM, THE COWARDLY THUGS SUBJECT HIM TO A TERRIBLE BEATING!
5
..UNTIL FINALLY HIS SENSES SWIM AND HE IS DROWNED IN WELCOME OBLIVION!
BOY, CAN HE TAKE IT!
YEAH! I THOUGHT HE WOULD NEVER DROP!
TAKE HIM IN TO THE NEXT ROOM!
6
TIME CREEPS BY, AND UNDER THE BLESSED SLEEP, THE BATMAN'S BODY SLOWLY GAINS REST AND RECOUPS ITS STRENGTH
GOT TO GET UP!... MUST! AH. THAT'S BETTER!... I ACHE ALL OVER! HEAR A VOICE!
..AND WITH MY "FEAR" DUST WE CAN TAKE OVER THE COUNTRY! IF WE SPRAY IT OVER THE CITY, THE COUNTRY, EVEN THE CAPITOL ITSELF, WHO WILL OPPOSE US?
7
ALL THE HIGH MEN IN PUBLIC OFFICE WILL BE AFRAID OF US! THEY WILL LET ME TAKE OVER THE REINS OF THE GOVERNMENT! I CAN BE DICTATOR OF AMERICA! UNDER THE INFLUENCE OF MY "FEAR DUST" THE WORLD WILL BOW!

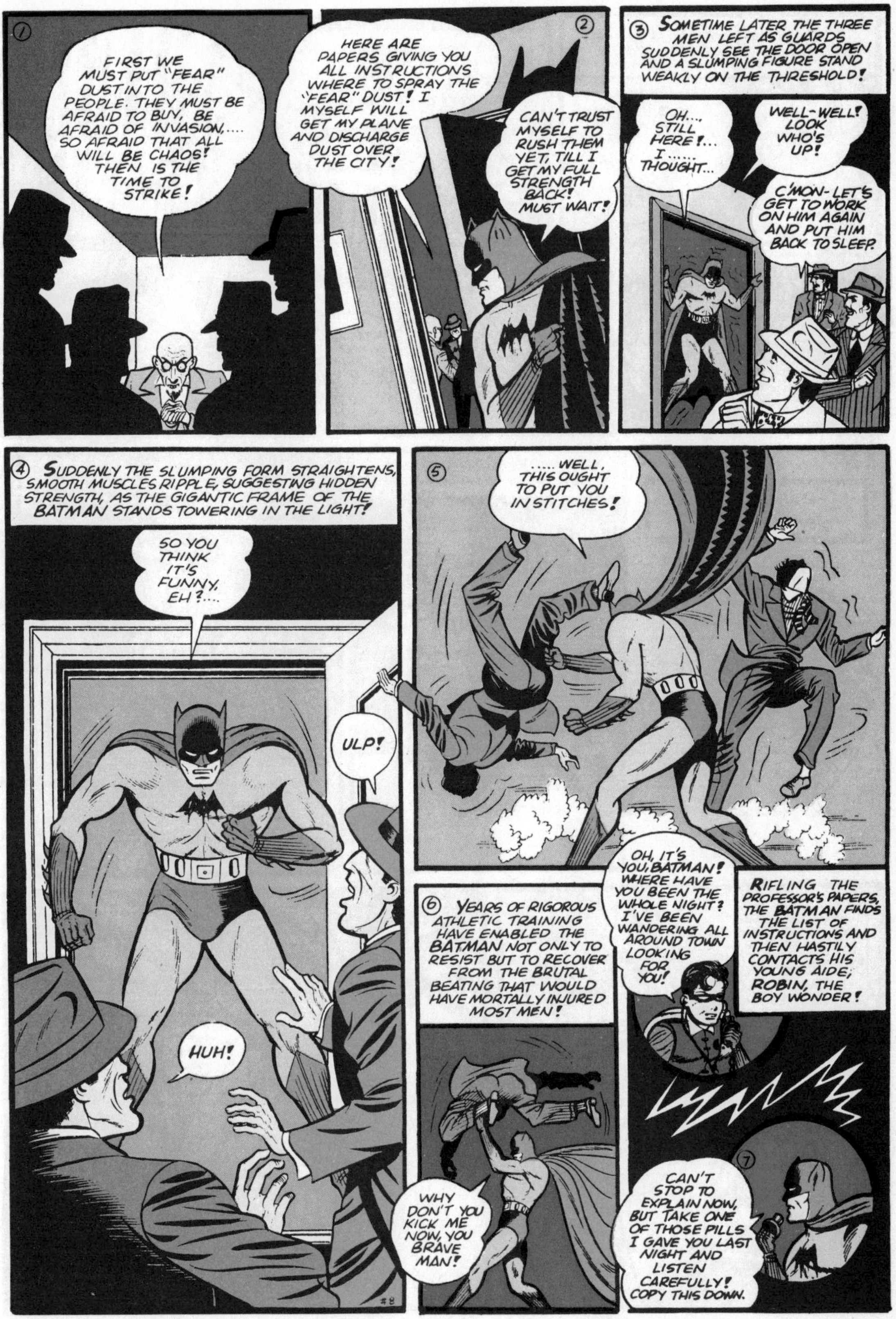
1
FIRST WE MUST PUT "FEAR" DUST INTO THE PEOPLE. THEY MUST BE AFRAID TO BUY, BE AFRAID OF INVASION,.... SO AFRAID THAT ALL WILL BE CHAOS! THEN IS THE TIME TO STRIKE!
2
HERE ARE PAPERS GIVING YOU ALL INSTRUCTIONS WHERE TO SPRAY THE "FEAR" DUST! I MYSELF WILL GET MY PLANE AND DISCHARGE DUST OVER THE CITY!
CAN'T TRUST MYSELF TO RUSH THEM YET, TILL I GET MY FULL STRENGTH BACK! MUST WAIT!
3 SOMETIME LATER THE THREE MEN LEFT AS GUARDS SUDDENLY SEE THE DOOR OPEN AND A SLUMPING FIGURE STAND WEAKLY ON THE THRESHOLD!
OH... STILL HERE!... I...... THOUGHT...
WELL-WELL! LOOK WHO'S UP!
C'MON- LET'S GET TO WORK ON HIM AGAIN AND PUT HIM BACK TO SLEEP.
4 SUDDENLY THE SLUMPING FORM STRAIGHTENS, SMOOTH MUSCLES RIPPLE, SUGGESTING HIDDEN STRENGTH, AS THE GIGANTIC FRAME OF THE BATMAN STANDS TOWERING IN THE LIGHT!
SO YOU THINK IT'S FUNNY, EH?....
ULP!
HUH!
5
.....WELL, THIS OUGHT TO PUT YOU IN STITCHES!
6 YEARS OF RIGOROUS ATHLETIC TRAINING HAVE ENABLED THE BATMAN NOT ONLY TO RESIST BUT TO RECOVER FROM THE BRUTAL BEATING THAT WOULD HAVE MORTALLY INJURED MOST MEN!
WHY DON'T YOU KICK ME NOW, YOU BRAVE MAN!
RIFLING THE PROFESSOR'S PAPERS, THE BATMAN FINDS THE LIST OF INSTRUCTIONS AND THEN HASTILY CONTACTS HIS YOUNG AIDE, ROBIN, THE BOY WONDER!
OH, IT'S YOU, BATMAN! WHERE HAVE YOU BEEN THE WHOLE NIGHT? I'VE BEEN WANDERING ALL AROUND TOWN LOOKING FOR YOU!
7
CAN'T STOP TO EXPLAIN NOW, BUT TAKE ONE OF THOSE PILLS I GAVE YOU LAST NIGHT AND LISTEN CAREFULLY! COPY THIS DOWN.
#8

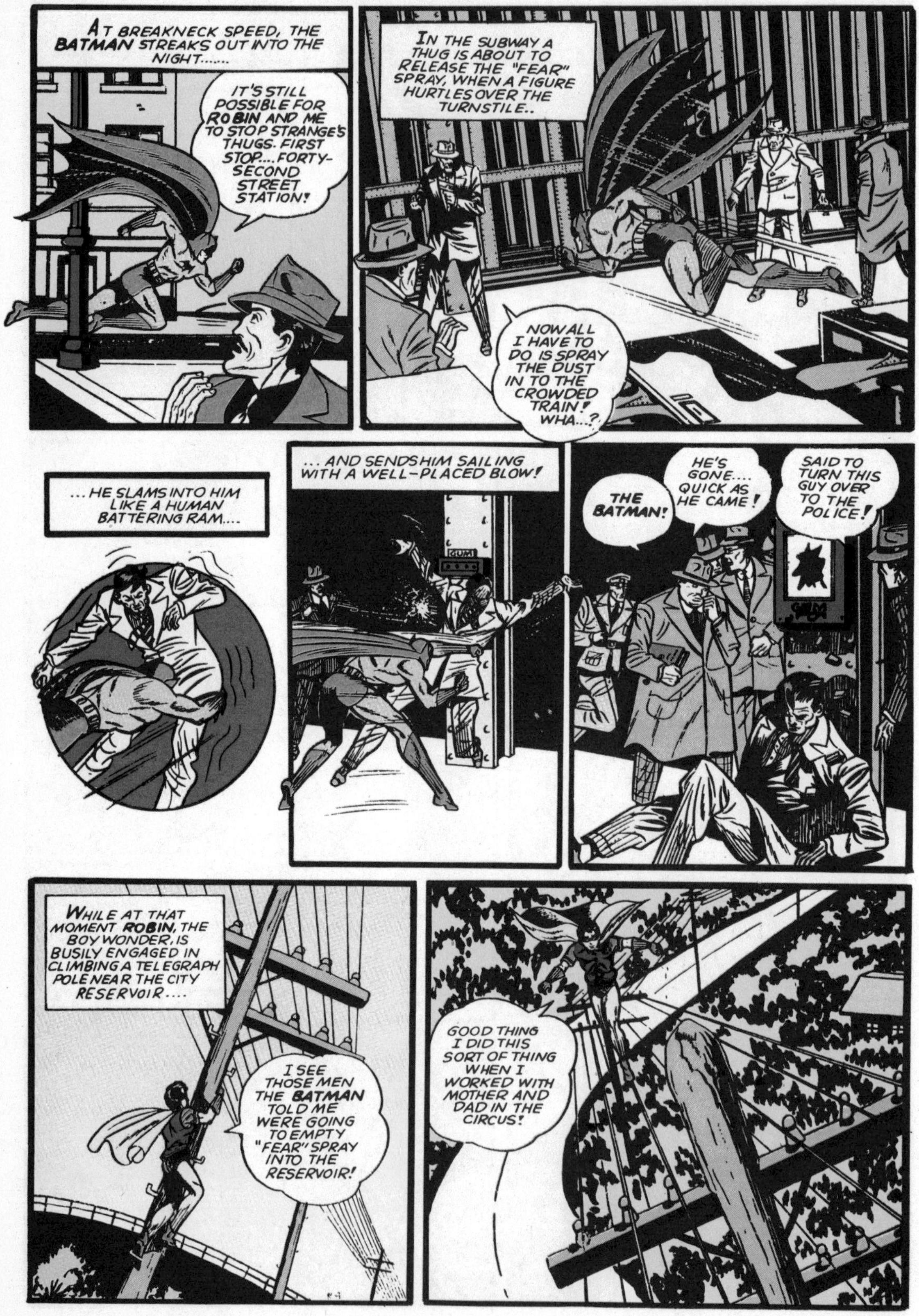

AT BREAKNECK SPEED, THE BATMAN STREAKS OUT INTO THE NIGHT.......
IT'S STILL POSSIBLE FOR ROBIN AND ME TO STOP STRANGE'S THUGS. FIRST STOP.... FORTY-SECOND STREET STATION!
IN THE SUBWAY A THUG IS ABOUT TO RELEASE THE "FEAR" SPRAY, WHEN A FIGURE HURTLES OVER THE TURNSTILE..
NOW ALL I HAVE TO DO IS SPRAY THE DUST IN TO THE CROWDED TRAIN! WHA...?
... HE SLAMS INTO HIM LIKE A HUMAN BATTERING RAM....
... AND SENDS HIM SAILING WITH A WELL-PLACED BLOW!
GUM
THE BATMAN!
HE'S GONE.... QUICK AS HE CAME!
SAID TO TURN THIS GUY OVER TO THE POLICE!
WHILE AT THAT MOMENT ROBIN, THE BOY WONDER, IS BUSILY ENGAGED IN CLIMBING A TELEGRAPH POLE NEAR THE CITY RESERVOIR....
I SEE THOSE MEN THE BATMAN TOLD ME WERE GOING TO EMPTY "FEAR" SPRAY INTO THE RESERVOIR!
GOOD THING I DID THIS SORT OF THING WHEN I WORKED WITH MOTHER AND DAD IN THE CIRCUS!

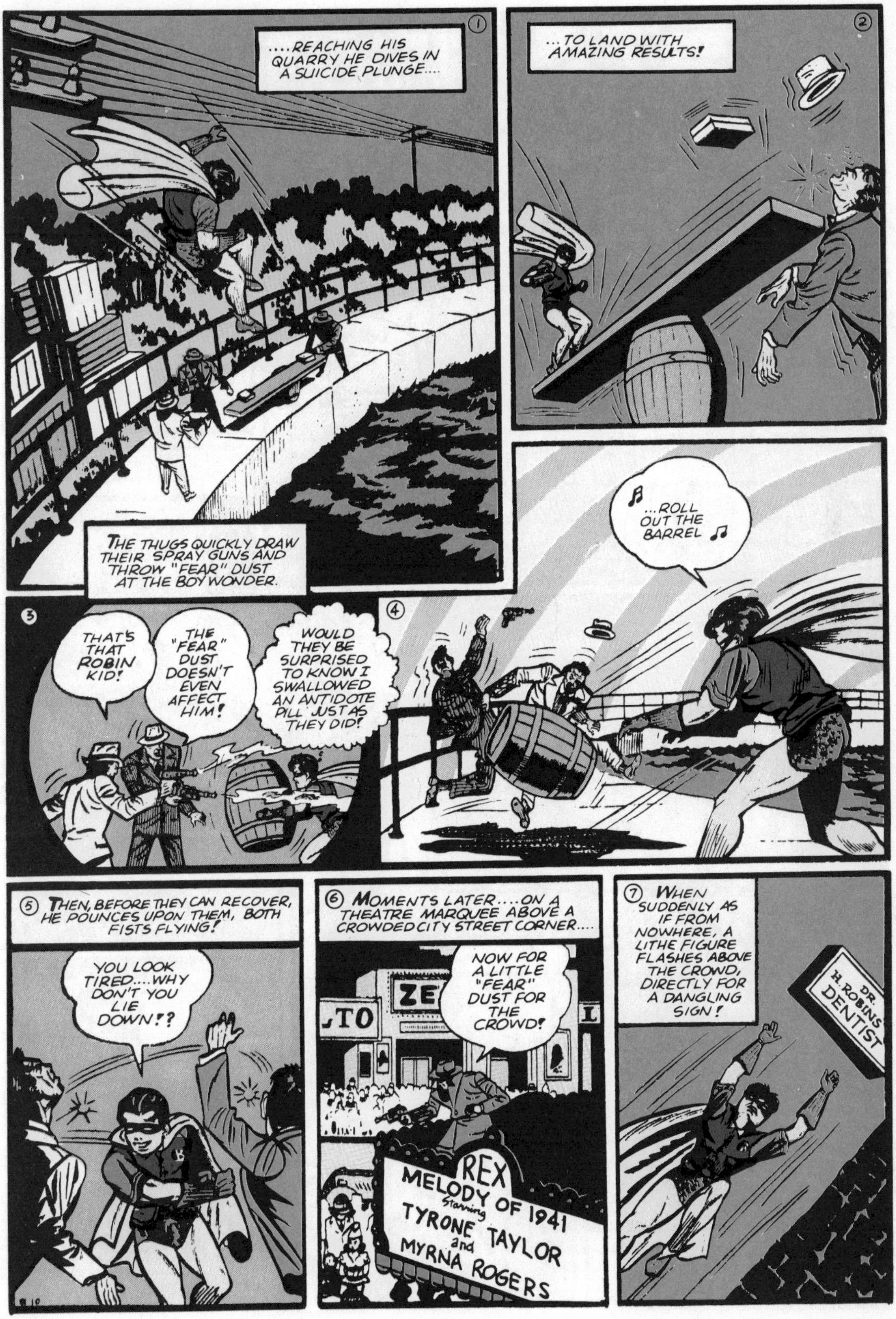
....REACHING HIS QUARRY HE DIVES IN A SUICIDE PLUNGE....
THE THUGS QUICKLY DRAW THEIR SPRAY GUNS AND THROW "FEAR" DUST AT THE BOY WONDER.
...TO LAND WITH AMAZING RESULTS!
THAT'S THAT ROBIN KID!
THE "FEAR" DUST DOESN'T EVEN AFFECT HIM!
WOULD THEY BE SURPRISED TO KNOW I SWALLOWED AN ANTIDOTE PILL JUST AS THEY DID!
...ROLL OUT THE BARREL
THEN, BEFORE THEY CAN RECOVER, HE POUNCES UPON THEM, BOTH FISTS FLYING!
YOU LOOK TIRED....WHY DON'T YOU LIE DOWN!?
MOMENTS LATER....ON A THEATRE MARQUEE ABOVE A CROWDED CITY STREET CORNER....
NOW FOR A LITTLE "FEAR" DUST FOR THE CROWD!
REX
MELODY OF 1941
Starring
TYRONE TAYLOR
and
MYRNA ROGERS
WHEN SUDDENLY AS IF FROM NOWHERE, A LITHE FIGURE FLASHES ABOVE THE CROWD, DIRECTLY FOR A DANGLING SIGN!
DR. H. ROBINS DENTIST

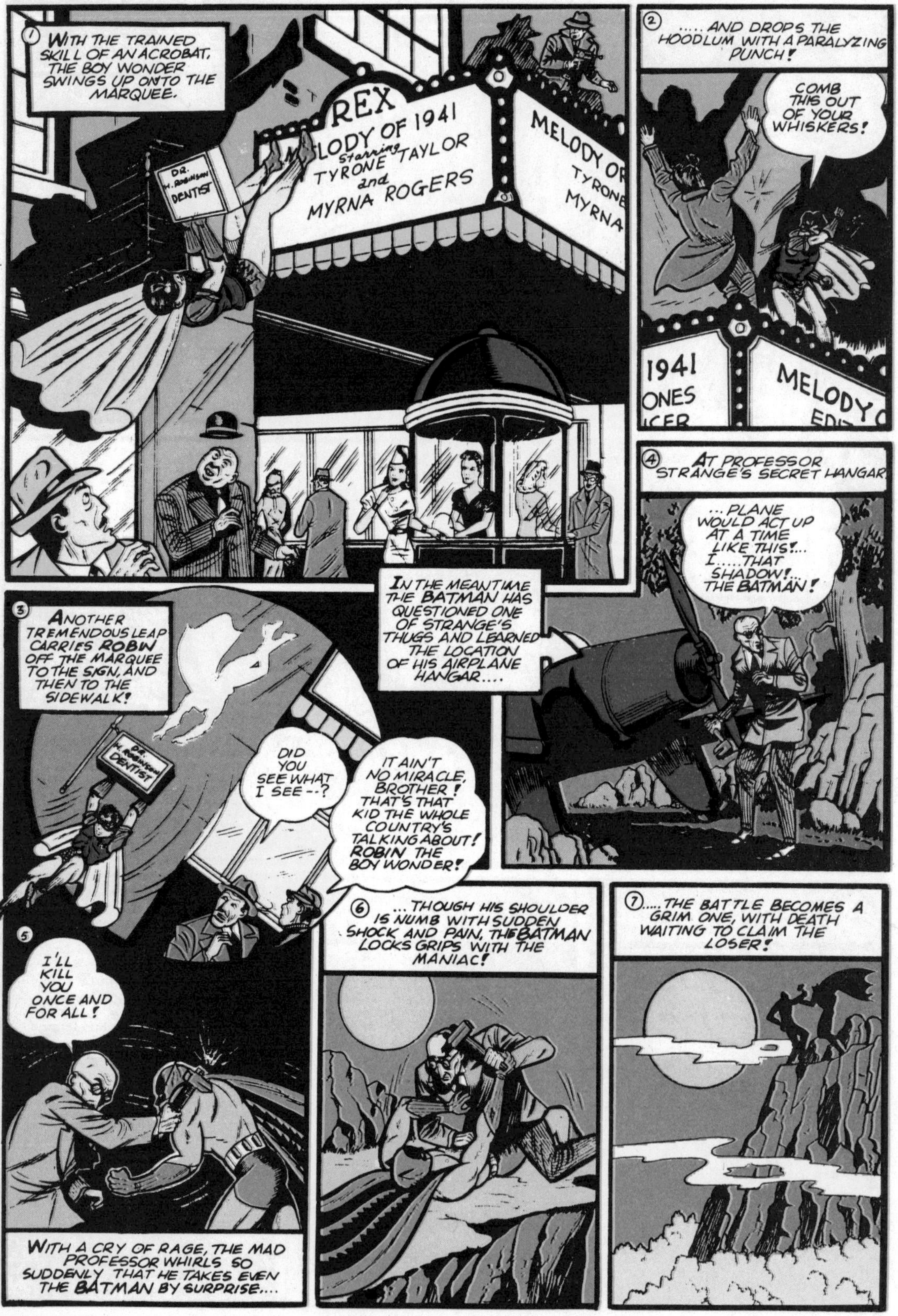
1 WITH THE TRAINED SKILL OF AN ACROBAT, THE BOY WONDER SWINGS UP ONTO THE MARQUEE.
REX
MELODY OF 1941 starring TYRONE TAYLOR and MYRNA ROGERS
DR. H. ROBINSON DENTIST
2 .....AND DROPS THE HOODLUM WITH A PARALYZING PUNCH!
COMB THIS OUT OF YOUR WHISKERS!
3 ANOTHER TREMENDOUS LEAP CARRIES ROBIN OFF THE MARQUEE TO THE SIGN, AND THEN TO THE SIDEWALK!
DID YOU SEE WHAT I SEE--?
IT AIN'T NO MIRACLE, BROTHER! THAT'S THAT KID THE WHOLE COUNTRY'S TALKING ABOUT! ROBIN THE BOY WONDER!
IN THE MEANTIME THE BATMAN HAS QUESTIONED ONE OF STRANGE'S THUGS AND LEARNED THE LOCATION OF HIS AIRPLANE HANGAR....
4 AT PROFESSOR STRANGE'S SECRET HANGAR
...PLANE WOULD ACT UP AT A TIME LIKE THIS!... I.....THAT SHADOW!... THE BATMAN!
5 I'LL KILL YOU ONCE AND FOR ALL!
WITH A CRY OF RAGE, THE MAD PROFESSOR WHIRLS SO SUDDENLY THAT HE TAKES EVEN THE BATMAN BY SURPRISE....
6 ...THOUGH HIS SHOULDER IS NUMB WITH SUDDEN SHOCK AND PAIN, THE BATMAN LOCKS GRIPS WITH THE MANIAC!
7 .....THE BATTLE BECOMES A GRIM ONE, WITH DEATH WAITING TO CLAIM THE LOSER!

ABRUPTLY, THE ARCH-CRIMINAL MANAGES TO LOOSEN HIS HAND, AND LASHES OUT AT THE BATMAN....

BLAST YOU!

MISSED! TSK, TSK!

....BUT THE NIMBLE BATMAN IS NOT TO BE CAUGHT NAPPING A SECOND TIME. THERE IS A CRACK LIKE THAT OF A RIFLE SHOT AS HIS FISTS LAND ON THE CRIMINAL'S CHIN......

BUT I WON'T!

...FOR A MOMENT HE TEETERS ON THE EDGE, CLAWING FOR BALANCE, AND THEN WITH A TRAILING SHRIEK TOPPLES TO HIS DOOM!

WELL....THIS TIME IT REALLY LOOKS AS IF IT IS THE END OF THE EVIL CAREER OF PROFESSOR HUGO STRANGE!

Y-A-A-A-A

THAT NIGHT, AS THE MOON SHEDS ITS LIGHT OVER A NOW PEACEFUL CITY, TWO FIGURES STAND ON A LONELY ROAD....

WELL...I GUESS WE CLEANED OUT THE "FEAR" GANG! NOW WHAT DO WE DO?

NOTHING MUCH LEFT TO DO BUT TO SET FREE THE KID THAT HELPED ME BREAK THIS CASE. HE'S TIED UP IN STRANGE'S HOUSE!

YOU KNOW...IT MUST HAVE BEEN A PECULIAR SIGHT TO SEE POLICEMEN AFRAID FOR THE FIRST TIME....

THEY COULDN'T HELP BEING AFRAID UNDER THE INFLUENCE OF THAT "FEAR" DUST ANY MORE THAN YOU COULD HELP CATCHING A COLD!

WHAT ABOUT THE PEOPLE THE "FEAR" DUST AFFECTED? WHAT CAN BE DONE ABOUT THEM?

I'LL GIVE THE PILLS TO A RESEARCH LABORATORY. THEY'LL FIND OUT WHAT THEY'RE MADE OF AND MAKE ENOUGH ANTIDOTE FOR THOSE POOR UNFORTUNATES!

THANKS FOR BEING WITH US AGAIN THIS MONTH! ROBIN AND I LOOK FORWARD TO THESE LITTLE GET-TOGETHERS WITH ALL YOU READERS EVERY MONTH IN DETECTIVE COMICS! LET'S MAKE IT A STANDING DATE!

BOB KANE

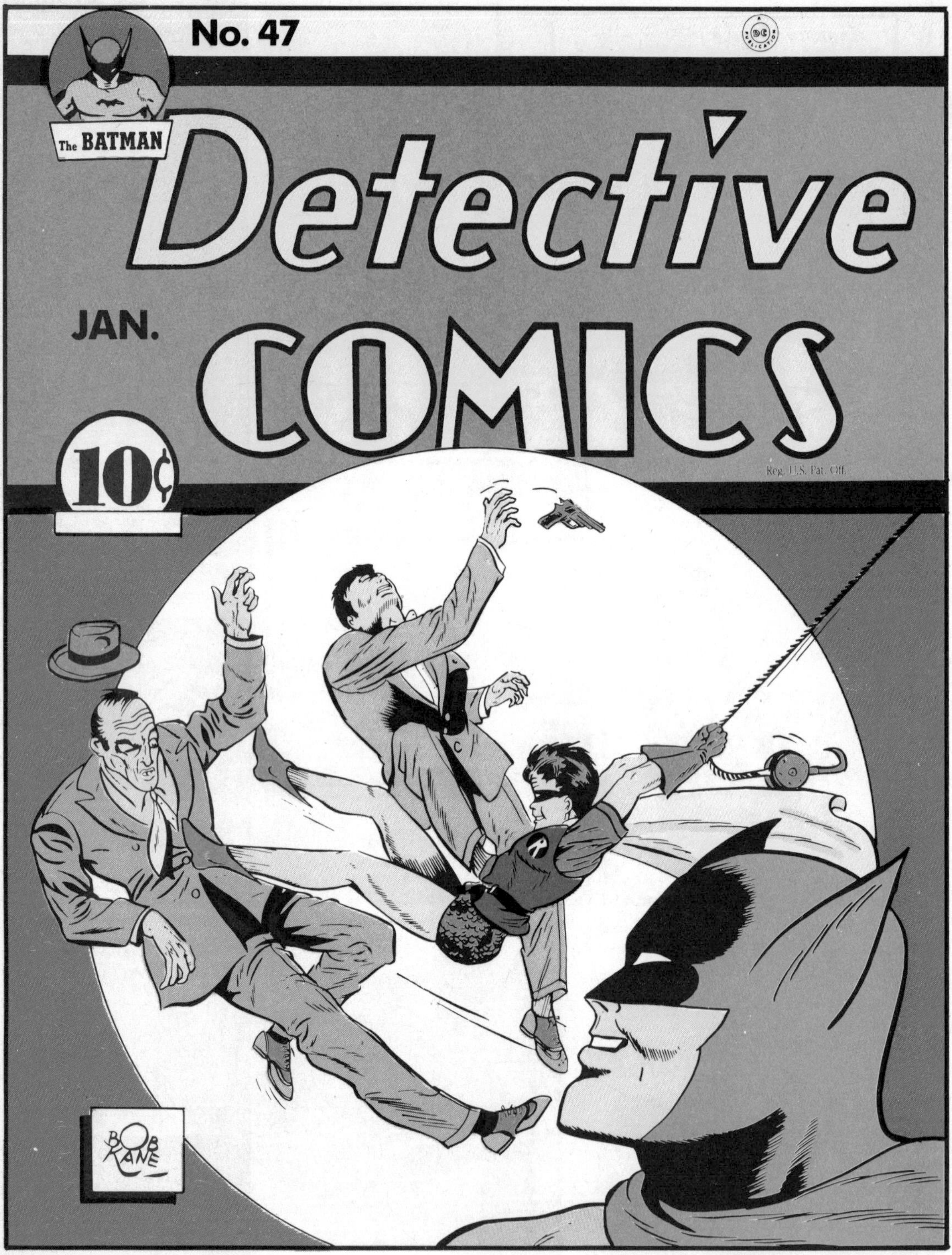
No. 47
A DC PUBLICATION
The BATMAN
Detective
JAN.
COMICS
10¢
Reg. U.S. Pat. Off.
BOB KANE

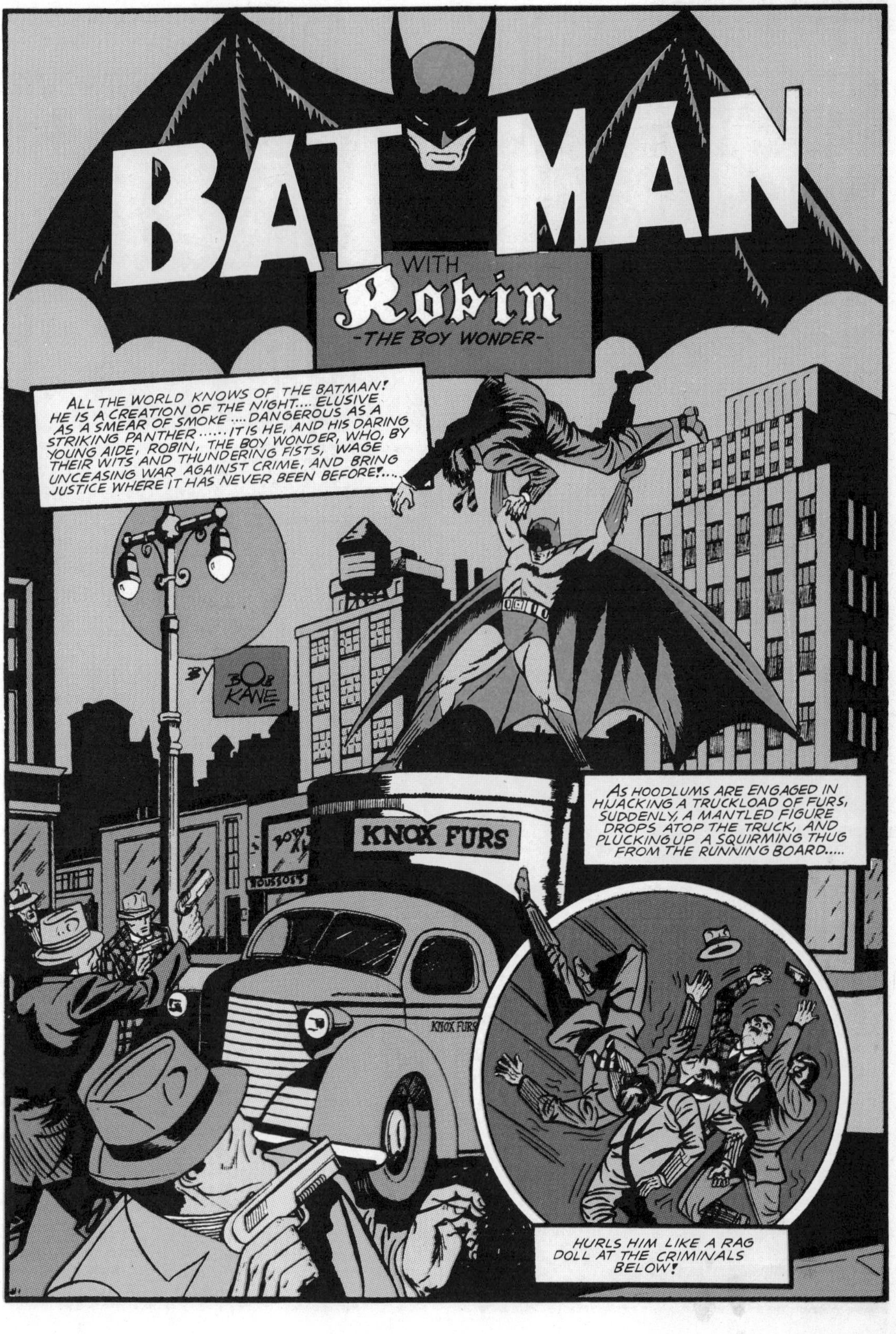
BATMAN
WITH
Robin
-THE BOY WONDER-
ALL THE WORLD KNOWS OF THE BATMAN! HE IS A CREATION OF THE NIGHT.... ELUSIVE AS A SMEAR OF SMOKE .... DANGEROUS AS A STRIKING PANTHER...... IT IS HE, AND HIS DARING YOUNG AIDE, ROBIN, THE BOY WONDER, WHO, BY THEIR WITS AND THUNDERING FISTS, WAGE UNCEASING WAR AGAINST CRIME, AND BRING JUSTICE WHERE IT HAS NEVER BEEN BEFORE!....
BY BOB KANE
AS HOODLUMS ARE ENGAGED IN HIJACKING A TRUCKLOAD OF FURS, SUDDENLY, A MANTLED FIGURE DROPS ATOP THE TRUCK, AND PLUCKING UP A SQUIRMING THUG FROM THE RUNNING BOARD.....
KNOX FURS
KNOX FURS
HURLS HIM LIKE A RAG DOLL AT THE CRIMINALS BELOW!

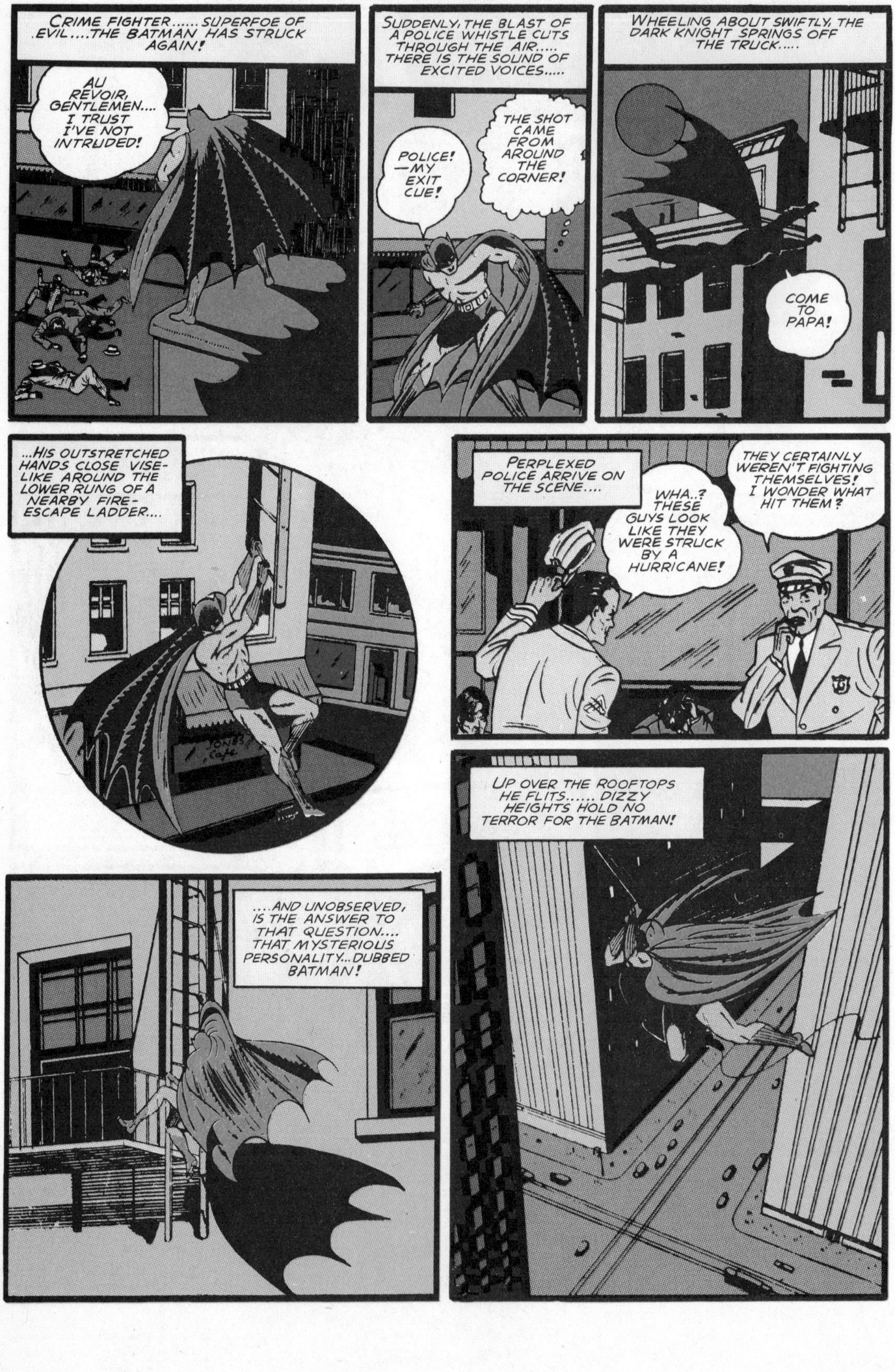
CRIME FIGHTER...... SUPERFOE OF EVIL.... THE BATMAN HAS STRUCK AGAIN!
AU REVOIR, GENTLEMEN.... I TRUST I'VE NOT INTRUDED!
SUDDENLY, THE BLAST OF A POLICE WHISTLE CUTS THROUGH THE AIR..... THERE IS THE SOUND OF EXCITED VOICES.....
POLICE! —MY EXIT CUE!
THE SHOT CAME FROM AROUND THE CORNER!
WHEELING ABOUT SWIFTLY, THE DARK KNIGHT SPRINGS OFF THE TRUCK.....
COME TO PAPA!
...HIS OUTSTRETCHED HANDS CLOSE VISE-LIKE AROUND THE LOWER RUNG OF A NEARBY FIRE-ESCAPE LADDER...
JONES Cafe
PERPLEXED POLICE ARRIVE ON THE SCENE....
WHA..? THESE GUYS LOOK LIKE THEY WERE STRUCK BY A HURRICANE!
THEY CERTAINLY WEREN'T FIGHTING THEMSELVES! I WONDER WHAT HIT THEM?
UP OVER THE ROOFTOPS HE FLITS...... DIZZY HEIGHTS HOLD NO TERROR FOR THE BATMAN!
....AND UNOBSERVED, IS THE ANSWER TO THAT QUESTION.... THAT MYSTERIOUS PERSONALITY...DUBBED BATMAN!

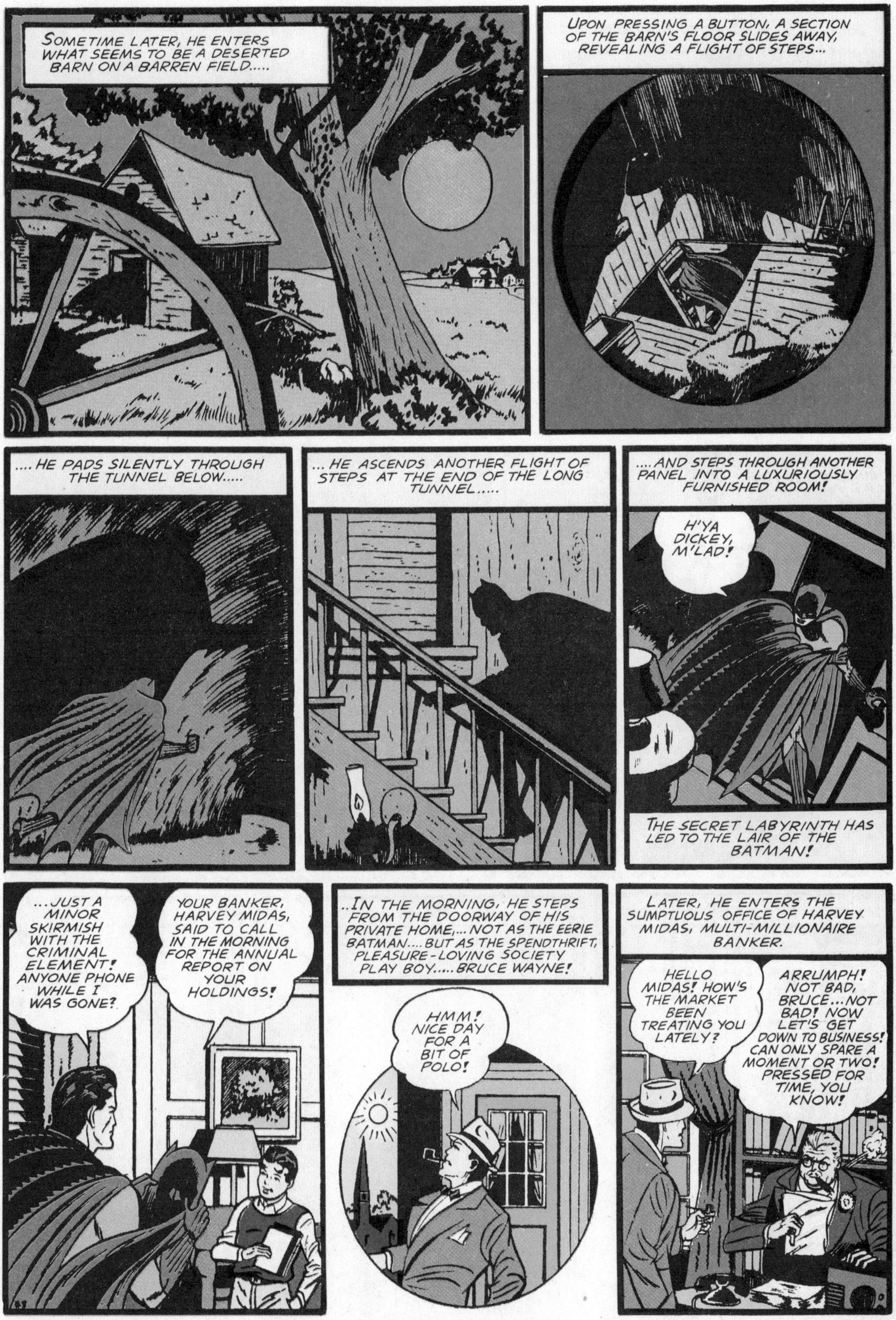
SOMETIME LATER, HE ENTERS WHAT SEEMS TO BE A DESERTED BARN ON A BARREN FIELD.....
UPON PRESSING A BUTTON, A SECTION OF THE BARN'S FLOOR SLIDES AWAY, REVEALING A FLIGHT OF STEPS...
....HE PADS SILENTLY THROUGH THE TUNNEL BELOW.....
...HE ASCENDS ANOTHER FLIGHT OF STEPS AT THE END OF THE LONG TUNNEL.....
....AND STEPS THROUGH ANOTHER PANEL INTO A LUXURIOUSLY FURNISHED ROOM!
H'YA DICKEY, M'LAD!
THE SECRET LABYRINTH HAS LED TO THE LAIR OF THE BATMAN!
...JUST A MINOR SKIRMISH WITH THE CRIMINAL ELEMENT! ANYONE PHONE WHILE I WAS GONE?
YOUR BANKER, HARVEY MIDAS, SAID TO CALL IN THE MORNING FOR THE ANNUAL REPORT ON YOUR HOLDINGS!
..IN THE MORNING, HE STEPS FROM THE DOORWAY OF HIS PRIVATE HOME,...NOT AS THE EERIE BATMAN....BUT AS THE SPENDTHRIFT, PLEASURE-LOVING SOCIETY PLAY BOY.....BRUCE WAYNE!
HMM! NICE DAY FOR A BIT OF POLO!
LATER, HE ENTERS THE SUMPTUOUS OFFICE OF HARVEY MIDAS, MULTI-MILLIONAIRE BANKER.
HELLO MIDAS! HOW'S THE MARKET BEEN TREATING YOU LATELY?
ARRUMPH! NOT BAD, BRUCE...NOT BAD! NOW LET'S GET DOWN TO BUSINESS! CAN ONLY SPARE A MOMENT OR TWO! PRESSED FOR TIME, YOU KNOW!

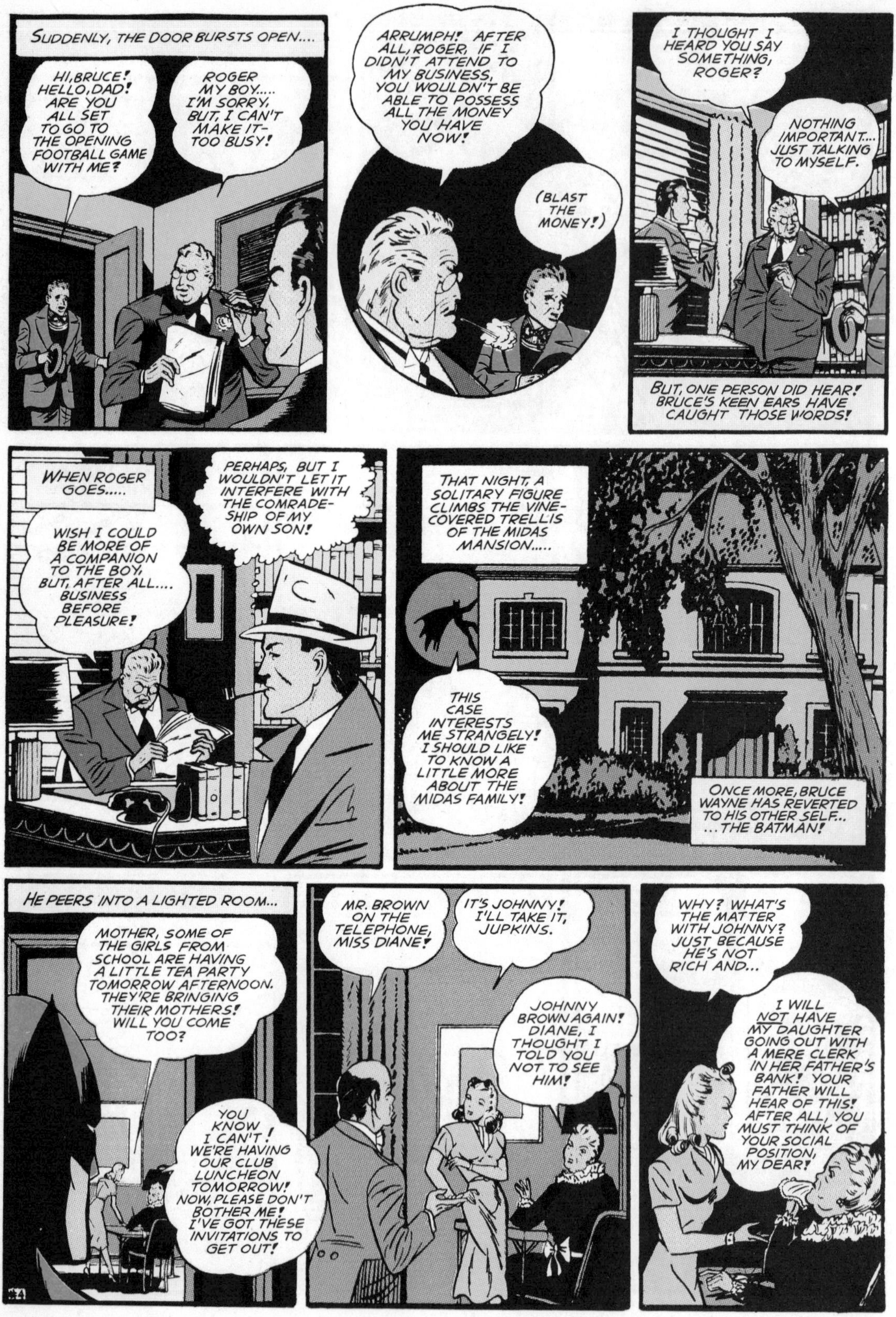
SUDDENLY, THE DOOR BURSTS OPEN....
HI, BRUCE! HELLO, DAD! ARE YOU ALL SET TO GO TO THE OPENING FOOTBALL GAME WITH ME?
ROGER MY BOY..... I'M SORRY, BUT, I CAN'T MAKE IT-- TOO BUSY!
ARRUMPH! AFTER ALL, ROGER, IF I DIDN'T ATTEND TO MY BUSINESS, YOU WOULDN'T BE ABLE TO POSSESS ALL THE MONEY YOU HAVE NOW!
(BLAST THE MONEY!)
I THOUGHT I HEARD YOU SAY SOMETHING, ROGER?
NOTHING IMPORTANT... JUST TALKING TO MYSELF.
BUT, ONE PERSON DID HEAR! BRUCE'S KEEN EARS HAVE CAUGHT THOSE WORDS!
WHEN ROGER GOES.....
WISH I COULD BE MORE OF A COMPANION TO THE BOY, BUT, AFTER ALL.... BUSINESS BEFORE PLEASURE!
PERHAPS, BUT I WOULDN'T LET IT INTERFERE WITH THE COMRADESHIP OF MY OWN SON!
THAT NIGHT, A SOLITARY FIGURE CLIMBS THE VINE-COVERED TRELLIS OF THE MIDAS MANSION.....
THIS CASE INTERESTS ME STRANGELY! I SHOULD LIKE TO KNOW A LITTLE MORE ABOUT THE MIDAS FAMILY!
ONCE MORE, BRUCE WAYNE HAS REVERTED TO HIS OTHER SELF... ...THE BATMAN!
HE PEERS INTO A LIGHTED ROOM...
MOTHER, SOME OF THE GIRLS FROM SCHOOL ARE HAVING A LITTLE TEA PARTY TOMORROW AFTERNOON. THEY'RE BRINGING THEIR MOTHERS! WILL YOU COME TOO?
YOU KNOW I CAN'T! WE'RE HAVING OUR CLUB LUNCHEON TOMORROW! NOW, PLEASE DON'T BOTHER ME! I'VE GOT THESE INVITATIONS TO GET OUT!
MR. BROWN ON THE TELEPHONE, MISS DIANE!
IT'S JOHNNY! I'LL TAKE IT, JUPKINS.
JOHNNY BROWN AGAIN! DIANE, I THOUGHT I TOLD YOU NOT TO SEE HIM!
WHY? WHAT'S THE MATTER WITH JOHNNY? JUST BECAUSE HE'S NOT RICH AND...
I WILL NOT HAVE MY DAUGHTER GOING OUT WITH A MERE CLERK IN HER FATHER'S BANK! YOUR FATHER WILL HEAR OF THIS! AFTER ALL, YOU MUST THINK OF YOUR SOCIAL POSITION, MY DEAR!

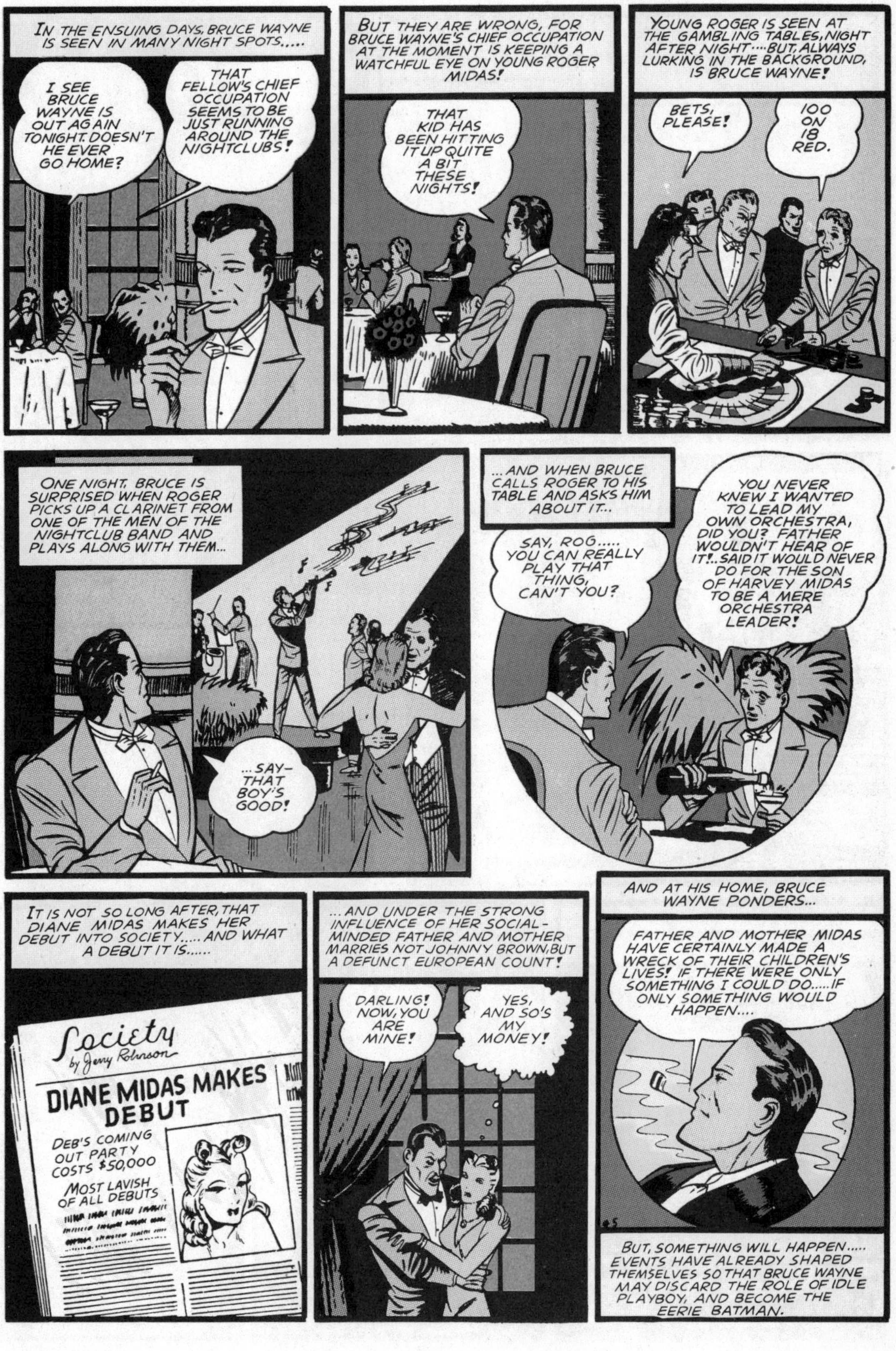
IN THE ENSUING DAYS, BRUCE WAYNE IS SEEN IN MANY NIGHT SPOTS.....
I SEE BRUCE WAYNE IS OUT AGAIN TONIGHT. DOESN'T HE EVER GO HOME?
THAT FELLOW'S CHIEF OCCUPATION SEEMS TO BE JUST RUNNING AROUND THE NIGHTCLUBS!
BUT THEY ARE WRONG, FOR BRUCE WAYNE'S CHIEF OCCUPATION AT THE MOMENT IS KEEPING A WATCHFUL EYE ON YOUNG ROGER MIDAS!
THAT KID HAS BEEN HITTING IT UP QUITE A BIT THESE NIGHTS!
YOUNG ROGER IS SEEN AT THE GAMBLING TABLES, NIGHT AFTER NIGHT....BUT, ALWAYS LURKING IN THE BACKGROUND, IS BRUCE WAYNE!
BETS, PLEASE!
100 ON 18 RED.
ONE NIGHT, BRUCE IS SURPRISED WHEN ROGER PICKS UP A CLARINET FROM ONE OF THE MEN OF THE NIGHTCLUB BAND AND PLAYS ALONG WITH THEM...
...SAY—THAT BOY'S GOOD!
...AND WHEN BRUCE CALLS ROGER TO HIS TABLE AND ASKS HIM ABOUT IT...
SAY, ROG..... YOU CAN REALLY PLAY THAT THING, CAN'T YOU?
YOU NEVER KNEW I WANTED TO LEAD MY OWN ORCHESTRA, DID YOU? FATHER WOULDN'T HEAR OF IT!..SAID IT WOULD NEVER DO FOR THE SON OF HARVEY MIDAS TO BE A MERE ORCHESTRA LEADER!
IT IS NOT SO LONG AFTER, THAT DIANE MIDAS MAKES HER DEBUT INTO SOCIETY..... AND WHAT A DEBUT IT IS.....
Society
by Jerry Robinson
DIANE MIDAS MAKES DEBUT
DEB'S COMING OUT PARTY COSTS $50,000
MOST LAVISH OF ALL DEBUTS
...AND UNDER THE STRONG INFLUENCE OF HER SOCIAL-MINDED FATHER AND MOTHER MARRIES NOT JOHNNY BROWN, BUT A DEFUNCT EUROPEAN COUNT!
DARLING! NOW, YOU ARE MINE!
YES, AND SO'S MY MONEY!
AND AT HIS HOME, BRUCE WAYNE PONDERS...
FATHER AND MOTHER MIDAS HAVE CERTAINLY MADE A WRECK OF THEIR CHILDREN'S LIVES! IF THERE WERE ONLY SOMETHING I COULD DO.....IF ONLY SOMETHING WOULD HAPPEN....
BUT, SOMETHING WILL HAPPEN..... EVENTS HAVE ALREADY SHAPED THEMSELVES SO THAT BRUCE WAYNE MAY DISCARD THE ROLE OF IDLE PLAYBOY, AND BECOME THE EERIE BATMAN.

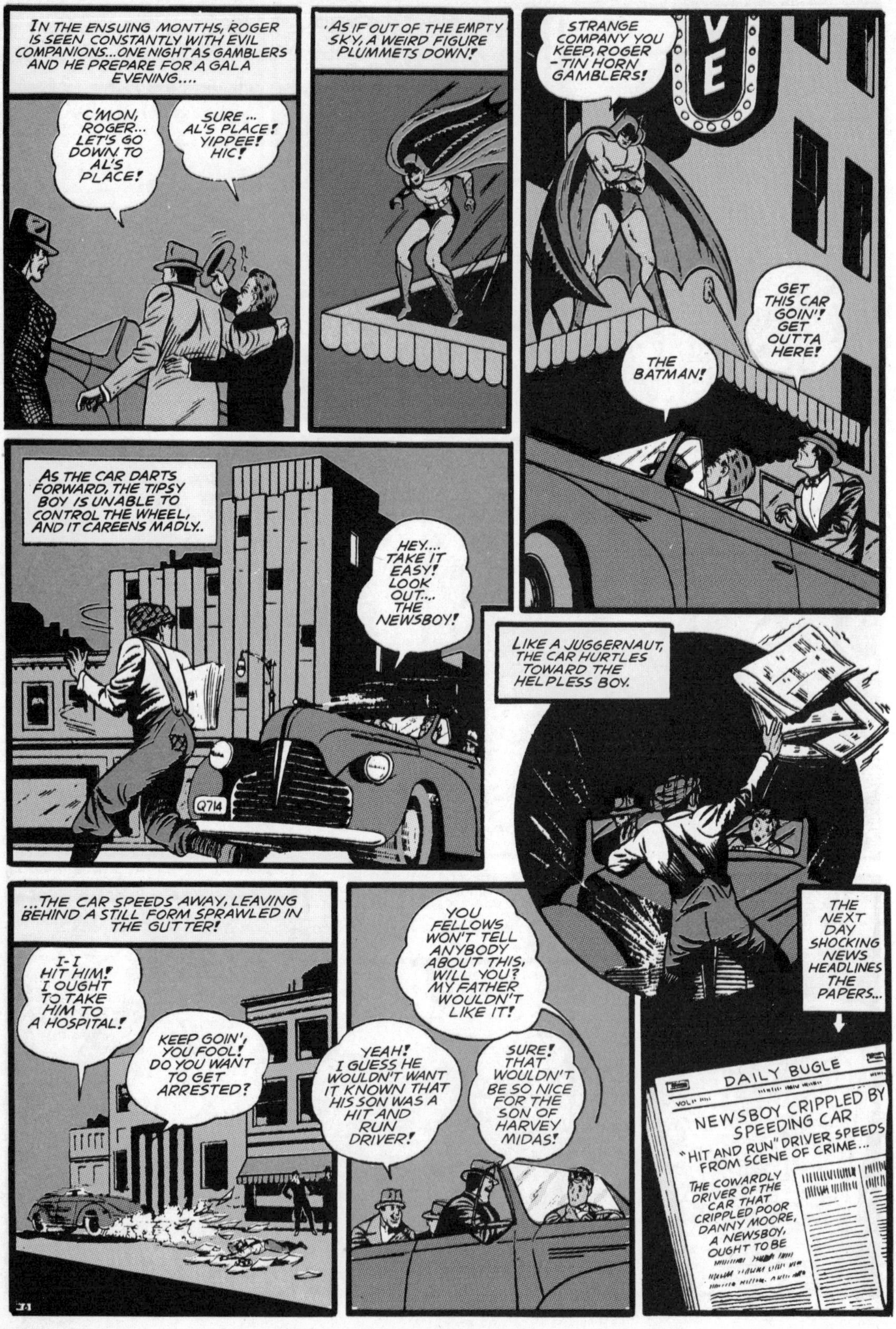
IN THE ENSUING MONTHS, ROGER IS SEEN CONSTANTLY WITH EVIL COMPANIONS...ONE NIGHT AS GAMBLERS AND HE PREPARE FOR A GALA EVENING....
C'MON, ROGER... LET'S GO DOWN TO AL'S PLACE!
SURE... AL'S PLACE! YIPPEE! HIC!
AS IF OUT OF THE EMPTY SKY, A WEIRD FIGURE PLUMMETS DOWN!
STRANGE COMPANY YOU KEEP, ROGER -TIN HORN GAMBLERS!
VE
GET THIS CAR GOIN'! GET OUTTA HERE!
THE BATMAN!
AS THE CAR DARTS FORWARD, THE TIPSY BOY IS UNABLE TO CONTROL THE WHEEL, AND IT CAREENS MADLY..
HEY.... TAKE IT EASY! LOOK OUT... THE NEWSBOY!
Q714
LIKE A JUGGERNAUT, THE CAR HURTLES TOWARD THE HELPLESS BOY.
...THE CAR SPEEDS AWAY, LEAVING BEHIND A STILL FORM SPRAWLED IN THE GUTTER!
I-I HIT HIM! I OUGHT TO TAKE HIM TO A HOSPITAL!
KEEP GOIN', YOU FOOL! DO YOU WANT TO GET ARRESTED?
YOU FELLOWS WON'T TELL ANYBODY ABOUT THIS, WILL YOU? MY FATHER WOULDN'T LIKE IT!
YEAH! I GUESS HE WOULDN'T WANT IT KNOWN THAT HIS SON WAS A HIT AND RUN DRIVER!
SURE! THAT WOULDN'T BE SO NICE FOR THE SON OF HARVEY MIDAS!
THE NEXT DAY SHOCKING NEWS HEADLINES THE PAPERS...
DAILY BUGLE
NEWSBOY CRIPPLED BY SPEEDING CAR
"HIT AND RUN" DRIVER SPEEDS FROM SCENE OF CRIME...
THE COWARDLY DRIVER OF THE CAR THAT CRIPPLED POOR DANNY MOORE, A NEWSBOY, OUGHT TO BE

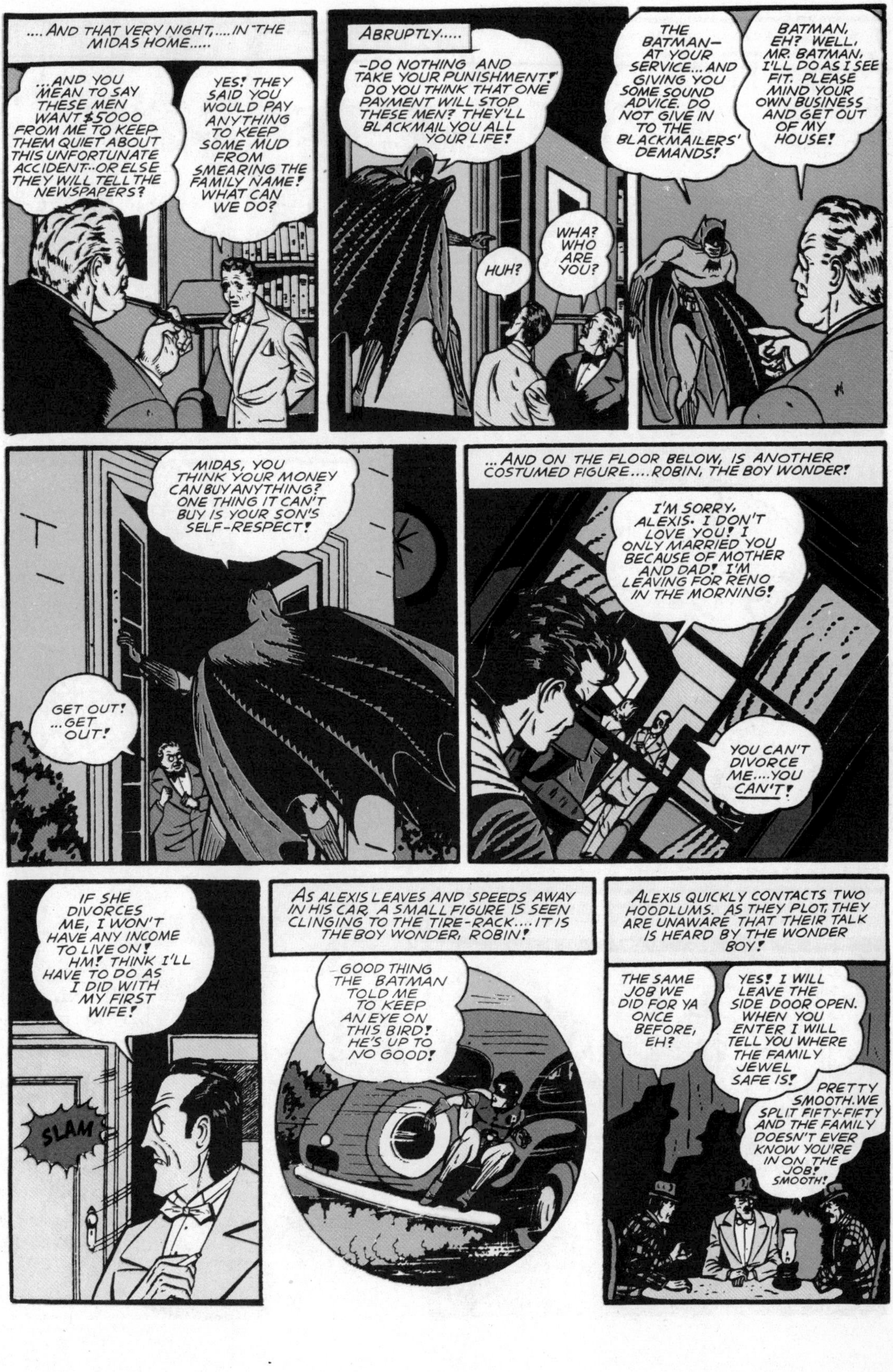
....AND THAT VERY NIGHT,....IN THE MIDAS HOME.....
...AND YOU MEAN TO SAY THESE MEN WANT $5000 FROM ME TO KEEP THEM QUIET ABOUT THIS UNFORTUNATE ACCIDENT--OR ELSE THEY WILL TELL THE NEWSPAPERS?
YES! THEY SAID YOU WOULD PAY ANYTHING TO KEEP SOME MUD FROM SMEARING THE FAMILY NAME! WHAT CAN WE DO?
ABRUPTLY.....
-DO NOTHING AND TAKE YOUR PUNISHMENT! DO YOU THINK THAT ONE PAYMENT WILL STOP THESE MEN? THEY'LL BLACKMAIL YOU ALL YOUR LIFE!
HUH?
WHA? WHO ARE YOU?
THE BATMAN-- AT YOUR SERVICE...AND GIVING YOU SOME SOUND ADVICE. DO NOT GIVE IN TO THE BLACKMAILERS' DEMANDS!
BATMAN, EH? WELL, MR. BATMAN, I'LL DO AS I SEE FIT. PLEASE MIND YOUR OWN BUSINESS AND GET OUT OF MY HOUSE!
MIDAS, YOU THINK YOUR MONEY CAN BUY ANYTHING? ONE THING IT CAN'T BUY IS YOUR SON'S SELF-RESPECT!
GET OUT! ...GET OUT!
...AND ON THE FLOOR BELOW, IS ANOTHER COSTUMED FIGURE....ROBIN, THE BOY WONDER!
I'M SORRY, ALEXIS. I DON'T LOVE YOU! I ONLY MARRIED YOU BECAUSE OF MOTHER AND DAD! I'M LEAVING FOR RENO IN THE MORNING!
YOU CAN'T DIVORCE ME....YOU CAN'T!
IF SHE DIVORCES ME, I WON'T HAVE ANY INCOME TO LIVE ON! HM! THINK I'LL HAVE TO DO AS I DID WITH MY FIRST WIFE!
SLAM
AS ALEXIS LEAVES AND SPEEDS AWAY IN HIS CAR, A SMALL FIGURE IS SEEN CLINGING TO THE TIRE-RACK....IT IS THE BOY WONDER, ROBIN!
GOOD THING THE BATMAN TOLD ME TO KEEP AN EYE ON THIS BIRD! HE'S UP TO NO GOOD!
ALEXIS QUICKLY CONTACTS TWO HOODLUMS. AS THEY PLOT, THEY ARE UNAWARE THAT THEIR TALK IS HEARD BY THE WONDER BOY!
THE SAME JOB WE DID FOR YA ONCE BEFORE, EH?
YES! I WILL LEAVE THE SIDE DOOR OPEN. WHEN YOU ENTER I WILL TELL YOU WHERE THE FAMILY JEWEL SAFE IS!
PRETTY SMOOTH. WE SPLIT FIFTY-FIFTY AND THE FAMILY DOESN'T EVER KNOW YOU'RE IN ON THE JOB! SMOOTH!

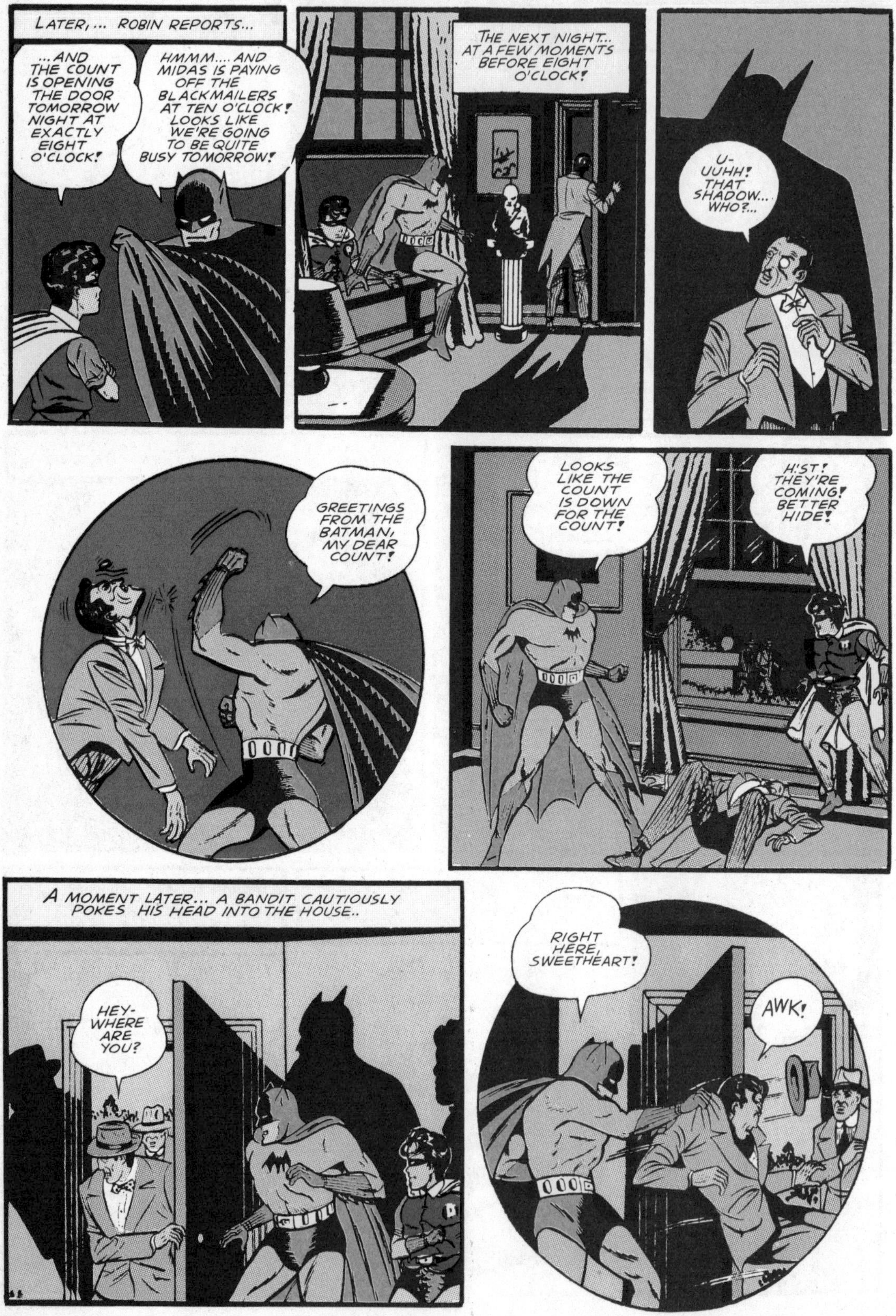
LATER, ... ROBIN REPORTS...
...AND THE COUNT IS OPENING THE DOOR TOMORROW NIGHT AT EXACTLY EIGHT O'CLOCK!
HMMM.... AND MIDAS IS PAYING OFF THE BLACKMAILERS AT TEN O'CLOCK! LOOKS LIKE WE'RE GOING TO BE QUITE BUSY TOMORROW!
THE NEXT NIGHT... AT A FEW MOMENTS BEFORE EIGHT O'CLOCK!
U-UUHH! THAT SHADOW... WHO?...
GREETINGS FROM THE BATMAN, MY DEAR COUNT!
LOOKS LIKE THE COUNT IS DOWN FOR THE COUNT!
H'ST! THEY'RE COMING! BETTER HIDE!
A MOMENT LATER... A BANDIT CAUTIOUSLY POKES HIS HEAD INTO THE HOUSE..
HEY-WHERE ARE YOU?
RIGHT HERE, SWEETHEART!
AWK!

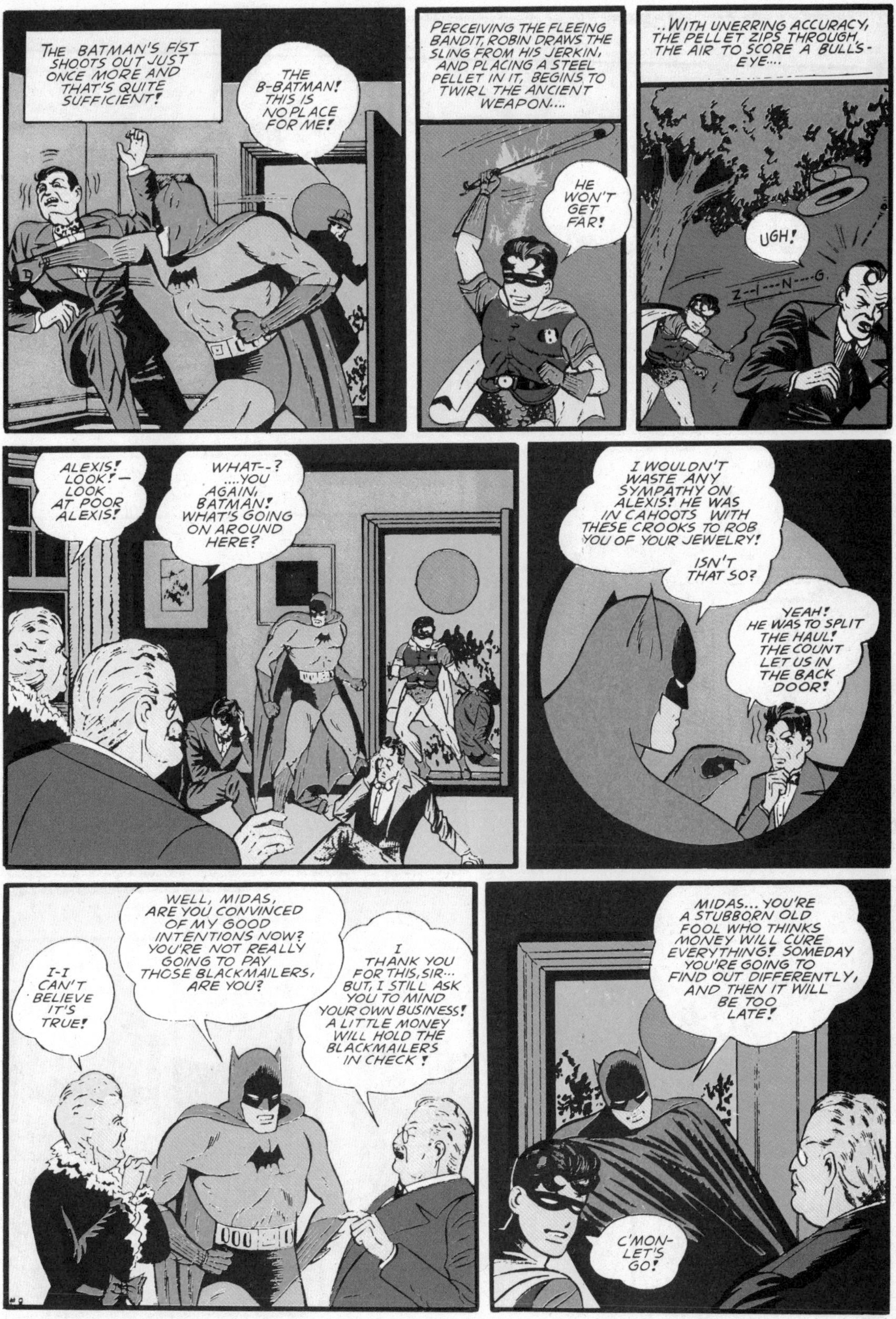
THE BATMAN'S FIST SHOOTS OUT JUST ONCE MORE AND THAT'S QUITE SUFFICIENT!
THE B-BATMAN! THIS IS NO PLACE FOR ME!
PERCEIVING THE FLEEING BANDIT, ROBIN DRAWS THE SLING FROM HIS JERKIN, AND PLACING A STEEL PELLET IN IT, BEGINS TO TWIRL THE ANCIENT WEAPON....
HE WON'T GET FAR!
..WITH UNERRING ACCURACY, THE PELLET ZIPS THROUGH THE AIR TO SCORE A BULL'S-EYE....
UGH!
Z--I---N----G.
ALEXIS! LOOK! — LOOK AT POOR ALEXIS!
WHAT--? ....YOU AGAIN, BATMAN! WHAT'S GOING ON AROUND HERE?
I WOULDN'T WASTE ANY SYMPATHY ON ALEXIS! HE WAS IN CAHOOTS WITH THESE CROOKS TO ROB YOU OF YOUR JEWELRY!
ISN'T THAT SO?
YEAH! HE WAS TO SPLIT THE HAUL! THE COUNT LET US IN THE BACK DOOR!
I-I CAN'T BELIEVE IT'S TRUE!
WELL, MIDAS, ARE YOU CONVINCED OF MY GOOD INTENTIONS NOW? YOU'RE NOT REALLY GOING TO PAY THOSE BLACKMAILERS, ARE YOU?
I THANK YOU FOR THIS, SIR... BUT, I STILL ASK YOU TO MIND YOUR OWN BUSINESS! A LITTLE MONEY WILL HOLD THE BLACKMAILERS IN CHECK!
MIDAS... YOU'RE A STUBBORN OLD FOOL WHO THINKS MONEY WILL CURE EVERYTHING! SOMEDAY YOU'RE GOING TO FIND OUT DIFFERENTLY, AND THEN IT WILL BE TOO LATE!
C'MON- LET'S GO!

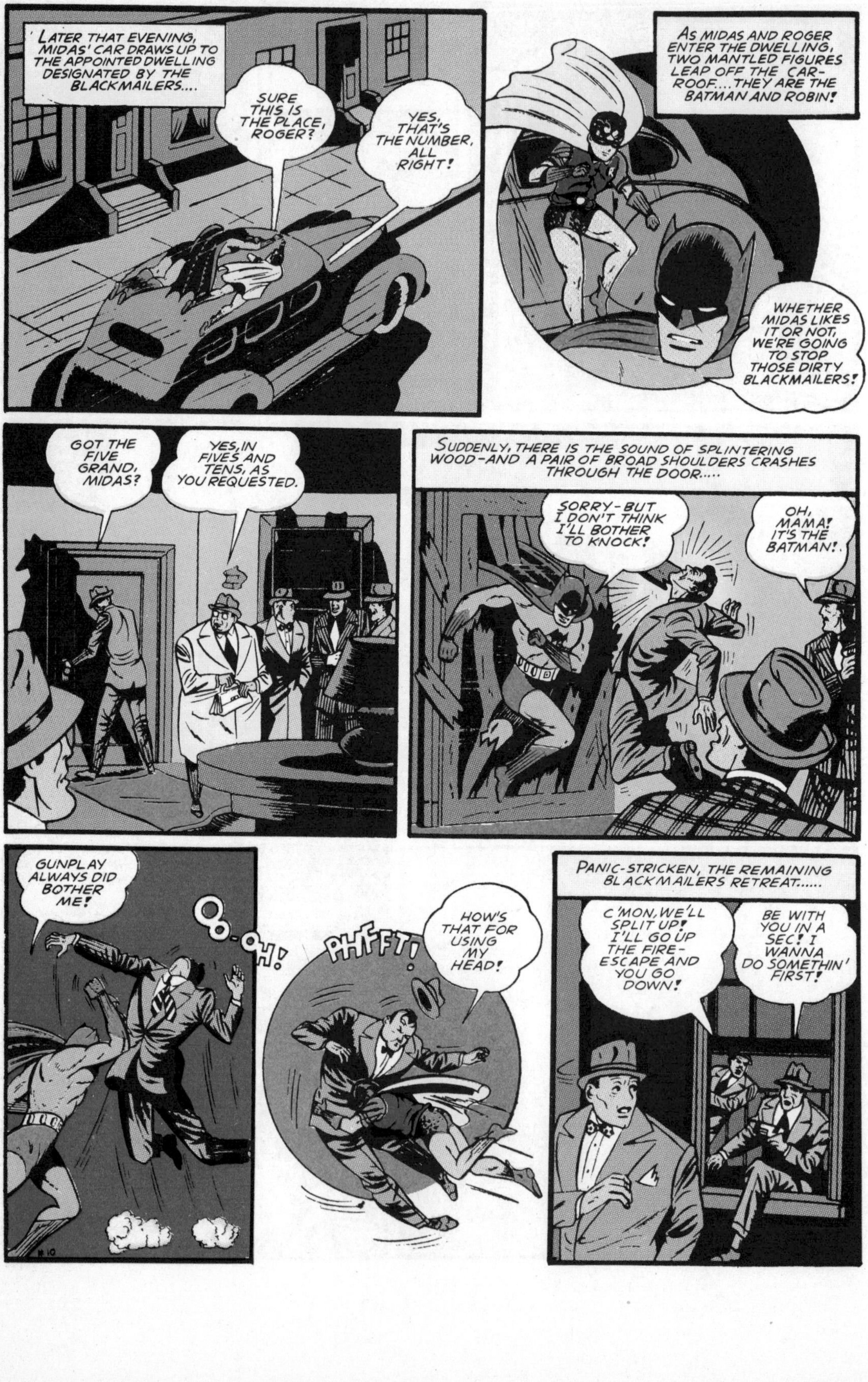
LATER THAT EVENING, MIDAS' CAR DRAWS UP TO THE APPOINTED DWELLING DESIGNATED BY THE BLACKMAILERS....
SURE THIS IS THE PLACE, ROGER?
YES, THAT'S THE NUMBER, ALL RIGHT!
AS MIDAS AND ROGER ENTER THE DWELLING, TWO MANTLED FIGURES LEAP OFF THE CAR-ROOF....THEY ARE THE BATMAN AND ROBIN!
WHETHER MIDAS LIKES IT OR NOT, WE'RE GOING TO STOP THOSE DIRTY BLACKMAILERS!
GOT THE FIVE GRAND, MIDAS?
YES, IN FIVES AND TENS, AS YOU REQUESTED.
SUDDENLY, THERE IS THE SOUND OF SPLINTERING WOOD-AND A PAIR OF BROAD SHOULDERS CRASHES THROUGH THE DOOR.....
SORRY-BUT I DON'T THINK I'LL BOTHER TO KNOCK!
OH, MAMA! IT'S THE BATMAN!
GUNPLAY ALWAYS DID BOTHER ME!
O-OH!
PHFFT!
HOW'S THAT FOR USING MY HEAD!
PANIC-STRICKEN, THE REMAINING BLACKMAILERS RETREAT......
C'MON, WE'LL SPLIT UP! I'LL GO UP THE FIRE-ESCAPE AND YOU GO DOWN!
BE WITH YOU IN A SEC! I WANNA DO SOMETHIN' FIRST!

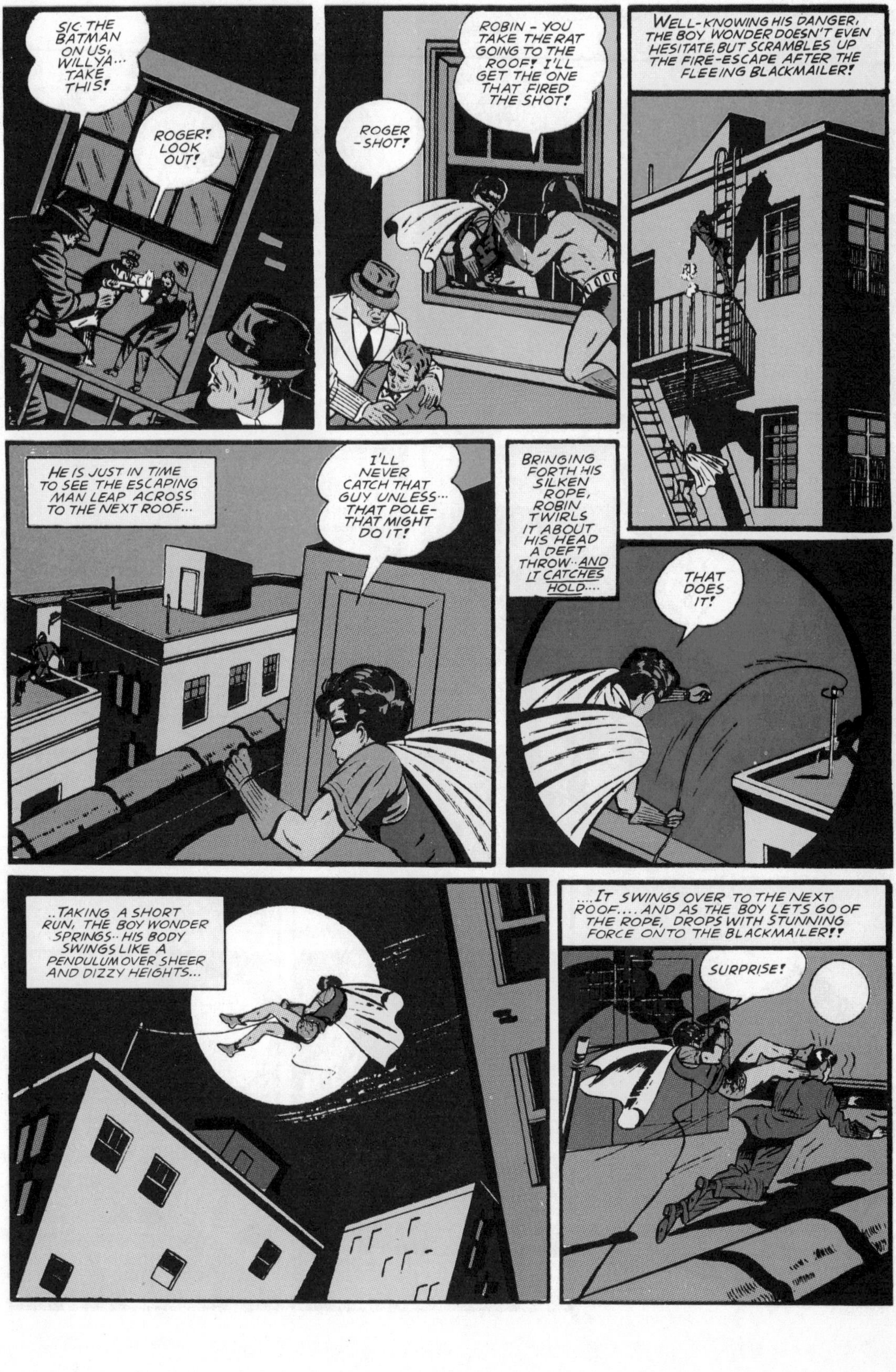
SIC THE BATMAN ON US, WILLYA... TAKE THIS!
ROGER! LOOK OUT!
ROBIN - YOU TAKE THE RAT GOING TO THE ROOF! I'LL GET THE ONE THAT FIRED THE SHOT!
ROGER -SHOT!
WELL-KNOWING HIS DANGER, THE BOY WONDER DOESN'T EVEN HESITATE, BUT SCRAMBLES UP THE FIRE-ESCAPE AFTER THE FLEEING BLACKMAILER!
HE IS JUST IN TIME TO SEE THE ESCAPING MAN LEAP ACROSS TO THE NEXT ROOF...
I'LL NEVER CATCH THAT GUY UNLESS... THAT POLE- THAT MIGHT DO IT!
BRINGING FORTH HIS SILKEN ROPE, ROBIN TWIRLS IT ABOUT HIS HEAD A DEFT THROW..AND IT CATCHES HOLD....
THAT DOES IT!
..TAKING A SHORT RUN, THE BOY WONDER SPRINGS.. HIS BODY SWINGS LIKE A PENDULUM OVER SHEER AND DIZZY HEIGHTS...
....IT SWINGS OVER TO THE NEXT ROOF.... AND AS THE BOY LETS GO OF THE ROPE, DROPS WITH STUNNING FORCE ONTO THE BLACKMAILER!!
SURPRISE!

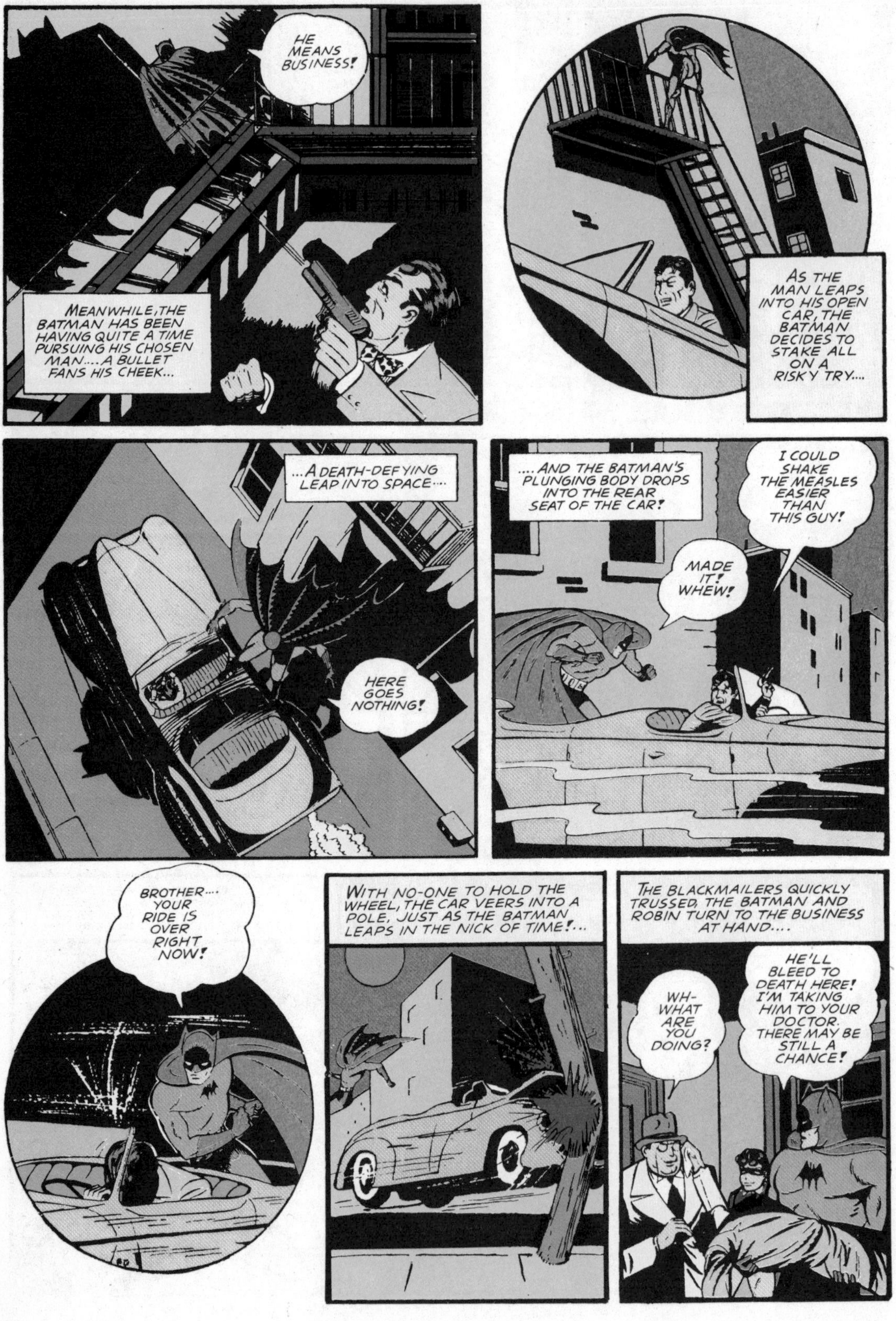
HE MEANS BUSINESS!
MEANWHILE, THE BATMAN HAS BEEN HAVING QUITE A TIME PURSUING HIS CHOSEN MAN.... A BULLET FANS HIS CHEEK...
AS THE MAN LEAPS INTO HIS OPEN CAR, THE BATMAN DECIDES TO STAKE ALL ON A RISKY TRY....
...A DEATH-DEFYING LEAP INTO SPACE....
HERE GOES NOTHING!
....AND THE BATMAN'S PLUNGING BODY DROPS INTO THE REAR SEAT OF THE CAR!
I COULD SHAKE THE MEASLES EASIER THAN THIS GUY!
MADE IT! WHEW!
BROTHER.... YOUR RIDE IS OVER RIGHT NOW!
WITH NO-ONE TO HOLD THE WHEEL, THE CAR VEERS INTO A POLE, JUST AS THE BATMAN LEAPS IN THE NICK OF TIME!...
THE BLACKMAILERS QUICKLY TRUSSED, THE BATMAN AND ROBIN TURN TO THE BUSINESS AT HAND....
WH-WHAT ARE YOU DOING?
HE'LL BLEED TO DEATH HERE! I'M TAKING HIM TO YOUR DOCTOR. THERE MAY BE STILL A CHANCE!

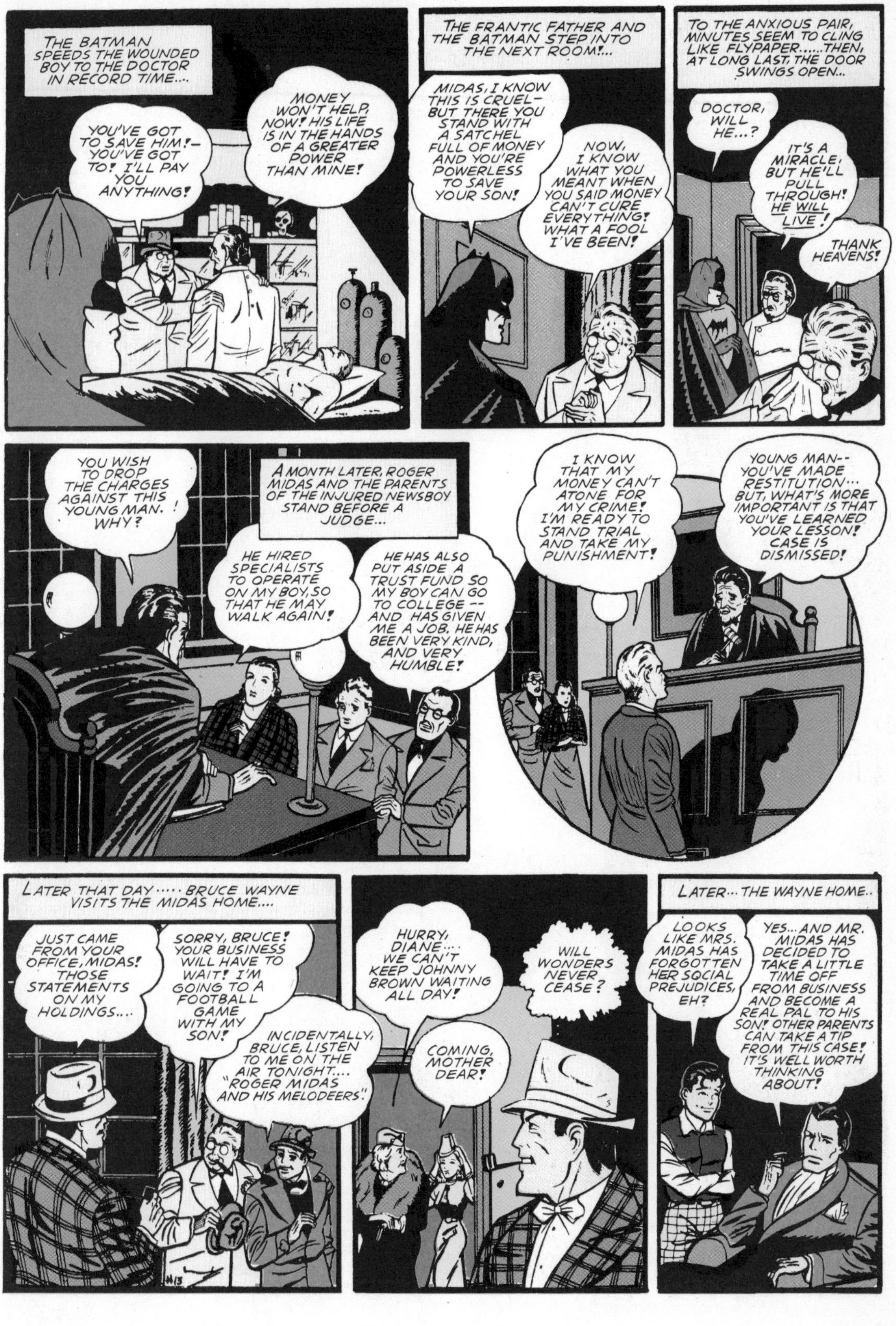

THE BATMAN SPEEDS THE WOUNDED BOY TO THE DOCTOR IN RECORD TIME....
YOU'VE GOT TO SAVE HIM!— YOU'VE GOT TO! I'LL PAY YOU ANYTHING!
MONEY WON'T HELP, NOW! HIS LIFE IS IN THE HANDS OF A GREATER POWER THAN MINE!
THE FRANTIC FATHER AND THE BATMAN STEP INTO THE NEXT ROOM!...
MIDAS, I KNOW THIS IS CRUEL— BUT THERE YOU STAND WITH A SATCHEL FULL OF MONEY AND YOU'RE POWERLESS TO SAVE YOUR SON!
NOW, I KNOW WHAT YOU MEANT WHEN YOU SAID MONEY CAN'T CURE EVERYTHING! WHAT A FOOL I'VE BEEN!
TO THE ANXIOUS PAIR, MINUTES SEEM TO CLING LIKE FLYPAPER.....THEN, AT LONG LAST, THE DOOR SWINGS OPEN...
DOCTOR, WILL HE...?
IT'S A MIRACLE, BUT HE'LL PULL THROUGH! HE WILL LIVE!
THANK HEAVENS!
YOU WISH TO DROP THE CHARGES AGAINST THIS YOUNG MAN. WHY?
A MONTH LATER, ROGER MIDAS AND THE PARENTS OF THE INJURED NEWSBOY STAND BEFORE A JUDGE...
HE HIRED SPECIALISTS TO OPERATE ON MY BOY, SO THAT HE MAY WALK AGAIN!
HE HAS ALSO PUT ASIDE A TRUST FUND SO MY BOY CAN GO TO COLLEGE -- AND HAS GIVEN ME A JOB. HE HAS BEEN VERY KIND, AND VERY HUMBLE!
I KNOW THAT MY MONEY CAN'T ATONE FOR MY CRIME! I'M READY TO STAND TRIAL AND TAKE MY PUNISHMENT!
YOUNG MAN-- YOU'VE MADE RESTITUTION... BUT, WHAT'S MORE IMPORTANT IS THAT YOU'VE LEARNED YOUR LESSON! CASE IS DISMISSED!
LATER THAT DAY..... BRUCE WAYNE VISITS THE MIDAS HOME....
JUST CAME FROM YOUR OFFICE, MIDAS! THOSE STATEMENTS ON MY HOLDINGS....
SORRY, BRUCE! YOUR BUSINESS WILL HAVE TO WAIT! I'M GOING TO A FOOTBALL GAME WITH MY SON!
INCIDENTALLY, BRUCE, LISTEN TO ME ON THE AIR TONIGHT.... "ROGER MIDAS AND HIS MELODEERS".
HURRY, DIANE.... WE CAN'T KEEP JOHNNY BROWN WAITING ALL DAY!
COMING, MOTHER DEAR!
WILL WONDERS NEVER CEASE?
LATER... THE WAYNE HOME..
LOOKS LIKE MRS. MIDAS HAS FORGOTTEN HER SOCIAL PREJUDICES, EH?
YES... AND MR. MIDAS HAS DECIDED TO TAKE A LITTLE TIME OFF FROM BUSINESS AND BECOME A REAL PAL TO HIS SON! OTHER PARENTS CAN TAKE A TIP FROM THIS CASE! IT'S WELL WORTH THINKING ABOUT!

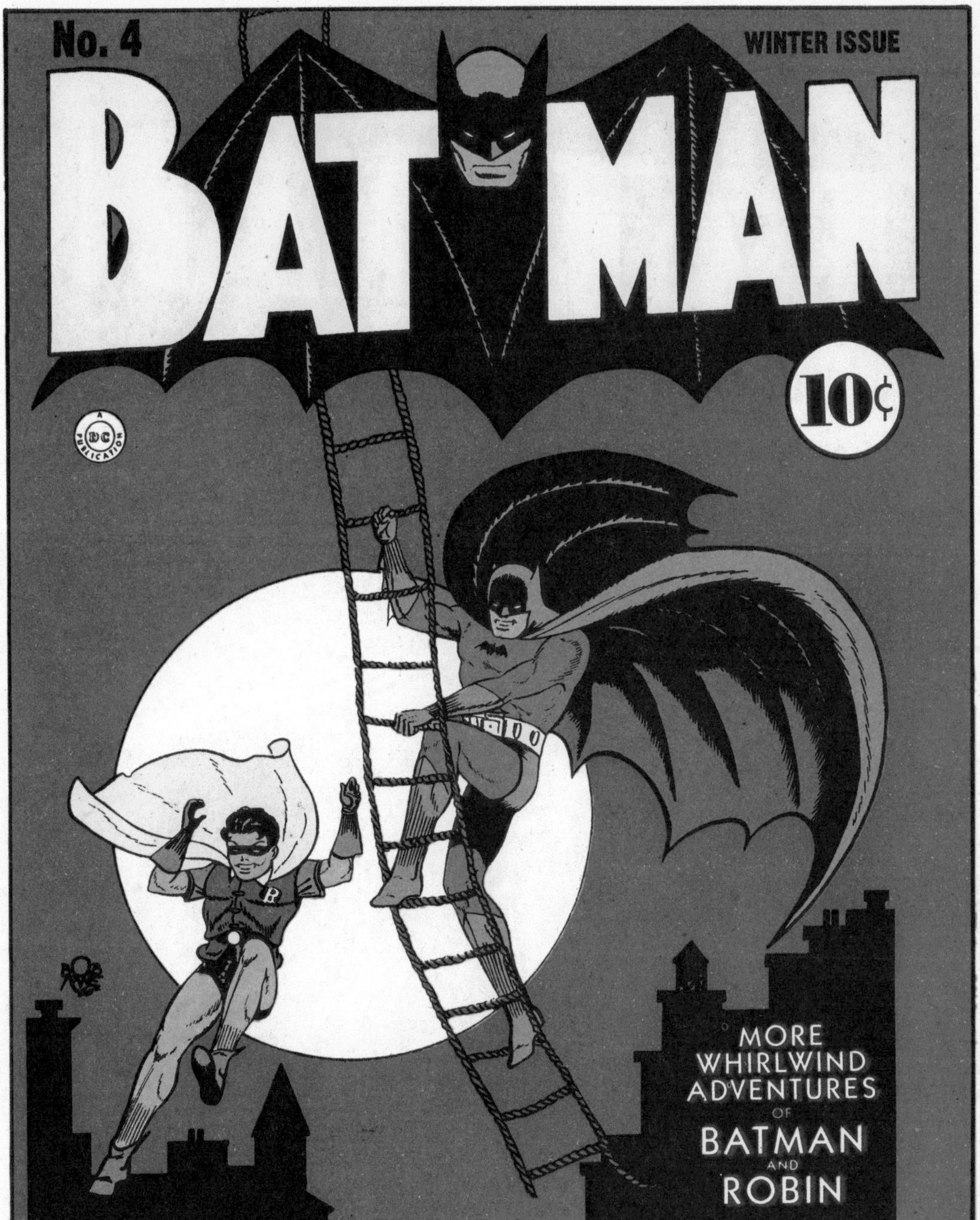
No. 4
WINTER ISSUE
BATMAN
10¢
A DC PUBLICATION
MORE WHIRLWIND ADVENTURES OF BATMAN AND ROBIN

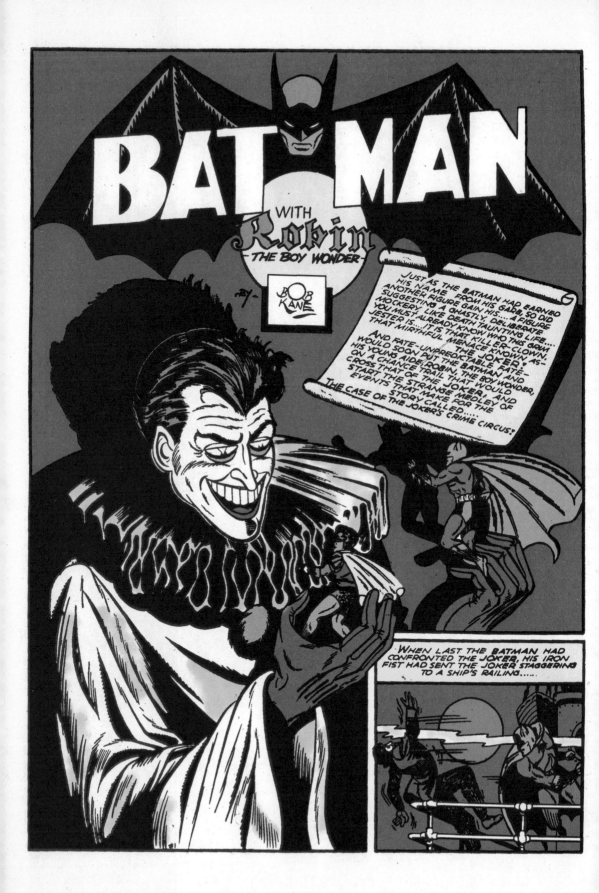

BAT MAN

WITH
Robin
-THE BOY WONDER-

-BY-
BOB KANE

JUST AS THE BATMAN HAD EARNED
HIS NAME FROM HIS GARB, SO DID
ANOTHER FIGURE GAIN HIS... A FIGURE
SUGGESTING A GHASTLY, DELIBERATE
MOCKERY, LIKE DEATH TAUNTING LIFE...
YOU MUST ALREADY KNOW WHO THIS GRIM
JESTER IS... IT IS THAT KILLER-CLOWN,
THAT MIRTHFUL MENACE KNOWN AS-
THE JOKER!

AND FATE-UNPREDICTABLE FATE-
WOULD SOON PUT THE BATMAN AND
HIS YOUNG AIDE, ROBIN, THE BOY WONDER,
ON A CHANCE TRAIL THAT WOULD
CROSS THAT OF THE JOKER, AND
START THE STRANGE MEDLEY OF
EVENTS THAT MAKE FOR THE
STORY CALLED...
THE CASE OF THE JOKER'S CRIME CIRCUS!

WHEN LAST THE BATMAN HAD
CONFRONTED THE JOKER, HIS IRON
FIST HAD SENT THE JOKER STAGGERING
TO A SHIP'S RAILING......

.....THE JOKER PLUMMETED DOWN TO HIT THE WATERS AND REMAIN BELOW......

I WONDER IF THIS IS REALLY THE END OF THE JOKER AT LAST?

.....AS THE LIGHTS OF THE SHIP TWINKLE LIKE FIREFLIES IN THE DISTANCE, A FIGURE RISES TO THE SURFACE OF THE WATER... IT IS THE JOKER?

.....HOURS LATER, A YACHT MAKES OUT HIS BOBBING FORM...

MAN AHEAD, SIR—LOOKS LIKE HE'S CLINGING TO A BIT OF DRIFTWOOD!

GIVE THE NECESSARY ORDER TO PICK HIM UP!

....THE JOKER IS TAKEN ASHORE......

QUEER SORT OF DUCK, WASN'T HE, SIR?

YES....AND THAT BLANK-WHITE FACE OF HIS...UGH!—IT GAVE ME THE CREEPS! WELL, AT LEAST, WE SAVED A MAN'S LIFE!

PERHAPS HE WOULD NOT HAVE MADE THAT STATEMENT WITH SUCH THANKFULNESS HAD HE KNOWN WHO THAT MAN WAS!

UNOBSERVED, HE STEALS TO THE EDGE OF TOWN TO A SEEMINGLY DESERTED, GLOOMY OLD MANSION DUBBED BY THE PEOPLE AS "HAUNTED"....

BUT THE STRANGE-LOOKING MANSION IS NOT REALLY "HAUNTED" AND DESERTED..... IN REALITY, IT IS THE HIDDEN SANCTUM OF THE JOKER...

#2

.....THEN, THE JOKER LAUGHS. A WILD, JEERING LAUGH THAT MAKES THE VERY SILENCE OF THE ROOM CRAWL WITH MENACE.

I'M ALIVE! HA HA! I'M ALIVE! HA HA HA HA!

THE CLEVEREST AND THE MOST DANGEROUS CRIMINAL IN THE ANNALS OF CRIME WAS STILL AT LIBERTY!

THE BATMAN THINKS I'M DEAD. HE'LL KNOW DIFFERENTLY WHEN WE MEET AGAIN! ...AND WE SHALL MEET AGAIN!

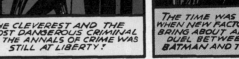

THE TIME WAS CLOSE WHEN NEW FACTORS WOULD BRING ABOUT AN ACTUAL DUEL BETWEEN THE BATMAN AND THE JOKER!

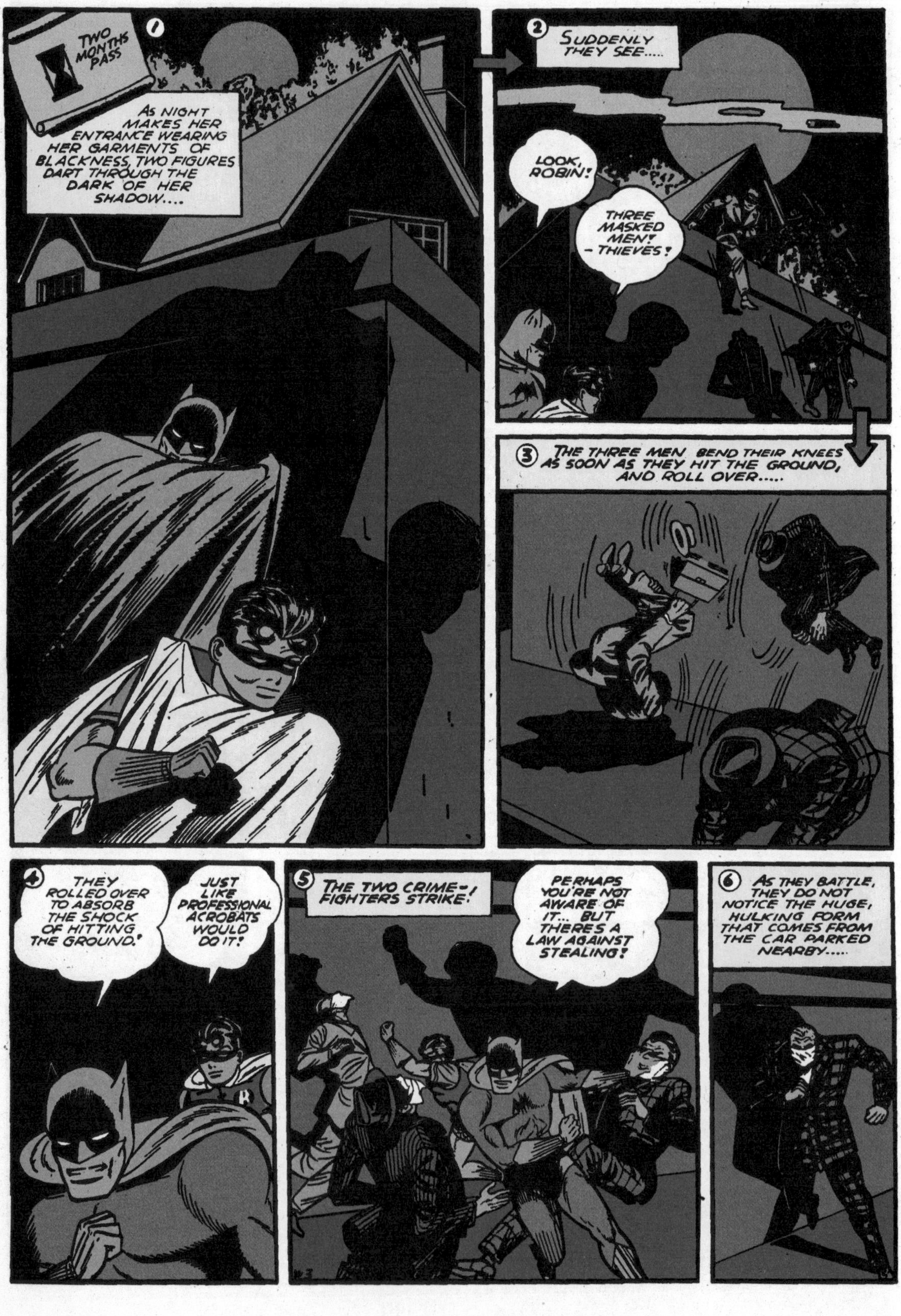
TWO MONTHS PASS
AS NIGHT MAKES HER ENTRANCE WEARING HER GARMENTS OF BLACKNESS, TWO FIGURES DART THROUGH THE DARK OF HER SHADOW....
SUDDENLY THEY SEE.....
LOOK, ROBIN!
THREE MASKED MEN! - THIEVES!
THE THREE MEN BEND THEIR KNEES AS SOON AS THEY HIT THE GROUND, AND ROLL OVER.....
THEY ROLLED OVER TO ABSORB THE SHOCK OF HITTING THE GROUND.
JUST LIKE PROFESSIONAL ACROBATS WOULD DO IT!
THE TWO CRIME-FIGHTERS STRIKE!
PERHAPS YOU'RE NOT AWARE OF IT... BUT THERE'S A LAW AGAINST STEALING!
AS THEY BATTLE, THEY DO NOT NOTICE THE HUGE, HULKING FORM THAT COMES FROM THE CAR PARKED NEARBY.....

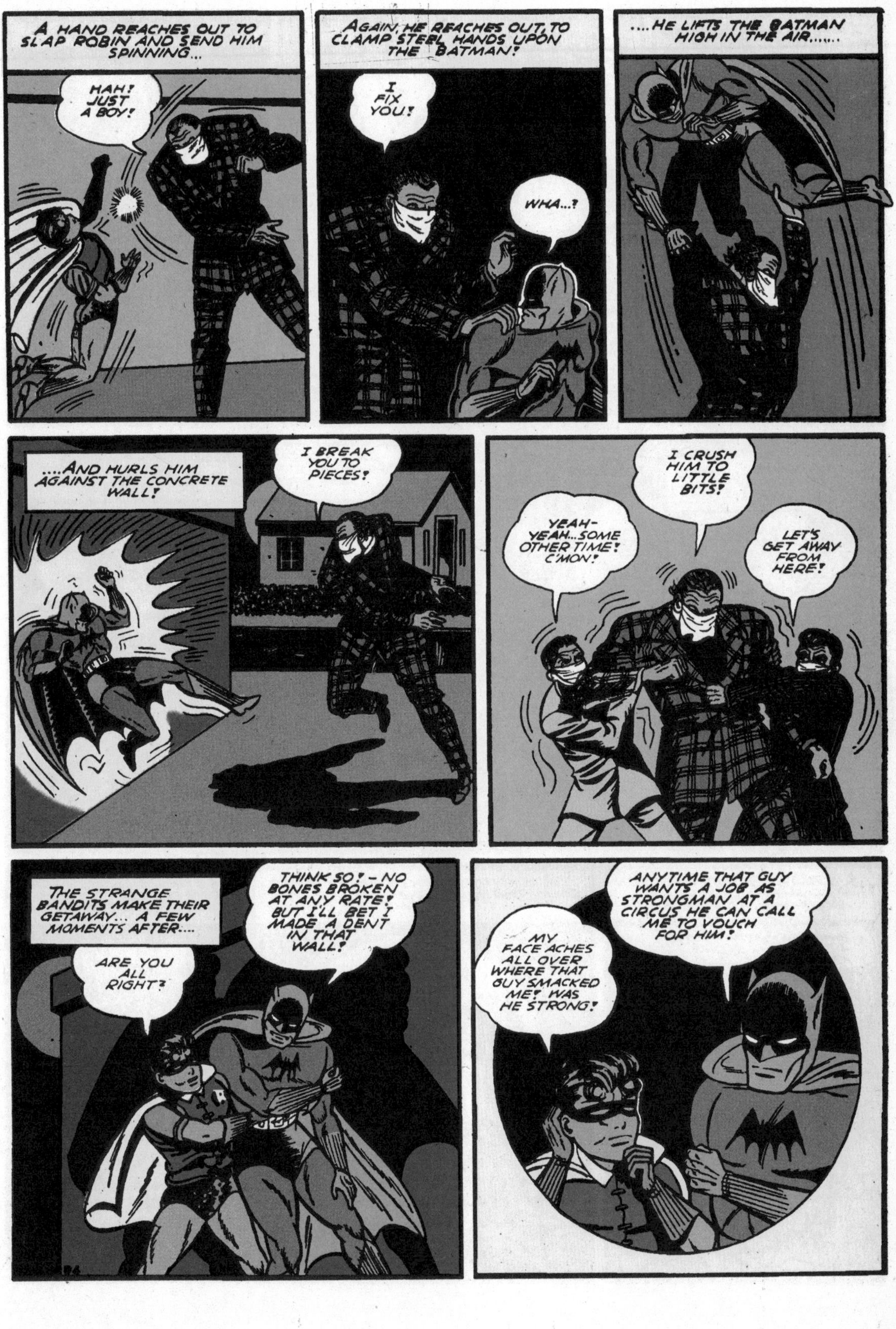
A HAND REACHES OUT TO SLAP ROBIN AND SEND HIM SPINNING...
HAH! JUST A BOY!
AGAIN, HE REACHES OUT, TO CLAMP STEEL HANDS UPON THE BATMAN!
I FIX YOU!
WHA...?
....HE LIFTS THE BATMAN HIGH IN THE AIR.......
....AND HURLS HIM AGAINST THE CONCRETE WALL!
I BREAK YOU TO PIECES!
I CRUSH HIM TO LITTLE BITS!
YEAH-YEAH...SOME OTHER TIME! C'MON!
LET'S GET AWAY FROM HERE!
THE STRANGE BANDITS MAKE THEIR GETAWAY... A FEW MOMENTS AFTER:...
THINK SO! - NO BONES BROKEN AT ANY RATE! BUT I'LL BET I MADE A DENT IN THAT WALL!
ARE YOU ALL RIGHT?
ANYTIME THAT GUY WANTS A JOB AS STRONGMAN AT A CIRCUS HE CAN CALL ME TO VOUCH FOR HIM!
MY FACE ACHES ALL OVER WHERE THAT GUY SMACKED ME! WAS HE STRONG!

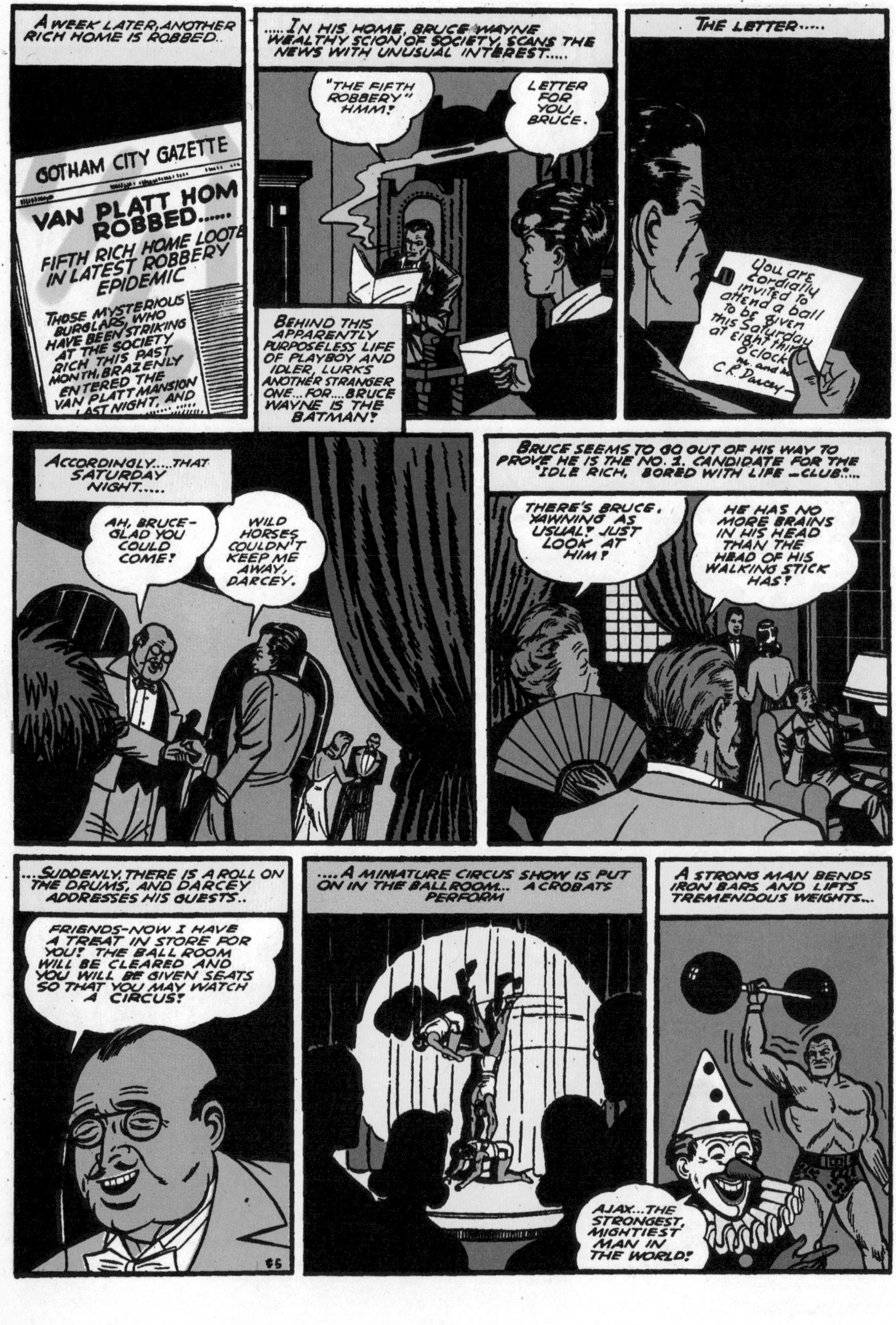
A WEEK LATER, ANOTHER RICH HOME IS ROBBED..
GOTHAM CITY GAZETTE
VAN PLATT HOM ROBBED......
FIFTH RICH HOME LOOTE IN LATEST ROBBERY EPIDEMIC
THOSE MYSTERIOUS BURGLARS, WHO HAVE BEEN STRIKING AT THE SOCIETY RICH THIS PAST MONTH, BRAZENLY ENTERED THE VAN PLATT MANSION LAST NIGHT, AND
.....IN HIS HOME, BRUCE WAYNE WEALTHY SCION OF SOCIETY, SCANS THE NEWS WITH UNUSUAL INTEREST.....
"THE FIFTH ROBBERY" HMM!
LETTER FOR YOU, BRUCE.
BEHIND THIS APPARENTLY PURPOSELESS LIFE OF PLAYBOY AND IDLER, LURKS ANOTHER STRANGER ONE... FOR.... BRUCE WAYNE IS THE BATMAN!
THE LETTER.....
You are cordially invited to attend a ball to be given this Saturday at eight thirty o'clock
C.R. Darcey
ACCORDINGLY.....THAT SATURDAY NIGHT.....
AH, BRUCE-GLAD YOU COULD COME!
WILD HORSES COULDN'T KEEP ME AWAY, DARCEY.
BRUCE SEEMS TO GO OUT OF HIS WAY TO PROVE HE IS THE NO. 1. CANDIDATE FOR THE 'IDLE RICH, BORED WITH LIFE -CLUB'....
THERE'S BRUCE, YAWNING AS USUAL! JUST LOOK AT HIM!
HE HAS NO MORE BRAINS IN HIS HEAD THAN THE HEAD OF HIS WALKING STICK HAS!
...SUDDENLY, THERE IS A ROLL ON THE DRUMS, AND DARCEY ADDRESSES HIS GUESTS..
FRIENDS-NOW I HAVE A TREAT IN STORE FOR YOU! THE BALL ROOM WILL BE CLEARED AND YOU WILL BE GIVEN SEATS SO THAT YOU MAY WATCH A CIRCUS!
.....A MINIATURE CIRCUS SHOW IS PUT ON IN THE BALLROOM... ACROBATS PERFORM
A STRONG MAN BENDS IRON BARS AND LIFTS TREMENDOUS WEIGHTS...
AJAX...THE STRONGEST, MIGHTIEST MAN IN THE WORLD!

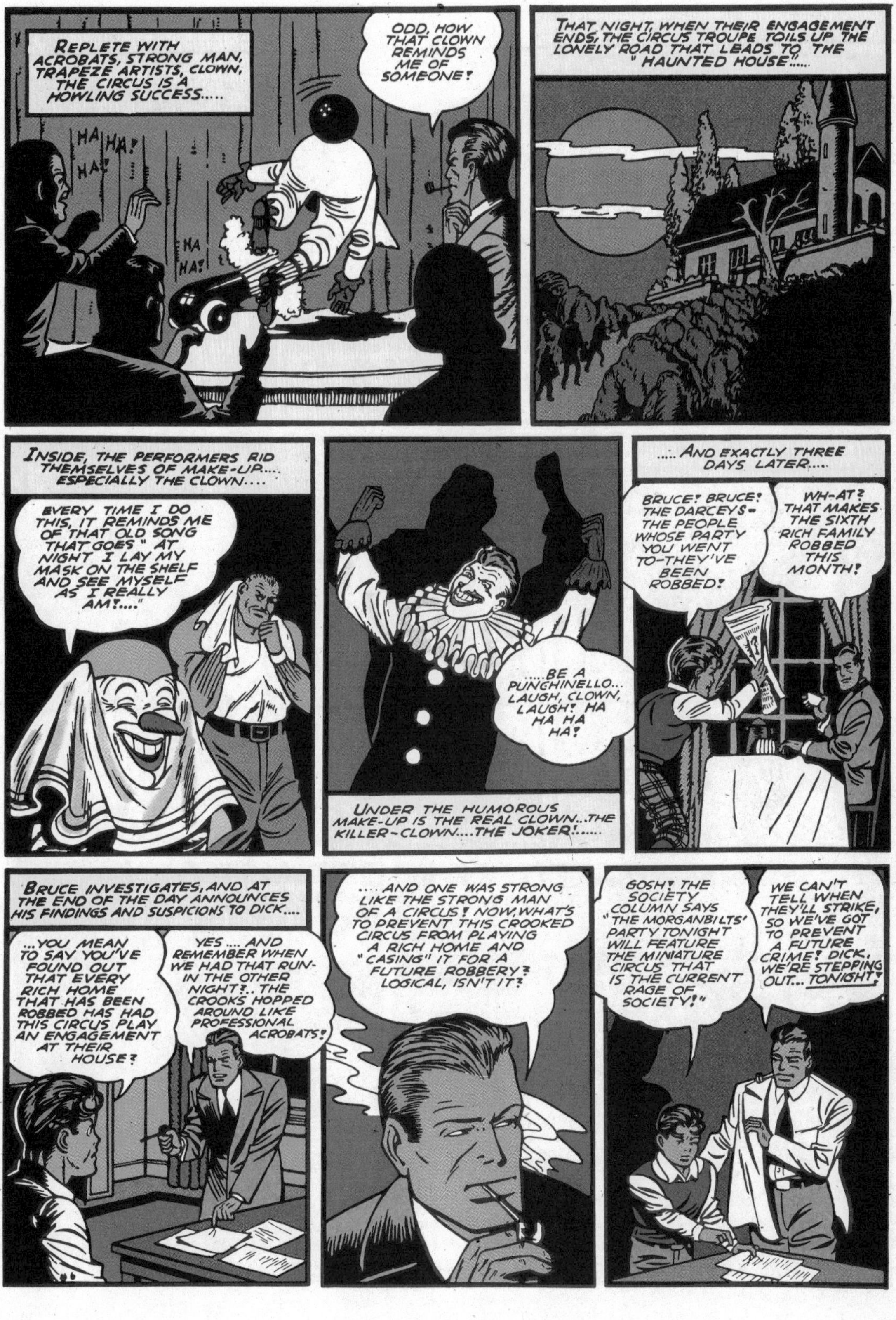
REPLETE WITH ACROBATS, STRONG MAN, TRAPEZE ARTISTS, CLOWN, THE CIRCUS IS A HOWLING SUCCESS.....
ODD, HOW THAT CLOWN REMINDS ME OF SOMEONE!
HA HA! HA!
HA HA!
THAT NIGHT, WHEN THEIR ENGAGEMENT ENDS, THE CIRCUS TROUPE TOILS UP THE LONELY ROAD THAT LEADS TO THE "HAUNTED HOUSE".....
INSIDE, THE PERFORMERS RID THEMSELVES OF MAKE-UP.... ESPECIALLY THE CLOWN....
EVERY TIME I DO THIS, IT REMINDS ME OF THAT OLD SONG THAT GOES "AT NIGHT I LAY MY MASK ON THE SHELF AND SEE MYSELF AS I REALLY AM!...."
.....BE A PUNCHINELLO... LAUGH, CLOWN, LAUGH! HA HA HA HA!
UNDER THE HUMOROUS MAKE-UP IS THE REAL CLOWN...THE KILLER-CLOWN....THE JOKER!.....
..... AND EXACTLY THREE DAYS LATER.....
BRUCE! BRUCE! THE DARCEYS-- THE PEOPLE WHOSE PARTY YOU WENT TO-THEY'VE BEEN ROBBED!
WH-AT? THAT MAKES THE SIXTH RICH FAMILY ROBBED THIS MONTH!
BRUCE INVESTIGATES, AND AT THE END OF THE DAY ANNOUNCES HIS FINDINGS AND SUSPICIONS TO DICK....
...YOU MEAN TO SAY YOU'VE FOUND OUT THAT EVERY RICH HOME THAT HAS BEEN ROBBED HAS HAD THIS CIRCUS PLAY AN ENGAGEMENT AT THEIR HOUSE?
YES .... AND REMEMBER WHEN WE HAD THAT RUN-IN THE OTHER NIGHT?.. THE CROOKS HOPPED AROUND LIKE PROFESSIONAL ACROBATS!
.... AND ONE WAS STRONG LIKE THE STRONG MAN OF A CIRCUS! NOW, WHAT'S TO PREVENT THIS CROOKED CIRCUS FROM PLAYING A RICH HOME AND "CASING" IT FOR A FUTURE ROBBERY? LOGICAL, ISN'T IT?
GOSH! THE SOCIETY COLUMN SAYS "THE MORGANBILTS' PARTY TONIGHT WILL FEATURE THE MINIATURE CIRCUS THAT IS THE CURRENT RAGE OF SOCIETY!"
WE CAN'T TELL WHEN THEY'LL STRIKE, SO WE'VE GOT TO PREVENT A FUTURE CRIME! DICK, WE'RE STEPPING OUT... TONIGHT!

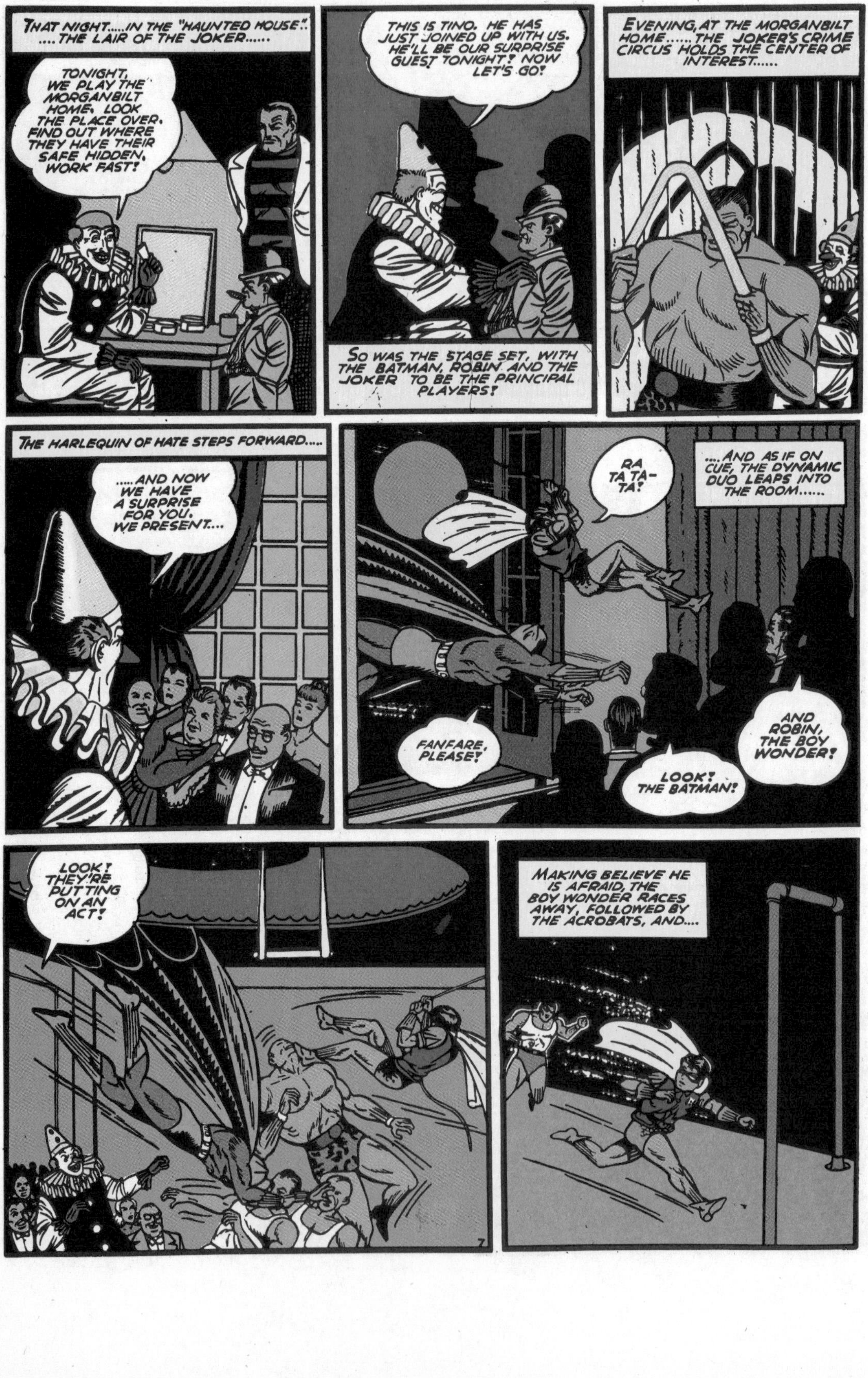
THAT NIGHT.....IN THE "HAUNTED HOUSE".
....THE LAIR OF THE JOKER......
TONIGHT, WE PLAY THE MORGANBILT HOME. LOOK THE PLACE OVER. FIND OUT WHERE THEY HAVE THEIR SAFE HIDDEN. WORK FAST!
THIS IS TINO. HE HAS JUST JOINED UP WITH US. HE'LL BE OUR SURPRISE GUEST TONIGHT! NOW LET'S GO!
SO WAS THE STAGE SET, WITH THE BATMAN, ROBIN AND THE JOKER TO BE THE PRINCIPAL PLAYERS!
EVENING, AT THE MORGANBILT HOME......THE JOKER'S CRIME CIRCUS HOLDS THE CENTER OF INTEREST......
THE HARLEQUIN OF HATE STEPS FORWARD.....
.....AND NOW WE HAVE A SURPRISE FOR YOU. WE PRESENT....
RA TA TA-TA!
....AND AS IF ON CUE, THE DYNAMIC DUO LEAPS INTO THE ROOM......
FANFARE, PLEASE!
LOOK! THE BATMAN!
AND ROBIN, THE BOY WONDER!
LOOK! THEY'RE PUTTING ON AN ACT!
MAKING BELIEVE HE IS AFRAID, THE BOY WONDER RACES AWAY, FOLLOWED BY THE ACROBATS, AND....

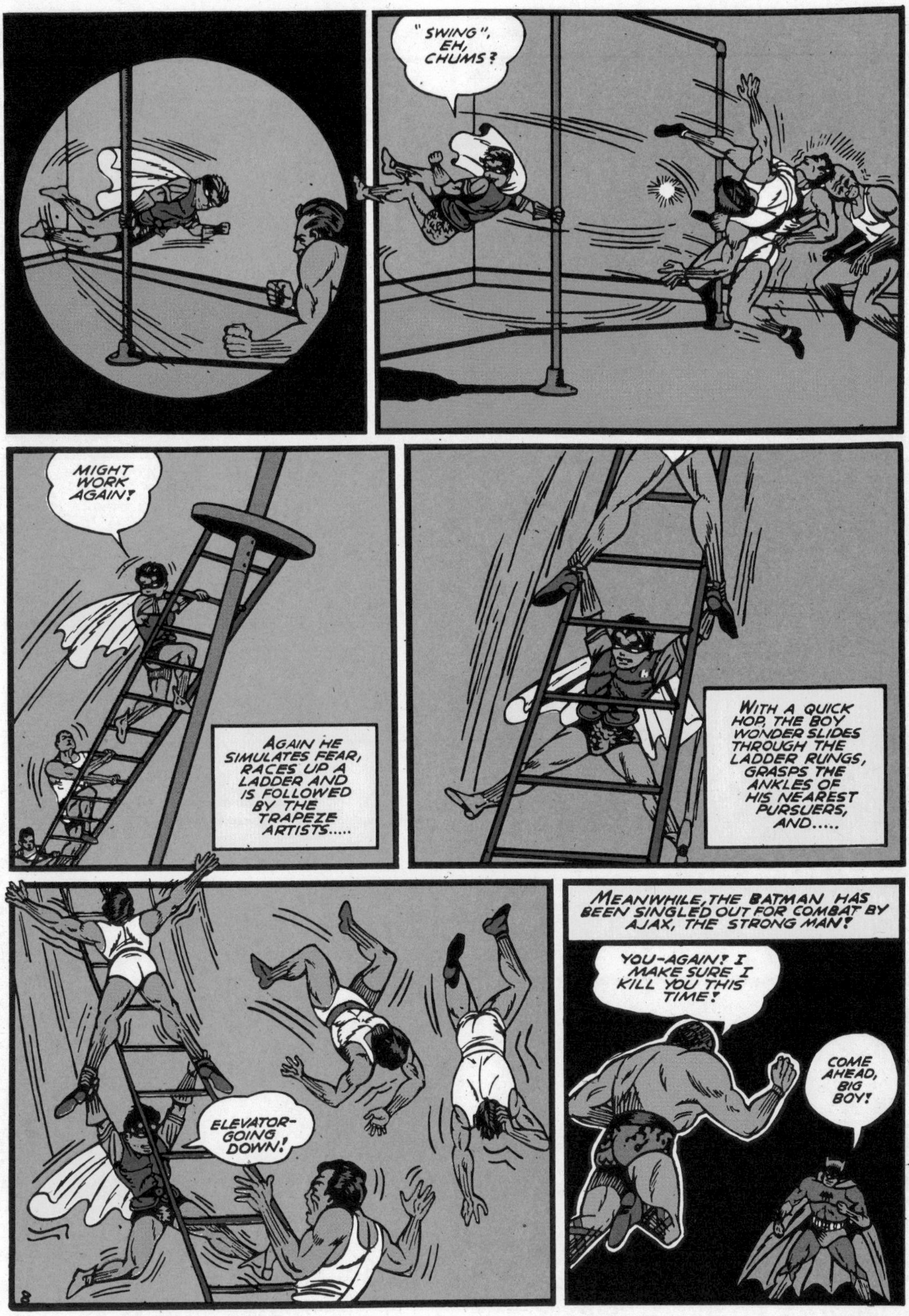
"SWING", EH, CHUMS?
MIGHT WORK AGAIN!
AGAIN HE SIMULATES FEAR, RACES UP A LADDER AND IS FOLLOWED BY THE TRAPEZE ARTISTS.....
WITH A QUICK HOP, THE BOY WONDER SLIDES THROUGH THE LADDER RUNGS, GRASPS THE ANKLES OF HIS NEAREST PURSUERS, AND.....
ELEVATOR-GOING DOWN!
8
MEANWHILE, THE BATMAN HAS BEEN SINGLED OUT FOR COMBAT BY AJAX, THE STRONG MAN!
YOU-AGAIN? I MAKE SURE I KILL YOU THIS TIME!
COME AHEAD, BIG BOY!

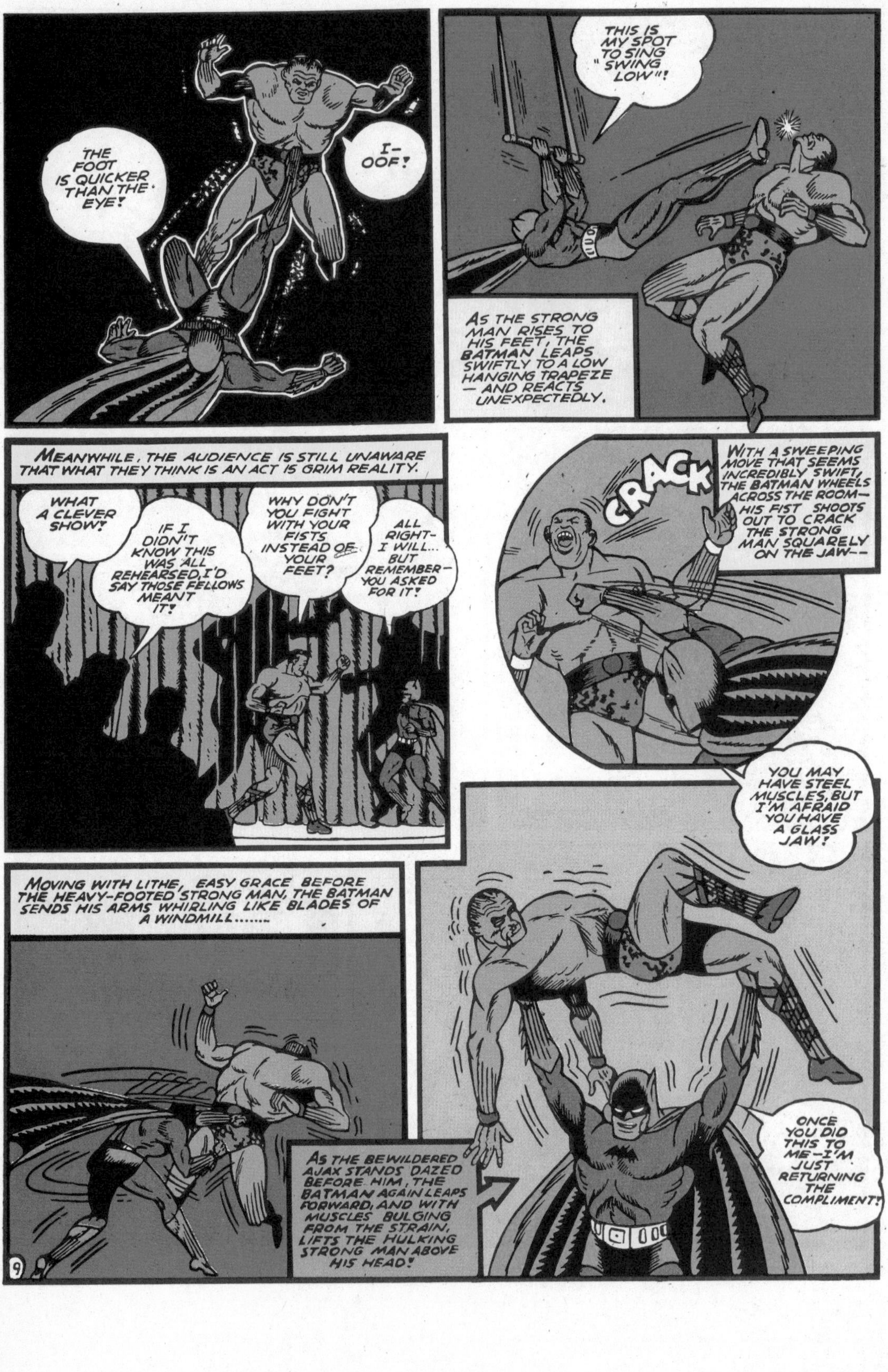
THE FOOT IS QUICKER THAN THE EYE!
I- OOF!
THIS IS MY SPOT TO SING "SWING LOW"!
AS THE STRONG MAN RISES TO HIS FEET, THE BATMAN LEAPS SWIFTLY TO A LOW HANGING TRAPEZE — AND REACTS UNEXPECTEDLY.
MEANWHILE, THE AUDIENCE IS STILL UNAWARE THAT WHAT THEY THINK IS AN ACT IS GRIM REALITY.
WHAT A CLEVER SHOW!
IF I DIDN'T KNOW THIS WAS ALL REHEARSED, I'D SAY THOSE FELLOWS MEANT IT!
WHY DON'T YOU FIGHT WITH YOUR FISTS INSTEAD OF YOUR FEET?
ALL RIGHT- I WILL... BUT REMEMBER- YOU ASKED FOR IT!
WITH A SWEEPING MOVE THAT SEEMS INCREDIBLY SWIFT, THE BATMAN WHEELS ACROSS THE ROOM— HIS FIST SHOOTS OUT TO CRACK THE STRONG MAN SQUARELY ON THE JAW--
CRACK
YOU MAY HAVE STEEL MUSCLES, BUT I'M AFRAID YOU HAVE A GLASS JAW!
MOVING WITH LITHE, EASY GRACE BEFORE THE HEAVY-FOOTED STRONG MAN, THE BATMAN SENDS HIS ARMS WHIRLING LIKE BLADES OF A WINDMILL.......
AS THE BEWILDERED AJAX STANDS DAZED BEFORE HIM, THE BATMAN AGAIN LEAPS FORWARD, AND WITH MUSCLES BULGING FROM THE STRAIN, LIFTS THE HULKING STRONG MAN ABOVE HIS HEAD!
ONCE YOU DID THIS TO ME—I'M JUST RETURNING THE COMPLIMENT!
9

WITH A SUDDEN, QUICK HEAVE OF HIS ARMS, THE *BATMAN* SLAMS THE GIANT BODY TO THE GROUND......

ONCE AGAIN, THE DARK KNIGHT HAS GIVEN PROOF OF THE OLD ADAGE.....BRUTE STRENGTH CANNOT AVAIL AGAINST A QUICK MIND AND A QUICK BODY.

....THE JOKER CHOOSES THAT MOMENT TO EFFECT HIS ESCAPE......

LOOK! THAT CLOWN—HE'S GETTING AWAY!

THE CLOWN!— NOW, I KNOW WHY HE REMINDED ME OF SOMEONE... HE'S THE JOKER-- ALIVE!

THE AUDIENCE LEARNS THE TRUTH...

...AND IF THE POLICE WILL QUESTION THESE MEN, YOU'LL FIND THIS ENTIRE CIRCUS IS RESPONSIBLE FOR THESE ROBBERIES!

C'MON, ROBIN!

DID YOU HEAR THAT?

NO WONDER THAT FIGHT LOOKED SO REAL!

KEEPING THE JOKER'S CAR IN SIGHT, THE BATMAN AND ROBIN FOLLOW HIM TO HIS LAIR!.....

SO, THIS IS HIS HIDEOUT!

SAY— THIS IS THE "HAUNTED HOUSE"?

AS THE BATMAN AND ROBIN DASH UP THE WINDING PATH, A FACE PEERS OUT AT THEM .....THE JOKER!

SO, THEY'RE COMING IN, ARE THEY? I'LL FIX THEM. I'LL SCARE THEM JUST AS I SCARE THE VILLAGERS WHEN THEY PRY INTO THIS HOUSE! HA HA HA!

AS THE BATMAN AND ROBIN ENTER THE MYSTERIOUS HOUSE, THE MASSIVE DOOR SUDDENLY SWINGS SHUT BEHIND THEM!

THE DOOR— LOCKED ITSELF!

SLAM!

THE TWO MOUNT CREAKY, OLD STAIRS.....

PLEASANT LITTLE PLACE, ISN'T IT?

YES— IT MAKES A LOVELY BREEDING GROUND FOR GHOSTS!

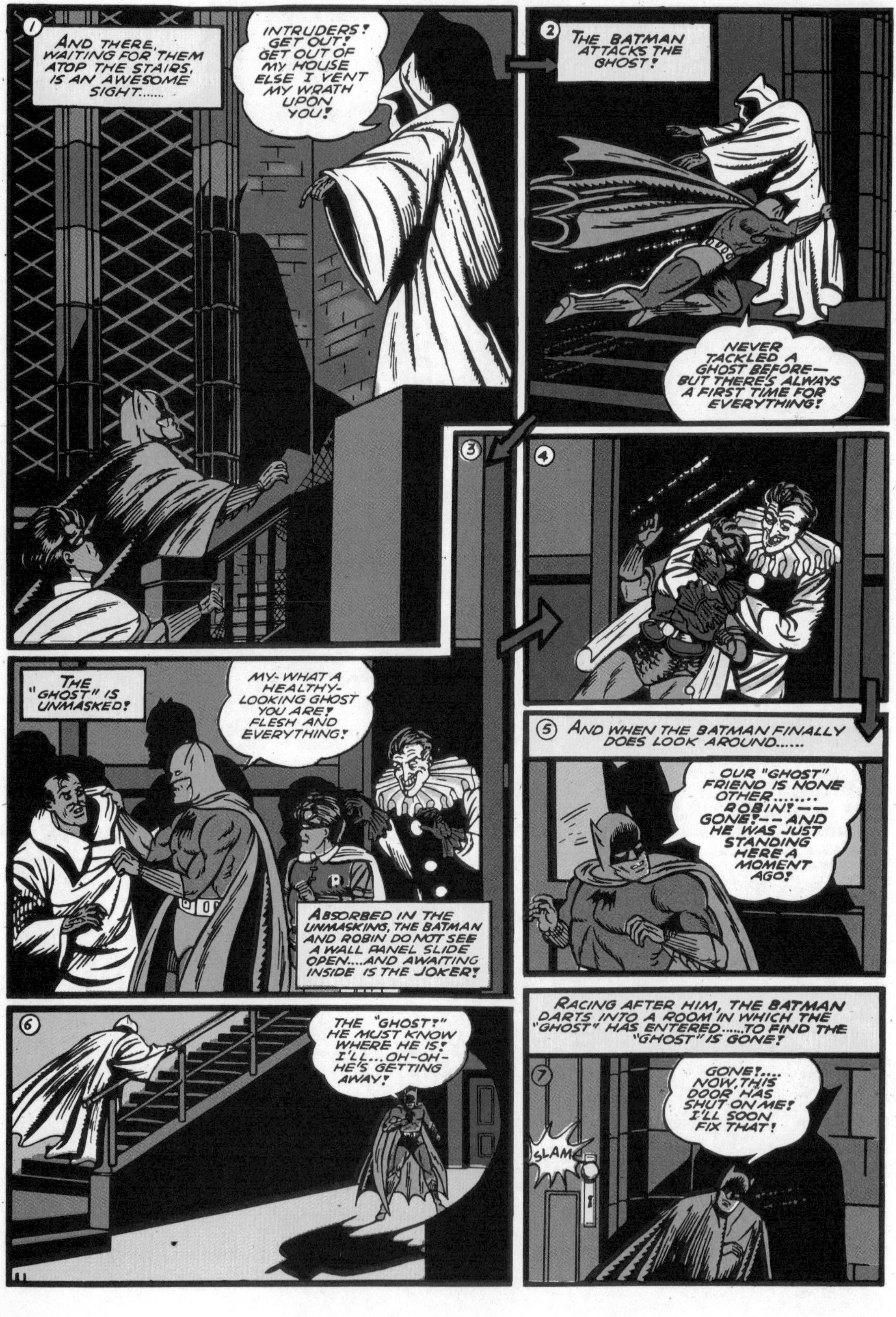
And there, waiting for them atop the stairs, is an awesome sight......
Intruders! Get out! Get out of my house else I vent my wrath upon you!
The Batman attacks the ghost!
Never tackled a ghost before—but there's always a first time for everything!
The "Ghost" is unmasked!
My- what a healthy- looking ghost you are! Flesh and everything!
Absorbed in the unmasking, the Batman and Robin do not see a wall panel slide open....and awaiting inside is the Joker!
And when the Batman finally does look around......
Our "Ghost" friend is none other........ Robin!— Gone!— And he was just standing here a moment ago!
The "Ghost!" He must know where he is! I'll...oh-oh- he's getting away!
Racing after him, the Batman darts into a room in which the "Ghost" has entered......to find the "Ghost" is gone!
Gone!.... Now, this door has shut on me! I'll soon fix that!
SLAM

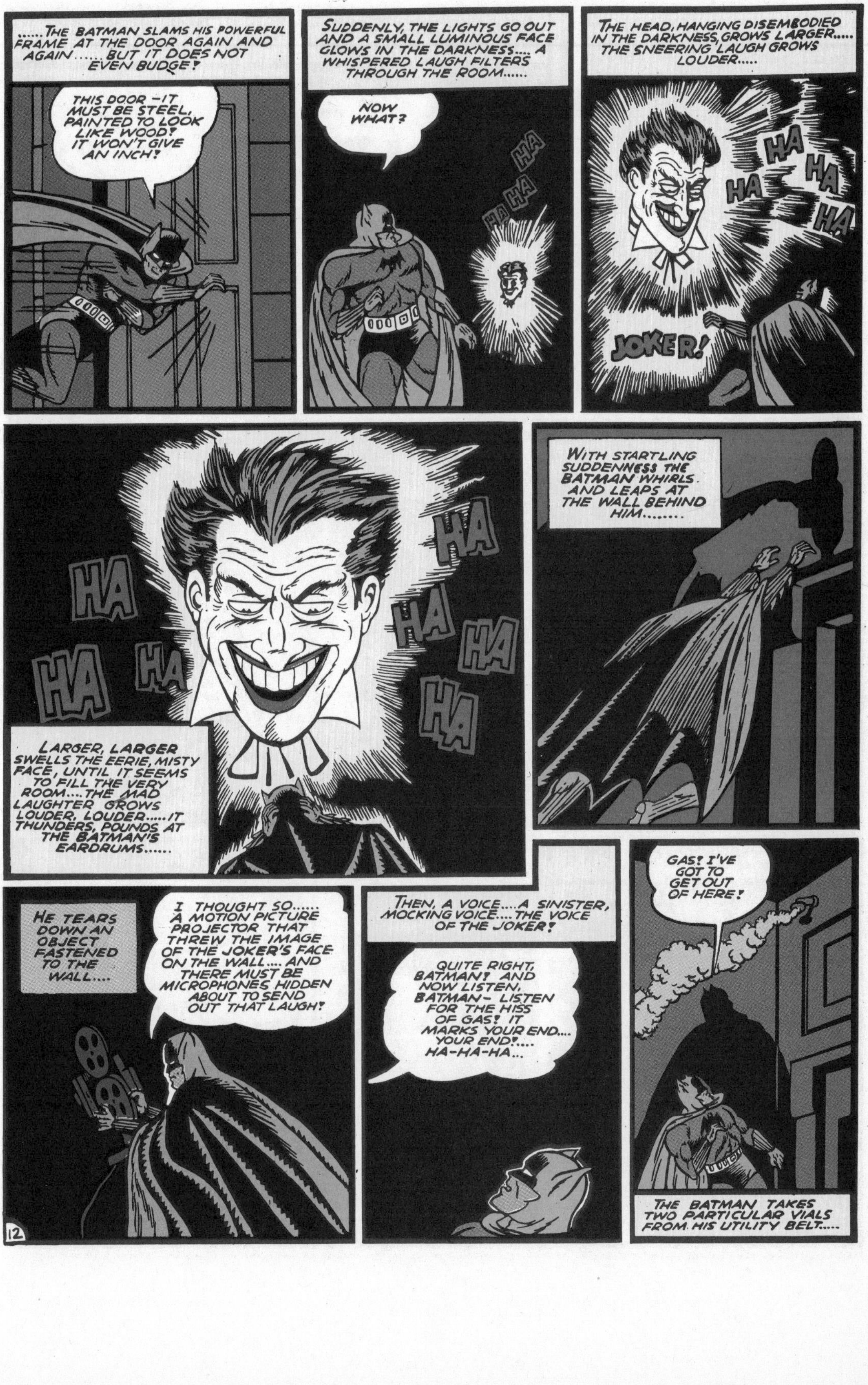
......THE BATMAN SLAMS HIS POWERFUL FRAME AT THE DOOR AGAIN AND AGAIN....... BUT IT DOES NOT EVEN BUDGE!
THIS DOOR -IT MUST BE STEEL, PAINTED TO LOOK LIKE WOOD! IT WON'T GIVE AN INCH!
SUDDENLY, THE LIGHTS GO OUT AND A SMALL LUMINOUS FACE GLOWS IN THE DARKNESS..... A WHISPERED LAUGH FILTERS THROUGH THE ROOM......
NOW WHAT?
HA HA HA HA
THE HEAD, HANGING DISEMBODIED IN THE DARKNESS, GROWS LARGER..... THE SNEERING LAUGH GROWS LOUDER.....
HA HA HA HA HA
JOKER!
HA HA HA HA HA HA HA HA
LARGER, LARGER SWELLS THE EERIE, MISTY FACE, UNTIL IT SEEMS TO FILL THE VERY ROOM.... THE MAD LAUGHTER GROWS LOUDER, LOUDER.....IT THUNDERS, POUNDS AT THE BATMAN'S EARDRUMS......
WITH STARTLING SUDDENNESS THE BATMAN WHIRLS AND LEAPS AT THE WALL BEHIND HIM........
HE TEARS DOWN AN OBJECT FASTENED TO THE WALL....
I THOUGHT SO...... A MOTION PICTURE PROJECTOR THAT THREW THE IMAGE OF THE JOKER'S FACE ON THE WALL.... AND THERE MUST BE MICROPHONES HIDDEN ABOUT TO SEND OUT THAT LAUGH!
THEN, A VOICE.... A SINISTER, MOCKING VOICE.... THE VOICE OF THE JOKER!
QUITE RIGHT, BATMAN! AND NOW LISTEN, BATMAN- LISTEN FOR THE HISS OF GAS! IT MARKS YOUR END.... YOUR END!.... HA-HA-HA...
GAS! I'VE GOT TO GET OUT OF HERE!
THE BATMAN TAKES TWO PARTICULAR VIALS FROM HIS UTILITY BELT.....
12

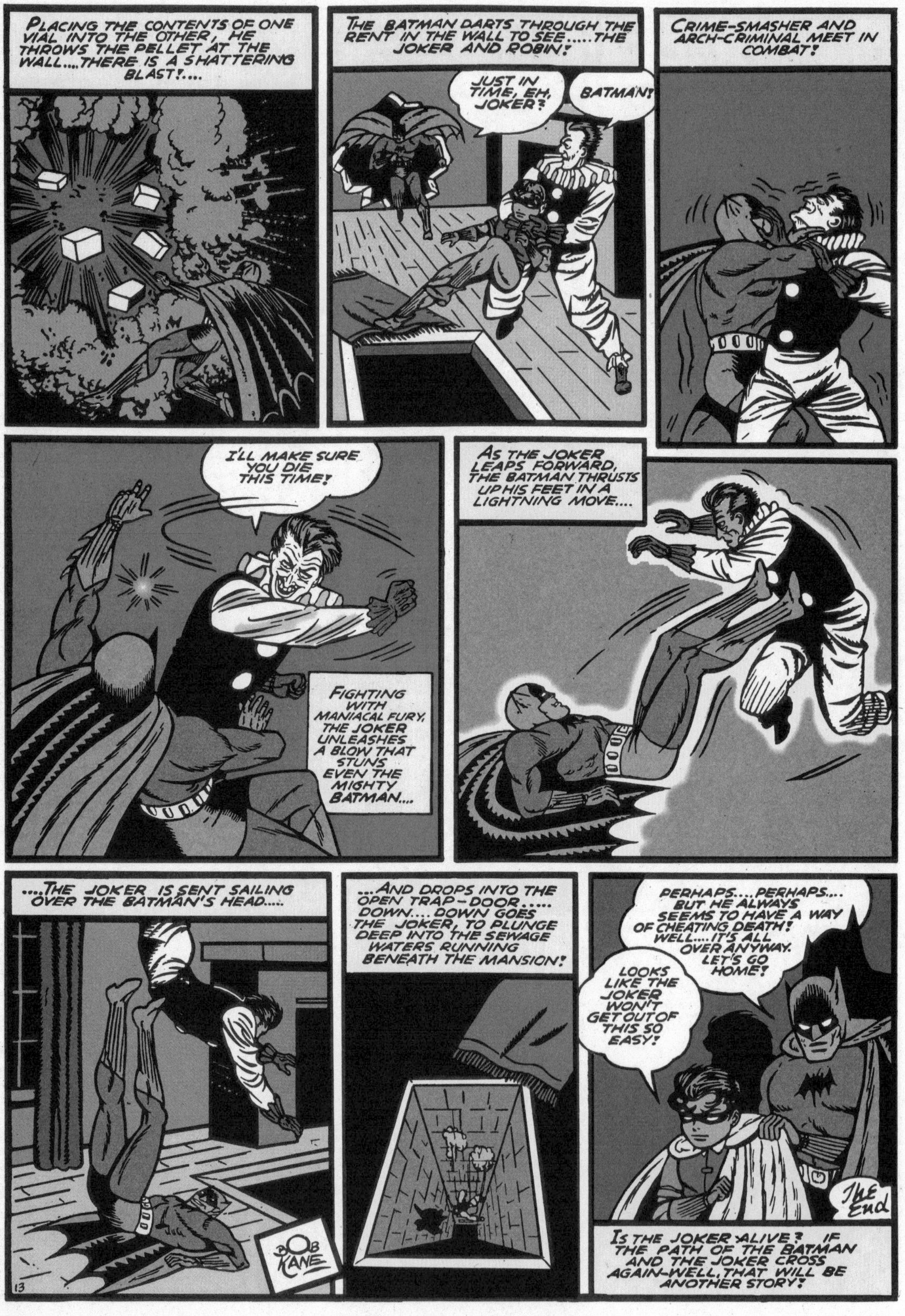
PLACING THE CONTENTS OF ONE VIAL INTO THE OTHER, HE THROWS THE PELLET AT THE WALL....THERE IS A SHATTERING BLAST!....
THE BATMAN DARTS THROUGH THE RENT IN THE WALL TO SEE.....THE JOKER AND ROBIN!
JUST IN TIME, EH, JOKER?
BATMAN!
CRIME-SMASHER AND ARCH-CRIMINAL MEET IN COMBAT!
I'LL MAKE SURE YOU DIE THIS TIME!
FIGHTING WITH MANIACAL FURY, THE JOKER UNLEASHES A BLOW THAT STUNS EVEN THE MIGHTY BATMAN....
AS THE JOKER LEAPS FORWARD, THE BATMAN THRUSTS UP HIS FEET IN A LIGHTNING MOVE....
....THE JOKER IS SENT SAILING OVER THE BATMAN'S HEAD.....
BOB KANE
13
...AND DROPS INTO THE OPEN TRAP-DOOR..... DOWN.... DOWN GOES THE JOKER, TO PLUNGE DEEP INTO THE SEWAGE WATERS RUNNING BENEATH THE MANSION!
LOOKS LIKE THE JOKER WON'T GET OUT OF THIS SO EASY!
PERHAPS....PERHAPS.... BUT HE ALWAYS SEEMS TO HAVE A WAY OF CHEATING DEATH! WELL....IT'S ALL OVER ANYWAY. LET'S GO HOME!
THE END
IS THE JOKER ALIVE? IF THE PATH OF THE BATMAN AND THE JOKER CROSS AGAIN-WELL, THAT WILL BE ANOTHER STORY!

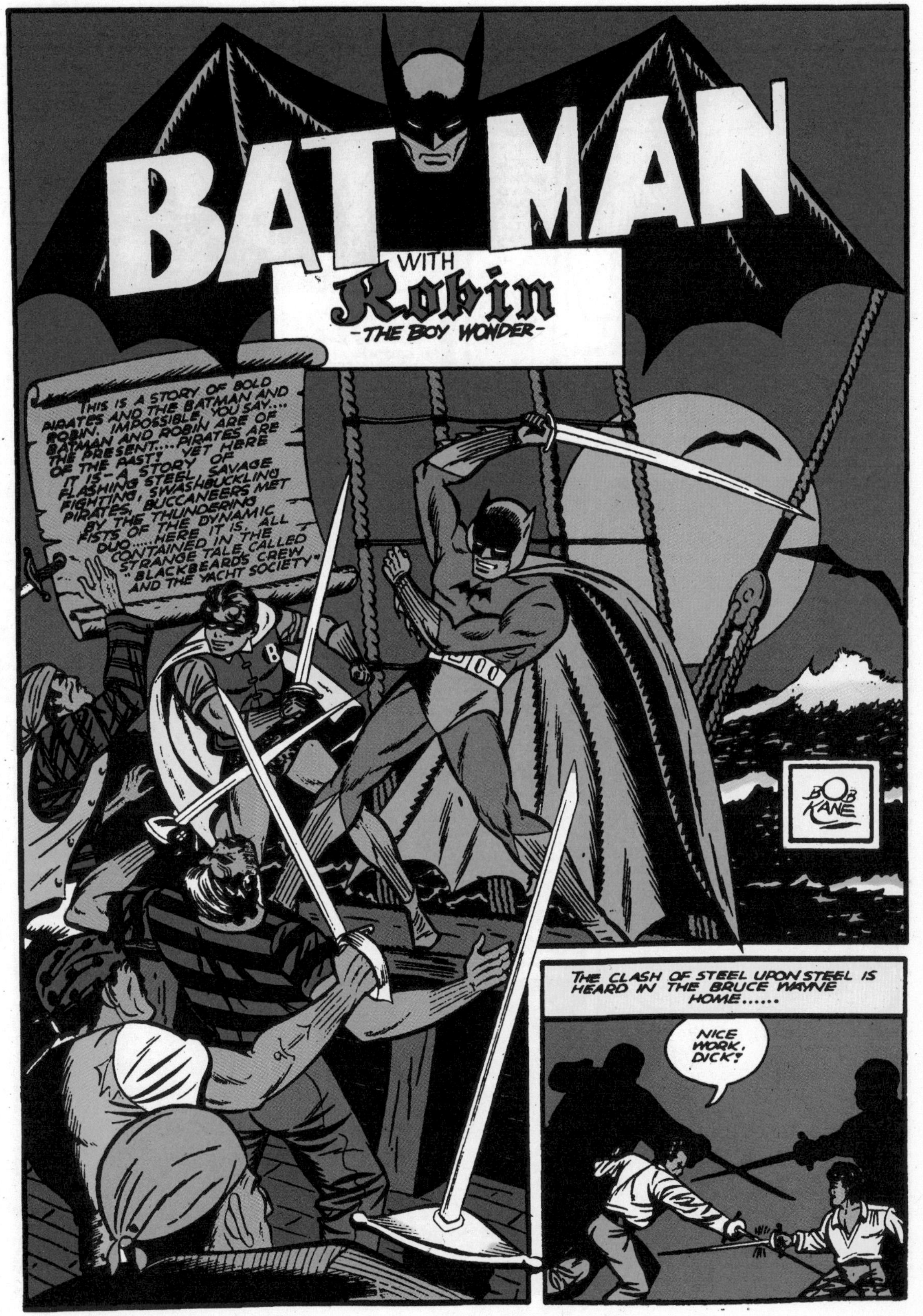
BATMAN
WITH
Robin
-THE BOY WONDER-
THIS IS A STORY OF BOLD PIRATES AND THE BATMAN AND ROBIN. IMPOSSIBLE, YOU SAY.... BATMAN AND ROBIN ARE OF THE PRESENT.... PIRATES ARE OF THE PAST! YET HERE IT IS--A STORY OF FLASHING STEEL, SAVAGE FIGHTING, SWASHBUCKLING PIRATES. BUCCANEERS MET BY THE THUNDERING FISTS OF THE DYNAMIC DUO.....HERE IT IS, ALL CONTAINED IN THE STRANGE TALE CALLED "BLACKBEARD'S CREW AND THE YACHT SOCIETY"
BOB KANE
THE CLASH OF STEEL UPON STEEL IS HEARD IN THE BRUCE WAYNE HOME......
NICE WORK, DICK!

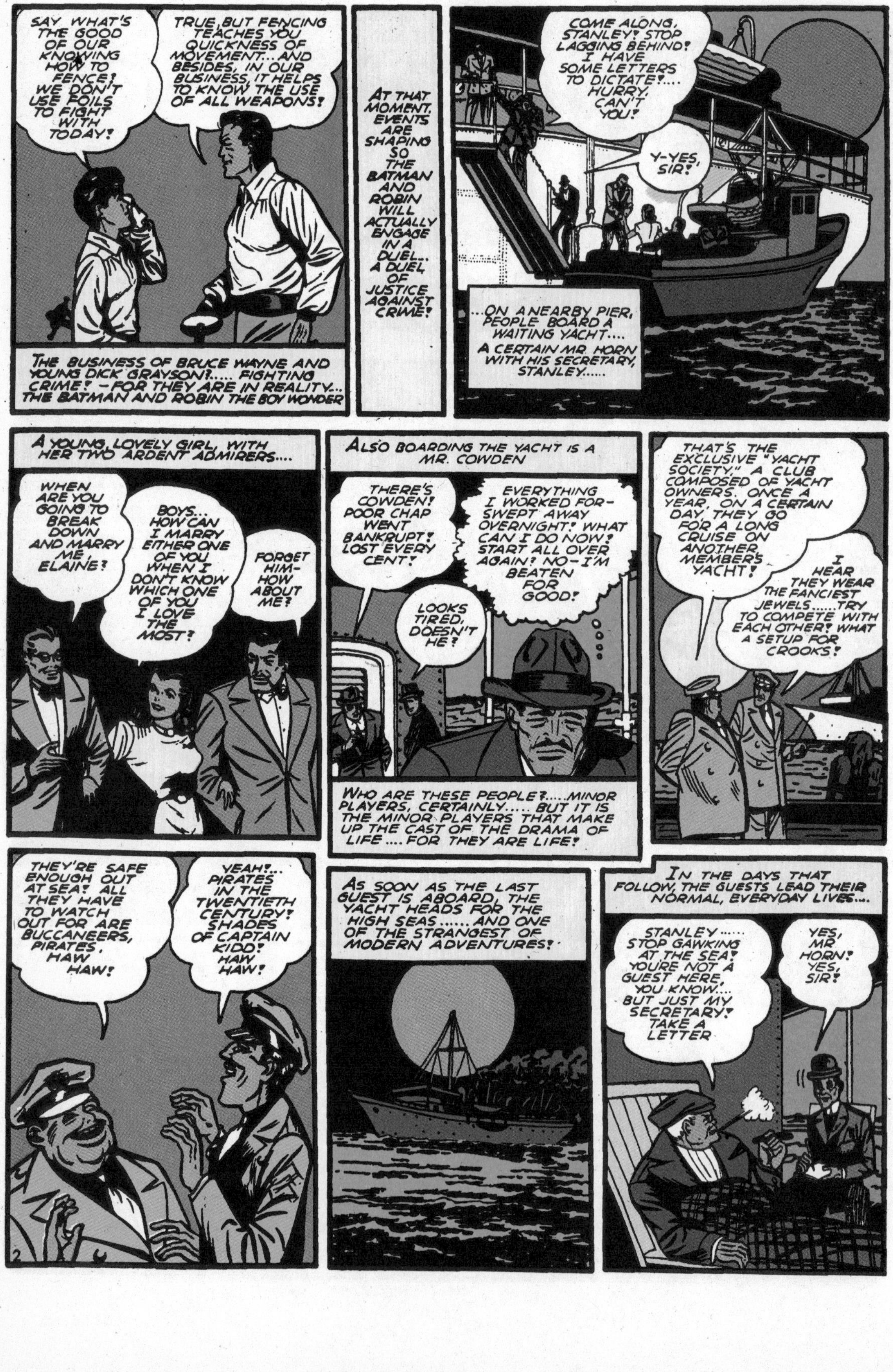
SAY WHAT'S THE GOOD OF OUR KNOWING HOW TO FENCE? WE DON'T USE FOILS TO FIGHT WITH TODAY!
TRUE, BUT FENCING TEACHES YOU QUICKNESS OF MOVEMENT... AND BESIDES, IN OUR BUSINESS, IT HELPS TO KNOW THE USE OF ALL WEAPONS!
THE BUSINESS OF BRUCE WAYNE AND YOUNG DICK GRAYSON?..... FIGHTING CRIME! – FOR THEY ARE IN REALITY... THE BATMAN AND ROBIN THE BOY WONDER
AT THAT MOMENT, EVENTS ARE SHAPING SO THE BATMAN AND ROBIN WILL ACTUALLY ENGAGE IN A DUEL... A DUEL OF JUSTICE AGAINST CRIME!
COME ALONG, STANLEY! STOP LAGGING BEHIND! I HAVE SOME LETTERS TO DICTATE!.... HURRY, CAN'T YOU!
Y-YES, SIR!
...ON A NEARBY PIER, PEOPLE BOARD A WAITING YACHT.... A CERTAIN MR. HORN WITH HIS SECRETARY, STANLEY.....
A YOUNG, LOVELY GIRL, WITH HER TWO ARDENT ADMIRERS....
WHEN ARE YOU GOING TO BREAK DOWN AND MARRY ME, ELAINE?
BOYS... HOW CAN I MARRY EITHER ONE OF YOU WHEN I DON'T KNOW WHICH ONE OF YOU I LOVE THE MOST?
FORGET HIM– HOW ABOUT ME?
ALSO BOARDING THE YACHT IS A MR. COWDEN
THERE'S COWDEN! POOR CHAP WENT BANKRUPT! LOST EVERY CENT!
EVERYTHING I WORKED FOR– SWEPT AWAY OVERNIGHT! WHAT CAN I DO NOW? START ALL OVER AGAIN? NO– I'M BEATEN FOR GOOD!
LOOKS TIRED, DOESN'T HE?
WHO ARE THESE PEOPLE?.....MINOR PLAYERS, CERTAINLY..... BUT IT IS THE MINOR PLAYERS THAT MAKE UP THE CAST OF THE DRAMA OF LIFE .... FOR THEY ARE LIFE!
THAT'S THE EXCLUSIVE "YACHT SOCIETY," A CLUB COMPOSED OF YACHT OWNERS. ONCE A YEAR, ON A CERTAIN DAY, THEY GO FOR A LONG CRUISE ON ANOTHER MEMBER'S YACHT!
I HEAR THEY WEAR THE FANCIEST JEWELS......TRY TO COMPETE WITH EACH OTHER! WHAT A SETUP FOR CROOKS!
THEY'RE SAFE ENOUGH OUT AT SEA! ALL THEY HAVE TO WATCH OUT FOR ARE BUCCANEERS, PIRATES, HAW HAW!
YEAH!... PIRATES IN THE TWENTIETH CENTURY! SHADES OF CAPTAIN KIDD! HAW HAW!
AS SOON AS THE LAST GUEST IS ABOARD, THE YACHT HEADS FOR THE HIGH SEAS ...... AND ONE OF THE STRANGEST OF MODERN ADVENTURES!
IN THE DAYS THAT FOLLOW, THE GUESTS LEAD THEIR NORMAL, EVERYDAY LIVES....
STANLEY...... STOP GAWKING AT THE SEA! YOU'RE NOT A GUEST HERE, YOU KNOW.... BUT JUST MY SECRETARY! TAKE A LETTER
YES, MR HORN! YES, SIR!
2

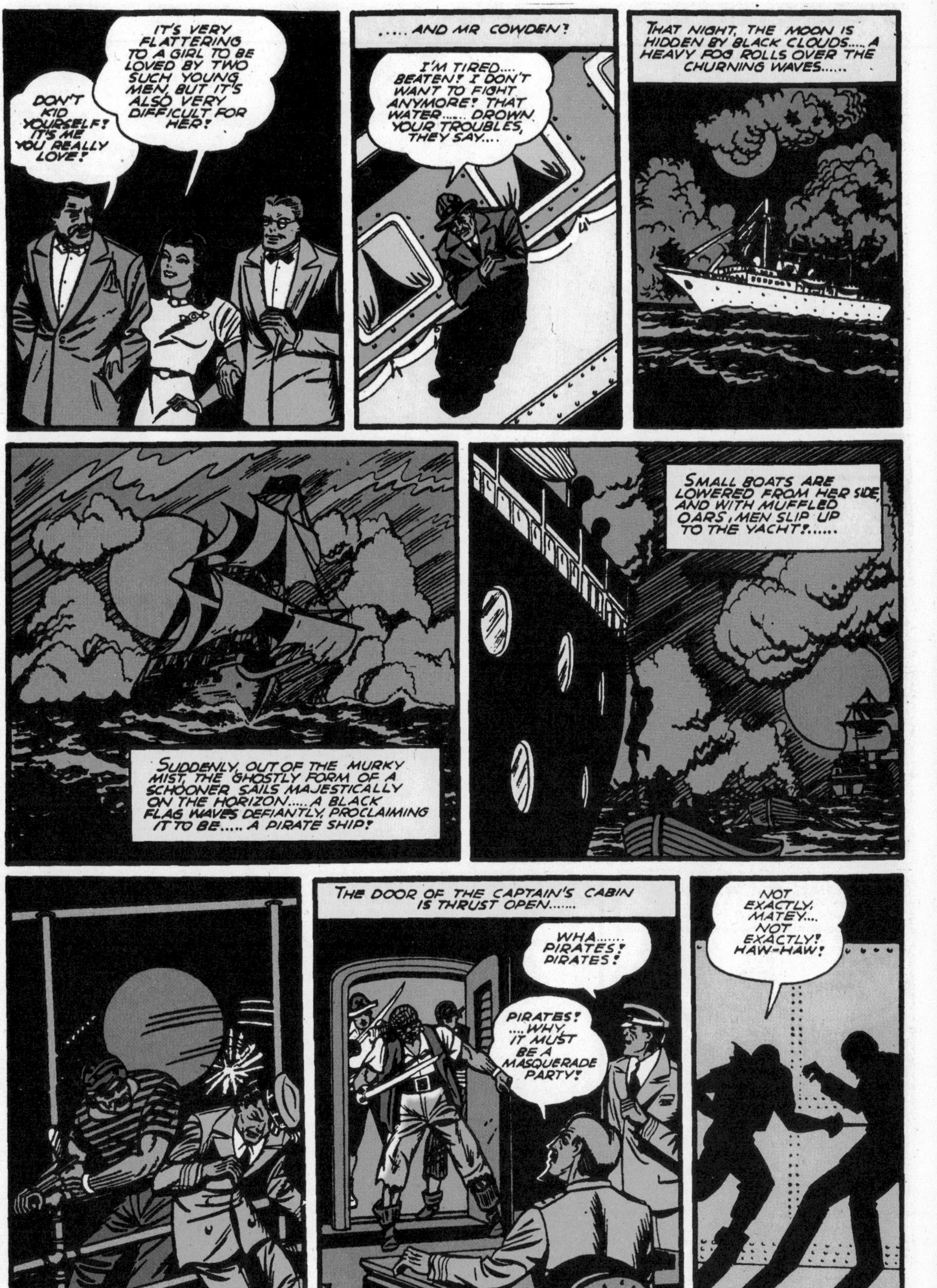
IT'S VERY FLATTERING TO A GIRL TO BE LOVED BY TWO SUCH YOUNG MEN, BUT IT'S ALSO VERY DIFFICULT FOR HER!
DON'T KID YOURSELF! IT'S ME YOU REALLY LOVE!
..... AND MR COWDEN?
I'M TIRED.... BEATEN! I DON'T WANT TO FIGHT ANYMORE! THAT WATER...... DROWN YOUR TROUBLES, THEY SAY...
THAT NIGHT, THE MOON IS HIDDEN BY BLACK CLOUDS..... A HEAVY FOG ROLLS OVER THE CHURNING WAVES......
SUDDENLY, OUT OF THE MURKY MIST, THE GHOSTLY FORM OF A SCHOONER SAILS MAJESTICALLY ON THE HORIZON..... A BLACK FLAG WAVES DEFIANTLY, PROCLAIMING IT TO BE..... A PIRATE SHIP!
SMALL BOATS ARE LOWERED FROM HER SIDE, AND WITH MUFFLED OARS, MEN SLIP UP TO THE YACHT!......
THE DOOR OF THE CAPTAIN'S CABIN IS THRUST OPEN.......
WHA....... PIRATES! PIRATES!
PIRATES! .....WHY, IT MUST BE A MASQUERADE PARTY!
NOT EXACTLY, MATEY.... NOT EXACTLY! HAW-HAW!

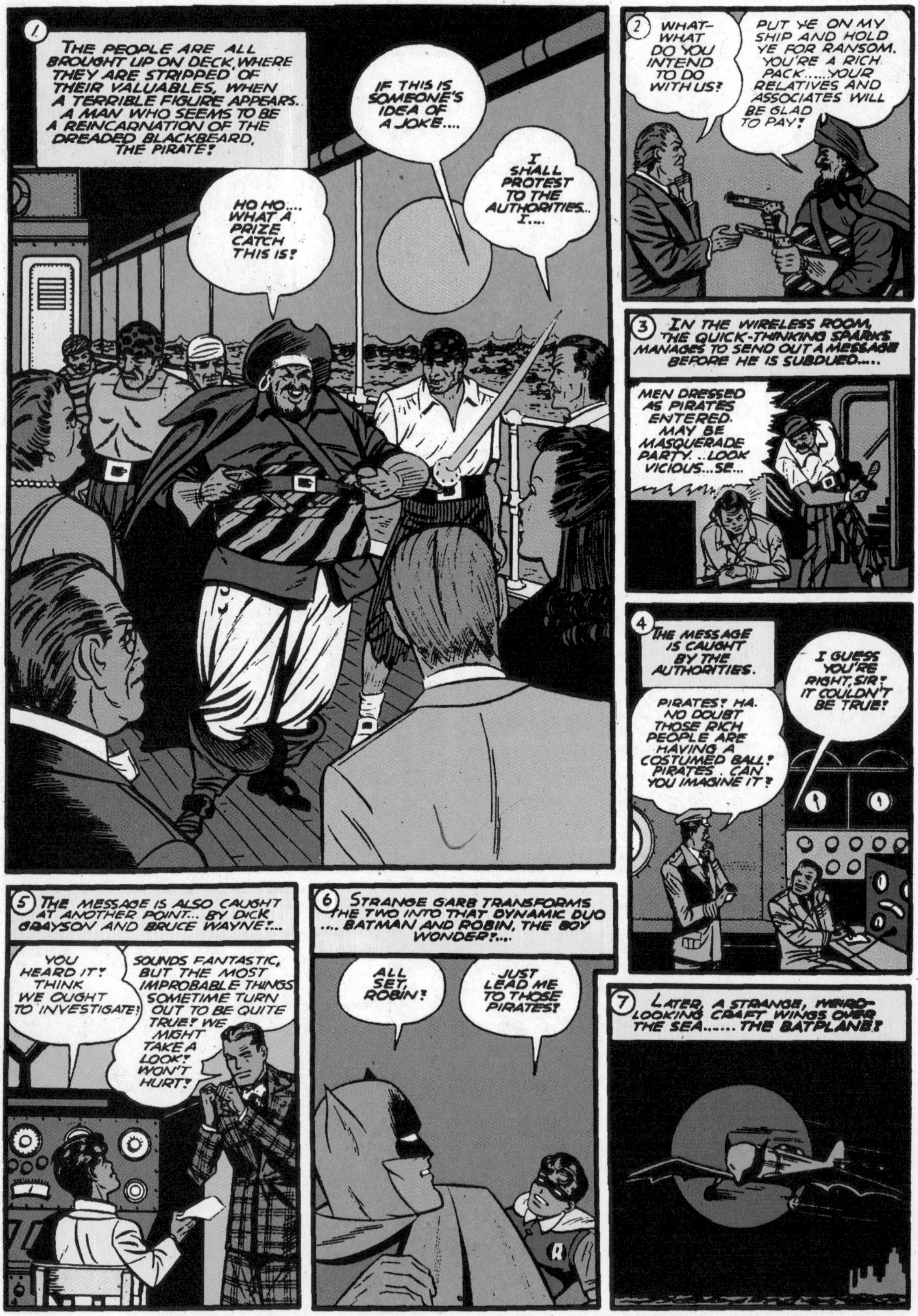
THE PEOPLE ARE ALL BROUGHT UP ON DECK, WHERE THEY ARE STRIPPED OF THEIR VALUABLES, WHEN A TERRIBLE FIGURE APPEARS. A MAN WHO SEEMS TO BE A REINCARNATION OF THE DREADED BLACKBEARD, THE PIRATE!
IF THIS IS SOMEONE'S IDEA OF A JOKE....
I SHALL PROTEST TO THE AUTHORITIES.. I....
HO HO.... WHAT A PRIZE CATCH THIS IS!
WHAT- WHAT DO YOU INTEND TO DO WITH US?
PUT YE ON MY SHIP AND HOLD YE FOR RANSOM. YOU'RE A RICH PACK.....YOUR RELATIVES AND ASSOCIATES WILL BE GLAD TO PAY!
IN THE WIRELESS ROOM, THE QUICK-THINKING SPARKS MANAGES TO SEND OUT A MESSAGE BEFORE HE IS SUBDUED.....
MEN DRESSED AS PIRATES ENTERED. MAY BE MASQUERADE PARTY. ..LOOK VICIOUS...SE...
THE MESSAGE IS CAUGHT BY THE AUTHORITIES.
PIRATES! HA. NO DOUBT THOSE RICH PEOPLE ARE HAVING A COSTUMED BALL! PIRATES. CAN YOU IMAGINE IT?
I GUESS YOU'RE RIGHT, SIR! IT COULDN'T BE TRUE!
THE MESSAGE IS ALSO CAUGHT AT ANOTHER POINT... BY DICK GRAYSON AND BRUCE WAYNE!...
YOU HEARD IT! THINK WE OUGHT TO INVESTIGATE!
SOUNDS FANTASTIC, BUT THE MOST IMPROBABLE THINGS SOMETIME TURN OUT TO BE QUITE TRUE! WE MIGHT TAKE A LOOK! WON'T HURT!
STRANGE GARB TRANSFORMS THE TWO INTO THAT DYNAMIC DUO .... BATMAN AND ROBIN, THE BOY WONDER!...
ALL SET, ROBIN!
JUST LEAD ME TO THOSE PIRATES!
LATER, A STRANGE, WEIRD-LOOKING CRAFT WINGS OVER THE SEA...... THE BATPLANE!

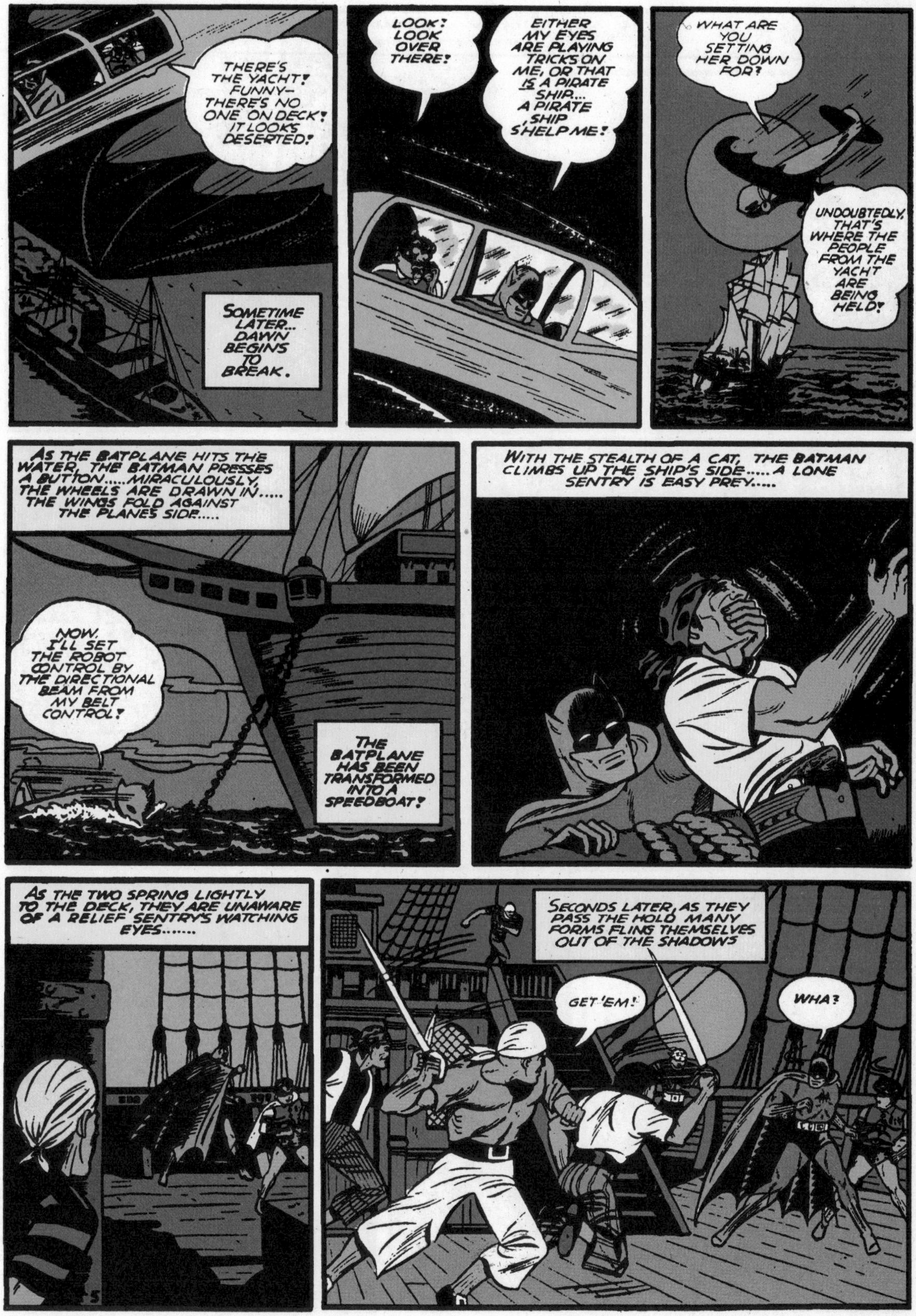
THERE'S THE YACHT! FUNNY— THERE'S NO ONE ON DECK! IT LOOKS DESERTED!
SOMETIME LATER... DAWN BEGINS TO BREAK.
LOOK! LOOK OVER THERE!
EITHER MY EYES ARE PLAYING TRICKS ON ME, OR THAT IS A PIRATE SHIP... A PIRATE SHIP S'HELP ME!
WHAT ARE YOU SETTING HER DOWN FOR?
UNDOUBTEDLY, THAT'S WHERE THE PEOPLE FROM THE YACHT ARE BEING HELD!
AS THE BATPLANE HITS THE WATER, THE BATMAN PRESSES A BUTTON.....MIRACULOUSLY, THE WHEELS ARE DRAWN IN..... THE WINGS FOLD AGAINST THE PLANES SIDE.....
NOW, I'LL SET THE ROBOT CONTROL BY THE DIRECTIONAL BEAM FROM MY BELT CONTROL!
THE BATPLANE HAS BEEN TRANSFORMED INTO A SPEEDBOAT!
WITH THE STEALTH OF A CAT, THE BATMAN CLIMBS UP THE SHIP'S SIDE.....A LONE SENTRY IS EASY PREY.....
AS THE TWO SPRING LIGHTLY TO THE DECK, THEY ARE UNAWARE OF A RELIEF SENTRY'S WATCHING EYES.......
SECONDS LATER, AS THEY PASS THE HOLD MANY FORMS FLING THEMSELVES OUT OF THE SHADOWS
GET 'EM!
WHA?

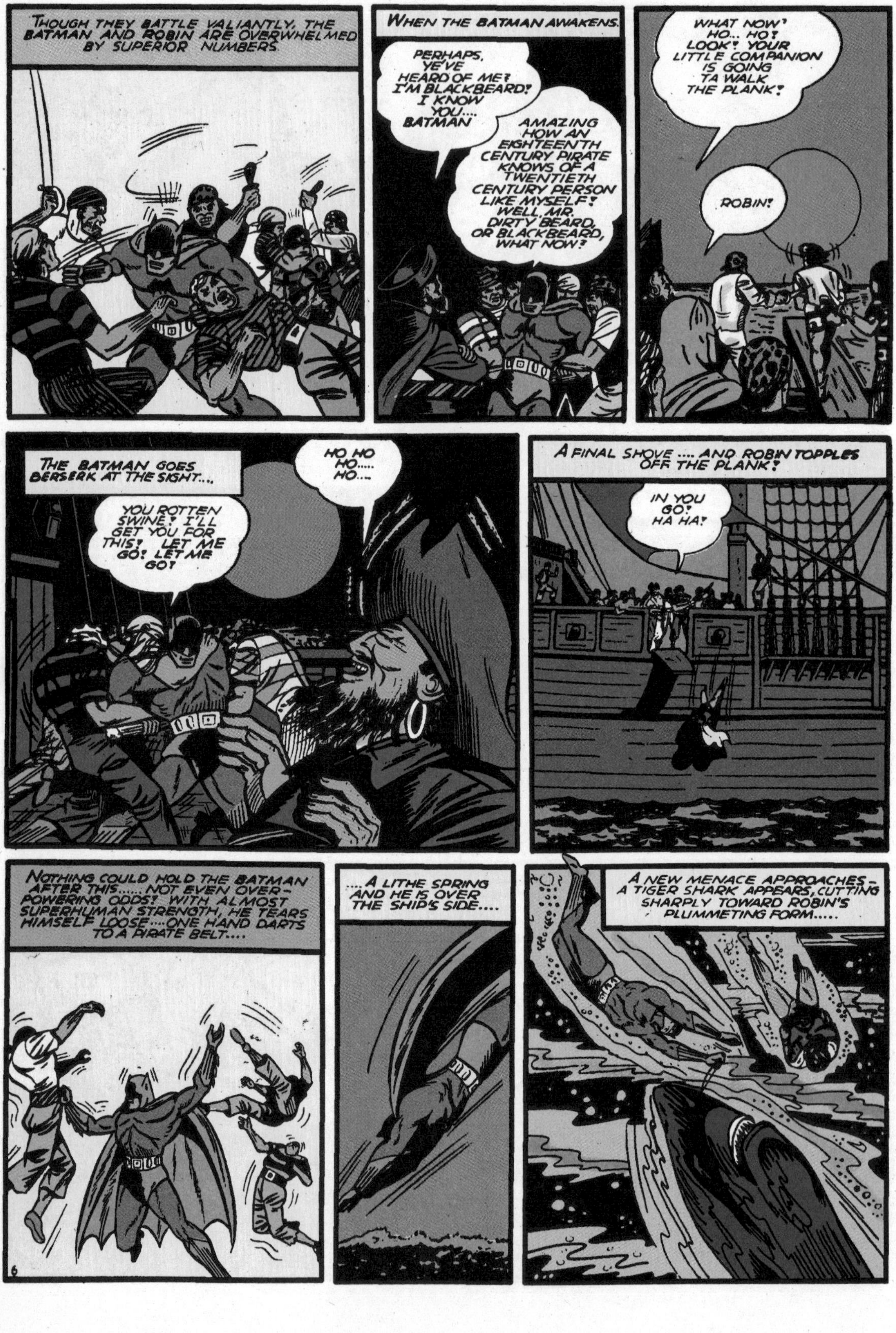
THOUGH THEY BATTLE VALIANTLY, THE BATMAN AND ROBIN ARE OVERWHELMED BY SUPERIOR NUMBERS.
WHEN THE BATMAN AWAKENS.
PERHAPS, YE'VE HEARD OF ME? I'M BLACKBEARD! I KNOW YOU.... BATMAN
AMAZING HOW AN EIGHTEENTH CENTURY PIRATE KNOWS OF A TWENTIETH CENTURY PERSON LIKE MYSELF! WELL, MR. DIRTY BEARD, OR BLACKBEARD, WHAT NOW?
WHAT NOW? HO... HO? LOOK! YOUR LITTLE COMPANION IS GOING TA WALK THE PLANK!
ROBIN!
THE BATMAN GOES BERSERK AT THE SIGHT....
HO HO HO.... HO....
YOU ROTTEN SWINE! I'LL GET YOU FOR THIS! LET ME GO! LET ME GO!
A FINAL SHOVE .... AND ROBIN TOPPLES OFF THE PLANK!
IN YOU GO! HA HA!
NOTHING COULD HOLD THE BATMAN AFTER THIS...... NOT EVEN OVER-POWERING ODDS! WITH ALMOST SUPERHUMAN STRENGTH, HE TEARS HIMSELF LOOSE....ONE HAND DARTS TO A PIRATE BELT....
....A LITHE SPRING AND HE IS OVER THE SHIP'S SIDE....
A NEW MENACE APPROACHES - A TIGER SHARK APPEARS, CUTTING SHARPLY TOWARD ROBIN'S PLUMMETING FORM.....

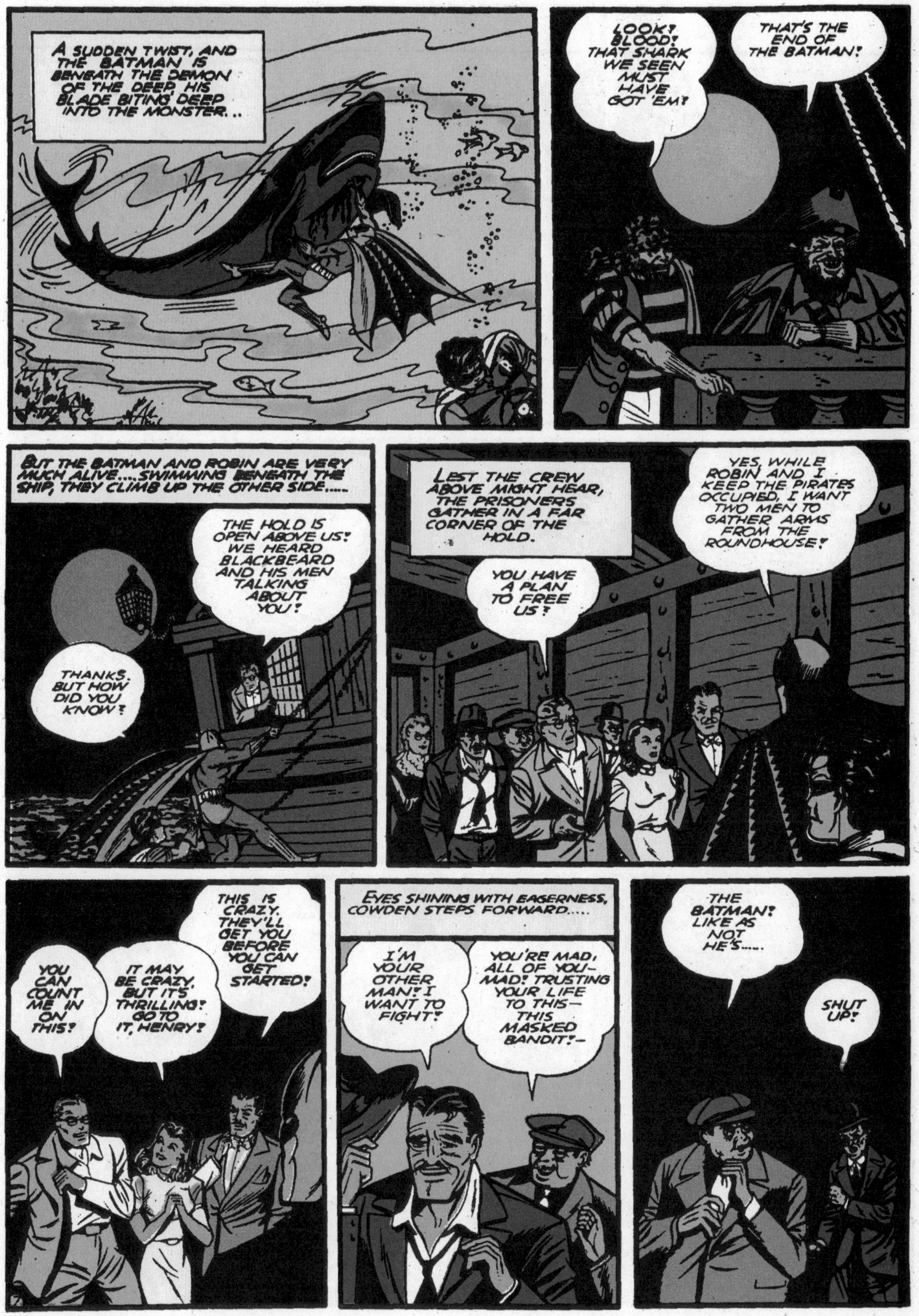
A SUDDEN TWIST, AND THE BATMAN IS BENEATH THE DEMON OF THE DEEP, HIS BLADE BITING DEEP INTO THE MONSTER...
LOOK! BLOOD! THAT SHARK WE SEEN MUST HAVE GOT 'EM!
THAT'S THE END OF THE BATMAN!
BUT THE BATMAN AND ROBIN ARE VERY MUCH ALIVE....SWIMMING BENEATH THE SHIP, THEY CLIMB UP THE OTHER SIDE.....
THE HOLD IS OPEN ABOVE US! WE HEARD BLACKBEARD AND HIS MEN TALKING ABOUT YOU!
THANKS. BUT HOW DID YOU KNOW?
LEST THE CREW ABOVE MIGHT HEAR, THE PRISONERS GATHER IN A FAR CORNER OF THE HOLD.
YOU HAVE A PLAN TO FREE US?
YES, WHILE ROBIN AND I KEEP THE PIRATES OCCUPIED, I WANT TWO MEN TO GATHER ARMS FROM THE ROUNDHOUSE!
YOU CAN COUNT ME IN ON THIS!
IT MAY BE CRAZY, BUT IT'S THRILLING! GO TO IT, HENRY!
THIS IS CRAZY. THEY'LL GET YOU BEFORE YOU CAN GET STARTED!
EYES SHINING WITH EAGERNESS, COWDEN STEPS FORWARD.....
I'M YOUR OTHER MAN! I WANT TO FIGHT!
YOU'RE MAD, ALL OF YOU--MAD! TRUSTING YOUR LIFE TO THIS--THIS MASKED BANDIT!--
THE BATMAN! LIKE AS NOT HE'S.....
SHUT UP!

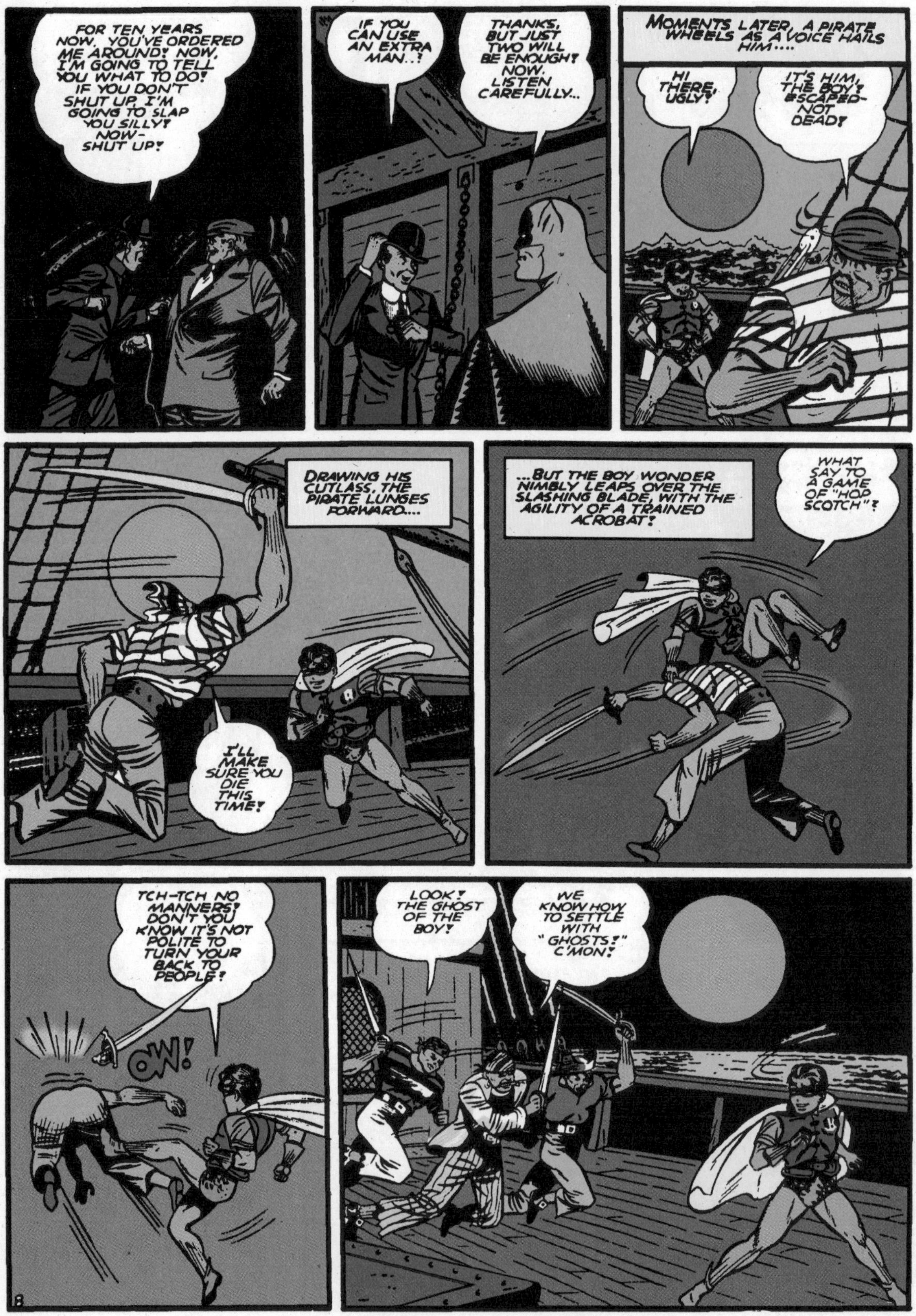

FOR TEN YEARS NOW, YOU'VE ORDERED ME AROUND! NOW, I'M GOING TO TELL YOU WHAT TO DO! IF YOU DON'T SHUT UP I'M GOING TO SLAP YOU SILLY! NOW- SHUT UP!
IF YOU CAN USE AN EXTRA MAN...?
THANKS, BUT JUST TWO WILL BE ENOUGH! NOW, LISTEN CAREFULLY...
MOMENTS LATER, A PIRATE WHEELS AS A VOICE HAILS HIM....
HI THERE, UGLY!
IT'S HIM, THE BOY! ESCAPED- NOT DEAD!
DRAWING HIS CUTLASS, THE PIRATE LUNGES FORWARD....
I'LL MAKE SURE YOU DIE THIS TIME!
...BUT THE BOY WONDER NIMBLY LEAPS OVER THE SLASHING BLADE, WITH THE AGILITY OF A TRAINED ACROBAT!
WHAT SAY TO A GAME OF "HOP SCOTCH"?
TCH-TCH NO MANNERS? DON'T YOU KNOW IT'S NOT POLITE TO TURN YOUR BACK TO PEOPLE?
OW!
8
LOOK! THE GHOST OF THE BOY!
WE KNOW HOW TO SETTLE WITH "GHOSTS!" C'MON!

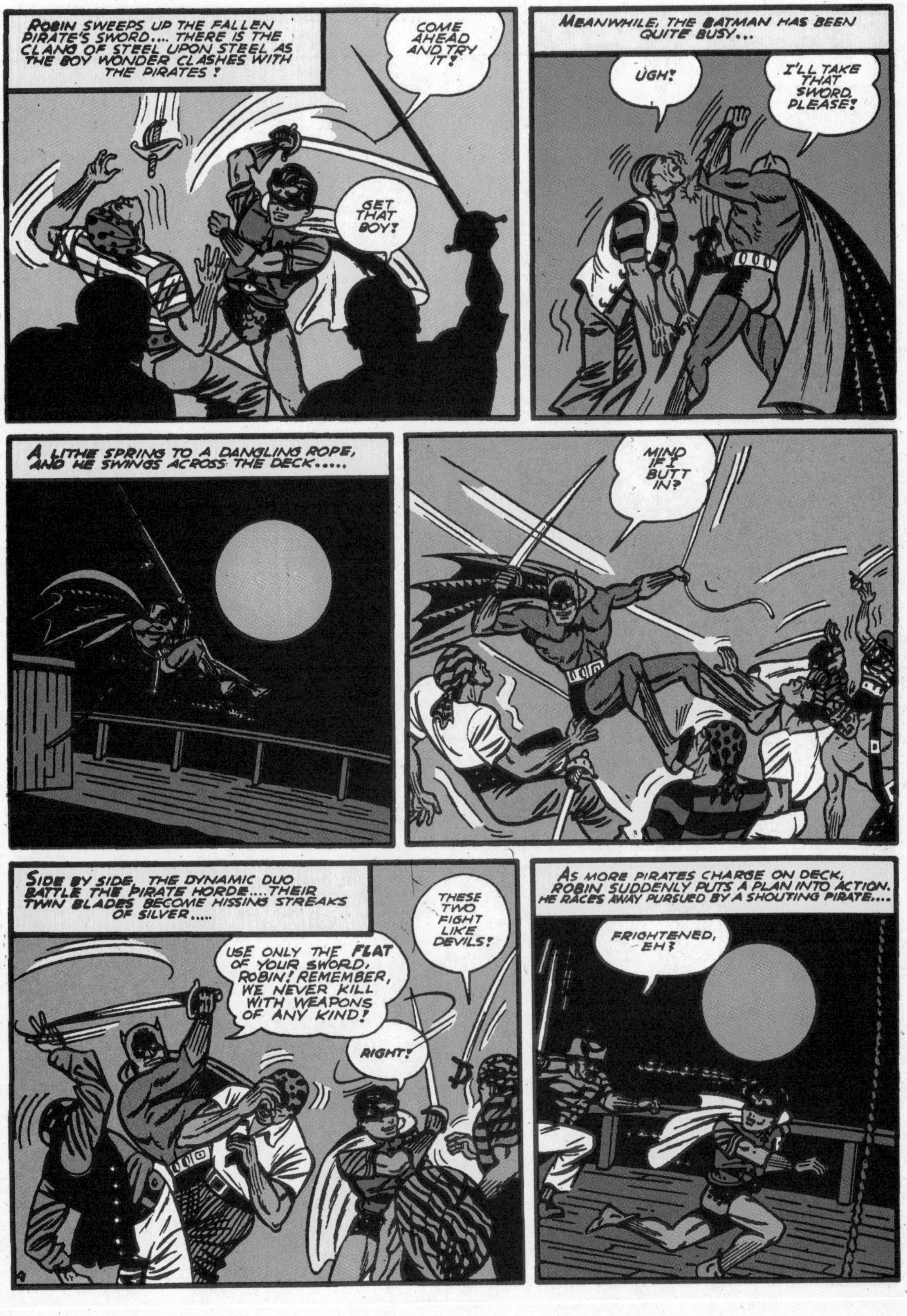
ROBIN SWEEPS UP THE FALLEN PIRATE'S SWORD.... THERE IS THE CLANG OF STEEL UPON STEEL AS THE BOY WONDER CLASHES WITH THE PIRATES!
COME AHEAD AND TRY IT!
GET THAT BOY!
MEANWHILE, THE BATMAN HAS BEEN QUITE BUSY...
UGH!
I'LL TAKE THAT SWORD, PLEASE!
A LITHE SPRING TO A DANGLING ROPE, AND HE SWINGS ACROSS THE DECK.....
MIND IF I BUTT IN?
SIDE BY SIDE, THE DYNAMIC DUO BATTLE THE PIRATE HORDE....THEIR TWIN BLADES BECOME HISSING STREAKS OF SILVER.....
THESE TWO FIGHT LIKE DEVILS!
USE ONLY THE FLAT OF YOUR SWORD, ROBIN! REMEMBER, WE NEVER KILL WITH WEAPONS OF ANY KIND!
RIGHT!
AS MORE PIRATES CHARGE ON DECK, ROBIN SUDDENLY PUTS A PLAN INTO ACTION. HE RACES AWAY PURSUED BY A SHOUTING PIRATE....
FRIGHTENED, EH?

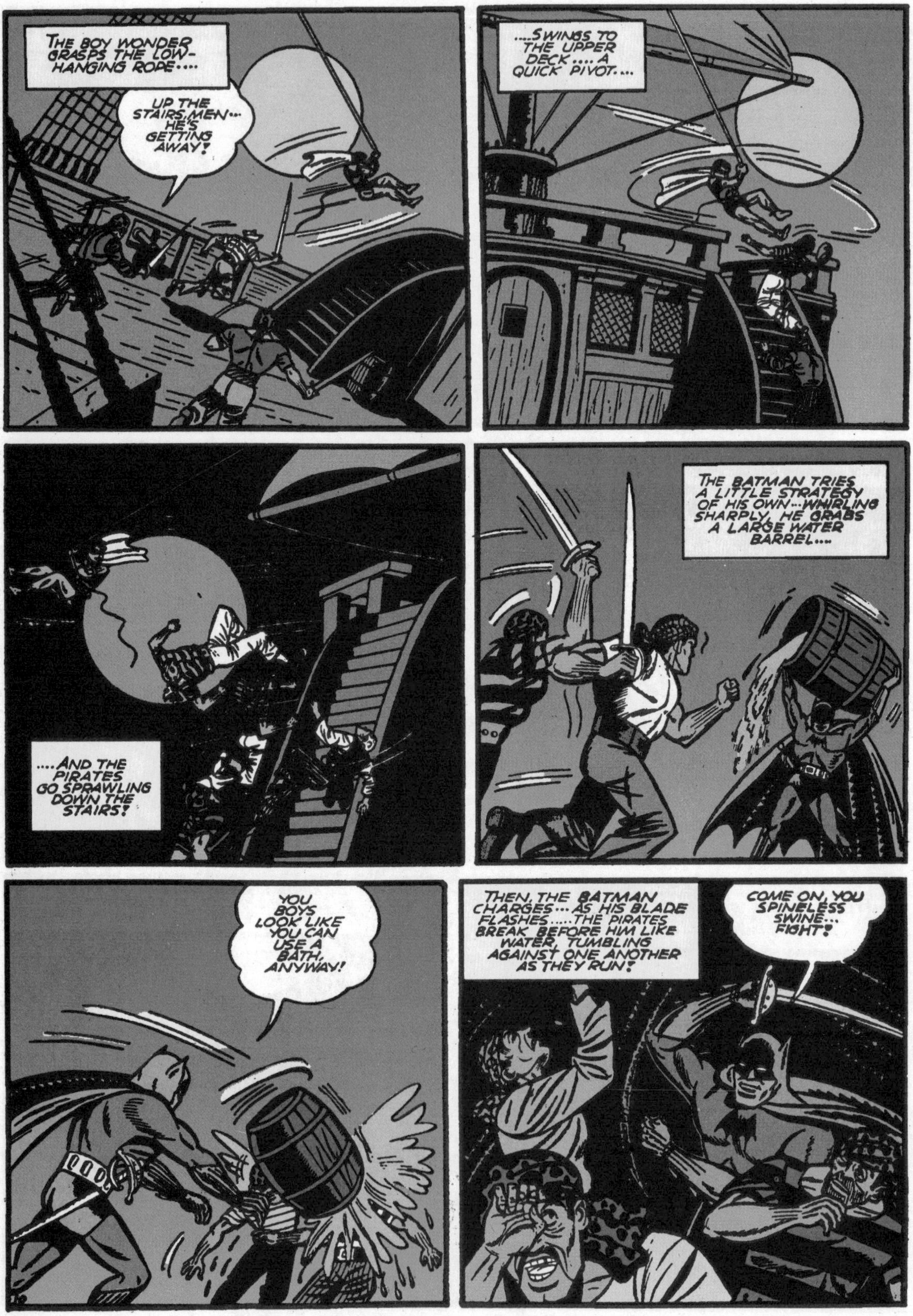
THE BOY WONDER GRASPS THE LOW-HANGING ROPE....
UP THE STAIRS MEN... HE'S GETTING AWAY!
....SWINGS TO THE UPPER DECK.... A QUICK PIVOT....
....AND THE PIRATES GO SPRAWLING DOWN THE STAIRS!
THE BATMAN TRIES A LITTLE STRATEGY OF HIS OWN...WHIRLING SHARPLY, HE GRABS A LARGE WATER BARREL....
YOU BOYS LOOK LIKE YOU CAN USE A BATH, ANYWAY!
THEN, THE BATMAN CHARGES... AS HIS BLADE FLASHES.....THE PIRATES BREAK BEFORE HIM LIKE WATER, TUMBLING AGAINST ONE ANOTHER AS THEY RUN!
COME ON, YOU SPINELESS SWINE... FIGHT!

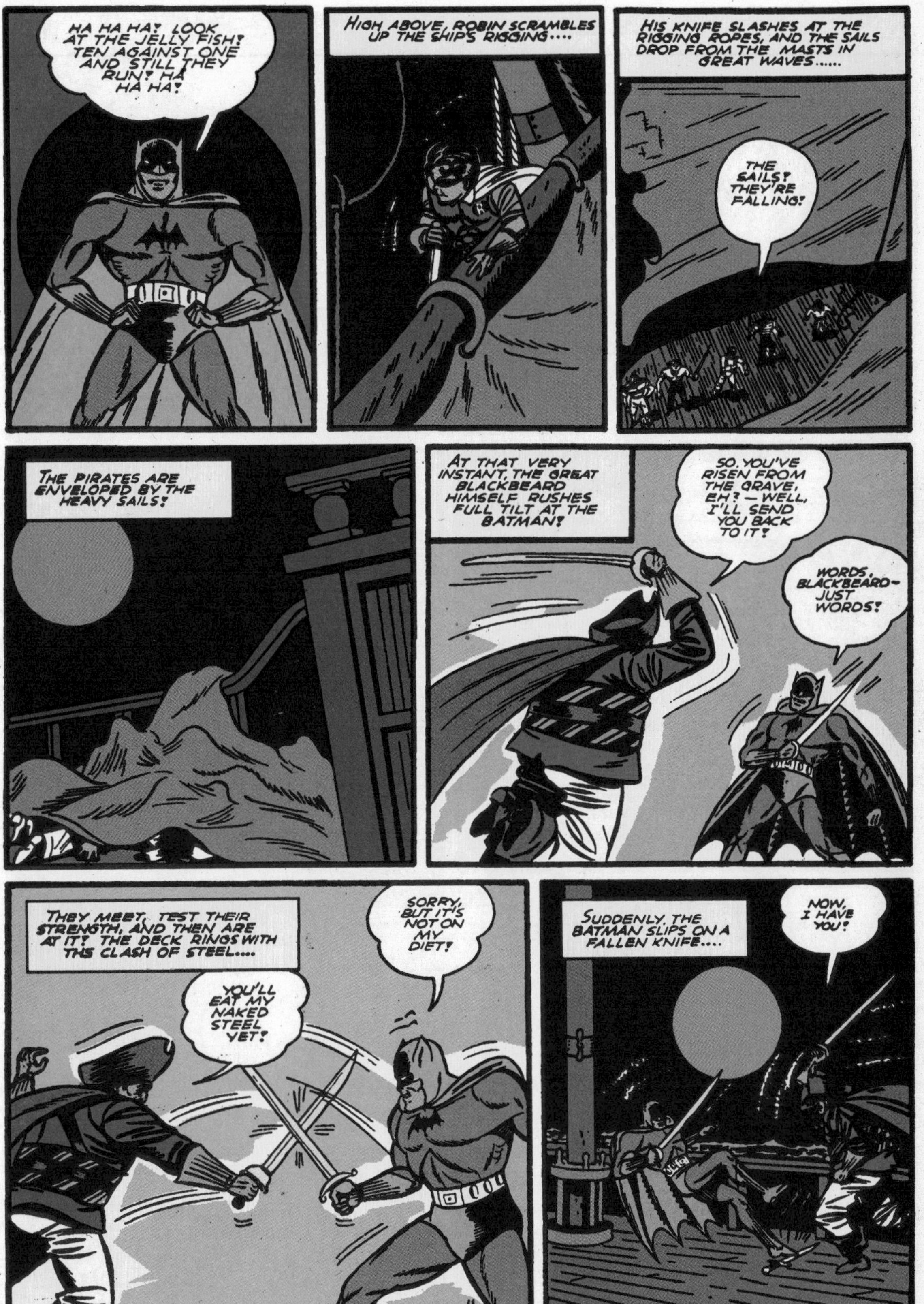

HA HA HA! LOOK AT THE JELLY FISH! TEN AGAINST ONE AND STILL THEY RUN! HA HA HA!
HIGH ABOVE, ROBIN SCRAMBLES UP THE SHIP'S RIGGING....
HIS KNIFE SLASHES AT THE RIGGING ROPES, AND THE SAILS DROP FROM THE MASTS IN GREAT WAVES......
THE SAILS? THEY'RE FALLING!
THE PIRATES ARE ENVELOPED BY THE HEAVY SAILS!
AT THAT VERY INSTANT, THE GREAT BLACKBEARD HIMSELF RUSHES FULL TILT AT THE BATMAN!
SO, YOU'VE RISEN FROM THE GRAVE, EH? — WELL, I'LL SEND YOU BACK TO IT!
WORDS, BLACKBEARD— JUST WORDS!
THEY MEET, TEST THEIR STRENGTH, AND THEN ARE AT IT! THE DECK RINGS WITH THE CLASH OF STEEL....
SORRY, BUT IT'S NOT ON MY DIET!
YOU'LL EAT MY NAKED STEEL YET!
SUDDENLY, THE BATMAN SLIPS ON A FALLEN KNIFE....
NOW, I HAVE YOU!

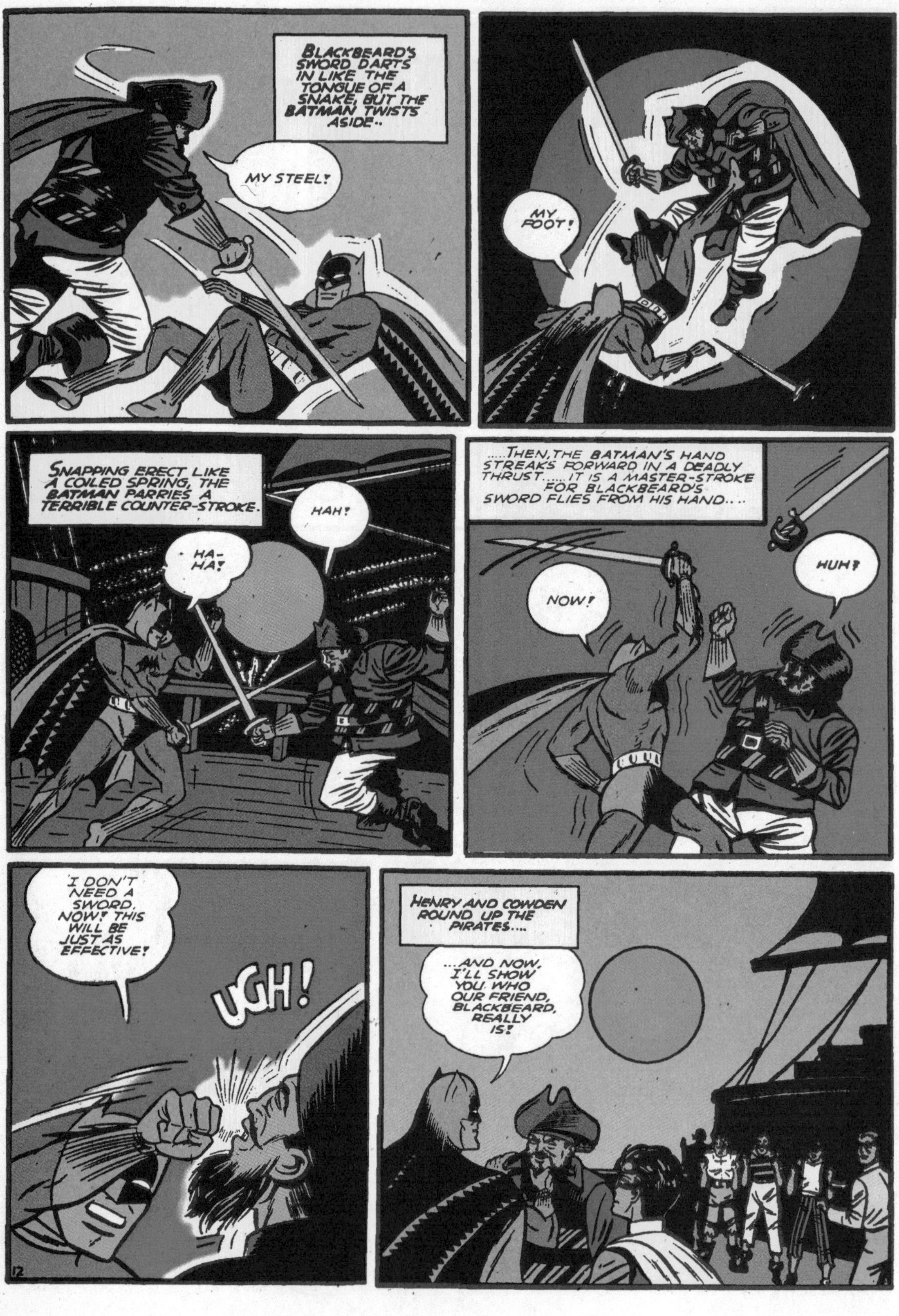
BLACKBEARD'S SWORD DARTS IN LIKE THE TONGUE OF A SNAKE, BUT THE BATMAN TWISTS ASIDE..
MY STEEL!
MY FOOT!
SNAPPING ERECT LIKE A COILED SPRING, THE BATMAN PARRIES A TERRIBLE COUNTER-STROKE.
HA-HA!
HAH!
....THEN, THE BATMAN'S HAND STREAKS FORWARD IN A DEADLY THRUST..... IT IS A MASTER-STROKE FOR BLACKBEARD'S SWORD FLIES FROM HIS HAND....
NOW!
HUH?
I DON'T NEED A SWORD NOW! THIS WILL BE JUST AS EFFECTIVE!
UGH!
HENRY AND COWDEN ROUND UP THE PIRATES....
...AND NOW, I'LL SHOW YOU WHO OUR FRIEND, BLACKBEARD, REALLY IS!

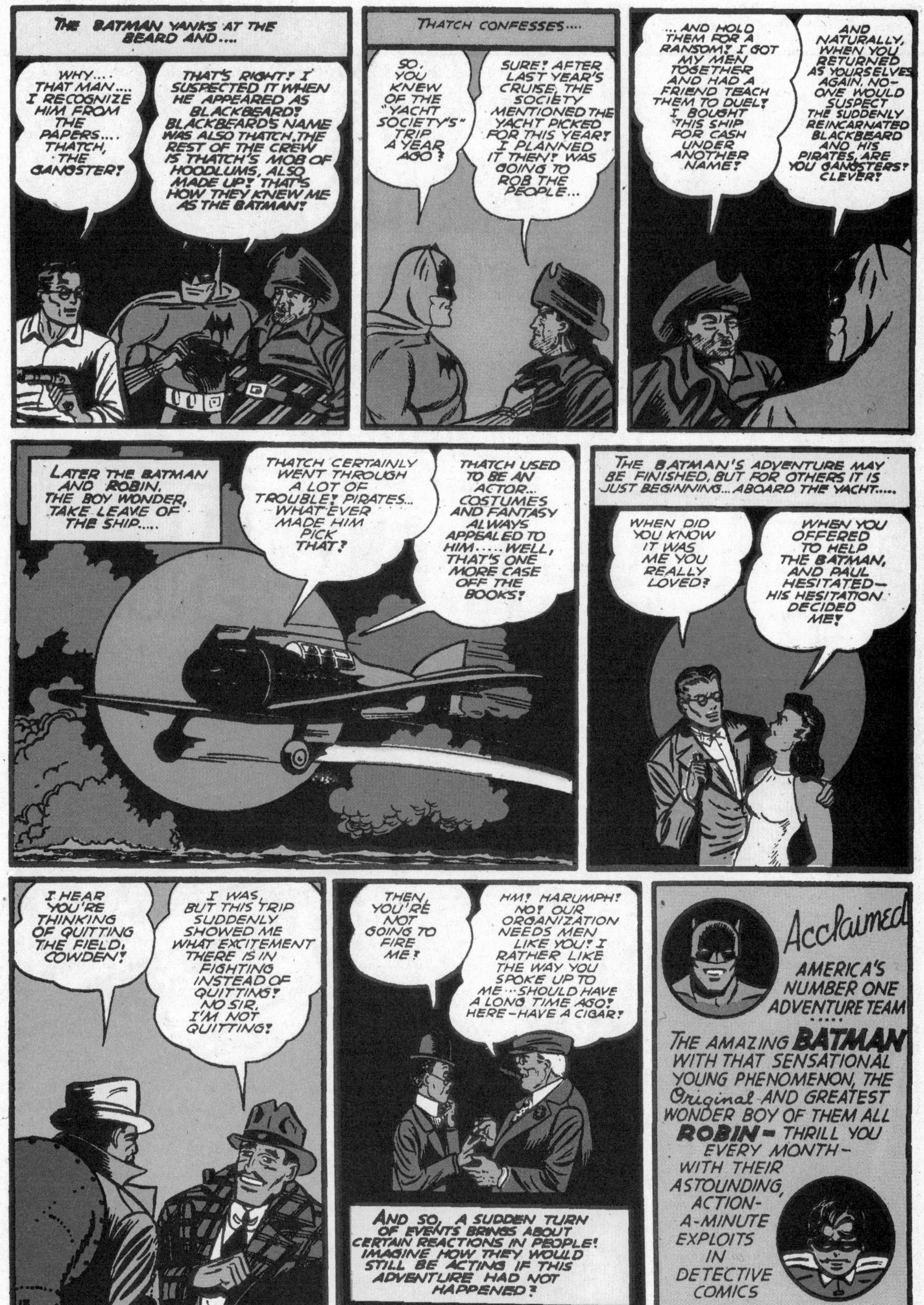
THE BATMAN YANKS AT THE BEARD AND....
WHY.... THAT MAN.... I RECOGNIZE HIM FROM THE PAPERS.... THATCH, THE GANGSTER?
THAT'S RIGHT! I SUSPECTED IT WHEN HE APPEARED AS BLACKBEARD! BLACKBEARD'S NAME WAS ALSO THATCH. THE REST OF THE CREW IS THATCH'S MOB OF HOODLUMS, ALSO MADE UP! THAT'S HOW THEY KNEW ME AS THE BATMAN!
THATCH CONFESSES....
SO, YOU KNEW OF THE "YACHT SOCIETY'S" TRIP A YEAR AGO?
SURE! AFTER LAST YEAR'S CRUISE, THE SOCIETY MENTIONED THE YACHT PICKED FOR THIS YEAR! I PLANNED IT THEN! WAS GOING TO ROB THE PEOPLE...
...AND HOLD THEM FOR A RANSOM! I GOT MY MEN TOGETHER AND HAD A FRIEND TEACH THEM TO DUEL! I BOUGHT THIS SHIP FOR CASH UNDER ANOTHER NAME!
AND NATURALLY, WHEN YOU RETURNED AS YOURSELVES AGAIN, NO-ONE WOULD SUSPECT THE SUDDENLY REINCARNATED BLACKBEARD AND HIS PIRATES ARE YOU GANGSTERS! CLEVER!
LATER THE BATMAN AND ROBIN, THE BOY WONDER, TAKE LEAVE OF THE SHIP....
THATCH CERTAINLY WENT THROUGH A LOT OF TROUBLE! PIRATES... WHAT EVER MADE HIM PICK THAT?
THATCH USED TO BE AN ACTOR... COSTUMES AND FANTASY ALWAYS APPEALED TO HIM..... WELL, THAT'S ONE MORE CASE OFF THE BOOKS!
THE BATMAN'S ADVENTURE MAY BE FINISHED, BUT FOR OTHERS IT IS JUST BEGINNING... ABOARD THE YACHT.....
WHEN DID YOU KNOW IT WAS ME YOU REALLY LOVED?
WHEN YOU OFFERED TO HELP THE BATMAN, AND PAUL HESITATED— HIS HESITATION DECIDED ME!
I HEAR YOU'RE THINKING OF QUITTING THE FIELD, COWDEN!
I WAS, BUT THIS TRIP SUDDENLY SHOWED ME WHAT EXCITEMENT THERE IS IN FIGHTING INSTEAD OF QUITTING! NO SIR, I'M NOT QUITTING!
THEN, YOU'RE NOT GOING TO FIRE ME?
HM! HARUMPH! NO! OUR ORGANIZATION NEEDS MEN LIKE YOU! I RATHER LIKE THE WAY YOU SPOKE UP TO ME... SHOULD HAVE A LONG TIME AGO! HERE-HAVE A CIGAR!
AND SO, A SUDDEN TURN OF EVENTS BRINGS ABOUT CERTAIN REACTIONS IN PEOPLE! IMAGINE HOW THEY WOULD STILL BE ACTING IF THIS ADVENTURE HAD NOT HAPPENED?
Acclaimed
AMERICA'S NUMBER ONE ADVENTURE TEAM
THE AMAZING BATMAN WITH THAT SENSATIONAL YOUNG PHENOMENON, THE Original AND GREATEST WONDER BOY OF THEM ALL ROBIN– THRILL YOU EVERY MONTH– WITH THEIR ASTOUNDING, ACTION-A-MINUTE EXPLOITS IN DETECTIVE COMICS

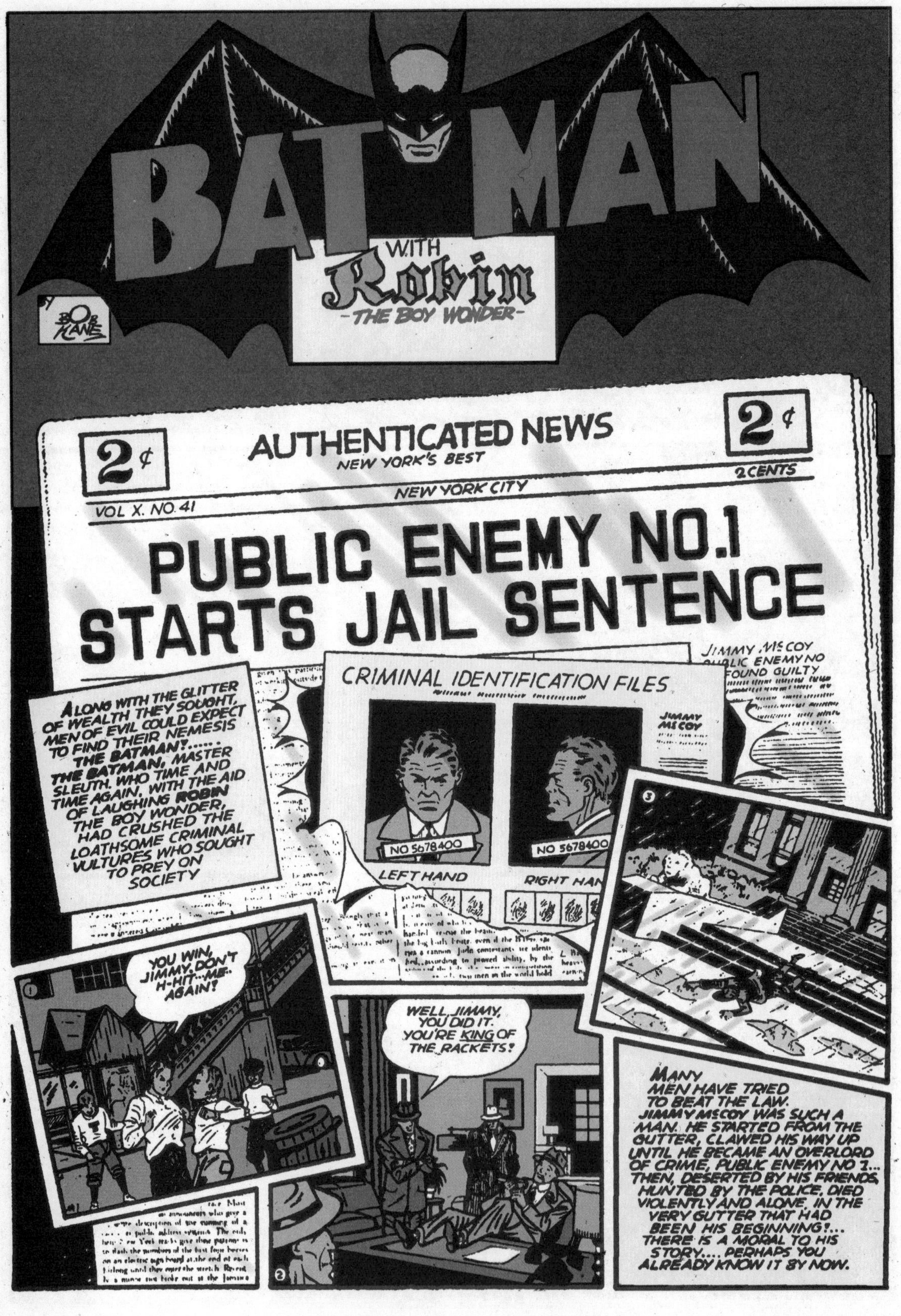
BATMAN
WITH Robin
-THE BOY WONDER-
BY BOB KANE
AUTHENTICATED NEWS
NEW YORK'S BEST
2¢
2¢
2 CENTS
VOL X. NO. 41
NEW YORK CITY
PUBLIC ENEMY NO. 1 STARTS JAIL SENTENCE
JIMMY McCOY PUBLIC ENEMY NO FOUND GUILTY
ALONG WITH THE GLITTER OF WEALTH THEY SOUGHT, MEN OF EVIL COULD EXPECT TO FIND THEIR NEMESIS THE BATMAN!..... THE BATMAN, MASTER SLEUTH, WHO TIME AND TIME AGAIN, WITH THE AID OF LAUGHING ROBIN THE BOY WONDER, HAD CRUSHED THE LOATHSOME CRIMINAL VULTURES WHO SOUGHT TO PREY ON SOCIETY
CRIMINAL IDENTIFICATION FILES
JIMMY McCOY
NO 5678400
NO 5678400
LEFT HAND
RIGHT HAN
YOU WIN, JIMMY, DON'T H-HIT-ME AGAIN!
WELL, JIMMY, YOU DID IT. YOU'RE KING OF THE RACKETS!
MANY MEN HAVE TRIED TO BEAT THE LAW. JIMMY McCOY WAS SUCH A MAN. HE STARTED FROM THE GUTTER, CLAWED HIS WAY UP UNTIL HE BECAME AN OVERLORD OF CRIME, PUBLIC ENEMY NO 1... THEN, DESERTED BY HIS FRIENDS, HUNTED BY THE POLICE, DIED VIOLENTLY AND ALONE, IN THE VERY GUTTER THAT HAD BEEN HIS BEGINNING!... THERE IS A MORAL TO HIS STORY.... PERHAPS YOU ALREADY KNOW IT BY NOW.

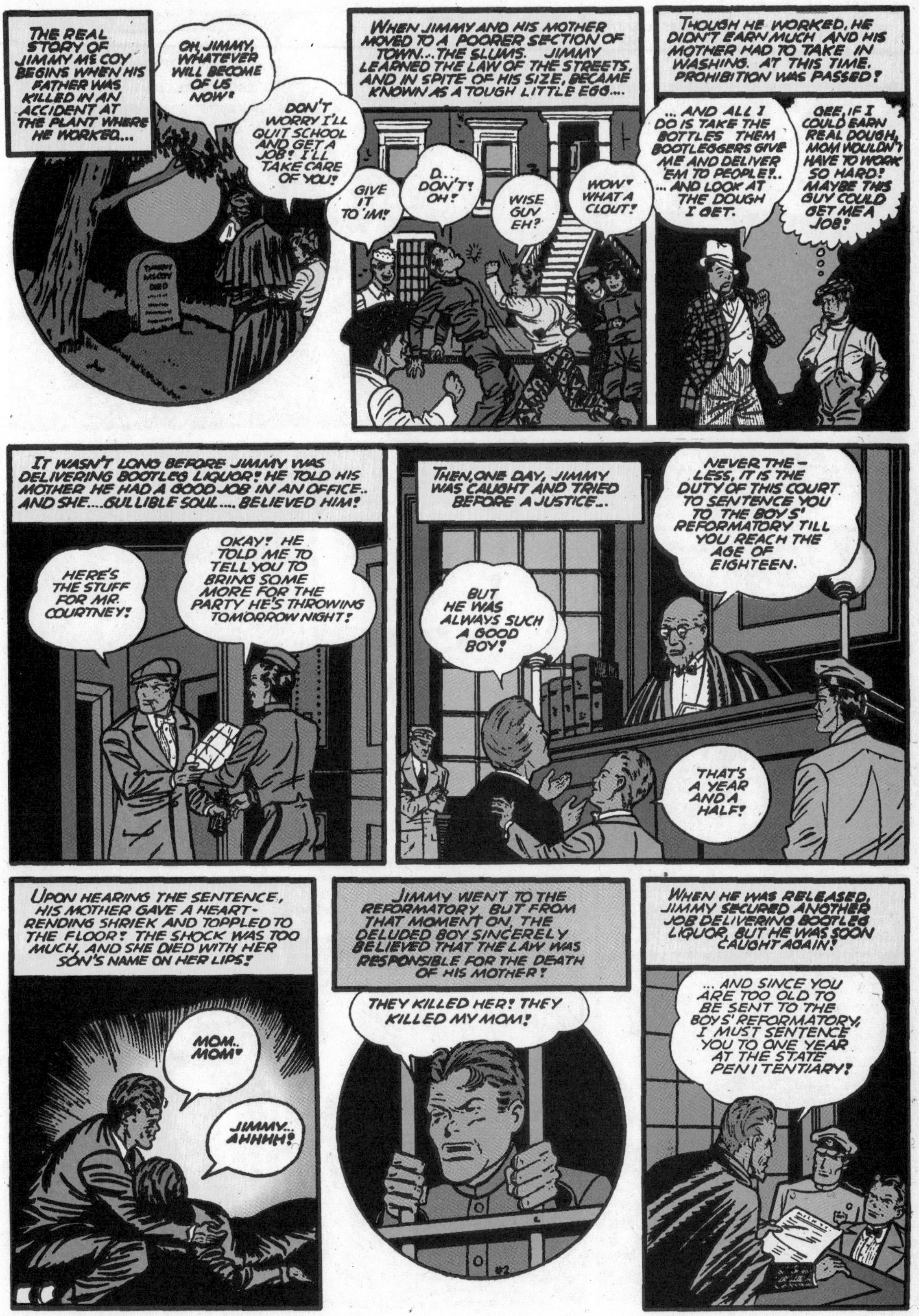
THE REAL STORY OF JIMMY McCOY BEGINS WHEN HIS FATHER WAS KILLED IN AN ACCIDENT AT THE PLANT WHERE HE WORKED...
OH, JIMMY, WHATEVER WILL BECOME OF US NOW!
DON'T WORRY I'LL QUIT SCHOOL AND GET A JOB! I'LL TAKE CARE OF YOU!
WHEN JIMMY AND HIS MOTHER MOVED TO A POORER SECTION OF TOWN...THE SLUMS. JIMMY LEARNED THE LAW OF THE STREETS, AND IN SPITE OF HIS SIZE, BECAME KNOWN AS A TOUGH LITTLE EGG....
GIVE IT TO 'IM!
D... DON'T! OH!
WISE GUY EH?
WOW! WHAT A CLOUT!
THOUGH HE WORKED, HE DIDN'T EARN MUCH AND HIS MOTHER HAD TO TAKE IN WASHING. AT THIS TIME, PROHIBITION WAS PASSED!
... AND ALL I DO IS TAKE THE BOTTLES THEM BOOTLEGGERS GIVE ME AND DELIVER 'EM TO PEOPLE!.. ... AND LOOK AT THE DOUGH I GET.
GEE, IF I COULD EARN REAL DOUGH, MOM WOULDN'T HAVE TO WORK SO HARD! MAYBE THIS GUY COULD GET ME A JOB!
IT WASN'T LONG BEFORE JIMMY WAS DELIVERING BOOTLEG LIQUOR! HE TOLD HIS MOTHER HE HAD A GOOD JOB IN AN OFFICE.. AND SHE....GULLIBLE SOUL.... BELIEVED HIM!
HERE'S THE STUFF FOR MR. COURTNEY!
OKAY! HE TOLD ME TO TELL YOU TO BRING SOME MORE FOR THE PARTY HE'S THROWING TOMORROW NIGHT!
THEN, ONE DAY, JIMMY WAS CAUGHT AND TRIED BEFORE A JUSTICE...
NEVERTHE-LESS, IT IS THE DUTY OF THIS COURT TO SENTENCE YOU TO THE BOYS' REFORMATORY TILL YOU REACH THE AGE OF EIGHTEEN.
BUT HE WAS ALWAYS SUCH A GOOD BOY!
THAT'S A YEAR AND A HALF!
UPON HEARING THE SENTENCE, HIS MOTHER GAVE A HEART-RENDING SHRIEK AND TOPPLED TO THE FLOOR! THE SHOCK WAS TOO MUCH, AND SHE DIED WITH HER SON'S NAME ON HER LIPS!
MOM.. MOM!
JIMMY... AHHHH!
JIMMY WENT TO THE REFORMATORY BUT FROM THAT MOMENT ON, THE DELUDED BOY SINCERELY BELIEVED THAT THE LAW WAS RESPONSIBLE FOR THE DEATH OF HIS MOTHER!
THEY KILLED HER! THEY KILLED MY MOM!
WHEN HE WAS RELEASED, JIMMY SECURED ANOTHER JOB DELIVERING BOOTLEG LIQUOR, BUT HE WAS SOON CAUGHT AGAIN!
... AND SINCE YOU ARE TOO OLD TO BE SENT TO THE BOYS' REFORMATORY, I MUST SENTENCE YOU TO ONE YEAR AT THE STATE PENITENTIARY!

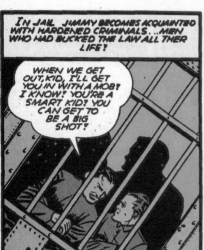

IN JAIL, JIMMY BECOMES ACQUAINTED WITH HARDENED CRIMINALS... MEN WHO HAD BUCKED THE LAW ALL THEIR LIFE!

WHEN WE GET OUT, KID, I'LL GET YOU IN WITH A MOB! I KNOW! YOU'RE A SMART KID! YOU CAN GET TO BE A BIG SHOT!

...AN' FROM NOW ON, YOU'RE GONNA BUY OUR BEER! -AN' IF YA DON'T....

IN THE YEARS THAT FOLLOWED, JIMMY McCOY CHANGED FROM AN EMBITTERED BOY, TO A SNEERING, CUNNING CRIMINAL.

JIMMY WASN'T CONTENT TO BE A MERE MOBSTER. HE ORGANIZED HIS OWN MOB AND IT WASN'T LONG BEFORE HE WAS BEING CALLED THE "KING OF RACKETS!"

I WANT YOU BOYS TO PAY A VISIT TO AUGIE DAVIS! TELL HIM I'M TAKING OVER THE NORTH SIDE! GET GOIN'!

THEN ONE DAY, JIMMY'S BUBBLE BURST!.... PROHIBITION WAS REPEALED!

WHAT ARE WE GONNA DO? BOOTLEGGIN' WON'T GET US DOUGH ANYMORE!

WE'LL EXPAND OUR "PROTECTION" RACKET! THERE'S WAYS WE CAN GET DOUGH FROM THE SUCKERS! STOP WORRYIN'!

BUT, THE PUBLIC WAS AFTER JIMMY AND HIS LIKE!... G-MEN CALLED HIM "PUBLIC ENEMY NO. 1"?

DAILY TIMES.
NEW YORK
VOL 14 NO 11   2 CENTS
2¢   2¢

GOVERNMENT TO INVESTIGATE JIMMY 'RED' McCOY

RACKET BOSS TO BE HELD FOR INCOME TAX EVASION.

JIMMY 'RED' McCOY ENTERING THE ATTORNEY'S OFFICE

INVESTIGATION OF JIMMY'S EARNINGS SHOWED HE HAD BEEN CARELESS ABOUT HIS ENTRIES. HE WAS FOUND GUILTY...

THE COURT FINDS YOU GUILTY OF TAX EVASION AND SENTENCES YOU TO TEN YEARS IN THE STATE PRISON!

WH-AT? WHY, YOU... YOU CAN'T DO THAT TO ME! I'M JIMMY McCOY! I CAN BUY AND SELL YOU!

BUT JIMMY'S THREATS DIDN'T HELP HIM... HE WAS SENT TO PRISON. THE YEARS PASSED..

THEN, THE DAY CAME WHEN HE WAS RELEASED..... JIMMY "RED" McCOY WAS FREE ONCE MORE!

NOW THAT I'M OUT, THE FIRST THING I'M GONNA DO IS GET MY OLD MOB TOGETHER! I'M GONNA RUN THIS TOWN JUST LIKE I USED TO!

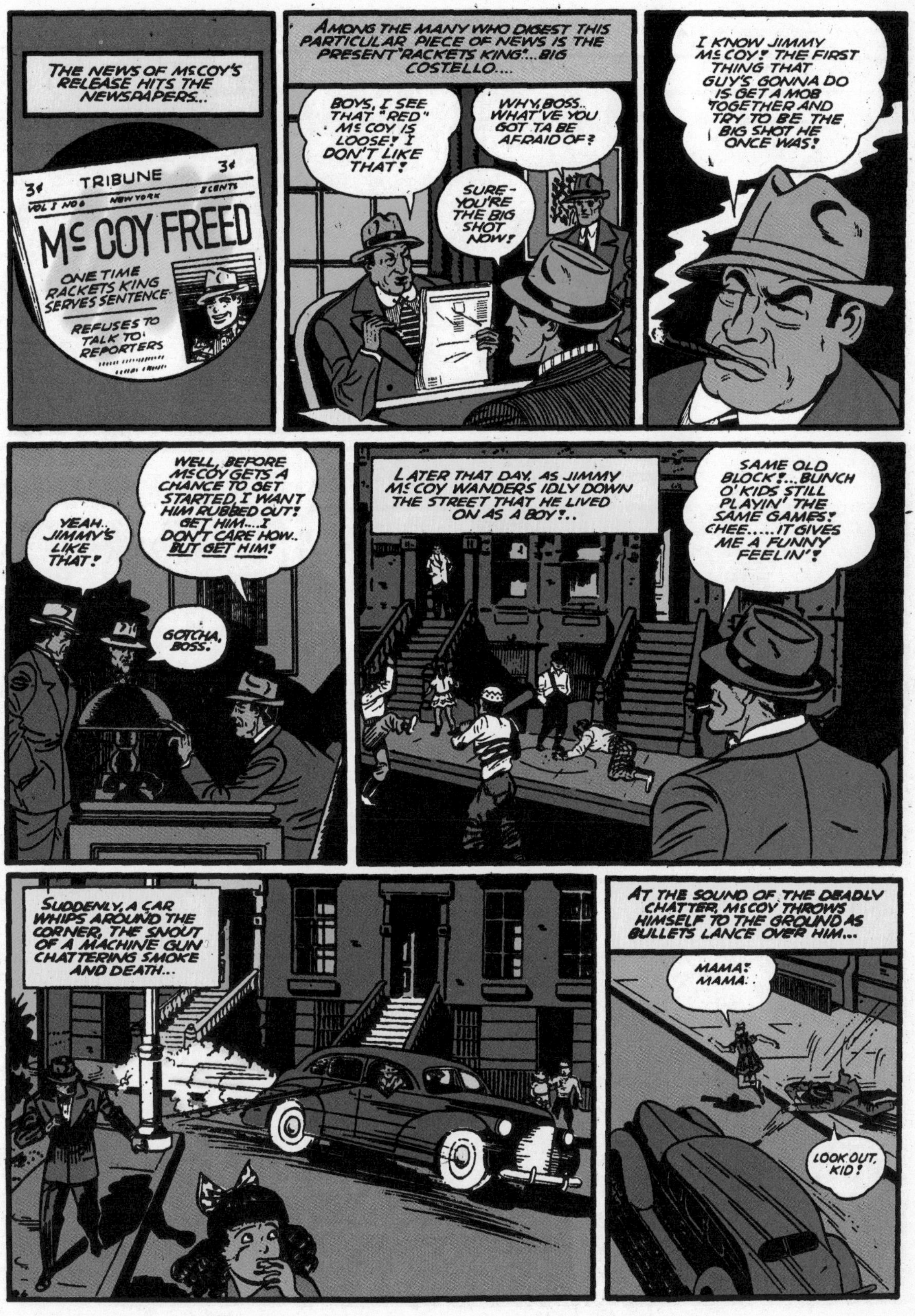
THE NEWS OF McCOY'S RELEASE HITS THE NEWSPAPERS...
TRIBUNE
3¢
3¢
McCOY FREED
ONE TIME RACKETS KING SERVES SENTENCE
REFUSES TO TALK TO REPORTERS
AMONG THE MANY WHO DIGEST THIS PARTICULAR PIECE OF NEWS IS THE PRESENT "RACKETS KING"... BIG COSTELLO....
BOYS, I SEE THAT "RED" McCOY IS LOOSE! I DON'T LIKE THAT!
WHY, BOSS.. WHAT'VE YOU GOT TA BE AFRAID OF?
SURE- YOU'RE THE BIG SHOT NOW!
I KNOW JIMMY McCOY! THE FIRST THING THAT GUY'S GONNA DO IS GET A MOB TOGETHER AND TRY TO BE THE BIG SHOT HE ONCE WAS!
YEAH.. JIMMY'S LIKE THAT!
WELL, BEFORE McCOY GETS A CHANCE TO GET STARTED, I WANT HIM RUBBED OUT! GET HIM....I DON'T CARE HOW.. BUT GET HIM!
GOTCHA, BOSS.
LATER THAT DAY, AS JIMMY McCOY WANDERS IDLY DOWN THE STREET THAT HE LIVED ON AS A BOY!..
SAME OLD BLOCK!... BUNCH O' KIDS STILL PLAYIN' THE SAME GAMES! CHEE.....IT GIVES ME A FUNNY FEELIN'!
SUDDENLY, A CAR WHIPS AROUND THE CORNER, THE SNOUT OF A MACHINE GUN CHATTERING SMOKE AND DEATH...
AT THE SOUND OF THE DEADLY CHATTER, McCOY THROWS HIMSELF TO THE GROUND AS BULLETS LANCE OVER HIM...
MAMA! MAMA!
LOOK OUT, KID!

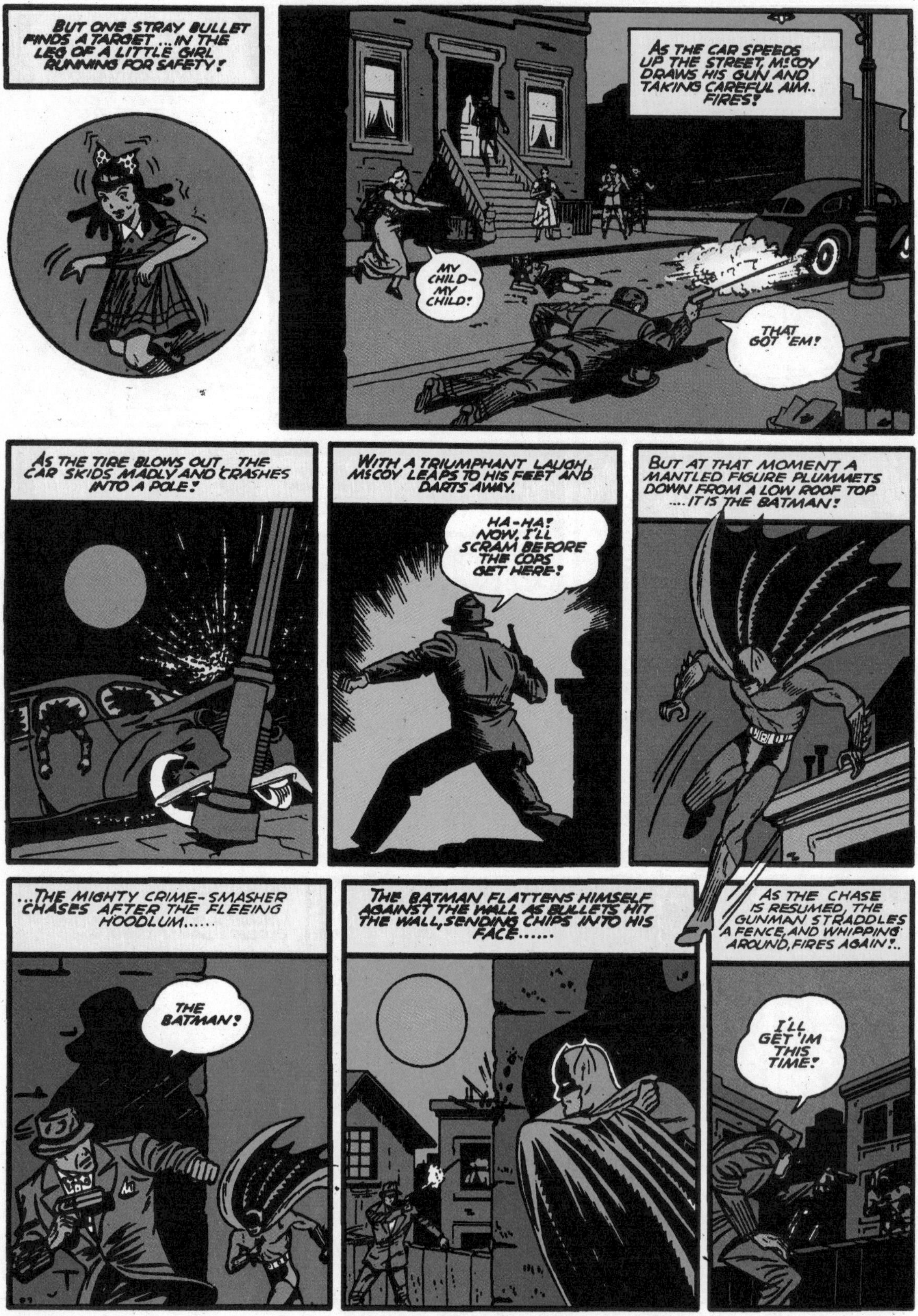
BUT ONE STRAY BULLET FINDS A TARGET ... IN THE LEG OF A LITTLE GIRL RUNNING FOR SAFETY!
AS THE CAR SPEEDS UP THE STREET, McCOY DRAWS HIS GUN AND TAKING CAREFUL AIM.. FIRES!
MY CHILD-- MY CHILD!
THAT GOT 'EM!
AS THE TIRE BLOWS OUT, THE CAR SKIDS MADLY AND CRASHES INTO A POLE!
WITH A TRIUMPHANT LAUGH, McCOY LEAPS TO HIS FEET AND DARTS AWAY.
HA-HA! NOW, I'LL SCRAM BEFORE THE COPS GET HERE!
BUT AT THAT MOMENT A MANTLED FIGURE PLUMMETS DOWN FROM A LOW ROOF TOP .... IT IS THE BATMAN!
...THE MIGHTY CRIME-SMASHER CHASES AFTER THE FLEEING HOODLUM.....
THE BATMAN!
THE BATMAN FLATTENS HIMSELF AGAINST THE WALL AS BULLETS HIT THE WALL, SENDING CHIPS INTO HIS FACE......
AS THE CHASE IS RESUMED, THE GUNMAN STRADDLES A FENCE, AND WHIPPING AROUND, FIRES AGAIN!..
I'LL GET 'IM THIS TIME!

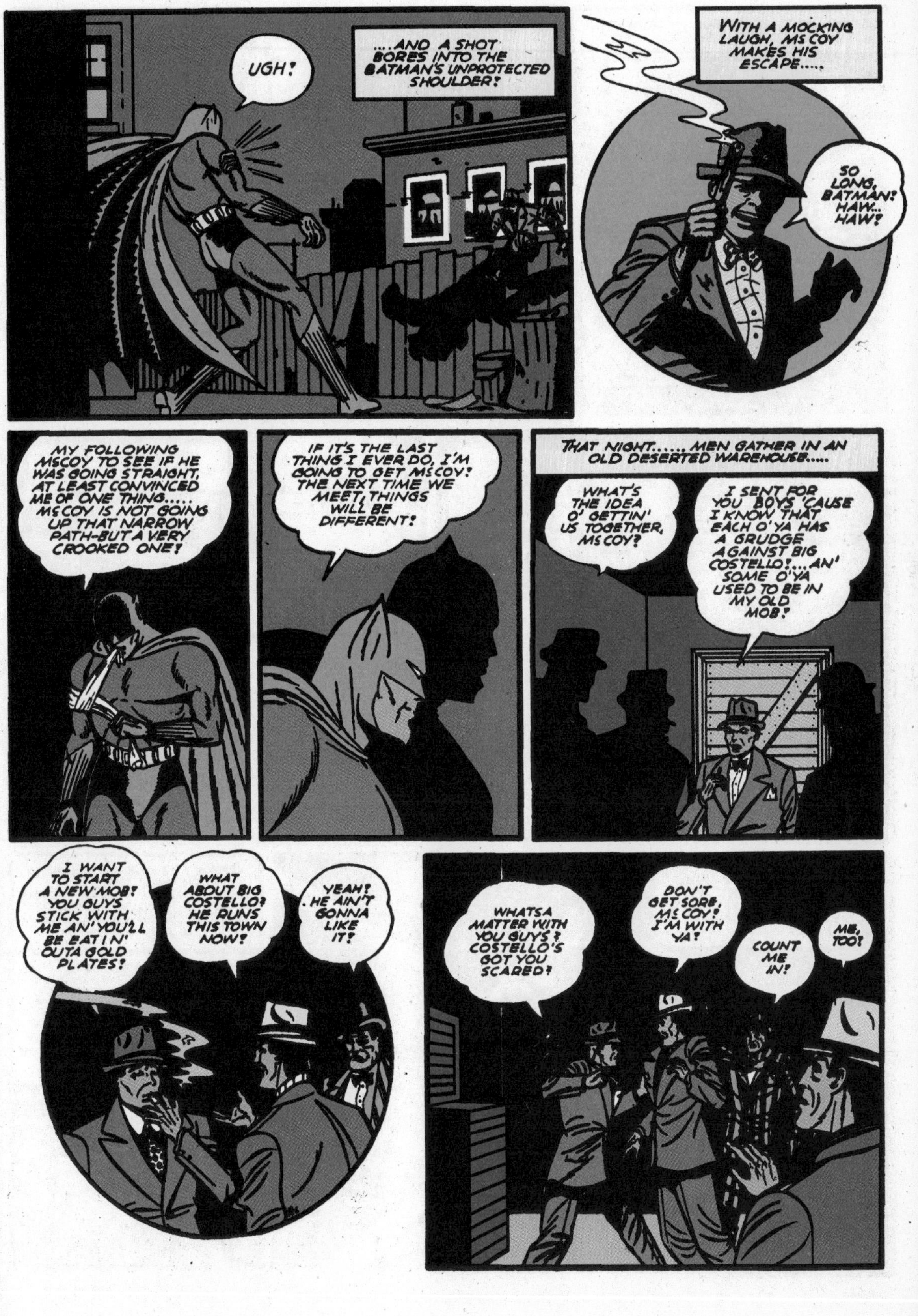
....AND A SHOT BORES INTO THE BATMAN'S UNPROTECTED SHOULDER!
UGH!
WITH A MOCKING LAUGH, MCCOY MAKES HIS ESCAPE.....
SO LONG, BATMAN! HAW... HAW!
MY FOLLOWING MCCOY TO SEE IF HE WAS GOING STRAIGHT, AT LEAST CONVINCED ME OF ONE THING..... MCCOY IS NOT GOING UP THAT NARROW PATH-BUT A VERY CROOKED ONE!
IF IT'S THE LAST THING I EVER DO, I'M GOING TO GET MCCOY! THE NEXT TIME WE MEET, THINGS WILL BE DIFFERENT!
THAT NIGHT...... MEN GATHER IN AN OLD DESERTED WAREHOUSE.....
WHAT'S THE IDEA O' GETTIN' US TOGETHER, MCCOY?
I SENT FOR YOU BOYS 'CAUSE I KNOW THAT EACH O'YA HAS A GRUDGE AGAINST BIG COSTELLO!...AN' SOME O'YA USED TO BE IN MY OLD MOB!
I WANT TO START A NEW MOB! YOU GUYS STICK WITH ME AN' YOU'LL BE EATIN' OUTA GOLD PLATES!
WHAT ABOUT BIG COSTELLO? HE RUNS THIS TOWN NOW!
YEAH! HE AIN'T GONNA LIKE IT!
WHATSA MATTER WITH YOU GUYS? COSTELLO'S GOT YOU SCARED?
DON'T GET SORE, MCCOY! I'M WITH YA!
COUNT ME IN!
ME, TOO!

AFTER LIGHTING HIS OWN CIGARETTE, A THUG HOLDS THE LIGHT FOR McCOY...

HERE'S A LIGHT, "RED."

HOLD THAT FOR ME!

AFTER LIGHTING UP, McCOY BLOWS THE FLAME!

HEY!... WHAT'S THE IDEA? YOU KNEW I WANTED A LIGHT!

SHUT UP! I NEVER LIGHT THREE ON A MATCH? IT'S BAD LUCK!

SAME OLD JIMMY McCOY... STILL SUPERSTITIOUS! I'LL BET YOU STILL HAVE THAT OLD LUCKY RABBIT'S FOOT!

YOU BET YOUR SWEET LIFE I HAVE. THE DAY I LOSE THAT MY LUCK'S GONNA RUN OUT!

BUT I'VE BEEN PAYING ANOTHER PROTECTIVE ASSOCIATION! I.....

SHUT UP! FROM NOW ON, WE'RE PROTECTIN' YA! GET ME?

IN THE ENSUING DAYS, JIMMY McCOY BEGINS TO MOVE IN ON COSTELLO'S TERRITORY...

CAN'T PAY UP, EH?.. OKAY, BOYS..... THROW THAT ACID OVER THE CLOTHES!!

NO ONE SEEMS SAFE FROM HIS MEN...

AS THE RIVAL GANGS CLASH, BATTLES ARE FOUGHT....THE SMOKING GUN HOLDS SWAY. ...!

BOOM

WHILE IN HIS APARTMENT, BRUCE WAYNE, WHO IS IN REALITY THE BATMAN, SPEAKS WITH HIS WARD, DICK GRAYSON, WHOSE OTHER SELF IS ROBIN, THE BOY WONDER!

READING ABOUT THE GANGWAR AGAIN?

YES, AND I'VE GOT A FEELING THAT McCOY IS THE ONE WHO IS BUCKING BIG COSTELLO!—BUT NOBODY CAN PROVE IT. STORE OWNERS ARE AFRAID TO TALK. DICK, YOU'VE GOT A JOB TO DO - LISTEN...

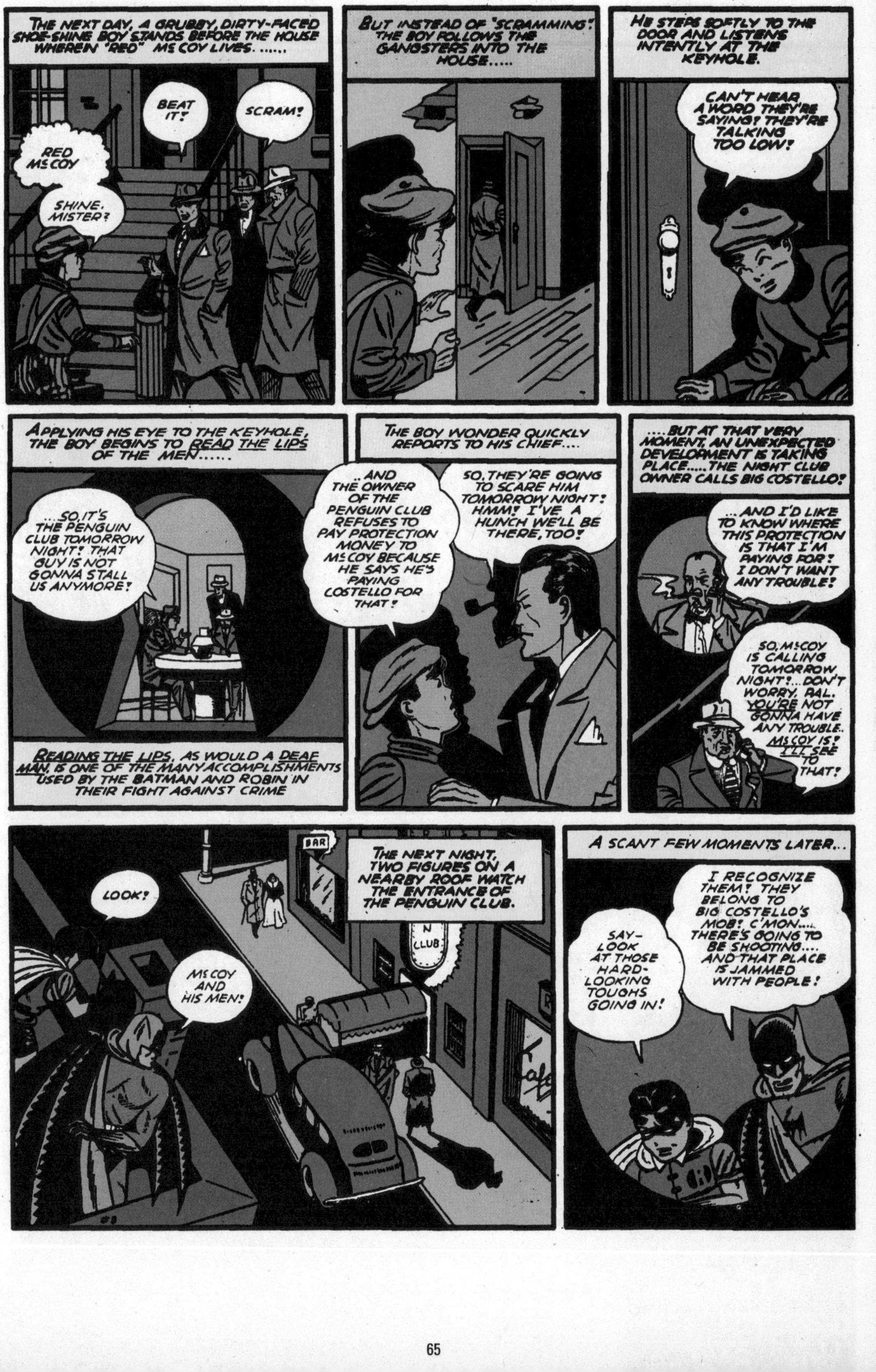
THE NEXT DAY, A GRUBBY, DIRTY-FACED SHOE-SHINE BOY STANDS BEFORE THE HOUSE WHEREIN "RED" McCOY LIVES.......
RED McCOY
SHINE, MISTER?
BEAT IT!
SCRAM!
BUT INSTEAD OF "SCRAMMING" THE BOY FOLLOWS THE GANGSTERS INTO THE HOUSE.....
HE STEPS SOFTLY TO THE DOOR AND LISTENS INTENTLY AT THE KEYHOLE.
CAN'T HEAR A WORD THEY'RE SAYING! THEY'RE TALKING TOO LOW!
APPLYING HIS EYE TO THE KEYHOLE, THE BOY BEGINS TO READ THE LIPS OF THE MEN......
...SO, IT'S THE PENGUIN CLUB TOMORROW NIGHT! THAT GUY IS NOT GONNA STALL US ANYMORE!
READING THE LIPS, AS WOULD A DEAF MAN, IS ONE OF THE MANY ACCOMPLISHMENTS USED BY THE BATMAN AND ROBIN IN THEIR FIGHT AGAINST CRIME
THE BOY WONDER QUICKLY REPORTS TO HIS CHIEF....
...AND THE OWNER OF THE PENGUIN CLUB REFUSES TO PAY PROTECTION MONEY TO McCOY BECAUSE HE SAYS HE'S PAYING COSTELLO FOR THAT!
SO, THEY'RE GOING TO SCARE HIM TOMORROW NIGHT! HMM! I'VE A HUNCH WE'LL BE THERE, TOO!
....BUT AT THAT VERY MOMENT, AN UNEXPECTED DEVELOPMENT IS TAKING PLACE.....THE NIGHT CLUB OWNER CALLS BIG COSTELLO!
...AND I'D LIKE TO KNOW WHERE THIS PROTECTION IS THAT I'M PAYING FOR! I DON'T WANT ANY TROUBLE!
SO, McCOY IS CALLING TOMORROW NIGHT?...DON'T WORRY, PAL. YOU'RE NOT GONNA HAVE ANY TROUBLE.. McCOY IS! I'LL SEE TO THAT!
THE NEXT NIGHT, TWO FIGURES ON A NEARBY ROOF WATCH THE ENTRANCE OF THE PENGUIN CLUB.
BAR
LOOK!
McCOY AND HIS MEN!
N CLUB
A SCANT FEW MOMENTS LATER...
SAY-LOOK AT THOSE HARD-LOOKING TOUGHS GOING IN!
I RECOGNIZE THEM! THEY BELONG TO BIG COSTELLO'S MOB! C'MON.... THERE'S GOING TO BE SHOOTING.... AND THAT PLACE IS JAMMED WITH PEOPLE!

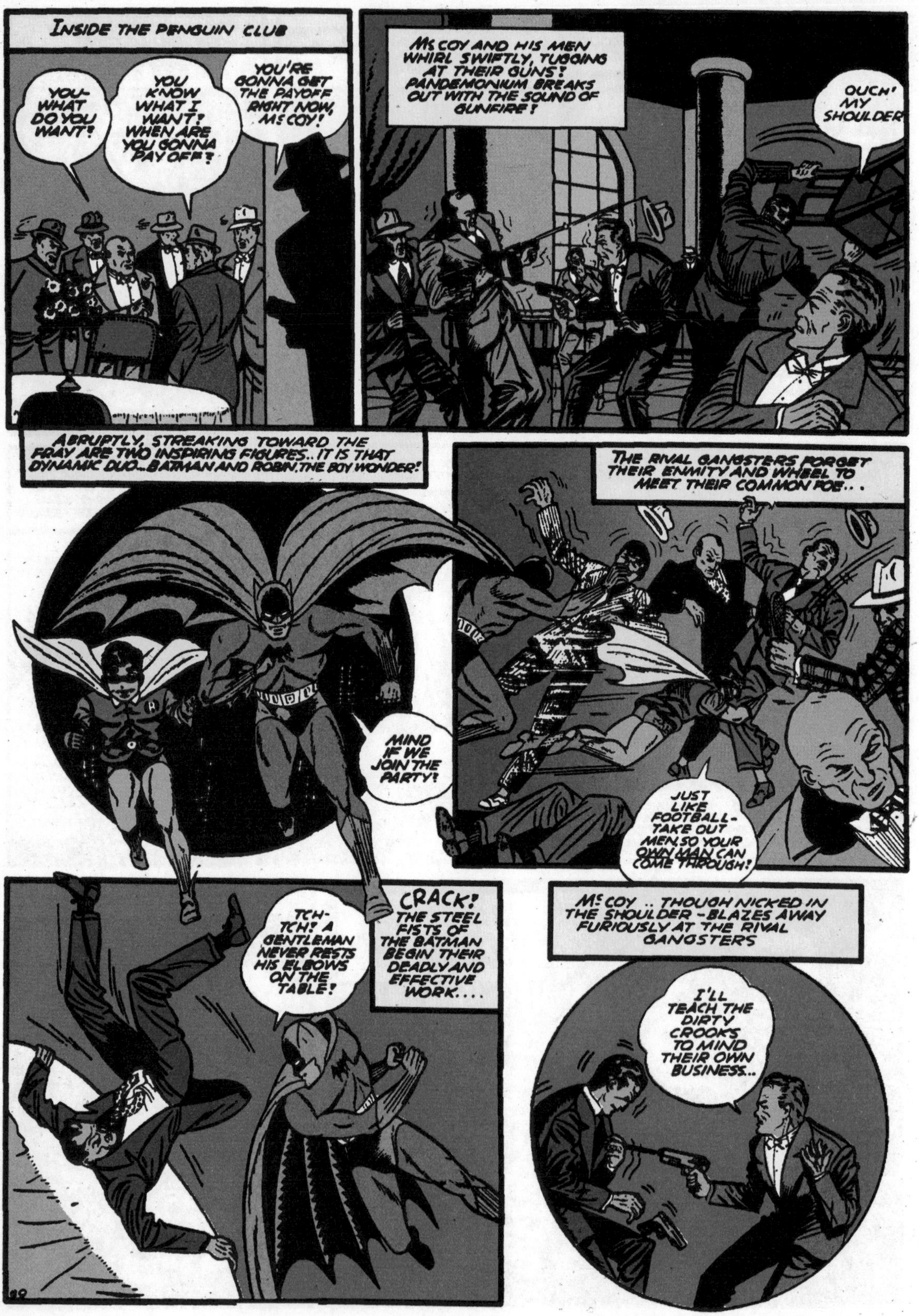
INSIDE THE PENGUIN CLUB
YOU- WHAT DO YOU WANT?
YOU KNOW WHAT I WANT! WHEN ARE YOU GONNA PAY OFF?
YOU'RE GONNA GET THE PAYOFF RIGHT NOW, MC COY!
MC COY AND HIS MEN WHIRL SWIFTLY, TUGGING AT THEIR GUNS! PANDEMONIUM BREAKS OUT WITH THE SOUND OF GUNFIRE!
OUCH! MY SHOULDER
ABRUPTLY, STREAKING TOWARD THE FRAY ARE TWO INSPIRING FIGURES...IT IS THAT DYNAMIC DUO...BATMAN AND ROBIN, THE BOY WONDER!
MIND IF WE JOIN THE PARTY?
THE RIVAL GANGSTERS FORGET THEIR ENMITY AND WHEEL TO MEET THEIR COMMON FOE...
JUST LIKE FOOTBALL- TAKE OUT MEN, SO YOUR OWN MAN CAN COME THROUGH!
TCH-TCH! A GENTLEMAN NEVER RESTS HIS ELBOWS ON THE TABLE!
CRACK! THE STEEL FISTS OF THE BATMAN BEGIN THEIR DEADLY AND EFFECTIVE WORK....
MC COY .. THOUGH NICKED IN THE SHOULDER - BLAZES AWAY FURIOUSLY AT THE RIVAL GANGSTERS
I'LL TEACH THE DIRTY CROOKS TO MIND THEIR OWN BUSINESS...

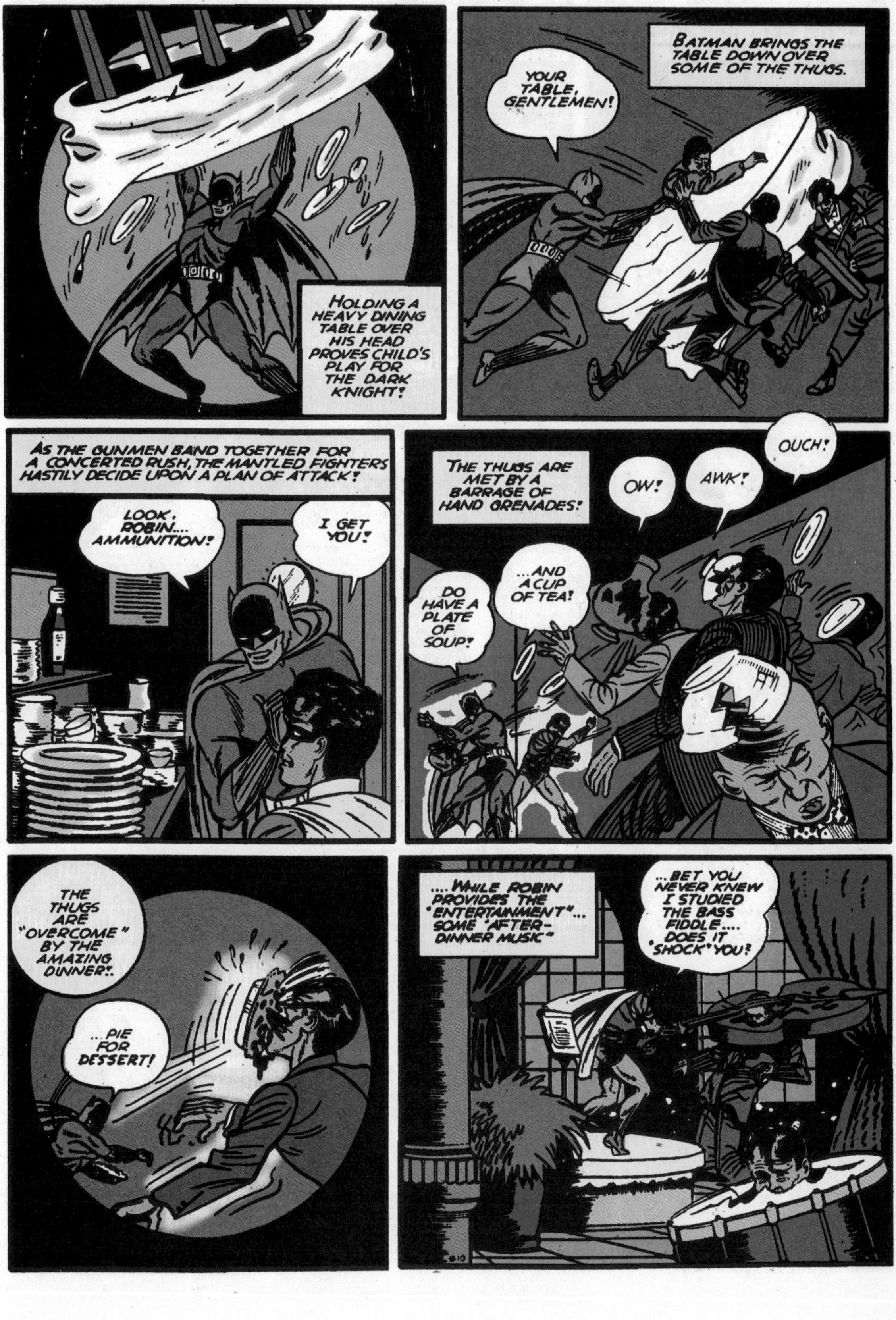
HOLDING A HEAVY DINING TABLE OVER HIS HEAD PROVES CHILD'S PLAY FOR THE DARK KNIGHT!
BATMAN BRINGS THE TABLE DOWN OVER SOME OF THE THUGS.
YOUR TABLE, GENTLEMEN!
AS THE GUNMEN BAND TOGETHER FOR A CONCERTED RUSH, THE MANTLED FIGHTERS HASTILY DECIDE UPON A PLAN OF ATTACK!
LOOK, ROBIN.... AMMUNITION!
I GET YOU!
THE THUGS ARE MET BY A BARRAGE OF HAND GRENADES!
OW!
AWK!
OUCH!
...AND A CUP OF TEA!
DO HAVE A PLATE OF SOUP!
THE THUGS ARE "OVERCOME" BY THE AMAZING DINNER!..
...PIE FOR DESSERT!
....WHILE ROBIN PROVIDES THE "ENTERTAINMENT"... SOME "AFTER-DINNER MUSIC"
...BET YOU NEVER KNEW I STUDIED THE BASS FIDDLE.... DOES IT "SHOCK" YOU?

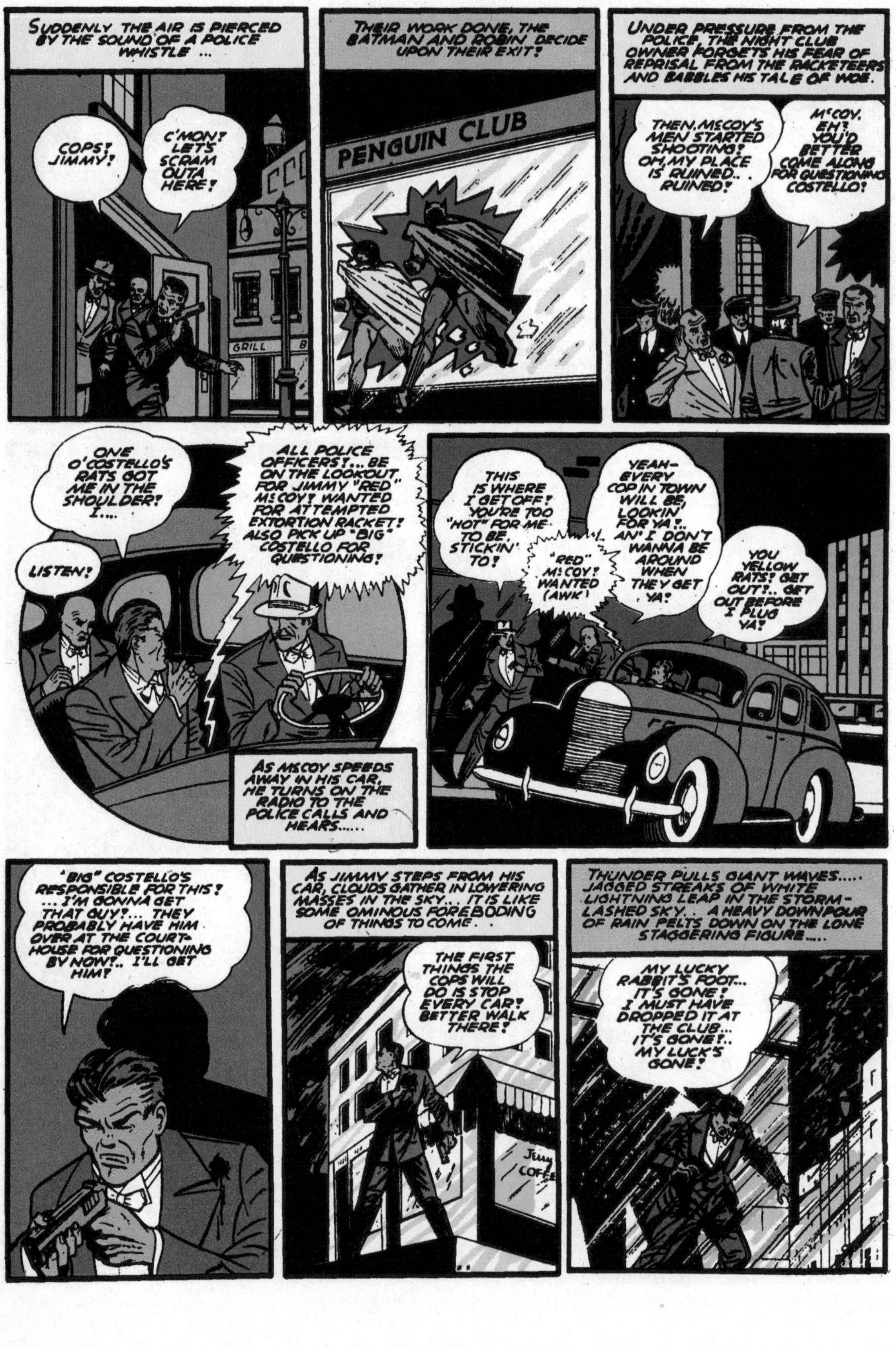
SUDDENLY THE AIR IS PIERCED BY THE SOUND OF A POLICE WHISTLE ...
COPS! JIMMY!
C'MON! LET'S SCRAM OUTA HERE!
GRILL
THEIR WORK DONE, THE BATMAN AND ROBIN DECIDE UPON THEIR EXIT!
PENGUIN CLUB
UNDER PRESSURE FROM THE POLICE, THE NIGHT CLUB OWNER FORGETS HIS FEAR OF REPRISAL FROM THE RACKETEERS AND BABBLES HIS TALE OF WOE.
THEN, MCCOY'S MEN STARTED SHOOTING! OH, MY PLACE IS RUINED.. RUINED!
McCOY, EH? YOU'D BETTER COME ALONG FOR QUESTIONING COSTELLO!
ONE O'COSTELLO'S RATS GOT ME IN THE SHOULDER! I....
LISTEN!
ALL POLICE OFFICERS!... BE ON THE LOOKOUT FOR JIMMY "RED" McCOY! WANTED FOR ATTEMPTED EXTORTION RACKET! ALSO PICK UP "BIG" COSTELLO FOR QUESTIONING!
AS MCCOY SPEEDS AWAY IN HIS CAR, HE TURNS ON THE RADIO TO THE POLICE CALLS AND HEARS.....
THIS IS WHERE I GET OFF! YOU'RE TOO "HOT" FOR ME TO BE STICKIN' TO!
"RED" McCOY! WANTED (AWK)
YEAH-EVERY COP IN TOWN WILL BE LOOKIN' FOR YA!.. AN' I DON'T WANNA BE AROUND WHEN THEY GET YA!
YOU YELLOW RATS! GET OUT!.. GET OUT BEFORE I PLUG YA!
"BIG" COSTELLO'S RESPONSIBLE FOR THIS! ... I'M GONNA GET THAT GUY!... THEY PROBABLY HAVE HIM OVER AT THE COURT-HOUSE FOR QUESTIONING BY NOW!.. I'LL GET HIM!
AS JIMMY STEPS FROM HIS CAR, CLOUDS GATHER IN LOWERING MASSES IN THE SKY... IT IS LIKE SOME OMINOUS FOREBODING OF THINGS TO COME . .
THE FIRST THINGS THE COPS WILL DO IS STOP EVERY CAR! BETTER WALK THERE!
THUNDER PULLS GIANT WAVES..... JAGGED STREAKS OF WHITE LIGHTNING LEAP IN THE STORM-LASHED SKY.. A HEAVY DOWNPOUR OF RAIN PELTS DOWN ON THE LONE STAGGERING FIGURE.....
MY LUCKY RABBIT'S FOOT... IT'S GONE! I MUST HAVE DROPPED IT AT THE CLUB... IT'S GONE!.. MY LUCK'S GONE!

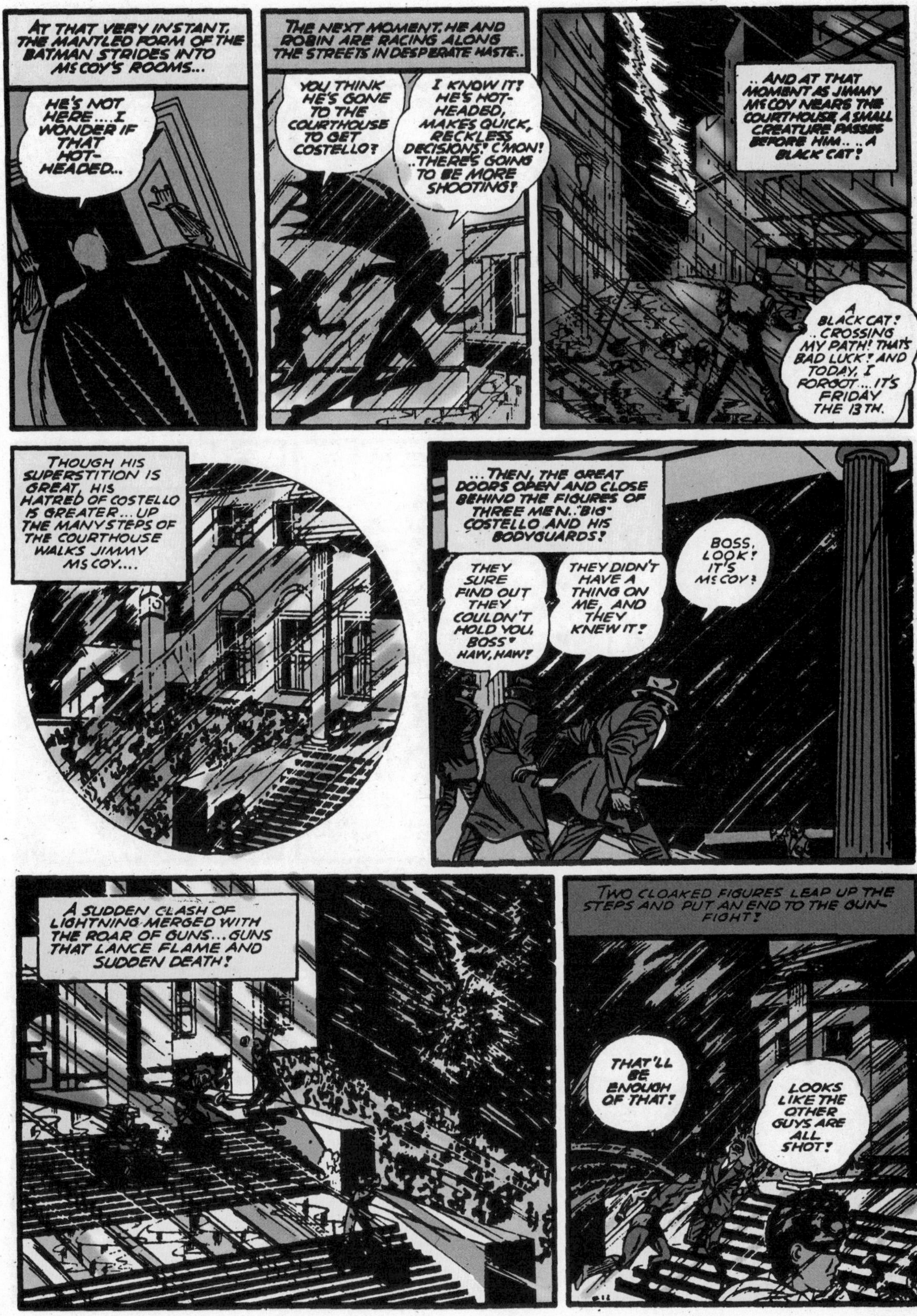
AT THAT VERY INSTANT, THE MANTLED FORM OF THE BATMAN STRIDES INTO MCCOY'S ROOMS...
HE'S NOT HERE....I WONDER IF THAT HOT-HEADED...
THE NEXT MOMENT, HE AND ROBIN ARE RACING ALONG THE STREETS IN DESPERATE HASTE..
YOU THINK HE'S GONE TO THE COURTHOUSE TO GET COSTELLO?
I KNOW IT! HE'S HOT-HEADED, MAKES QUICK, RECKLESS DECISIONS! C'MON! ..THERE'S GOING TO BE MORE SHOOTING!
..AND AT THAT MOMENT AS JIMMY MCCOY NEARS THE COURTHOUSE, A SMALL CREATURE PASSES BEFORE HIM.... A BLACK CAT!
A BLACK CAT! ..CROSSING MY PATH! THAT'S BAD LUCK! AND TODAY, I FORGOT... IT'S FRIDAY THE 13TH.
THOUGH HIS SUPERSTITION IS GREAT, HIS HATRED OF COSTELLO IS GREATER... UP THE MANY STEPS OF THE COURTHOUSE WALKS JIMMY MCCOY....
...THEN, THE GREAT DOORS OPEN AND CLOSE BEHIND THE FIGURES OF THREE MEN.."BIG" COSTELLO AND HIS BODYGUARDS!
THEY SURE FIND OUT THEY COULDN'T HOLD YOU, BOSS! HAW, HAW!
THEY DIDN'T HAVE A THING ON ME, AND THEY KNEW IT!
BOSS, LOOK! IT'S MCCOY!
A SUDDEN CLASH OF LIGHTNING MERGED WITH THE ROAR OF GUNS... GUNS THAT LANCE FLAME AND SUDDEN DEATH!
TWO CLOAKED FIGURES LEAP UP THE STEPS AND PUT AN END TO THE GUN-FIGHT!
THAT'LL BE ENOUGH OF THAT!
LOOKS LIKE THE OTHER GUYS ARE ALL SHOT!

OKAY, McCOY!.... I'M TAKING YOU IN! YOU'RE GOING TO A CELL AGAIN!

I'M NOT GOIN' TO ANY JAIL ANYMORE! HA HA! YOU'RE JUST A LITTLE TOO LATE! HA HA!

SUDDENLY, McCOY'S LAUGHTER IS CHOKED OFF BY A RACKING COUGH... HE CLAWS CONVULSIVELY AT HIS CHEST..

JUST A LITTLE TOO LATE! HA HA (COUGH) AHHH!!

...AND TUMBLES DOWN THE STEPS......

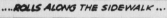
....ROLLS ALONG THE SIDEWALK ...

...AND SPRAWLS OVER THE CURB AND THE GUTTER!

JIMMY McCOY'S INFAMOUS CAREER HAS COME TO AN END AT LAST!

IT IS THE NEXT DAY IN THE WAYNE HOME!...

SOMETHING THAT SUGGESTED HE WAS A BOY TRYING TO ACT LIKE A BIG SHOT! YES, I FELT IT, TOO! TOO BAD.....HE HAD TALENT. HE WOULD HAVE GONE FAR IN BUSINESS!

YOU KNOW—EVEN THOUGH McCOY WAS A CRIMINAL THERE WAS SOMETHING ..SOMETHING ABOUT HIM—

BRUCE..... IF YOU COULD SPEAK TO EVERY GIRL AND BOY RIGHT NOW, WHAT WOULD YOU SAY?

JUST THIS: DON'T BE IMPRESSED BY THE POWER OF CRIMINALS, OF THEIR SLEEK CLOTHES, THEIR LUXURIOUS SURROUNDINGS! THEIRS IS A LIFE OF FEAR... FEAR OF THE POLICE, FEAR THAT THEY, TOO, WILL END AS JIMMY McCOY DID!

LEST ALL OF YOU FORGET, THINK BACK NOW TO THAT DREADFUL NIGHT, THAT TERRIBLE SCENE WHEN JIMMY McCOY LAY FACE DOWN IN THE GUTTER, AS THE RAIN PELTED DOWN ON HIS SPRAWLED FIGURE! THINK BACK AND BE WISE!

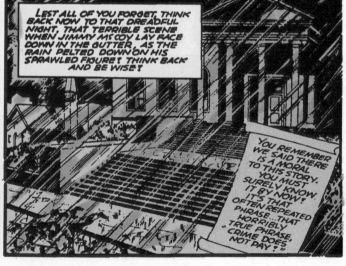

YOU REMEMBER WE SAID THERE IS A MORAL TO THIS STORY. YOU MUST SURELY KNOW IT BY NOW! IT'S THAT OFTEN REPEATED PHRASE...THAT HORRIBLY TRUE PHRASE.. "CRIME DOES NOT PAY!"

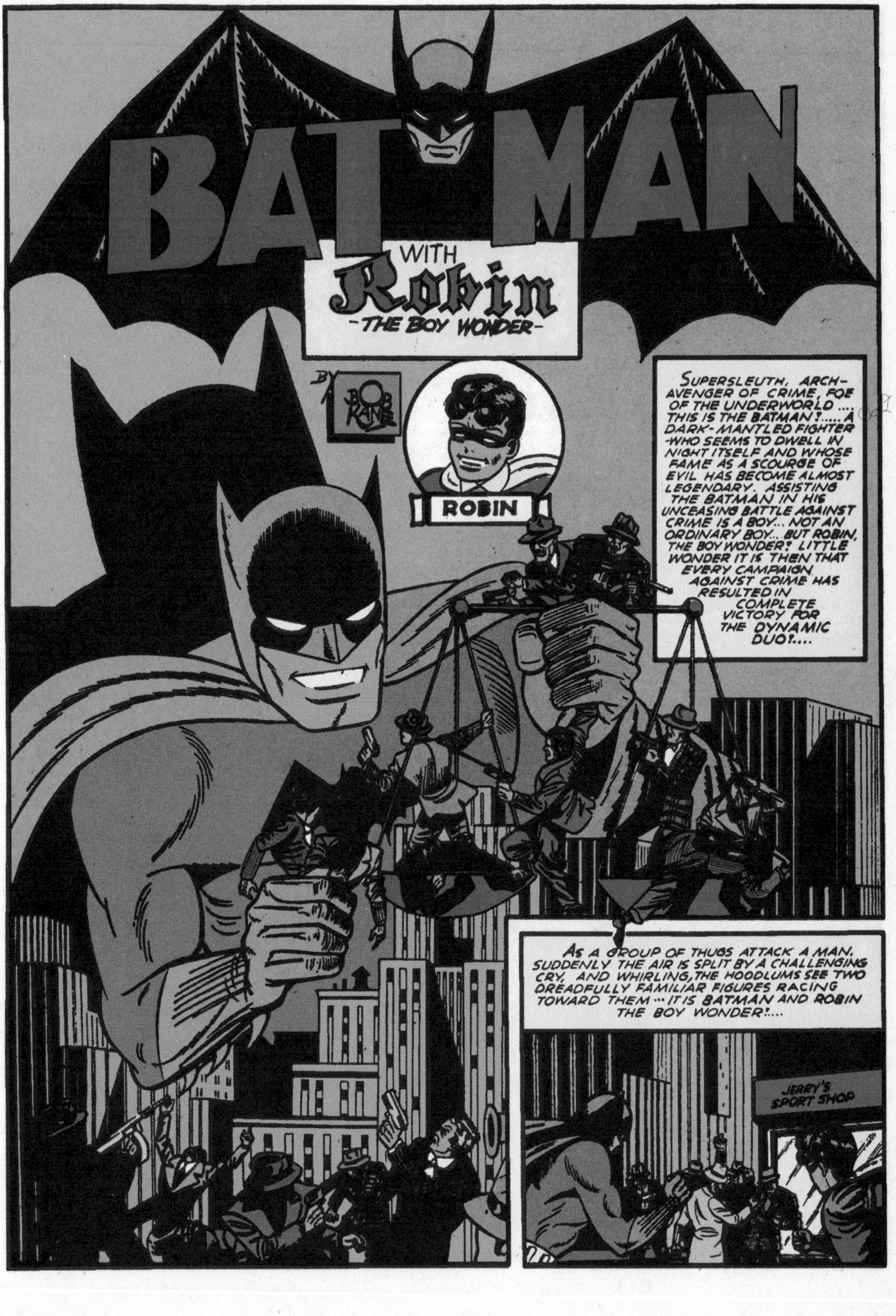
BATMAN
WITH Robin -THE BOY WONDER-
BY BOB KANE
ROBIN
SUPERSLEUTH, ARCH-AVENGER OF CRIME, FOE OF THE UNDERWORLD .... THIS IS THE BATMAN!..... A DARK-MANTLED FIGHTER -WHO SEEMS TO DWELL IN NIGHT ITSELF AND WHOSE FAME AS A SCOURGE OF EVIL HAS BECOME ALMOST LEGENDARY. ASSISTING THE BATMAN IN HIS UNCEASING BATTLE AGAINST CRIME IS A BOY... NOT AN ORDINARY BOY... BUT ROBIN, THE BOY WONDER! LITTLE WONDER IT IS THEN THAT EVERY CAMPAIGN AGAINST CRIME HAS RESULTED IN COMPLETE VICTORY FOR THE DYNAMIC DUO!....
AS A GROUP OF THUGS ATTACK A MAN, SUDDENLY THE AIR IS SPLIT BY A CHALLENGING CRY, AND WHIRLING, THE HOODLUMS SEE TWO DREADFULLY FAMILIAR FIGURES RACING TOWARD THEM ... IT IS BATMAN AND ROBIN THE BOY WONDER!....
JERRY'S SPORT SHOP

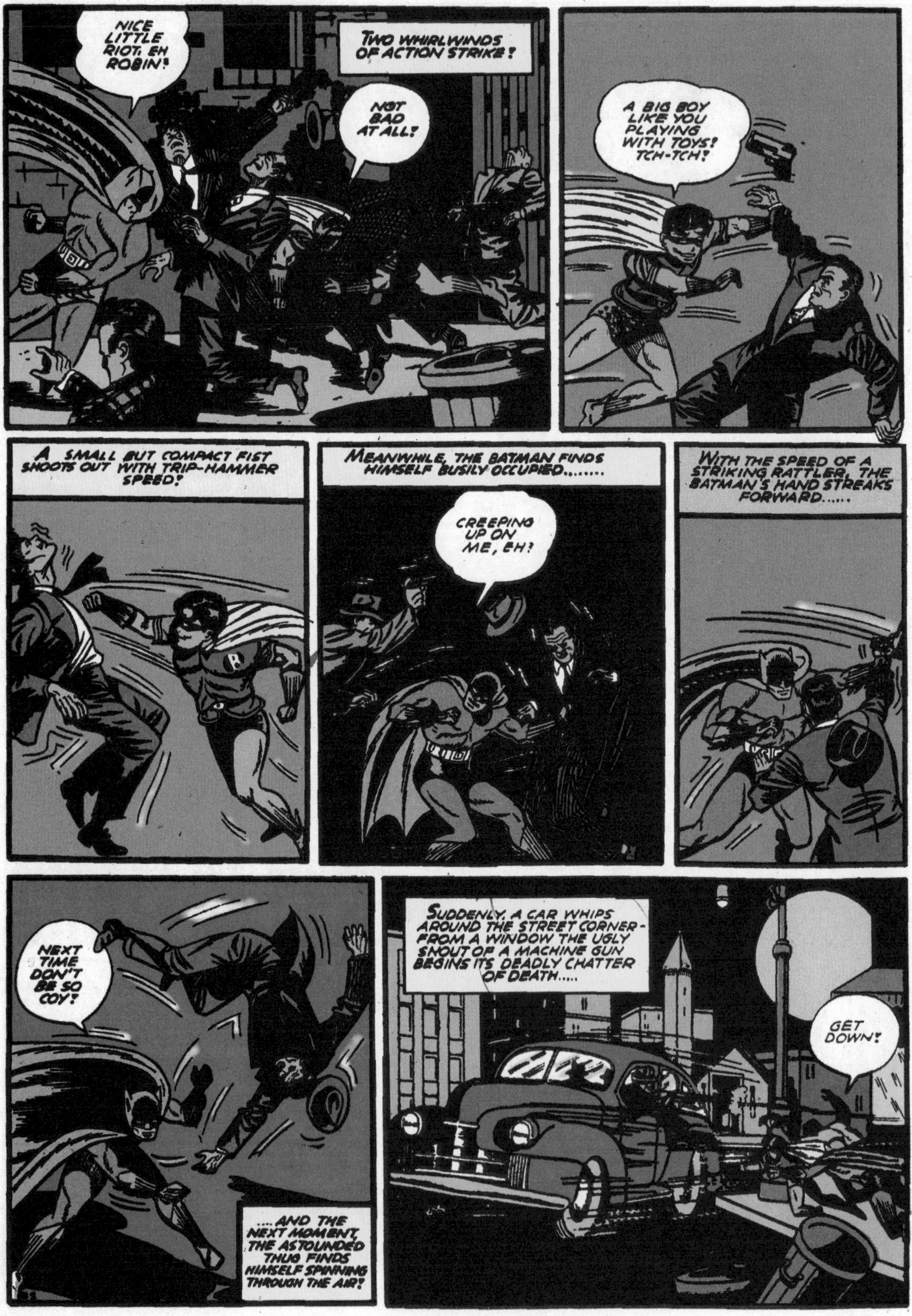
NICE LITTLE RIOT, EH ROBIN?
TWO WHIRLWINDS OF ACTION STRIKE!
NOT BAD AT ALL!
A BIG BOY LIKE YOU PLAYING WITH TOYS! TCH-TCH!
A SMALL BUT COMPACT FIST SHOOTS OUT WITH TRIP-HAMMER SPEED!
MEANWHILE, THE BATMAN FINDS HIMSELF BUSILY OCCUPIED.......
CREEPING UP ON ME, EH?
WITH THE SPEED OF A STRIKING RATTLER, THE BATMAN'S HAND STREAKS FORWARD......
NEXT TIME DON'T BE SO COY!
....AND THE NEXT MOMENT, THE ASTOUNDED THUG FINDS HIMSELF SPINNING THROUGH THE AIR!
SUDDENLY, A CAR WHIPS AROUND THE STREET CORNER - FROM A WINDOW THE UGLY SNOUT OF A MACHINE GUN BEGINS ITS DEADLY CHATTER OF DEATH.....
GET DOWN!

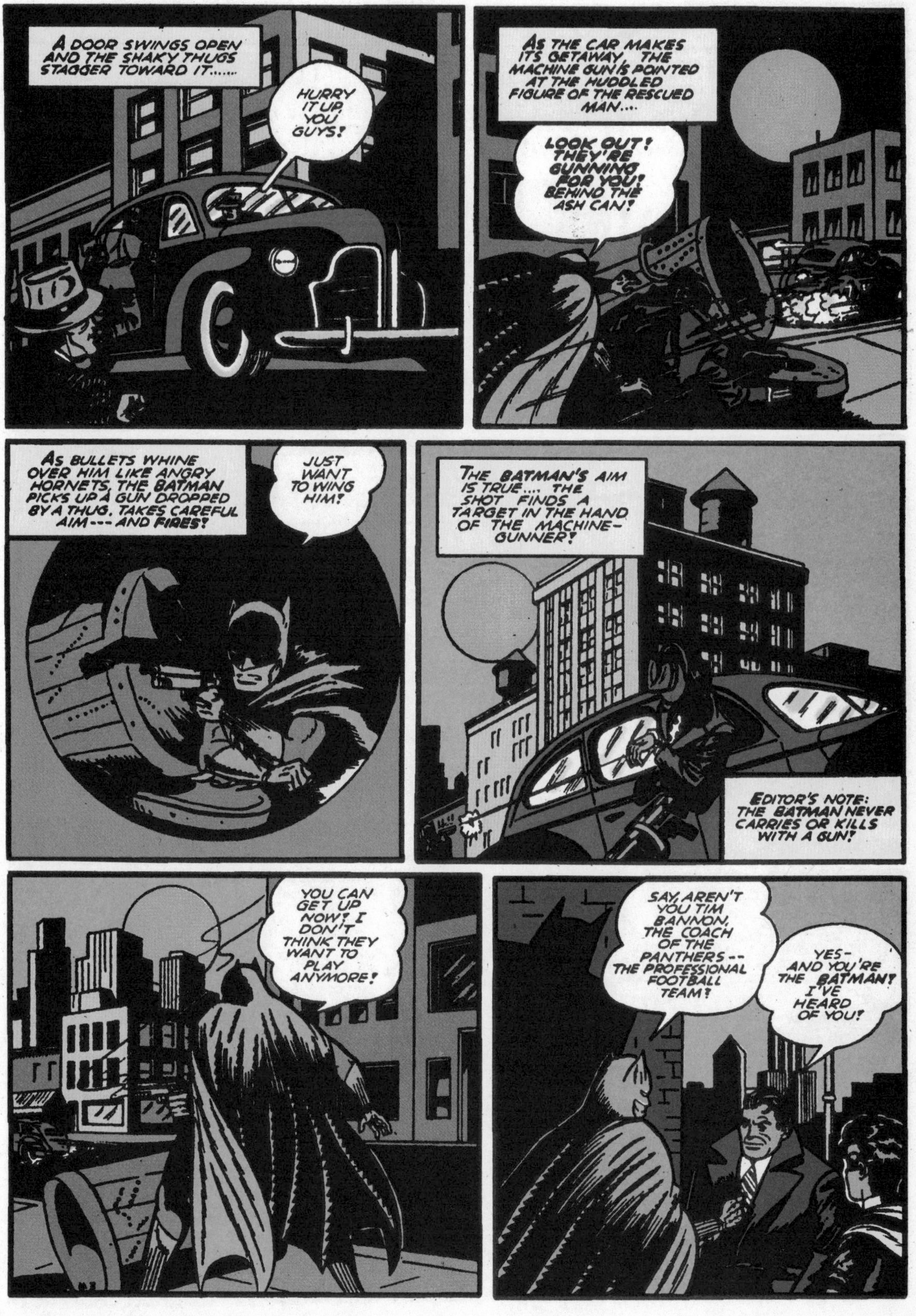
A DOOR SWINGS OPEN AND THE SHAKY THUGS STAGGER TOWARD IT......
HURRY IT UP, YOU GUYS!
AS THE CAR MAKES ITS GETAWAY, THE MACHINE GUN IS POINTED AT THE HUDDLED FIGURE OF THE RESCUED MAN....
LOOK OUT! THEY'RE GUNNING FOR YOU! BEHIND THE ASH CAN!
AS BULLETS WHINE OVER HIM LIKE ANGRY HORNETS, THE BATMAN PICKS UP A GUN DROPPED BY A THUG, TAKES CAREFUL AIM--- AND FIRES!
JUST WANT TO WING HIM!
THE BATMAN'S AIM IS TRUE.... THE SHOT FINDS A TARGET IN THE HAND OF THE MACHINE-GUNNER!
EDITOR'S NOTE: THE BATMAN NEVER CARRIES OR KILLS WITH A GUN!
YOU CAN GET UP NOW! I DON'T THINK THEY WANT TO PLAY ANYMORE!
SAY, AREN'T YOU TIM BANNON, THE COACH OF THE PANTHERS -- THE PROFESSIONAL FOOTBALL TEAM?
YES- AND YOU'RE THE BATMAN! I'VE HEARD OF YOU!

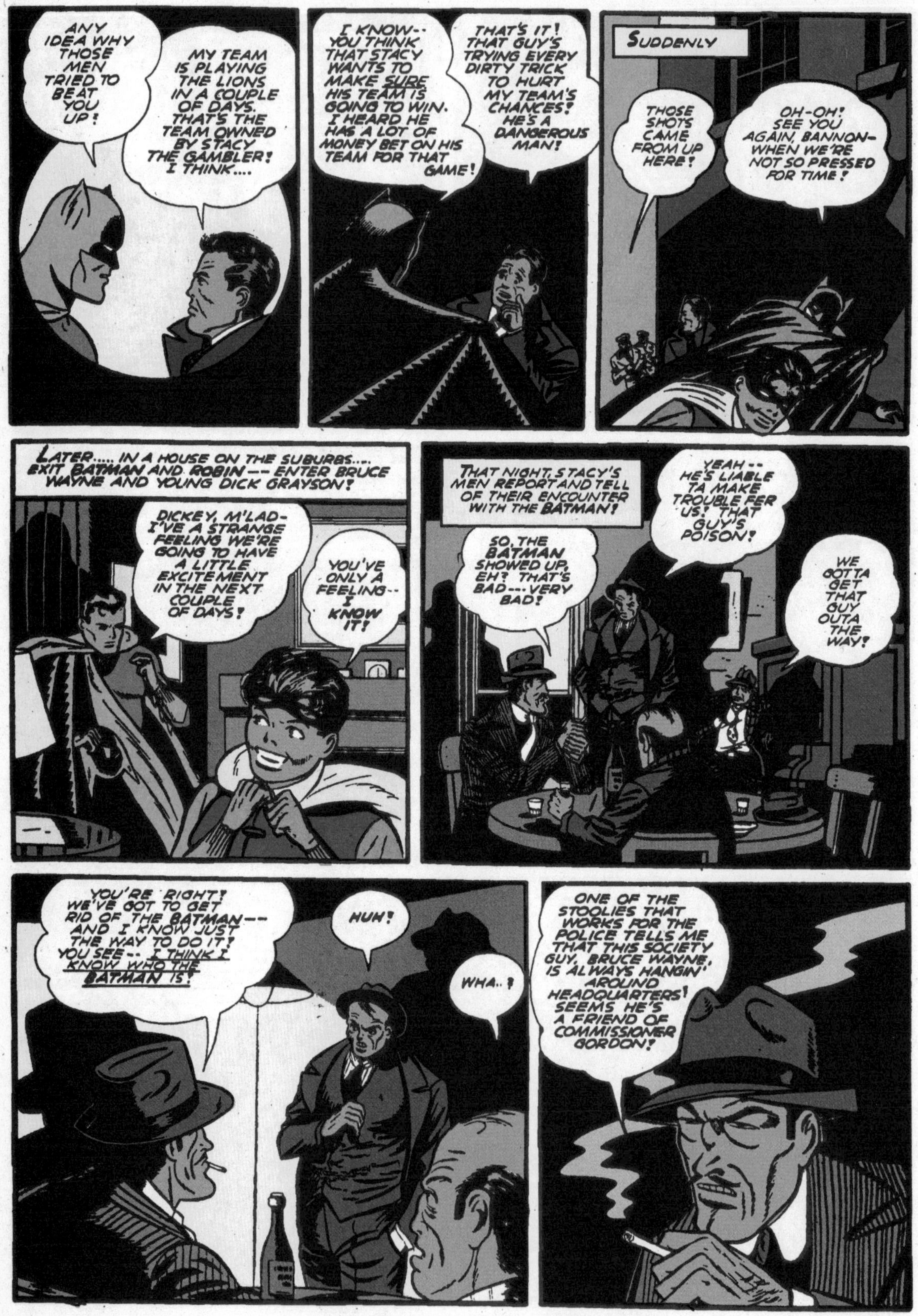
ANY IDEA WHY THOSE MEN TRIED TO BEAT YOU UP?
MY TEAM IS PLAYING THE LIONS IN A COUPLE OF DAYS. THAT'S THE TEAM OWNED BY STACY THE GAMBLER! I THINK....
I KNOW-- YOU THINK THAT STACY WANTS TO MAKE SURE HIS TEAM IS GOING TO WIN. I HEARD HE HAS A LOT OF MONEY BET ON HIS TEAM FOR THAT GAME!
THAT'S IT! THAT GUY'S TRYING EVERY DIRTY TRICK TO HURT MY TEAM'S CHANCES! HE'S A DANGEROUS MAN!
SUDDENLY
THOSE SHOTS CAME FROM UP HERE!
OH-OH! SEE YOU AGAIN, BANNON- WHEN WE'RE NOT SO PRESSED FOR TIME!
LATER..... IN A HOUSE ON THE SUBURBS.... EXIT BATMAN AND ROBIN -- ENTER BRUCE WAYNE AND YOUNG DICK GRAYSON!
DICKEY, M'LAD- I'VE A STRANGE FEELING WE'RE GOING TO HAVE A LITTLE EXCITEMENT IN THE NEXT COUPLE OF DAYS!
YOU'VE ONLY A FEELING-- I KNOW IT!
THAT NIGHT, STACY'S MEN REPORT AND TELL OF THEIR ENCOUNTER WITH THE BATMAN!
SO, THE BATMAN SHOWED UP, EH? THAT'S BAD--- VERY BAD!
YEAH -- HE'S LIABLE TA MAKE TROUBLE FER US! THAT GUY'S POISON!
WE GOTTA GET THAT GUY OUTA THE WAY!
YOU'RE RIGHT! WE'VE GOT TO GET RID OF THE BATMAN-- AND I KNOW JUST THE WAY TO DO IT! YOU SEE -- I THINK I KNOW WHO THE BATMAN IS!
HUH!
WHA..?
ONE OF THE STOOLIES THAT WORKS FOR THE POLICE TELLS ME THAT THIS SOCIETY GUY, BRUCE WAYNE, IS ALWAYS HANGIN' AROUND HEADQUARTERS! SEEMS HE'S A FRIEND OF COMMISSIONER GORDON!

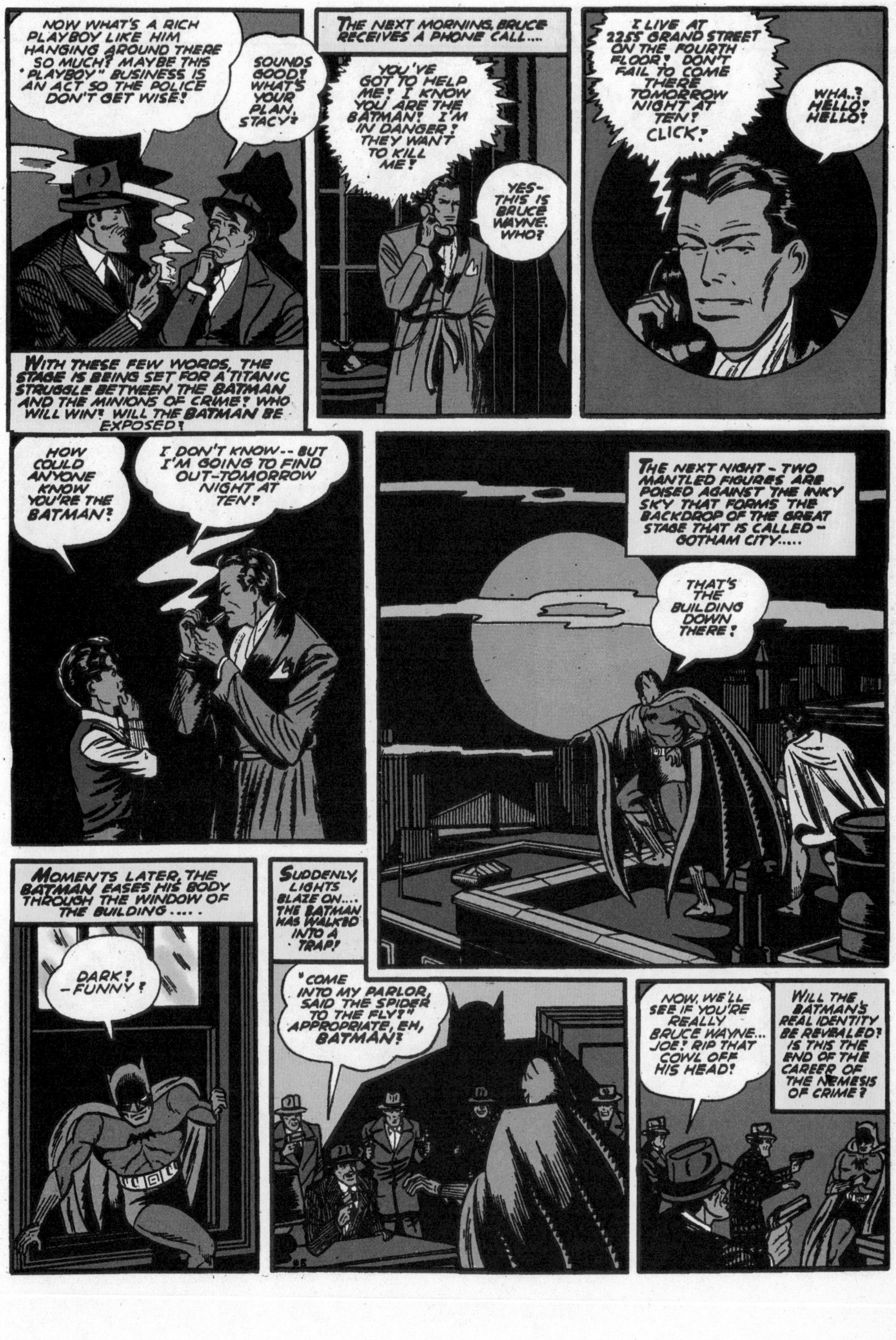
NOW WHAT'S A RICH PLAYBOY LIKE HIM HANGING AROUND THERE SO MUCH? MAYBE THIS "PLAYBOY" BUSINESS IS AN ACT SO THE POLICE DON'T GET WISE!
SOUNDS GOOD! WHAT'S YOUR PLAN, STACY?
WITH THESE FEW WORDS, THE STAGE IS BEING SET FOR A TITANIC STRUGGLE BETWEEN THE BATMAN AND THE MINIONS OF CRIME! WHO WILL WIN? WILL THE BATMAN BE EXPOSED?
THE NEXT MORNING, BRUCE RECEIVES A PHONE CALL....
YOU'VE GOT TO HELP ME! I KNOW YOU ARE THE BATMAN! I'M IN DANGER! THEY WANT TO KILL ME!
YES- THIS IS BRUCE WAYNE. WHO?
I LIVE AT 2255 GRAND STREET ON THE FOURTH FLOOR! DON'T FAIL TO COME THERE TOMORROW NIGHT AT TEN! CLICK!
WHA..? HELLO! HELLO!
HOW COULD ANYONE KNOW YOU'RE THE BATMAN?
I DON'T KNOW-- BUT I'M GOING TO FIND OUT-TOMORROW NIGHT AT TEN!
THE NEXT NIGHT - TWO MANTLED FIGURES ARE POISED AGAINST THE INKY SKY THAT FORMS THE BACKDROP OF THE GREAT STAGE THAT IS CALLED - GOTHAM CITY.....
THAT'S THE BUILDING DOWN THERE!
MOMENTS LATER, THE BATMAN EASES HIS BODY THROUGH THE WINDOW OF THE BUILDING.....
DARK! - FUNNY!
SUDDENLY, LIGHTS BLAZE ON.... THE BATMAN HAS WALKED INTO A TRAP!
"COME INTO MY PARLOR, SAID THE SPIDER TO THE FLY!" APPROPRIATE, EH, BATMAN!
NOW, WE'LL SEE IF YOU'RE REALLY BRUCE WAYNE... JOE! RIP THAT COWL OFF HIS HEAD!
WILL THE BATMAN'S REAL IDENTITY BE REVEALED? IS THIS THE END OF THE CAREER OF THE NEMESIS OF CRIME?

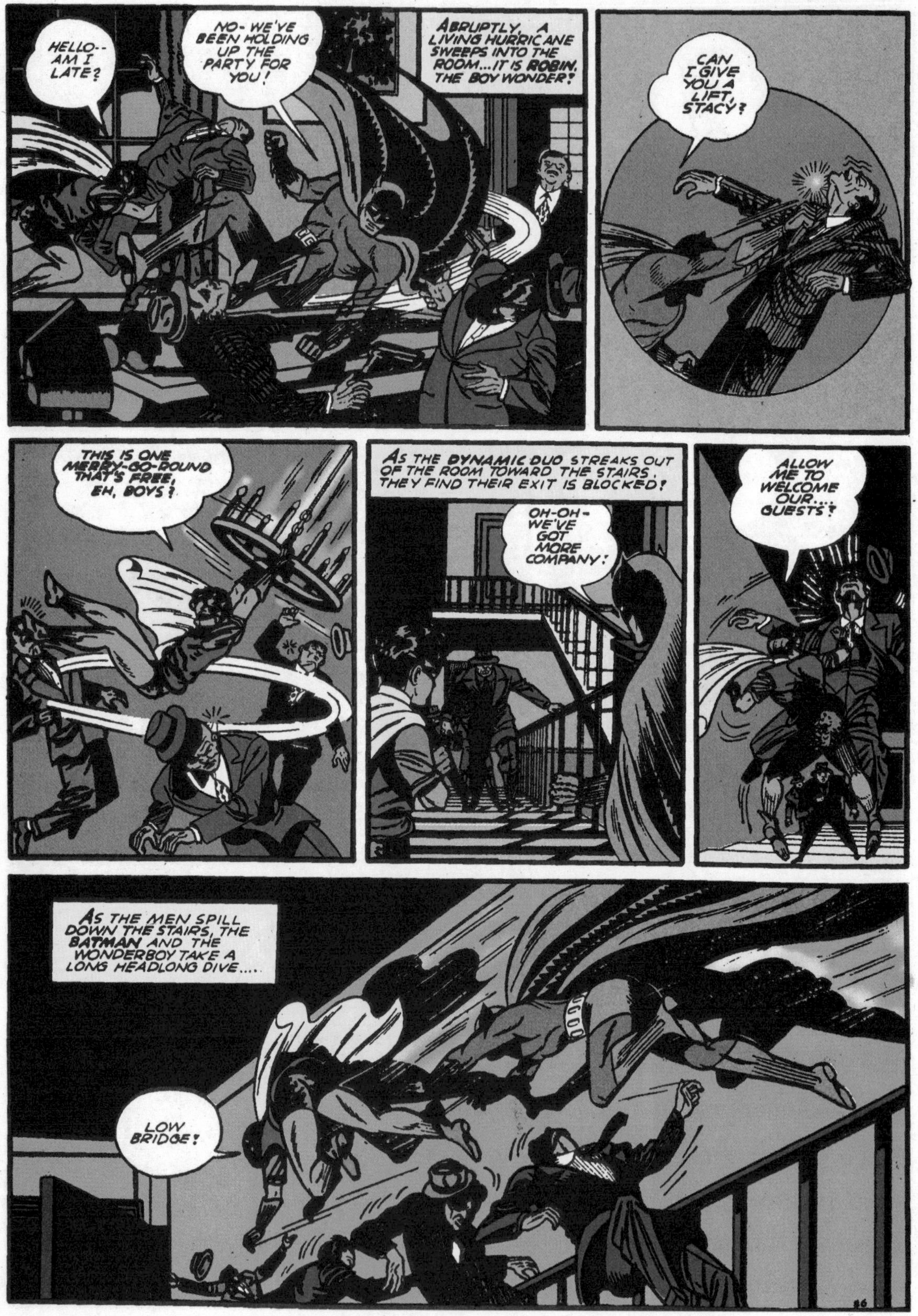
HELLO-- AM I LATE?
NO- WE'VE BEEN HOLDING UP THE PARTY FOR YOU!
ABRUPTLY, A LIVING HURRICANE SWEEPS INTO THE ROOM...IT IS ROBIN, THE BOY WONDER!
CAN I GIVE YOU A LIFT, STACY?
THIS IS ONE MERRY-GO-ROUND THAT'S FREE, EH, BOYS?
AS THE DYNAMIC DUO STREAKS OUT OF THE ROOM TOWARD THE STAIRS, THEY FIND THEIR EXIT IS BLOCKED!
OH-OH- WE'VE GOT MORE COMPANY!
ALLOW ME TO WELCOME OUR.... GUESTS!
AS THE MEN SPILL DOWN THE STAIRS, THE BATMAN AND THE WONDERBOY TAKE A LONG HEADLONG DIVE....
LOW BRIDGE!

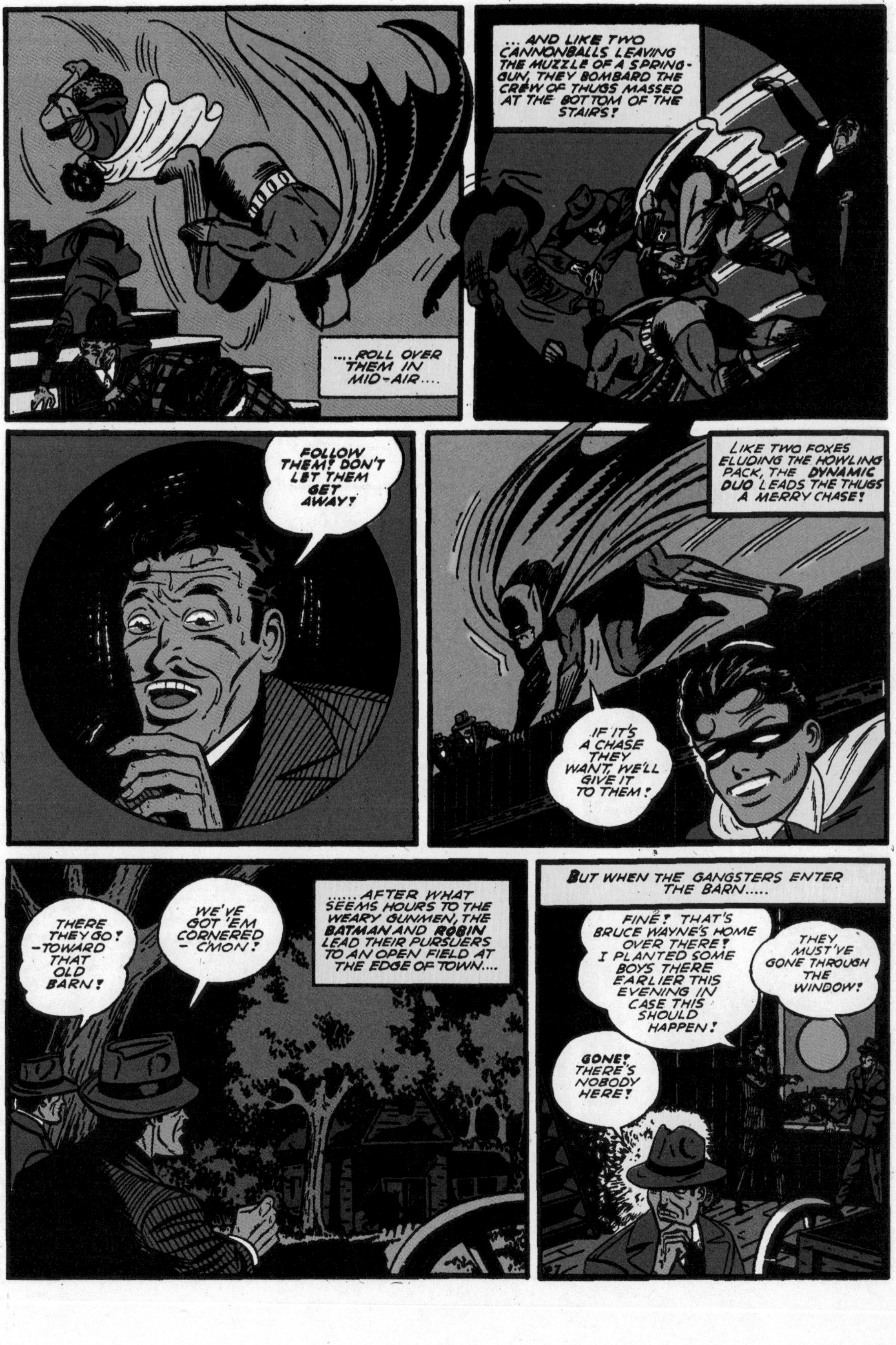

....ROLL OVER THEM IN MID-AIR....
...AND LIKE TWO CANNONBALLS LEAVING THE MUZZLE OF A SPRING-GUN, THEY BOMBARD THE CREW OF THUGS MASSED AT THE BOTTOM OF THE STAIRS!
FOLLOW THEM! DON'T LET THEM GET AWAY!
LIKE TWO FOXES ELUDING THE HOWLING PACK, THE DYNAMIC DUO LEADS THE THUGS A MERRY CHASE!
IF IT'S A CHASE THEY WANT, WE'LL GIVE IT TO THEM!
.....AFTER WHAT SEEMS HOURS TO THE WEARY GUNMEN, THE BATMAN AND ROBIN LEAD THEIR PURSUERS TO AN OPEN FIELD AT THE EDGE OF TOWN....
THERE THEY GO! -TOWARD THAT OLD BARN!
WE'VE GOT 'EM CORNERED - C'MON!
BUT WHEN THE GANGSTERS ENTER THE BARN.....
GONE! THERE'S NOBODY HERE!
THEY MUST'VE GONE THROUGH THE WINDOW!
FINE! THAT'S BRUCE WAYNE'S HOME OVER THERE! I PLANTED SOME BOYS THERE EARLIER THIS EVENING IN CASE THIS SHOULD HAPPEN!

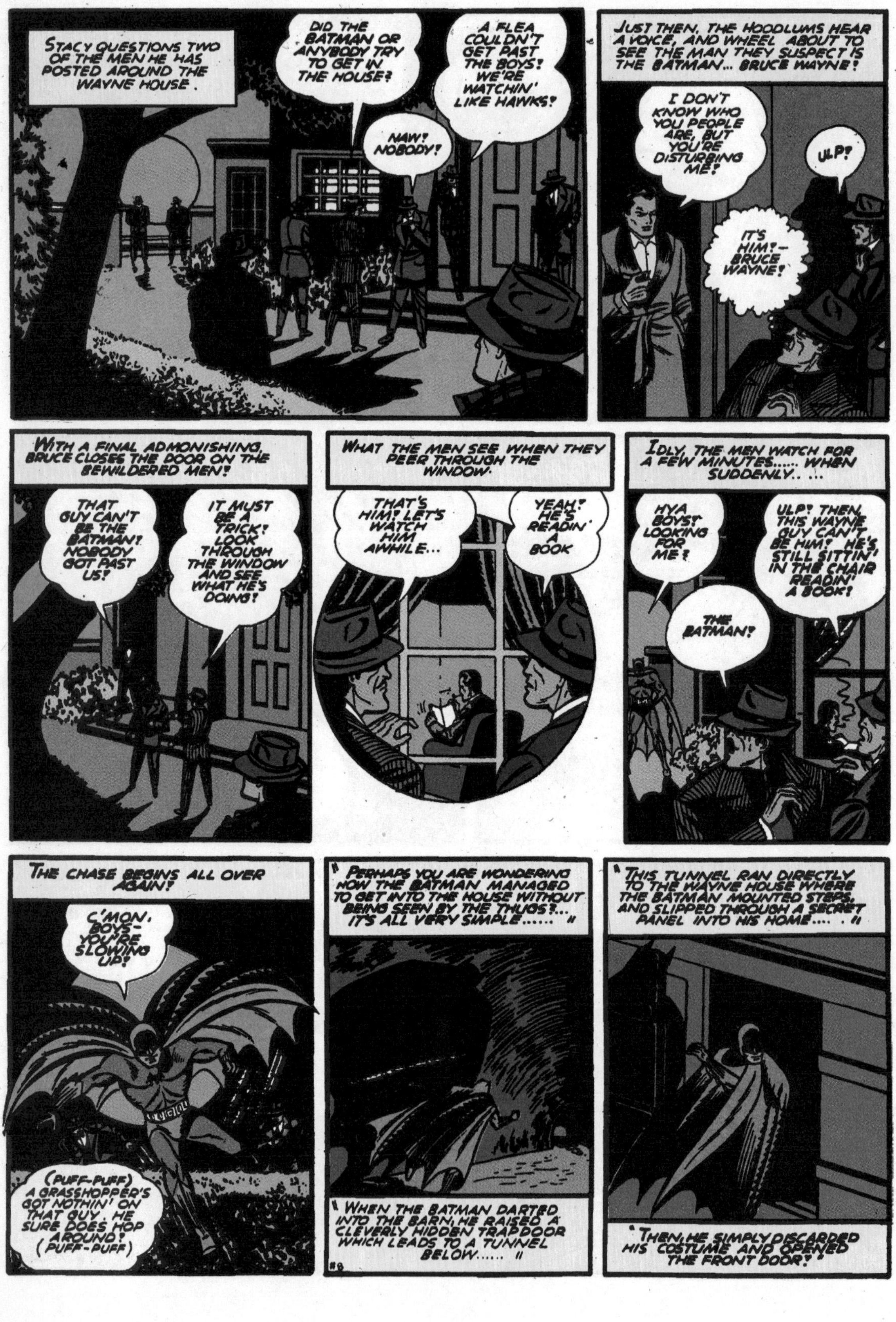
STACY QUESTIONS TWO OF THE MEN HE HAS POSTED AROUND THE WAYNE HOUSE.
DID THE BATMAN OR ANYBODY TRY TO GET IN THE HOUSE?
NAW! NOBODY!
A FLEA COULDN'T GET PAST THE BOYS! WE'RE WATCHIN' LIKE HAWKS!
JUST THEN, THE HOODLUMS HEAR A VOICE, AND WHEEL ABOUT TO SEE THE MAN THEY SUSPECT IS THE BATMAN... BRUCE WAYNE!
I DON'T KNOW WHO YOU PEOPLE ARE, BUT YOU'RE DISTURBING ME!
ULP!
IT'S HIM!— BRUCE WAYNE!
WITH A FINAL ADMONISHING, BRUCE CLOSES THE DOOR ON THE BEWILDERED MEN!
THAT GUY CAN'T BE THE BATMAN! NOBODY GOT PAST US!
IT MUST BE A TRICK! LOOK THROUGH THE WINDOW AND SEE WHAT HE'S DOING!
WHAT THE MEN SEE WHEN THEY PEER THROUGH THE WINDOW.
THAT'S HIM! LET'S WATCH HIM AWHILE...
YEAH! HE'S READIN' A BOOK
IDLY, THE MEN WATCH FOR A FEW MINUTES...... WHEN SUDDENLY.. ...
HYA BOYS! LOOKING FOR ME?
THE BATMAN!
ULP! THEN, THIS WAYNE GUY CAN'T BE HIM! HE'S STILL SITTIN' IN THE CHAIR READIN' A BOOK!
THE CHASE BEGINS ALL OVER AGAIN!
C'MON, BOYS— YOU'RE SLOWING UP!
(PUFF-PUFF) A GRASSHOPPER'S GOT NOTHIN' ON THAT GUY. HE SURE DOES HOP AROUND! (PUFF-PUFF)
" PERHAPS YOU ARE WONDERING HOW THE BATMAN MANAGED TO GET INTO THE HOUSE WITHOUT BEING SEEN BY THE THUGS?... IT'S ALL VERY SIMPLE...... "
" WHEN THE BATMAN DARTED INTO THE BARN, HE RAISED A CLEVERLY HIDDEN TRAPDOOR WHICH LEADS TO A TUNNEL BELOW...... "
" THIS TUNNEL RAN DIRECTLY TO THE WAYNE HOUSE WHERE THE BATMAN MOUNTED STEPS, AND SLIPPED THROUGH A SECRET PANEL INTO HIS HOME..... . "
" THEN, HE SIMPLY DISCARDED HIS COSTUME AND OPENED THE FRONT DOOR! "

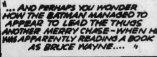

"...AND PERHAPS YOU WONDER HOW THE BATMAN MANAGED TO APPEAR TO LEAD THE THUGS ANOTHER MERRY CHASE—WHEN HE WAS APPARENTLY READING A BOOK AS BRUCE WAYNE...."

ALL SET TO SLIP THE DUMMY ON!

SIT OVER THERE BY THE WINDOW! THEY'LL BE LOOKING IN NEXT!

"EXPLANATION...AN ESPECIALLY CONSTRUCTED LIFE-LIKE DUMMY WHICH IS SLIPPED OVER ROBIN'S FORM... "

"...AND WHEN ROBIN WORKS HIS HANDS IN THE SLEEVES, IT SEEMS TO THE OBSERVER TO BE THE ACTIONS OF BRUCE WAYNE HIMSELF! "

"WHILE ROBIN MANIPULATED THE DUMMY, BRUCE SLIPPED ON HIS COSTUME AND RACED THROUGH THE TUNNEL AND OUT IN THE NIGHT! "

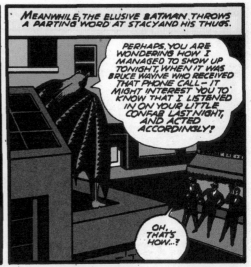

MEANWHILE, THE ELUSIVE BATMAN THROWS A PARTING WORD AT STACY AND HIS THUGS.

PERHAPS, YOU ARE WONDERING HOW I MANAGED TO SHOW UP TONIGHT, WHEN IT WAS BRUCE WAYNE WHO RECEIVED THAT PHONE CALL—IT MIGHT INTEREST YOU TO KNOW THAT I LISTENED IN ON YOUR LITTLE CONFAB LAST NIGHT, AND ACTED ACCORDINGLY!

OH, THAT'S HOW...?

THAT VERY NIGHT, STACY AND HIS MEN ARE WEARY AND FOOTSORE AFTER A FUTILE EFFORT TO CATCH THE BATMAN!

WELL, STACY, ARE YA CONVINCED NOW THAT BRUCE WAYNE AIN'T THE BATMAN?

YEAH-YEAH!—BUT THAT ISN'T GOING TO STOP ME FROM GOING AHEAD WITH MY PLANS! I'VE GOT TOO MUCH MONEY BET TO STOP NOW!

OKAY! WE KNOW WHAT TO DO!

THE MORNING OF THE BIG GAME.....

WHAT'S THE IDEA OF SLIPPING OVER TO SEE STOCKTON, THE STAR QUARTERBACK OF THE PANTHERS?

JUST WANT TO MAKE SURE THAT STACY'S MEN HAVEN'T INTIMIDATED HIM—THREATENED TO HURT HIM UNLESS HE FUMBLES A FEW PLAYS!

BUT WHEN THEY STEP INSIDE..

BARTON! STOCKTON'S ROOM-MATE... STABBED TO DEATH!...

AND STOCKTON'S NOT AROUND? THEY'VE KIDNAPPED HIM? STACY'S MEN HAVE KIDNAPPED HIM TO KEEP HIM FROM PLAYING!

SEATING HIMSELF BEFORE A MIRROR, THE BATMAN PROPS UP A PICTURE OF THE KIDNAPPED STAR..

SAY—WHAT ARE YOU DOING?

STOCKTON'S MY HEIGHT AND ABOUT MY BUILD. I THINK IT WILL WORK!

DEFT FINGERS APPLY MAKEUP FROM THE UTILITY BELT...SLOWLY MOULD AND CHANGE THE CONTOURS OF THE FACE...

MMM! NOSE NEEDS A LITTLE MORE PUTTY TO GET THAT SHAPE!

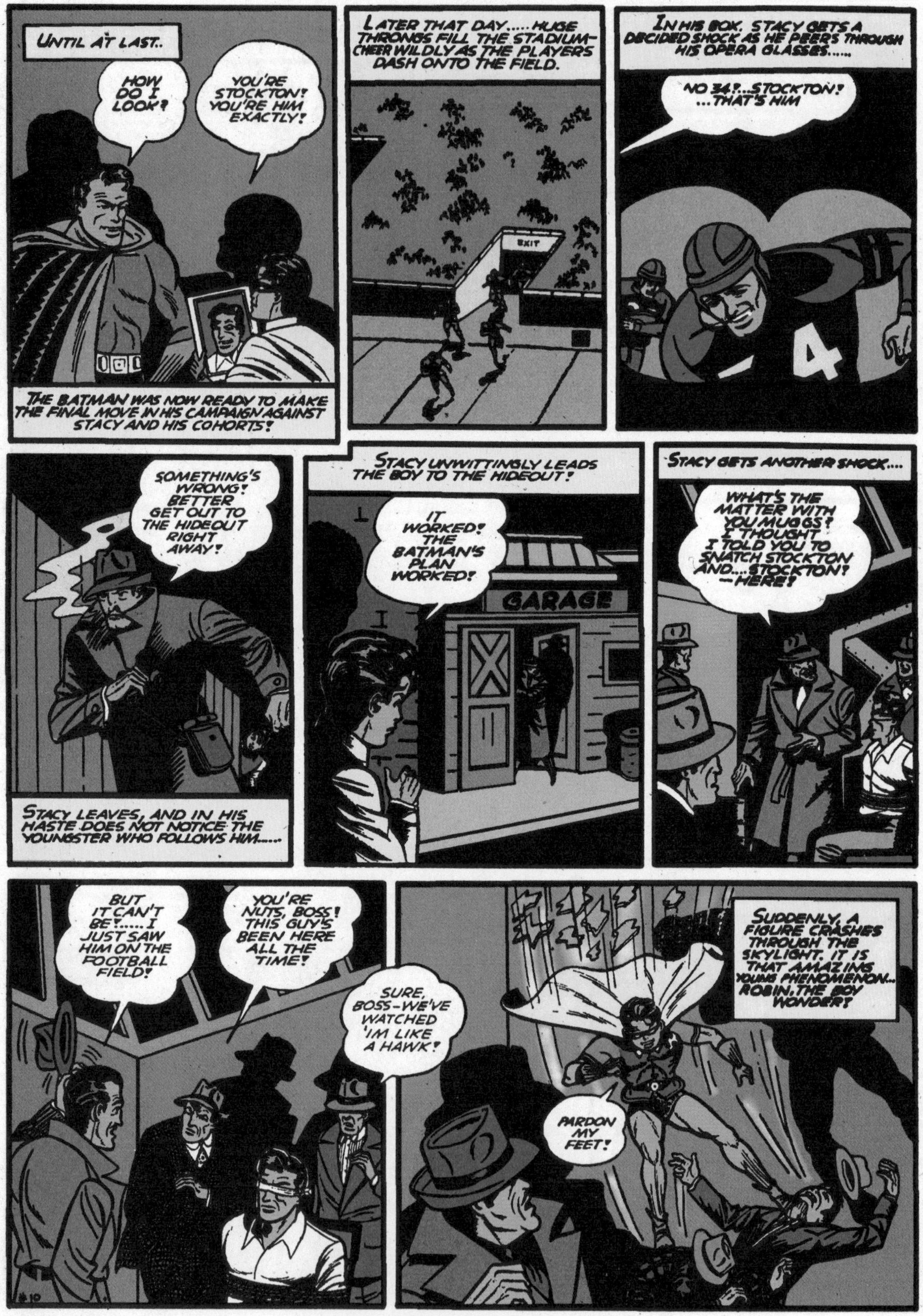
UNTIL AT LAST..
HOW DO I LOOK?
YOU'RE STOCKTON! YOU'RE HIM EXACTLY!
THE BATMAN WAS NOW READY TO MAKE THE FINAL MOVE IN HIS CAMPAIGN AGAINST STACY AND HIS COHORTS!
LATER THAT DAY..... HUGE THRONGS FILL THE STADIUM-CHEER WILDLY AS THE PLAYERS DASH ONTO THE FIELD.
EXIT
IN HIS BOX, STACY GETS A DECIDED SHOCK AS HE PEERS THROUGH HIS OPERA GLASSES......
NO 34?...STOCKTON! ...THAT'S HIM
SOMETHING'S WRONG! BETTER GET OUT TO THE HIDEOUT RIGHT AWAY!
STACY LEAVES, AND IN HIS HASTE DOES NOT NOTICE THE YOUNGSTER WHO FOLLOWS HIM.....
STACY UNWITTINGLY LEADS THE BOY TO THE HIDEOUT!
IT WORKED! THE BATMAN'S PLAN WORKED!
GARAGE
STACY GETS ANOTHER SHOCK....
WHAT'S THE MATTER WITH YOU MUGGS? I THOUGHT I TOLD YOU TO SNATCH STOCKTON AND....STOCKTON? —HERE?
BUT IT CAN'T BE?.....I JUST SAW HIM ON THE FOOTBALL FIELD!
YOU'RE NUTS, BOSS! THIS GUY'S BEEN HERE ALL THE TIME!
SURE, BOSS-WE'VE WATCHED 'IM LIKE A HAWK!
SUDDENLY, A FIGURE CRASHES THROUGH THE SKYLIGHT. IT IS THAT AMAZING YOUNG PHENOMENON... ROBIN, THE BOY WONDER!
PARDON MY FEET!

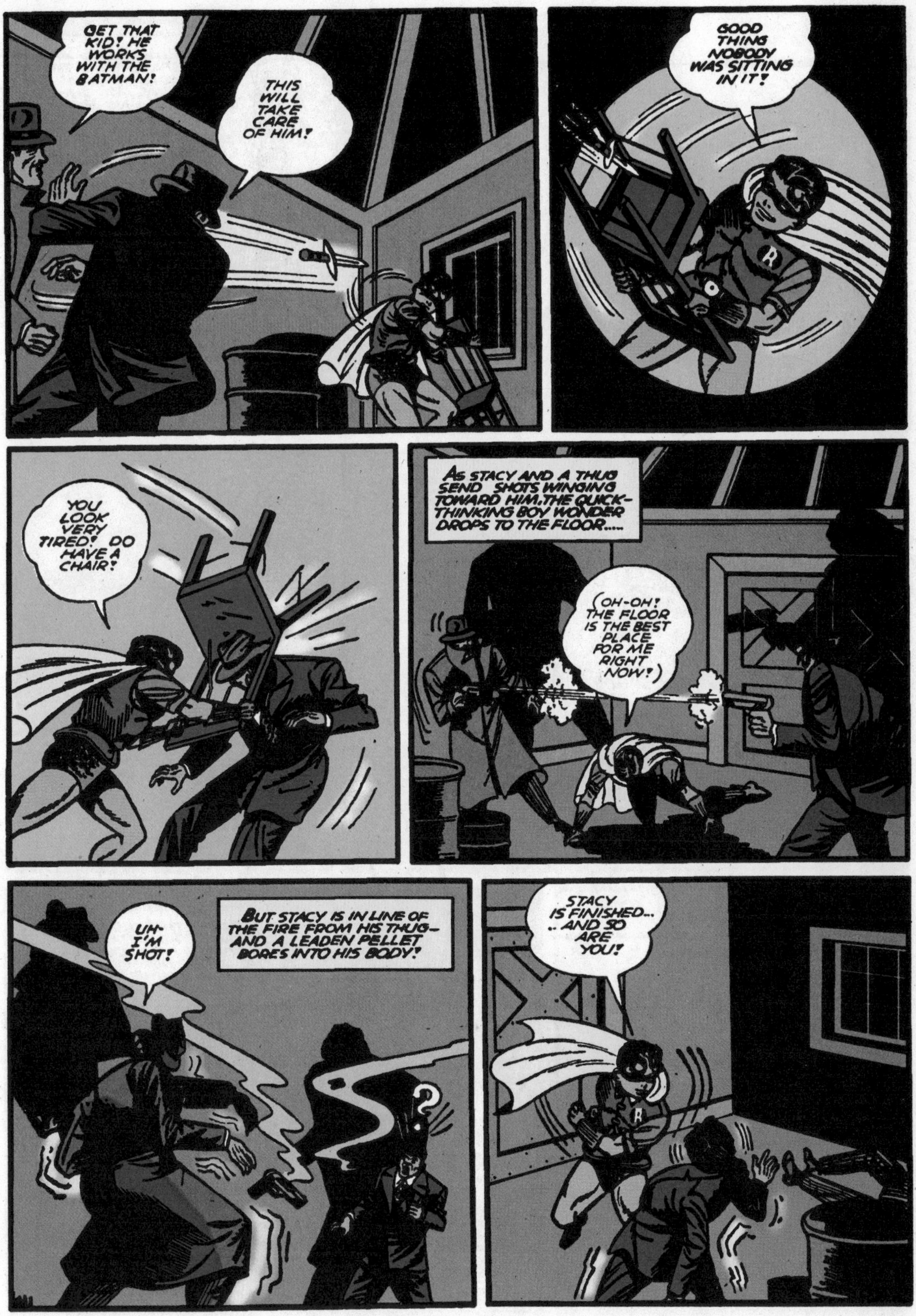
GET THAT KID! HE WORKS WITH THE BATMAN!
THIS WILL TAKE CARE OF HIM!
GOOD THING NOBODY WAS SITTING IN IT!
YOU LOOK VERY TIRED! DO HAVE A CHAIR!
AS STACY AND A THUG SEND SHOTS WINGING TOWARD HIM, THE QUICK-THINKING BOY WONDER DROPS TO THE FLOOR.....
(OH-OH! THE FLOOR IS THE BEST PLACE FOR ME RIGHT NOW!)
UH- I'M SHOT!
BUT STACY IS IN LINE OF THE FIRE FROM HIS THUG- AND A LEADEN PELLET BORES INTO HIS BODY!
STACY IS FINISHED... .. AND SO ARE YOU!

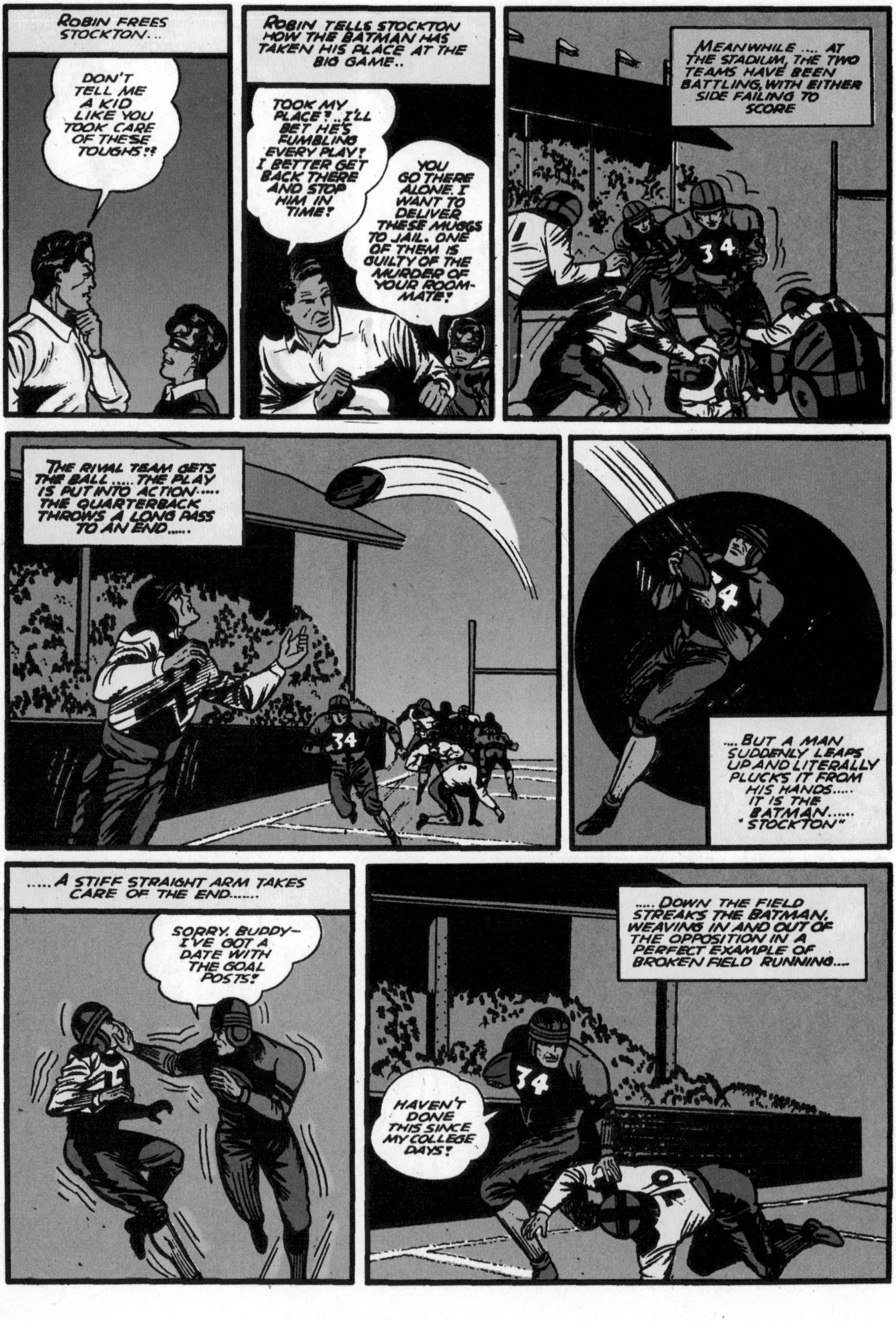

ROBIN FREES STOCKTON...
DON'T TELL ME A KID LIKE YOU TOOK CARE OF THESE TOUGHS!?
ROBIN TELLS STOCKTON HOW THE BATMAN HAS TAKEN HIS PLACE AT THE BIG GAME..
TOOK MY PLACE? ..I'LL BET HE'S FUMBLING EVERY PLAY! I BETTER GET BACK THERE AND STOP HIM IN TIME!
YOU GO THERE ALONE. I WANT TO DELIVER THESE MUGGS TO JAIL. ONE OF THEM IS GUILTY OF THE MURDER OF YOUR ROOM-MATE!
MEANWHILE .... AT THE STADIUM, THE TWO TEAMS HAVE BEEN BATTLING, WITH EITHER SIDE FAILING TO SCORE
THE RIVAL TEAM GETS THE BALL ..... THE PLAY IS PUT INTO ACTION..... THE QUARTERBACK THROWS A LONG PASS TO AN END......
....BUT A MAN SUDDENLY LEAPS UP AND LITERALLY PLUCKS IT FROM HIS HANDS..... IT IS THE BATMAN...... "STOCKTON"
.....A STIFF STRAIGHT ARM TAKES CARE OF THE END.......
SORRY, BUDDY-- I'VE GOT A DATE WITH THE GOAL POSTS!
.....DOWN THE FIELD STREAKS THE BATMAN, WEAVING IN AND OUT OF THE OPPOSITION IN A PERFECT EXAMPLE OF BROKEN FIELD RUNNING....
HAVEN'T DONE THIS SINCE MY COLLEGE DAYS!

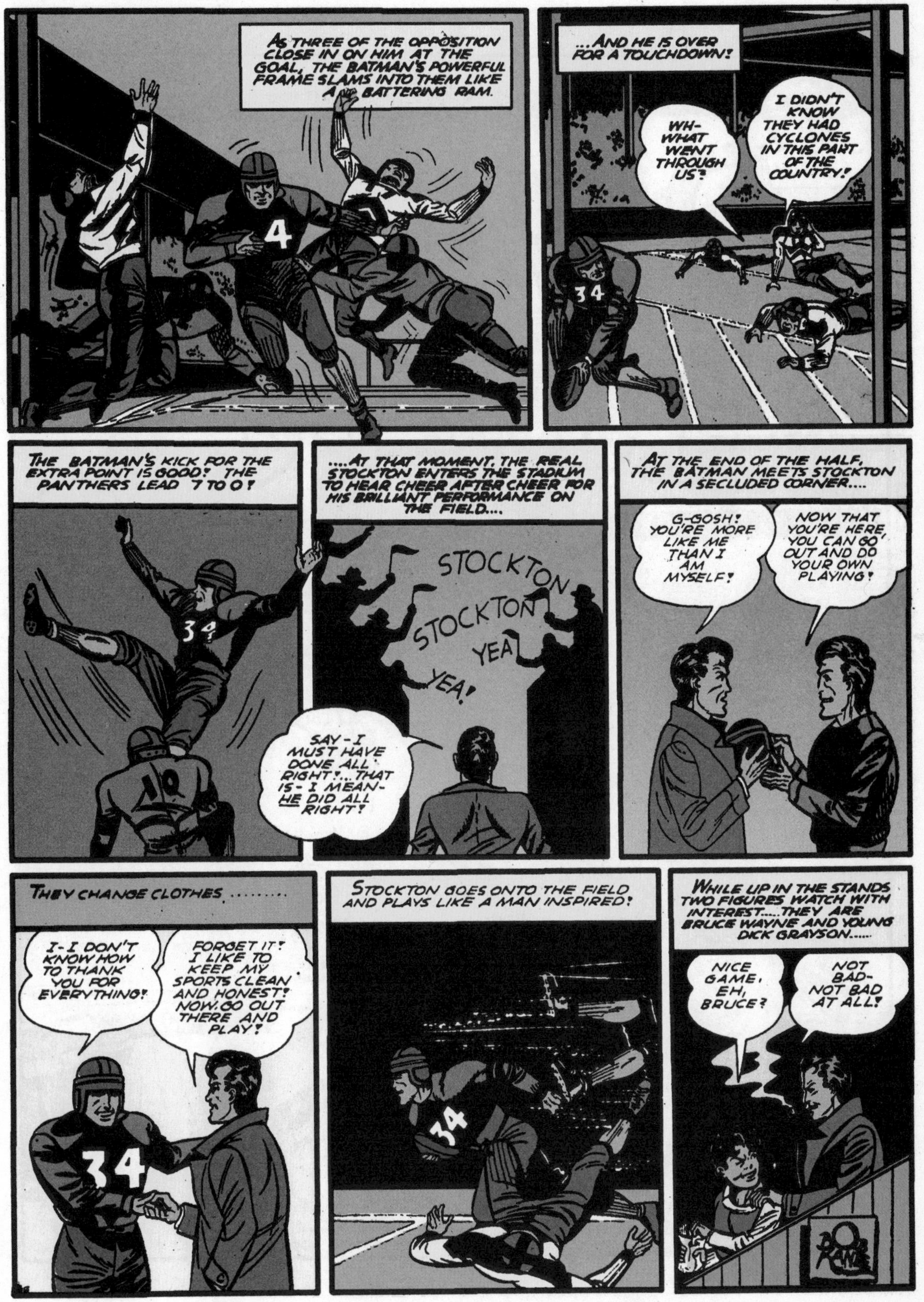
AS THREE OF THE OPPOSITION CLOSE IN ON HIM AT THE GOAL, THE BATMAN'S POWERFUL FRAME SLAMS INTO THEM LIKE A BATTERING RAM.
...AND HE IS OVER FOR A TOUCHDOWN!
WH-WHAT WENT THROUGH US?
I DIDN'T KNOW THEY HAD CYCLONES IN THIS PART OF THE COUNTRY!
THE BATMAN'S KICK FOR THE EXTRA POINT IS GOOD! THE PANTHERS LEAD 7 TO 0!
....AT THAT MOMENT, THE REAL STOCKTON ENTERS THE STADIUM TO HEAR CHEER AFTER CHEER FOR HIS BRILLIANT PERFORMANCE ON THE FIELD....
STOCKTON
STOCKTON
YEA
YEA!
SAY-I MUST HAVE DONE ALL RIGHT!...THAT IS- I MEAN- HE DID ALL RIGHT!
AT THE END OF THE HALF, THE BATMAN MEETS STOCKTON IN A SECLUDED CORNER....
G-GOSH! YOU'RE MORE LIKE ME THAN I AM MYSELF!
NOW THAT YOU'RE HERE, YOU CAN GO OUT AND DO YOUR OWN PLAYING!
THEY CHANGE CLOTHES ....
I-I DON'T KNOW HOW TO THANK YOU FOR EVERYTHING!
FORGET IT! I LIKE TO KEEP MY SPORTS CLEAN AND HONEST! NOW, GO OUT THERE AND PLAY!
STOCKTON GOES ONTO THE FIELD AND PLAYS LIKE A MAN INSPIRED!
WHILE UP IN THE STANDS TWO FIGURES WATCH WITH INTEREST.....THEY ARE BRUCE WAYNE AND YOUNG DICK GRAYSON......
NICE GAME, EH, BRUCE?
NOT BAD- NOT BAD AT ALL!
BOB KANE

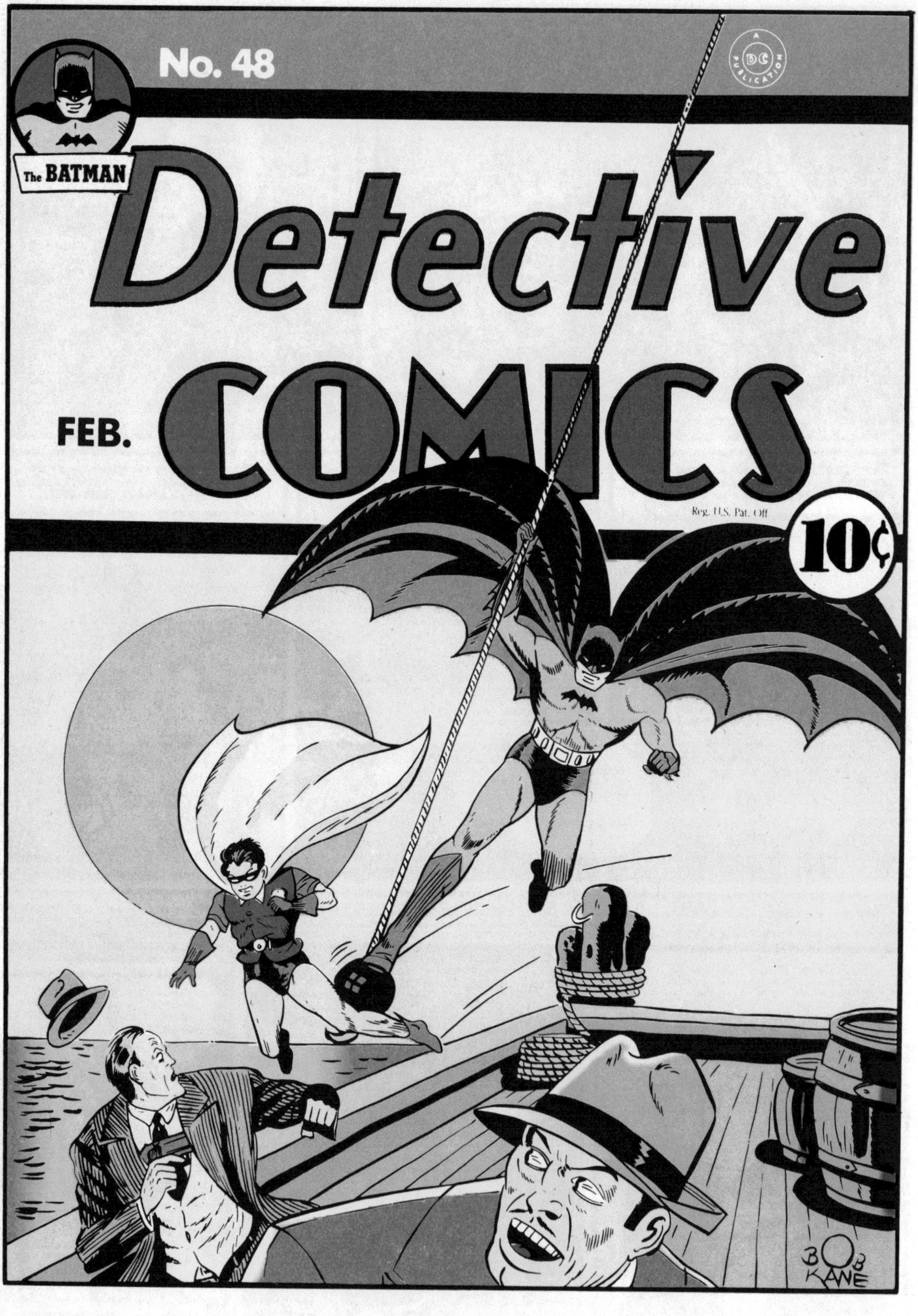

No. 48
The BATMAN
A DC PUBLICATION
Detective
COMICS
FEB.
Reg. U.S. Pat. Off
10¢
BOB KANE

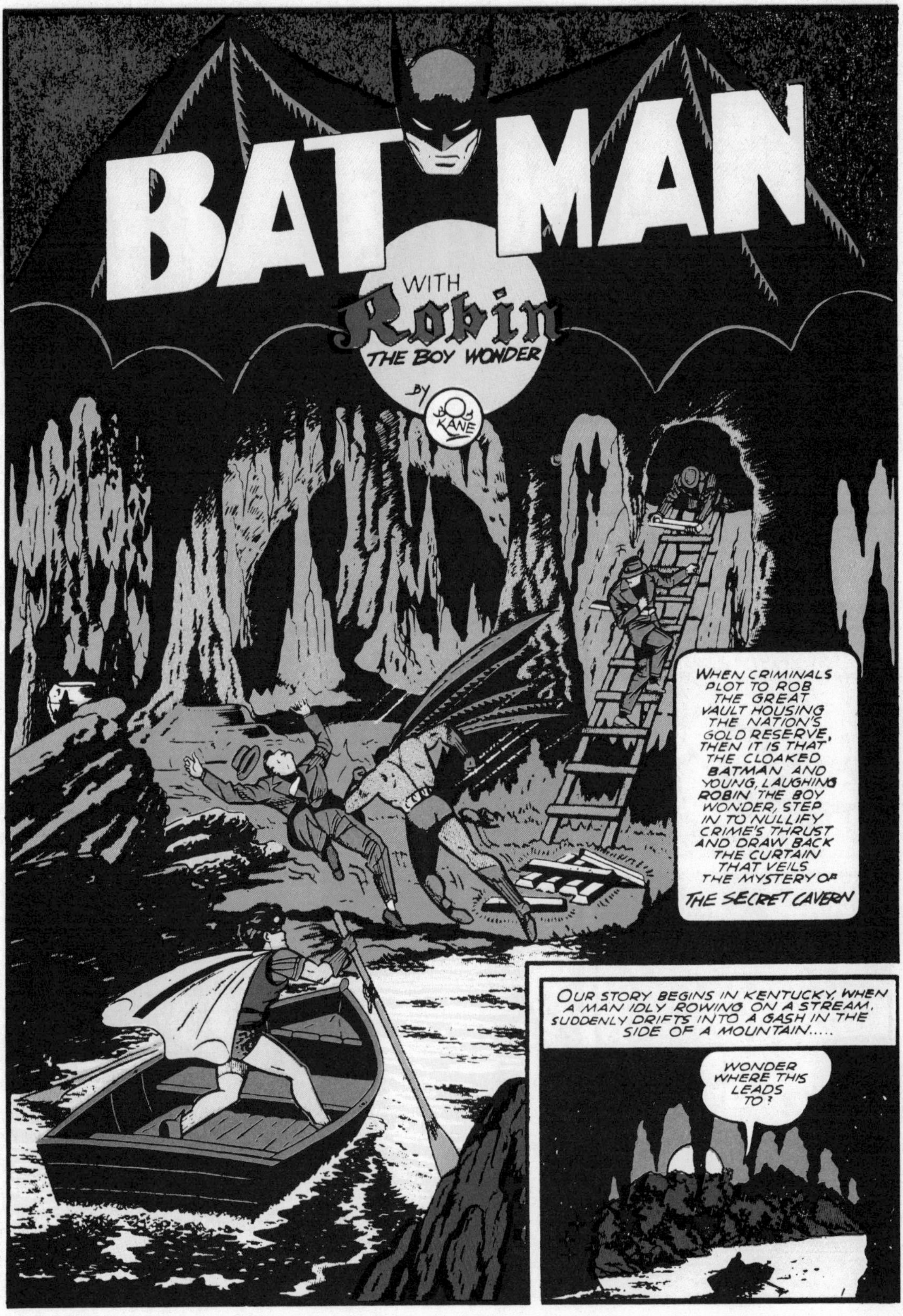
BATMAN
WITH Robin THE BOY WONDER
BY BOB KANE
WHEN CRIMINALS PLOT TO ROB THE GREAT VAULT HOUSING THE NATION'S GOLD RESERVE, THEN IT IS THAT THE CLOAKED BATMAN AND YOUNG, LAUGHING ROBIN THE BOY WONDER, STEP IN TO NULLIFY CRIME'S THRUST AND DRAW BACK THE CURTAIN THAT VEILS THE MYSTERY OF THE SECRET CAVERN
OUR STORY BEGINS IN KENTUCKY, WHEN A MAN IDLY ROWING ON A STREAM, SUDDENLY DRIFTS INTO A GASH IN THE SIDE OF A MOUNTAIN.....
WONDER WHERE THIS LEADS TO?

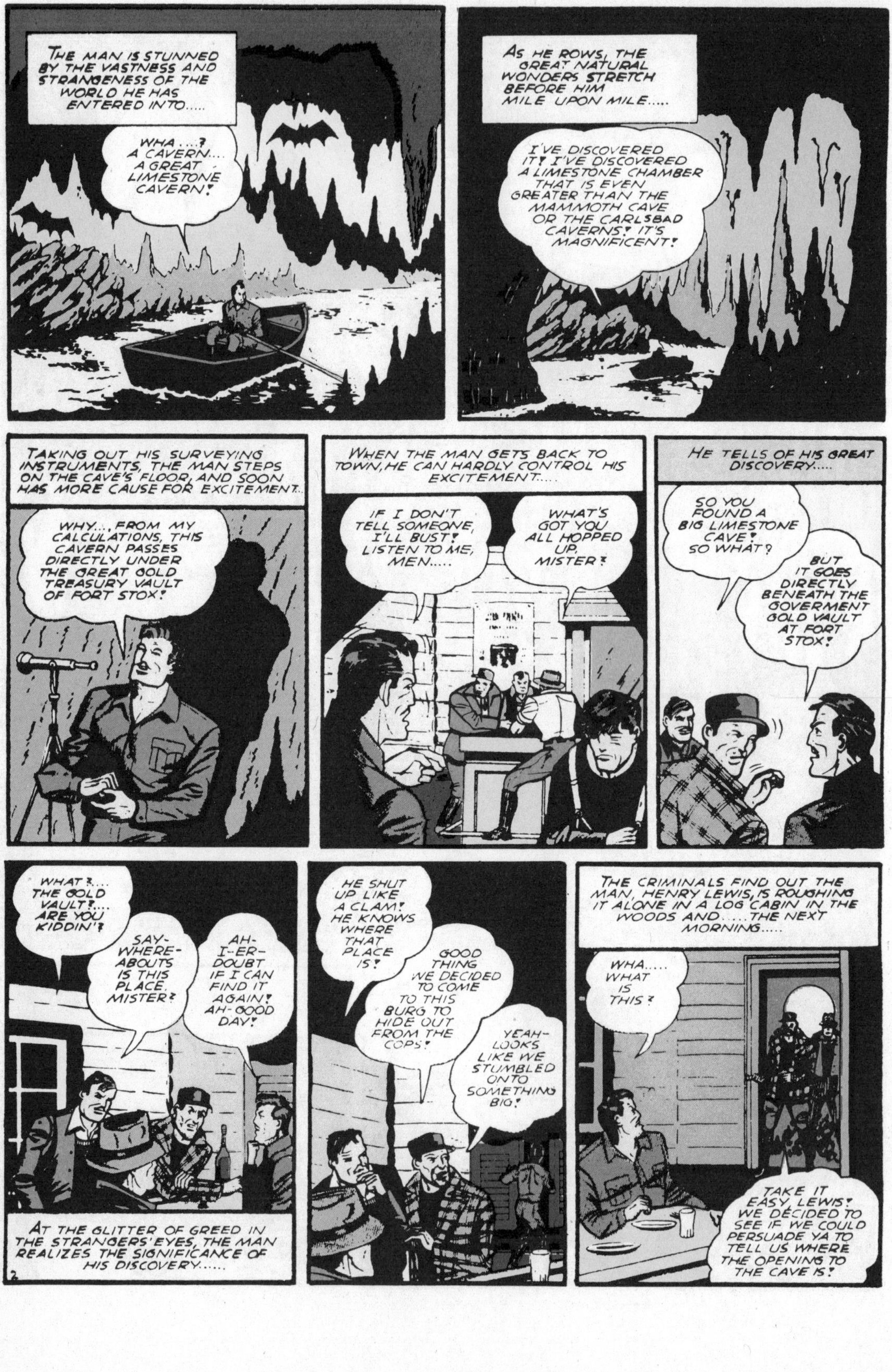

THE MAN IS STUNNED BY THE VASTNESS AND STRANGENESS OF THE WORLD HE HAS ENTERED INTO.....
WHA....? A CAVERN.... A GREAT LIMESTONE CAVERN!
AS HE ROWS, THE GREAT NATURAL WONDERS STRETCH BEFORE HIM MILE UPON MILE.....
I'VE DISCOVERED IT! I'VE DISCOVERED A LIMESTONE CHAMBER THAT IS EVEN GREATER THAN THE MAMMOTH CAVE OR THE CARLSBAD CAVERNS! IT'S MAGNIFICENT!
TAKING OUT HIS SURVEYING INSTRUMENTS, THE MAN STEPS ON THE CAVE'S FLOOR, AND SOON HAS MORE CAUSE FOR EXCITEMENT...
WHY..., FROM MY CALCULATIONS, THIS CAVERN PASSES DIRECTLY UNDER THE GREAT GOLD TREASURY VAULT OF FORT STOX!
WHEN THE MAN GETS BACK TO TOWN, HE CAN HARDLY CONTROL HIS EXCITEMENT.....
IF I DON'T TELL SOMEONE, I'LL BUST! LISTEN TO ME, MEN.....
WHAT'S GOT YOU ALL HOPPED UP, MISTER?
HE TELLS OF HIS GREAT DISCOVERY.....
SO YOU FOUND A BIG LIMESTONE CAVE! SO WHAT?
BUT IT GOES DIRECTLY BENEATH THE GOVERMENT GOLD VAULT AT FORT STOX!
WHAT?.... THE GOLD VAULT?.... ARE YOU KIDDIN'?
SAY- WHERE- ABOUTS IS THIS PLACE, MISTER?
AH- I--ER- DOUBT IF I CAN FIND IT AGAIN! AH-GOOD DAY!
AT THE GLITTER OF GREED IN THE STRANGERS' EYES, THE MAN REALIZES THE SIGNIFICANCE OF HIS DISCOVERY......
HE SHUT UP LIKE A CLAM! HE KNOWS WHERE THAT PLACE IS!
GOOD THING WE DECIDED TO COME TO THIS BURG TO HIDE OUT FROM THE COPS!
YEAH- LOOKS LIKE WE STUMBLED ONTO SOMETHING BIG!
THE CRIMINALS FIND OUT THE MAN, HENRY LEWIS, IS ROUGHING IT ALONE IN A LOG CABIN IN THE WOODS AND.....THE NEXT MORNING.....
WHA..... WHAT IS THIS?
TAKE IT EASY, LEWIS! WE DECIDED TO SEE IF WE COULD PERSUADE YA TO TELL US WHERE THE OPENING TO THE CAVE IS!

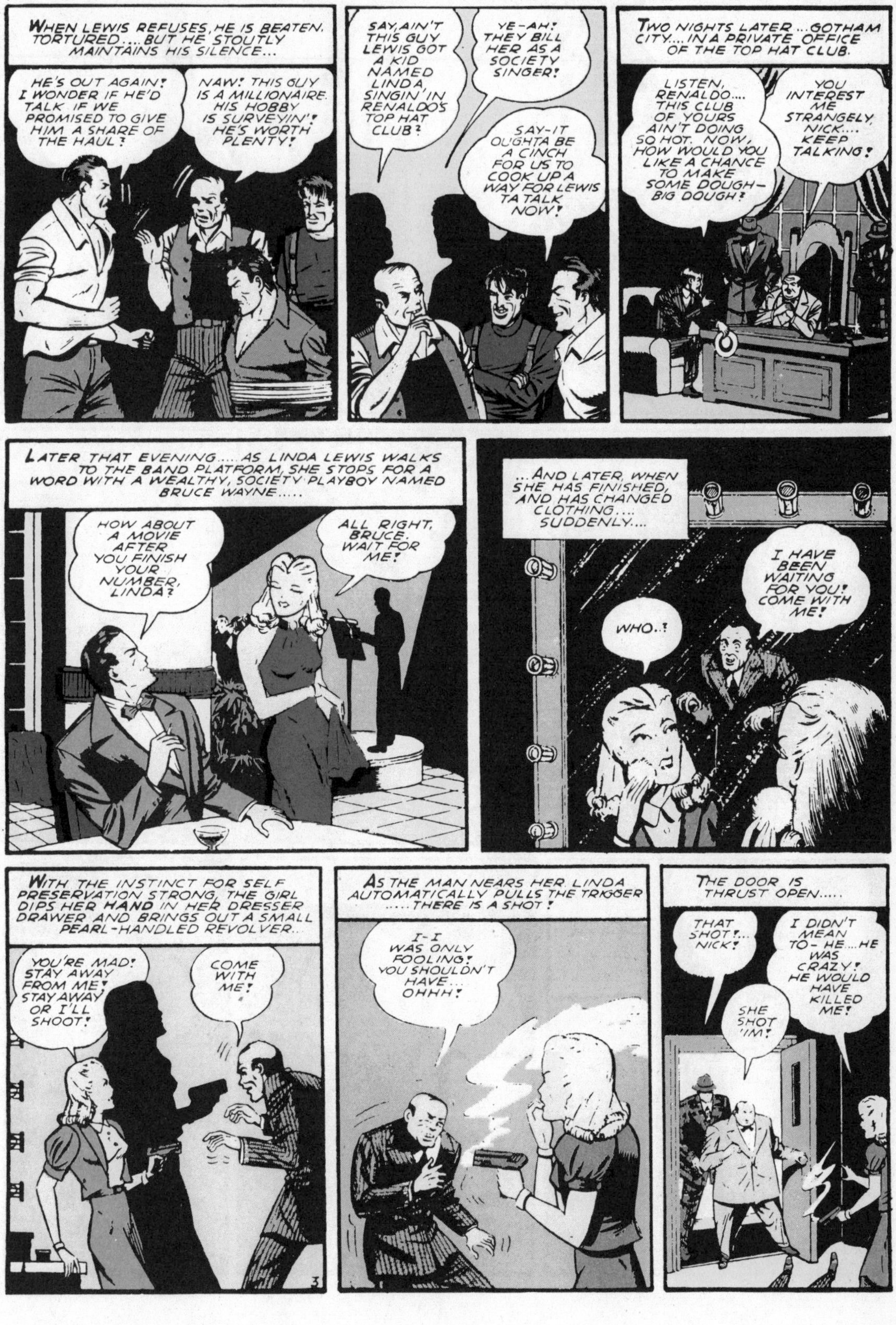
WHEN LEWIS REFUSES, HE IS BEATEN. TORTURED.... BUT HE STOUTLY MAINTAINS HIS SILENCE...
HE'S OUT AGAIN! I WONDER IF HE'D TALK IF WE PROMISED TO GIVE HIM A SHARE OF THE HAUL?
NAW! THIS GUY IS A MILLIONAIRE. HIS HOBBY IS SURVEYIN'! HE'S WORTH PLENTY!
SAY, AIN'T THIS GUY LEWIS GOT A KID NAMED LINDA, SINGIN' IN RENALDO'S TOP HAT CLUB?
YE-AH! THEY BILL HER AS A SOCIETY SINGER!
SAY-IT OUGHTA BE A CINCH FOR US TO COOK UP A WAY FOR LEWIS TA TALK NOW!
TWO NIGHTS LATER ... GOTHAM CITY.... IN A PRIVATE OFFICE OF THE TOP HAT CLUB.
LISTEN, RENALDO.... THIS CLUB OF YOURS AIN'T DOING SO HOT. NOW, HOW WOULD YOU LIKE A CHANCE TO MAKE SOME DOUGH— BIG DOUGH?
YOU INTEREST ME STRANGELY, NICK.... KEEP TALKING!
LATER THAT EVENING..... AS LINDA LEWIS WALKS TO THE BAND PLATFORM, SHE STOPS FOR A WORD WITH A WEALTHY, SOCIETY PLAYBOY NAMED BRUCE WAYNE.....
HOW ABOUT A MOVIE AFTER YOU FINISH YOUR NUMBER, LINDA?
ALL RIGHT, BRUCE. WAIT FOR ME!
...AND LATER, WHEN SHE HAS FINISHED, AND HAS CHANGED CLOTHING.... SUDDENLY....
WHO..?
I HAVE BEEN WAITING FOR YOU! COME WITH ME!
WITH THE INSTINCT FOR SELF PRESERVATION STRONG, THE GIRL DIPS HER HAND IN HER DRESSER DRAWER AND BRINGS OUT A SMALL PEARL-HANDLED REVOLVER...
YOU'RE MAD! STAY AWAY FROM ME! STAY AWAY OR I'LL SHOOT!
COME WITH ME!
AS THE MAN NEARS HER, LINDA AUTOMATICALLY PULLS THE TRIGGER .....THERE IS A SHOT!
I-I WAS ONLY FOOLING! YOU SHOULDN'T HAVE... OHHH!
THE DOOR IS THRUST OPEN.....
THAT SHOT!... NICK!
SHE SHOT 'IM!
I DIDN'T MEAN TO- HE....HE WAS CRAZY! HE WOULD HAVE KILLED ME!

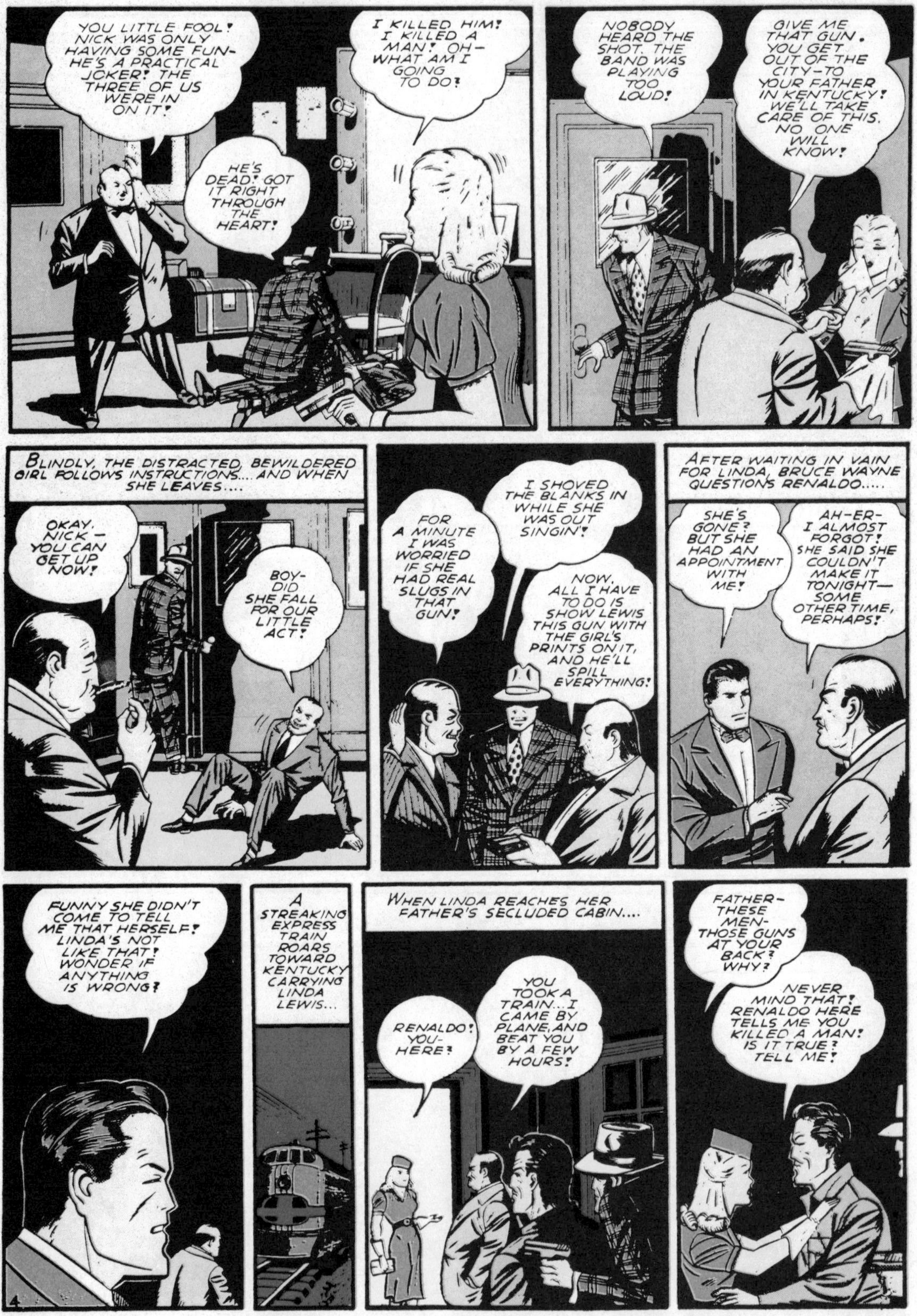

YOU LITTLE FOOL! NICK WAS ONLY HAVING SOME FUN- HE'S A PRACTICAL JOKER! THE THREE OF US WERE IN ON IT!
I KILLED HIM! I KILLED A MAN! OH- WHAT AM I GOING TO DO?
HE'S DEAD! GOT IT RIGHT THROUGH THE HEART!
NOBODY HEARD THE SHOT. THE BAND WAS PLAYING TOO LOUD!
GIVE ME THAT GUN. YOU GET OUT OF THE CITY-TO YOUR FATHER IN KENTUCKY! WE'LL TAKE CARE OF THIS. NO ONE WILL KNOW!
BLINDLY, THE DISTRACTED, BEWILDERED GIRL FOLLOWS INSTRUCTIONS.... AND WHEN SHE LEAVES....
OKAY, NICK - YOU CAN GET UP NOW!
BOY- DID SHE FALL FOR OUR LITTLE ACT!
FOR A MINUTE I WAS WORRIED IF SHE HAD REAL SLUGS IN THAT GUN!
I SHOVED THE BLANKS IN WHILE SHE WAS OUT SINGIN'!
NOW, ALL I HAVE TO DO IS SHOW LEWIS THIS GUN WITH THE GIRL'S PRINTS ON IT, AND HE'LL SPILL EVERYTHING!
AFTER WAITING IN VAIN FOR LINDA, BRUCE WAYNE QUESTIONS RENALDO.....
SHE'S GONE? BUT SHE HAD AN APPOINTMENT WITH ME!
AH-ER- I ALMOST FORGOT! SHE SAID SHE COULDN'T MAKE IT TONIGHT— SOME OTHER TIME, PERHAPS!
FUNNY SHE DIDN'T COME TO TELL ME THAT HERSELF! LINDA'S NOT LIKE THAT! WONDER IF ANYTHING IS WRONG?
A STREAKING EXPRESS TRAIN ROARS TOWARD KENTUCKY CARRYING LINDA LEWIS...
WHEN LINDA REACHES HER FATHER'S SECLUDED CABIN....
RENALDO! YOU- HERE?
YOU TOOK A TRAIN... I CAME BY PLANE, AND BEAT YOU BY A FEW HOURS!
FATHER- THESE MEN- THOSE GUNS AT YOUR BACK? WHY?
NEVER MIND THAT! RENALDO HERE TELLS ME YOU KILLED A MAN! IS IT TRUE? TELL ME!
4

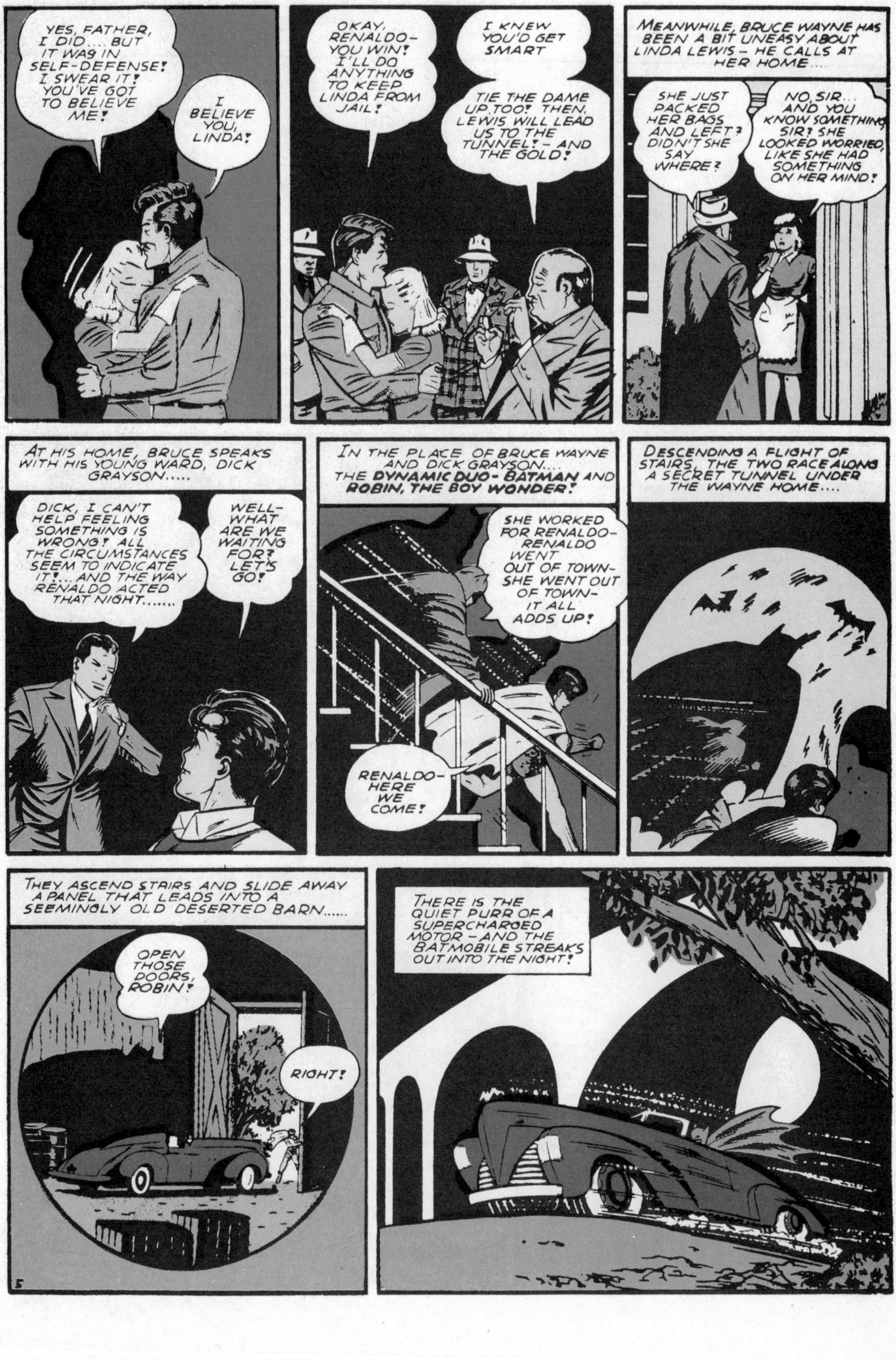
YES, FATHER, I DID.... BUT IT WAS IN SELF-DEFENSE! I SWEAR IT! YOU'VE GOT TO BELIEVE ME!
I BELIEVE YOU, LINDA!
OKAY, RENALDO-- YOU WIN! I'LL DO ANYTHING TO KEEP LINDA FROM JAIL!
I KNEW YOU'D GET SMART
TIE THE DAME UP, TOO! THEN, LEWIS WILL LEAD US TO THE TUNNEL! - AND THE GOLD!
MEANWHILE, BRUCE WAYNE HAS BEEN A BIT UNEASY ABOUT LINDA LEWIS - HE CALLS AT HER HOME....
SHE JUST PACKED HER BAGS AND LEFT? DIDN'T SHE SAY WHERE?
NO, SIR... AND YOU KNOW SOMETHING, SIR? SHE LOOKED WORRIED, LIKE SHE HAD SOMETHING ON HER MIND!
AT HIS HOME, BRUCE SPEAKS WITH HIS YOUNG WARD, DICK GRAYSON.....
DICK, I CAN'T HELP FEELING SOMETHING IS WRONG! ALL THE CIRCUMSTANCES SEEM TO INDICATE IT!... AND THE WAY RENALDO ACTED THAT NIGHT.......
WELL-- WHAT ARE WE WAITING FOR? LET'S GO!
IN THE PLACE OF BRUCE WAYNE AND DICK GRAYSON.... THE DYNAMIC DUO- BATMAN AND ROBIN, THE BOY WONDER!
SHE WORKED FOR RENALDO-- RENALDO WENT OUT OF TOWN-- SHE WENT OUT OF TOWN-- IT ALL ADDS UP!
RENALDO-- HERE WE COME!
DESCENDING A FLIGHT OF STAIRS, THE TWO RACE ALONG A SECRET TUNNEL UNDER THE WAYNE HOME....
THEY ASCEND STAIRS AND SLIDE AWAY A PANEL THAT LEADS INTO A SEEMINGLY OLD DESERTED BARN......
OPEN THOSE DOORS, ROBIN!
RIGHT!
5
THERE IS THE QUIET PURR OF A SUPERCHARGED MOTOR - AND THE BATMOBILE STREAKS OUT INTO THE NIGHT!

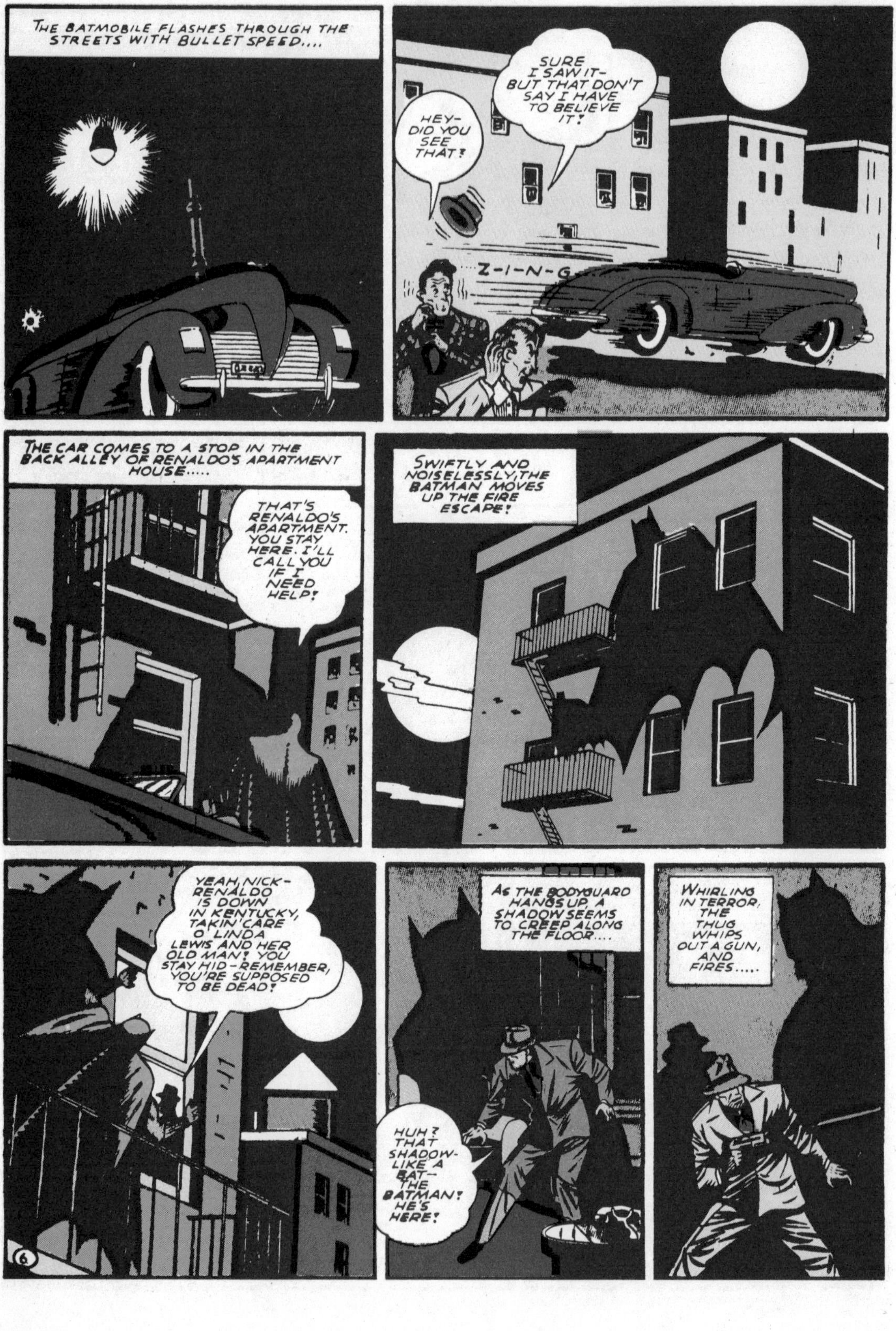
THE BATMOBILE FLASHES THROUGH THE STREETS WITH BULLET SPEED....
HEY- DID YOU SEE THAT?
SURE I SAW IT- BUT THAT DON'T SAY I HAVE TO BELIEVE IT!
Z-I-N-G
THE CAR COMES TO A STOP IN THE BACK ALLEY OF RENALDO'S APARTMENT HOUSE....
THAT'S RENALDO'S APARTMENT. YOU STAY HERE. I'LL CALL YOU IF I NEED HELP!
SWIFTLY AND NOISELESSLY, THE BATMAN MOVES UP THE FIRE ESCAPE!
YEAH, NICK- RENALDO IS DOWN IN KENTUCKY, TAKIN' CARE O' LINDA LEWIS AND HER OLD MAN! YOU STAY HID-REMEMBER, YOU'RE SUPPOSED TO BE DEAD!
6
AS THE BODYGUARD HANGS UP, A SHADOW SEEMS TO CREEP ALONG THE FLOOR....
HUH? THAT SHADOW- LIKE A BAT- THE BATMAN! HE'S HERE!
WHIRLING IN TERROR, THE THUG WHIPS OUT A GUN, AND FIRES.....

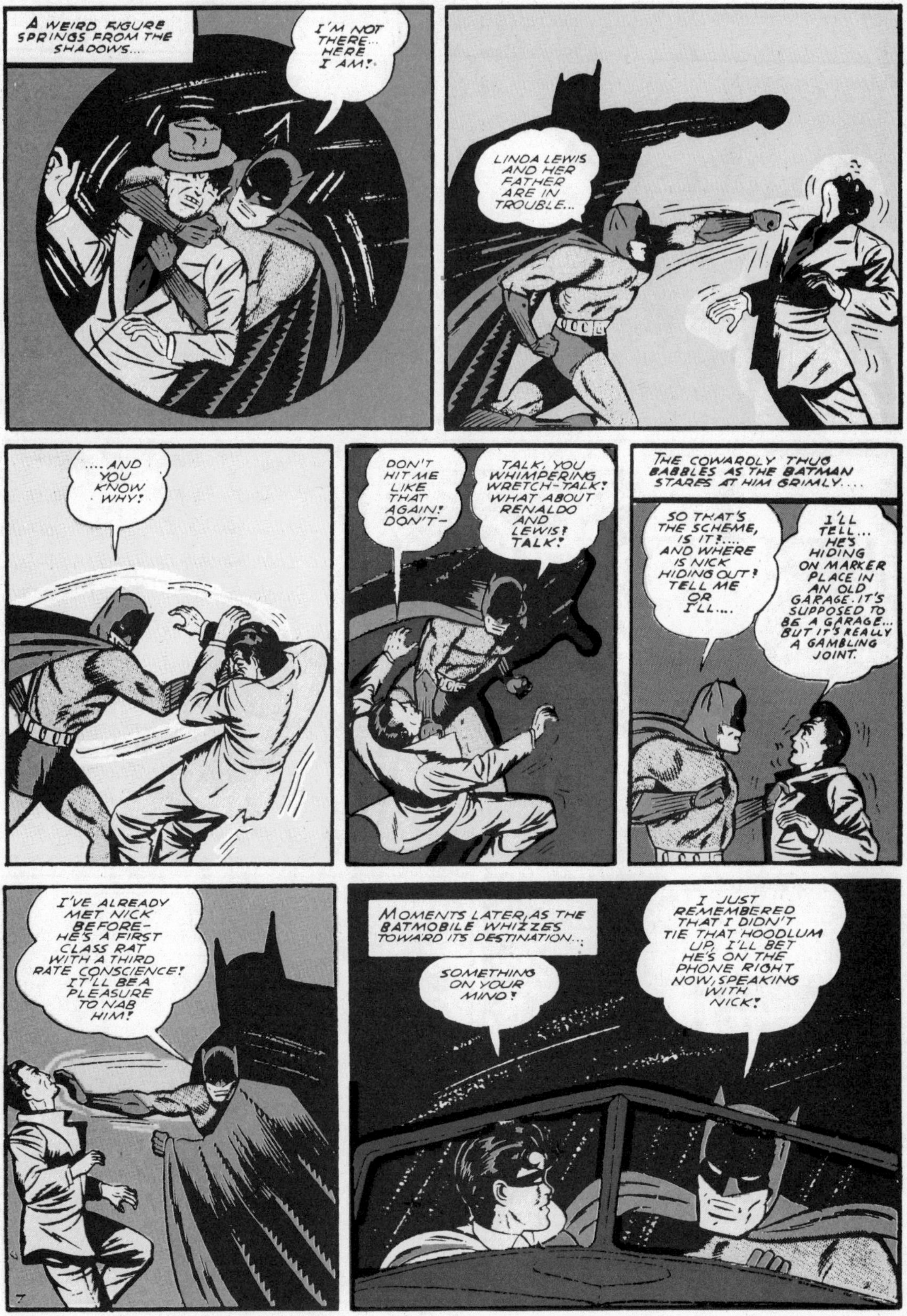
A WEIRD FIGURE SPRINGS FROM THE SHADOWS...
I'M NOT THERE... HERE I AM!
LINDA LEWIS AND HER FATHER ARE IN TROUBLE...
....AND YOU KNOW WHY!
DON'T HIT ME LIKE THAT AGAIN! DON'T-
TALK, YOU WHIMPERING WRETCH-TALK! WHAT ABOUT RENALDO AND LEWIS? TALK!
THE COWARDLY THUG BABBLES AS THE BATMAN STARES AT HIM GRIMLY....
SO THAT'S THE SCHEME, IS IT?.... AND WHERE IS NICK HIDING OUT? TELL ME OR I'LL....
I'LL TELL... HE'S HIDING ON MARKER PLACE IN AN OLD GARAGE. IT'S SUPPOSED TO BE A GARAGE... BUT IT'S REALLY A GAMBLING JOINT.
I'VE ALREADY MET NICK BEFORE- HE'S A FIRST CLASS RAT WITH A THIRD RATE CONSCIENCE! IT'LL BE A PLEASURE TO NAB HIM!
MOMENTS LATER, AS THE BATMOBILE WHIZZES TOWARD ITS DESTINATION...
SOMETHING ON YOUR MIND?
I JUST REMEMBERED THAT I DIDN'T TIE THAT HOODLUM UP. I'LL BET HE'S ON THE PHONE RIGHT NOW, SPEAKING WITH NICK!
7

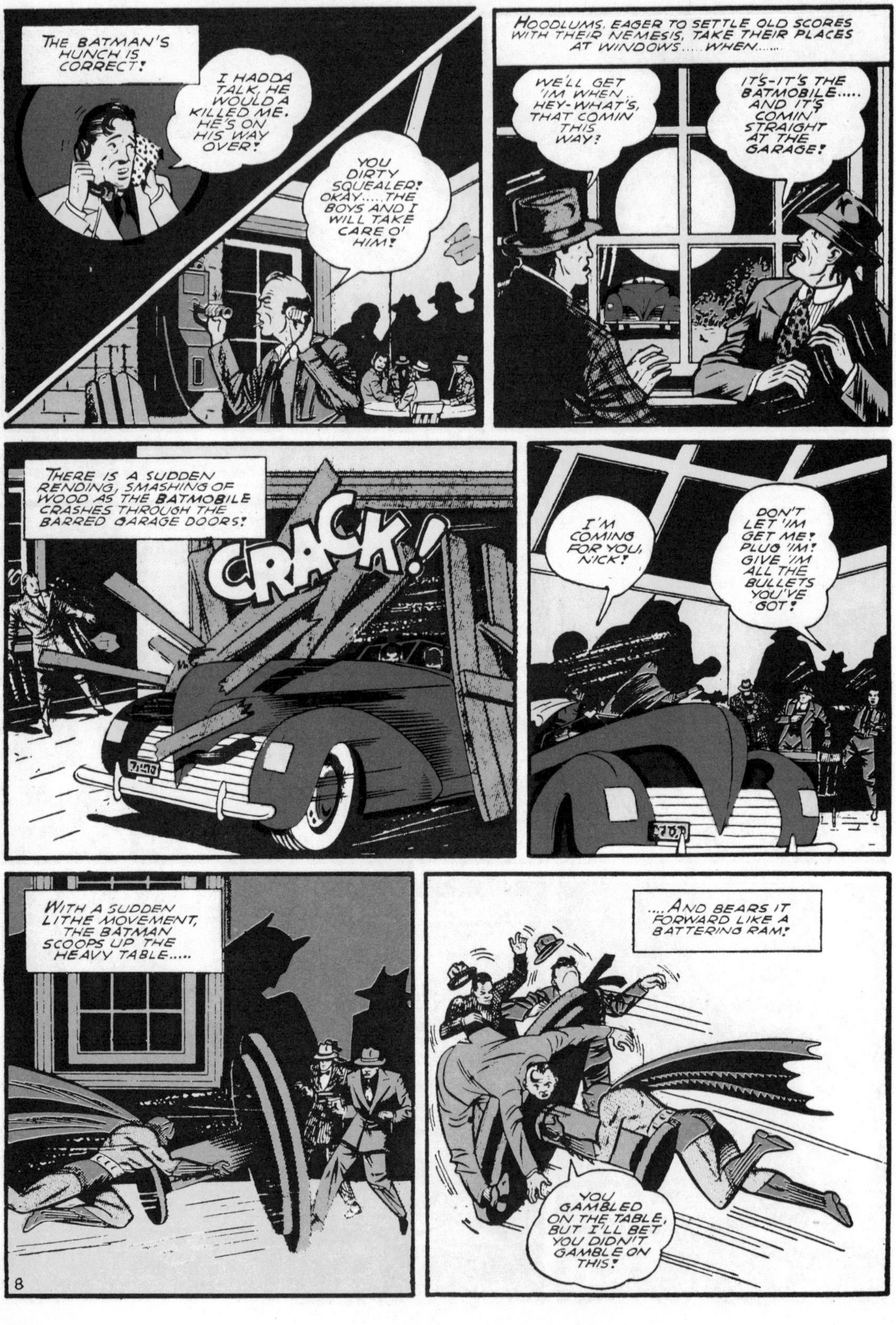
THE BATMAN'S HUNCH IS CORRECT!
I HADDA TALK, HE WOULD A KILLED ME. HE'S ON HIS WAY OVER!
YOU DIRTY SQUEALER! OKAY.....THE BOYS AND I WILL TAKE CARE O' HIM!
HOODLUMS, EAGER TO SETTLE OLD SCORES WITH THEIR NEMESIS, TAKE THEIR PLACES AT WINDOWS.....WHEN.......
WE'LL GET 'IM WHEN.. HEY-WHAT'S, THAT COMIN THIS WAY?
IT'S-IT'S THE BATMOBILE..... AND IT'S COMIN' STRAIGHT AT THE GARAGE!
THERE IS A SUDDEN RENDING, SMASHING OF WOOD AS THE BATMOBILE CRASHES THROUGH THE BARRED GARAGE DOORS!
CRACK!
I'M COMING FOR YOU, NICK!
DON'T LET 'IM GET ME! PLUG 'IM! GIVE 'IM ALL THE BULLETS YOU'VE GOT!
WITH A SUDDEN LITHE MOVEMENT, THE BATMAN SCOOPS UP THE HEAVY TABLE.....
8
....AND BEARS IT FORWARD LIKE A BATTERING RAM!
YOU GAMBLED ON THE TABLE, BUT I'LL BET YOU DIDN'T GAMBLE ON THIS!

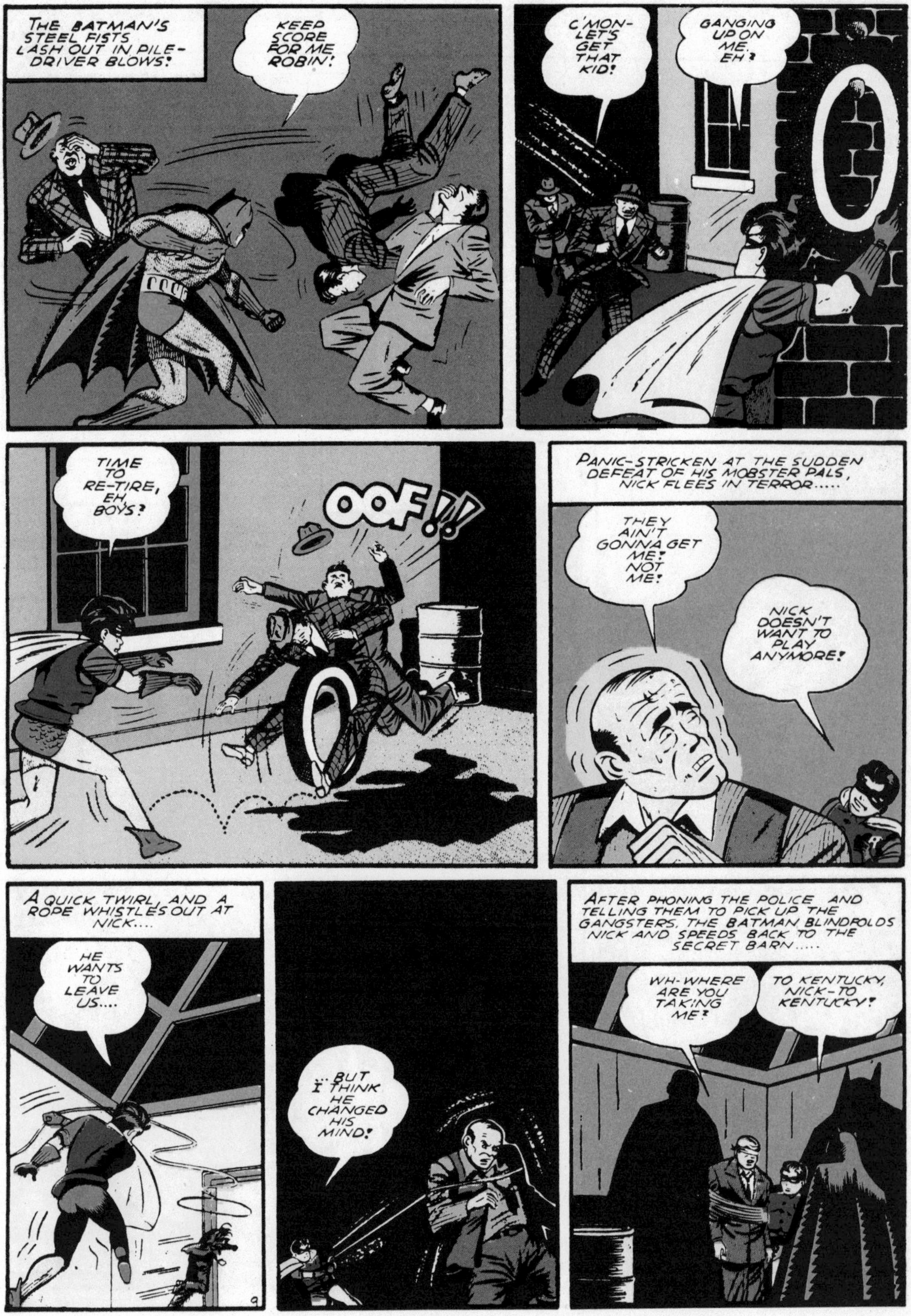
THE BATMAN'S STEEL FISTS LASH OUT IN PILE-DRIVER BLOWS!
KEEP SCORE FOR ME ROBIN!
C'MON-LET'S GET THAT KID!
GANGING UP ON ME, EH?
TIME TO RE-TIRE, EH, BOYS?
OOF!!
PANIC-STRICKEN AT THE SUDDEN DEFEAT OF HIS MOBSTER PALS, NICK FLEES IN TERROR.....
THEY AIN'T GONNA GET ME! NOT ME!
NICK DOESN'T WANT TO PLAY ANYMORE!
A QUICK TWIRL, AND A ROPE WHISTLES OUT AT NICK....
HE WANTS TO LEAVE US....
...BUT I THINK HE CHANGED HIS MIND!
AFTER PHONING THE POLICE AND TELLING THEM TO PICK UP THE GANGSTERS, THE BATMAN BLINDFOLDS NICK AND SPEEDS BACK TO THE SECRET BARN.....
WH-WHERE ARE YOU TAKING ME?
TO KENTUCKY, NICK-TO KENTUCKY!

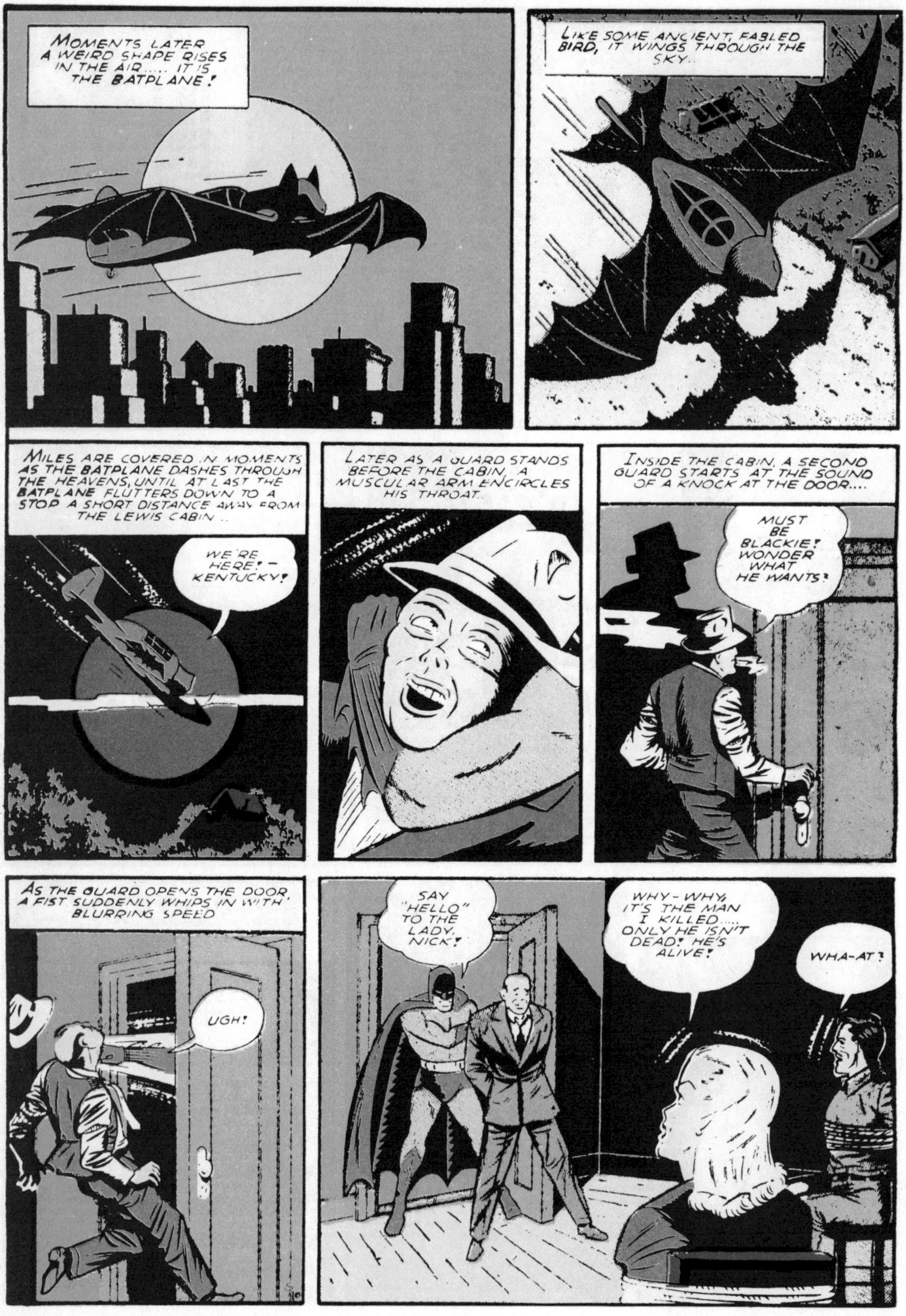
MOMENTS LATER A WEIRD SHAPE RISES IN THE AIR..... IT IS THE BATPLANE!
LIKE SOME ANCIENT, FABLED BIRD, IT WINGS THROUGH THE SKY..
MILES ARE COVERED IN MOMENTS AS THE BATPLANE DASHES THROUGH THE HEAVENS, UNTIL AT LAST THE BATPLANE FLUTTERS DOWN TO A STOP A SHORT DISTANCE AWAY FROM THE LEWIS CABIN..
WE'RE HERE! — KENTUCKY!
LATER AS A GUARD STANDS BEFORE THE CABIN, A MUSCULAR ARM ENCIRCLES HIS THROAT..
INSIDE THE CABIN, A SECOND GUARD STARTS AT THE SOUND OF A KNOCK AT THE DOOR....
MUST BE BLACKIE! WONDER WHAT HE WANTS?
AS THE GUARD OPENS THE DOOR, A FIST SUDDENLY WHIPS IN WITH BLURRING SPEED
UGH!
SAY "HELLO" TO THE LADY, NICK!
WHY-WHY, IT'S THE MAN I KILLED..... ONLY HE ISN'T DEAD! HE'S ALIVE!
WHA-AT?

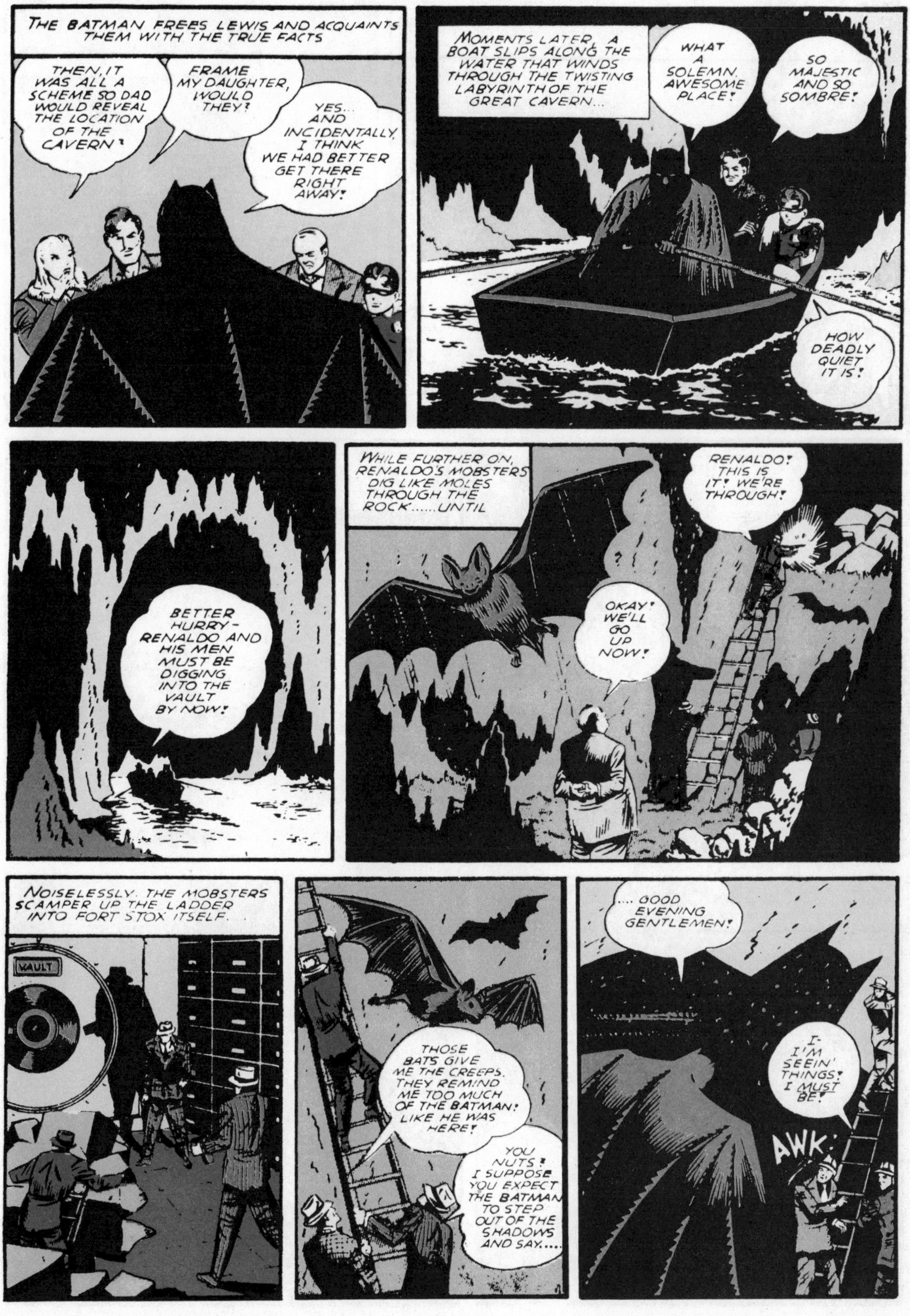
THE BATMAN FREES LEWIS AND ACQUAINTS THEM WITH THE TRUE FACTS
THEN, IT WAS ALL A SCHEME SO DAD WOULD REVEAL THE LOCATION OF THE CAVERN?
FRAME MY DAUGHTER, WOULD THEY?
YES... AND INCIDENTALLY, I THINK WE HAD BETTER GET THERE RIGHT AWAY!
MOMENTS LATER, A BOAT SLIPS ALONG THE WATER THAT WINDS THROUGH THE TWISTING LABYRINTH OF THE GREAT CAVERN...
WHAT A SOLEMN, AWESOME PLACE!
SO MAJESTIC AND SO SOMBRE!
HOW DEADLY QUIET IT IS!
BETTER HURRY- RENALDO AND HIS MEN MUST BE DIGGING INTO THE VAULT BY NOW!
WHILE FURTHER ON, RENALDO'S MOBSTERS DIG LIKE MOLES THROUGH THE ROCK......UNTIL
RENALDO! THIS IS IT! WE'RE THROUGH!
OKAY! WE'LL GO UP NOW!
NOISELESSLY, THE MOBSTERS SCAMPER UP THE LADDER INTO FORT STOX ITSELF.
VAULT
THOSE BATS GIVE ME THE CREEPS. THEY REMIND ME TOO MUCH OF THE BATMAN! LIKE HE WAS HERE!
YOU NUTS? I SUPPOSE YOU EXPECT THE BATMAN TO STEP OUT OF THE SHADOWS AND SAY....
....GOOD EVENING GENTLEMEN!
I- I'M SEEIN' THINGS! I MUST BE!
AWK!

AS ROBIN USES AN OAR. WITH A PURPOSE OTHER THAN THAT FOR THE ONE IT WAS INTENDED, THE BATMAN SPRINGS FORWARD TOWARD THE UPRIGHT LADDER...
NOW, YOU'RE SEEING THINGS... STARS!
DOWN COMES THE LADDER, AND THE GUNMEN WITH IT!
JUST LIKE HUMPTY-DUMPTY-YOU HAD A GREAT FALL!
THE MEN RISE SHAKILY TO THEIR FEET.....
....ONLY TO GO DOWN AGAIN!
YOU CERTAINLY DO HAVE YOUR UPS AND DOWNS, DON'T YOU?
MEANWHILE, THE BOY WONDER GIVES A GOOD ACCOUNTING OF HIMSELF.....
A LITTLE SOMETHING FOR YOU, BUDDY!
12
....AND YOU'RE NO EXCEPTION, HORSEFACE!

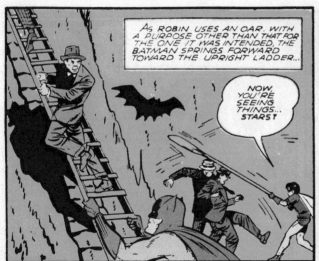

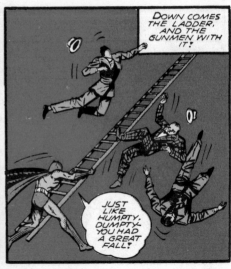

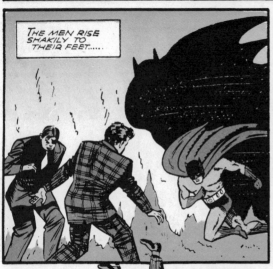

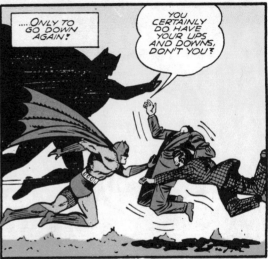

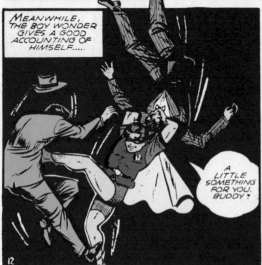

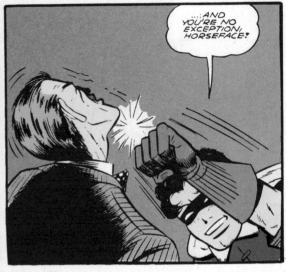

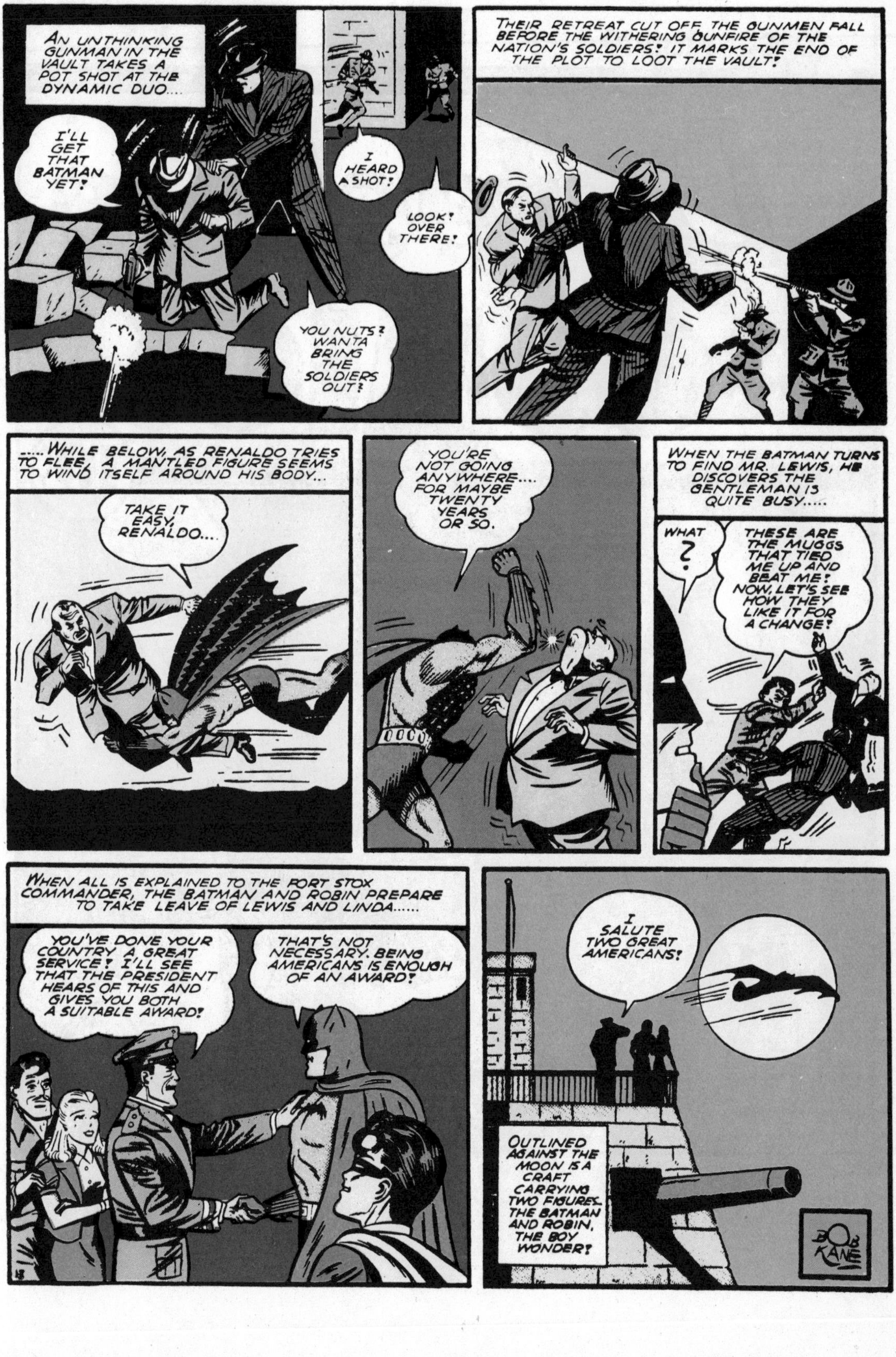
AN UNTHINKING GUNMAN IN THE VAULT TAKES A POT SHOT AT THE DYNAMIC DUO....
I'LL GET THAT BATMAN YET!
I HEARD A SHOT!
LOOK! OVER THERE!
YOU NUTS? WANTA BRING THE SOLDIERS OUT?
THEIR RETREAT CUT OFF THE GUNMEN FALL BEFORE THE WITHERING GUNFIRE OF THE NATION'S SOLDIERS! IT MARKS THE END OF THE PLOT TO LOOT THE VAULT!
.....WHILE BELOW, AS RENALDO TRIES TO FLEE, A MANTLED FIGURE SEEMS TO WIND ITSELF AROUND HIS BODY...
TAKE IT EASY, RENALDO....
YOU'RE NOT GOING ANYWHERE.... FOR MAYBE TWENTY YEARS OR SO.
WHEN THE BATMAN TURNS TO FIND MR. LEWIS, HE DISCOVERS THE GENTLEMAN IS QUITE BUSY.....
WHAT ?
THESE ARE THE MUGGS THAT TIED ME UP AND BEAT ME! NOW, LET'S SEE HOW THEY LIKE IT FOR A CHANGE!
WHEN ALL IS EXPLAINED TO THE FORT STOX COMMANDER, THE BATMAN AND ROBIN PREPARE TO TAKE LEAVE OF LEWIS AND LINDA......
YOU'VE DONE YOUR COUNTRY A GREAT SERVICE! I'LL SEE THAT THE PRESIDENT HEARS OF THIS AND GIVES YOU BOTH A SUITABLE AWARD!
THAT'S NOT NECESSARY. BEING AMERICANS IS ENOUGH OF AN AWARD!
I SALUTE TWO GREAT AMERICANS!
OUTLINED AGAINST THE MOON IS A CRAFT CARRYING TWO FIGURES. THE BATMAN AND ROBIN, THE BOY WONDER!
BOB KANE

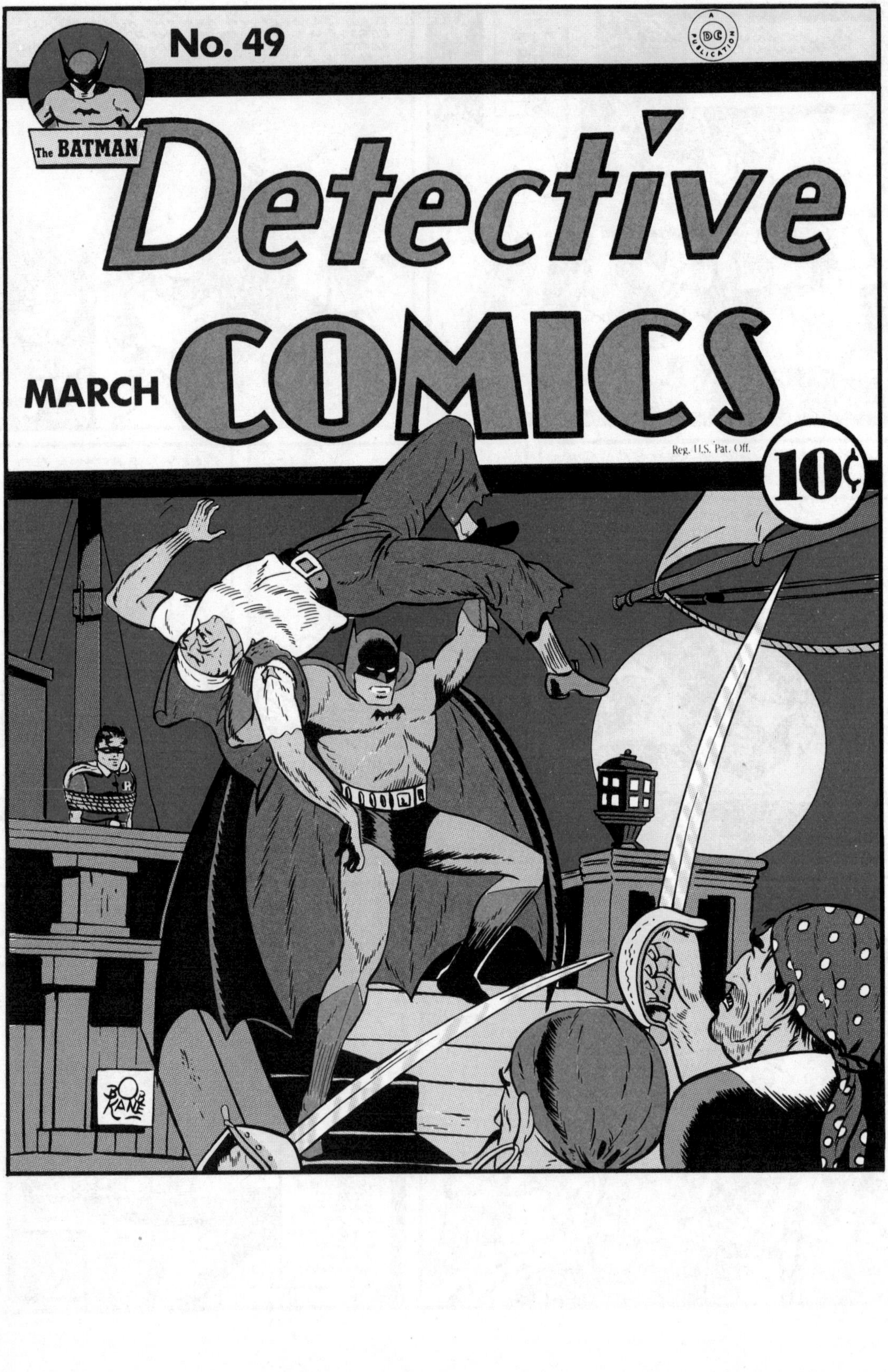
No. 49
A DC PUBLICATION
The BATMAN
Detective
MARCH
COMICS
Reg. U.S. Pat. Off.
10¢
BOB KANE

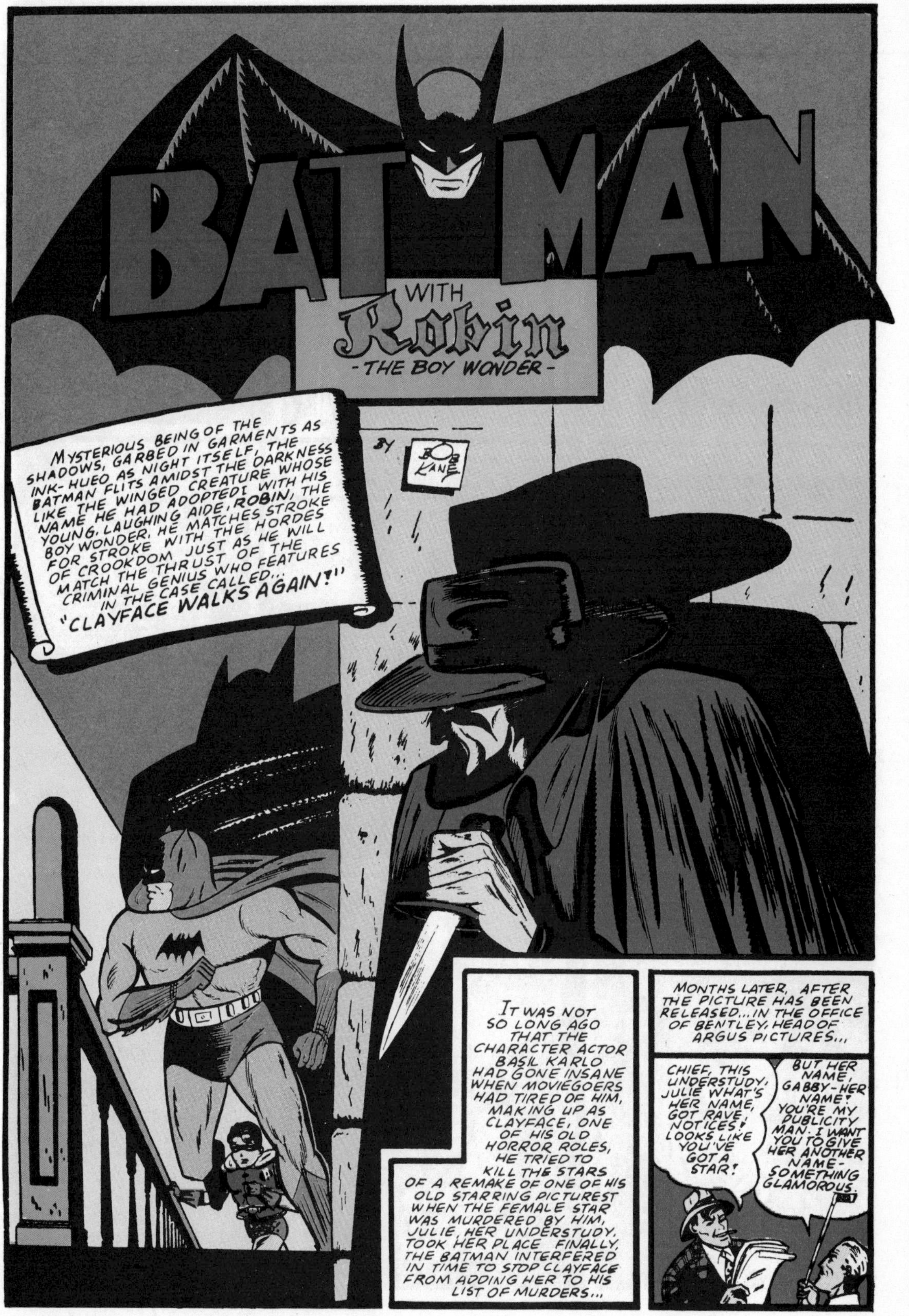
BATMAN
WITH Robin
-THE BOY WONDER-
MYSTERIOUS BEING OF THE SHADOWS, GARBED IN GARMENTS AS INK-HUEO AS NIGHT ITSELF, THE BATMAN FLITS AMIDST THE DARKNESS LIKE THE WINGED CREATURE WHOSE NAME HE HAD ADOPTED! WITH HIS YOUNG, LAUGHING AIDE, ROBIN, THE BOY WONDER, HE MATCHES STROKE FOR STROKE WITH THE HORDES OF CROOKDOM JUST AS HE WILL MATCH THE THRUST OF THE CRIMINAL GENIUS WHO FEATURES IN THE CASE CALLED... "CLAYFACE WALKS AGAIN!"
BY BOB KANE
IT WAS NOT SO LONG AGO THAT THE CHARACTER ACTOR BASIL KARLO HAD GONE INSANE WHEN MOVIEGOERS HAD TIRED OF HIM, MAKING UP AS CLAYFACE, ONE OF HIS OLD HORROR ROLES, HE TRIED TO KILL THE STARS OF A REMAKE OF ONE OF HIS OLD STARRING PICTUREST WHEN THE FEMALE STAR WAS MURDERED BY HIM, JULIE, HER UNDERSTUDY, TOOK HER PLACE FINALLY, THE BATMAN INTERFERED IN TIME TO STOP CLAYFACE FROM ADDING HER TO HIS LIST OF MURDERS...
MONTHS LATER, AFTER THE PICTURE HAS BEEN RELEASED... IN THE OFFICE OF BENTLEY, HEAD OF ARGUS PICTURES...
CHIEF, THIS UNDERSTUDY, JULIE WHAT'S HER NAME, GOT RAVE NOTICES! LOOKS LIKE YOU'VE GOT A STAR!
BUT HER NAME, GABBY-HER NAME! YOU'RE MY PUBLICITY MAN. I WANT YOU TO GIVE HER ANOTHER NAME-SOMETHING GLAMOROUS.

SHE TOOK THE PUBLIC BY STORM, AND...

"STORM" THAT'S IT! — BUT LET'S SPELL IT "S-T-O-R-M-E!"

SNAP!

"STORME"- NOT BAD! NOW A FIRST NAME. ONE THAT WILL BE IN CONTRAST! SOMETHING GENTLE, KIND, SWEET!

WHO WAS IT IN BOOKS THAT WAS GENTLE, KIND?

"PORTIA"? SHAKESPEARE'S "PORTIA!" HOW DO YOU LIKE THIS? "PORTIA STORME!"

ITS A NATURAL! A NATURAL! CALL UP THE NEWSPAPERS, THE MOVIE MAGS! SPREAD THAT NAME FROM HERE TO TIMBUCTOO!

SNAP!

A STAR IS BORN!

GOTHAM GAZETTE
PORTIA STORME

SCREEN STARS 10¢

DO NEWS

MOVIE MAG 10¢

PORTIA STORME

MOVI

PORTIA STORME

PORTIA STORME

A STAR IS BORN

Starring PORTIA STORME TRUE STORY

A FEW DAYS LATER, JULIE, NOW PORTIA STORME, TALKS WITH HER FIANCE, BRUCE WAYNE...

YOU'RE ON YOUR WAY UP, A NEW STAR, A NEW NAME!

...AND A NEW CAREER! OH, BRUCE, IF ONLY YOU WOULD DO SOMETHING!

...IF ONLY YOU'D FIND YOURSELF A CAREER INSTEAD OF BEING THE PUBLIC'S NUMBER ONE PLAYBOY!

SORRY, HONEY. I'M HAVING TOO GOOD A TIME TO BE BOTHERED WITH ANYTHING REMOTELY CONNECTED WITH WORK! (YOU'D BE MIGHTY SURPRISED IF YOU KNEW I HAD A CAREER- AS THE BATMAN!)

THEN I'M SORRY, BRUCE. UNTIL YOU DECIDE TO MAKE SOMETHING OF YOURSELF, I'M AFRAID OUR ENGAGEMENT IS OFF!

I-I SEE.

I'M NOT WALKING OUT ON YOU, BRUCE. ANYTIME YOU DECIDE TO CHANGE YOUR WAYS, I'LL COME BACK TO YOU GLADLY!

I UNDERSTAND! IT'S ALL RIGHT!

IN CASE YOU EVER NEED ME FOR ANYTHING, JUST HOLLER. IF EVER THERE'S ANYTHING I CAN DO...

THANK YOU, BRUCE, BUT I DON'T THINK I'LL EVER BE IN MUCH TROUBLE.

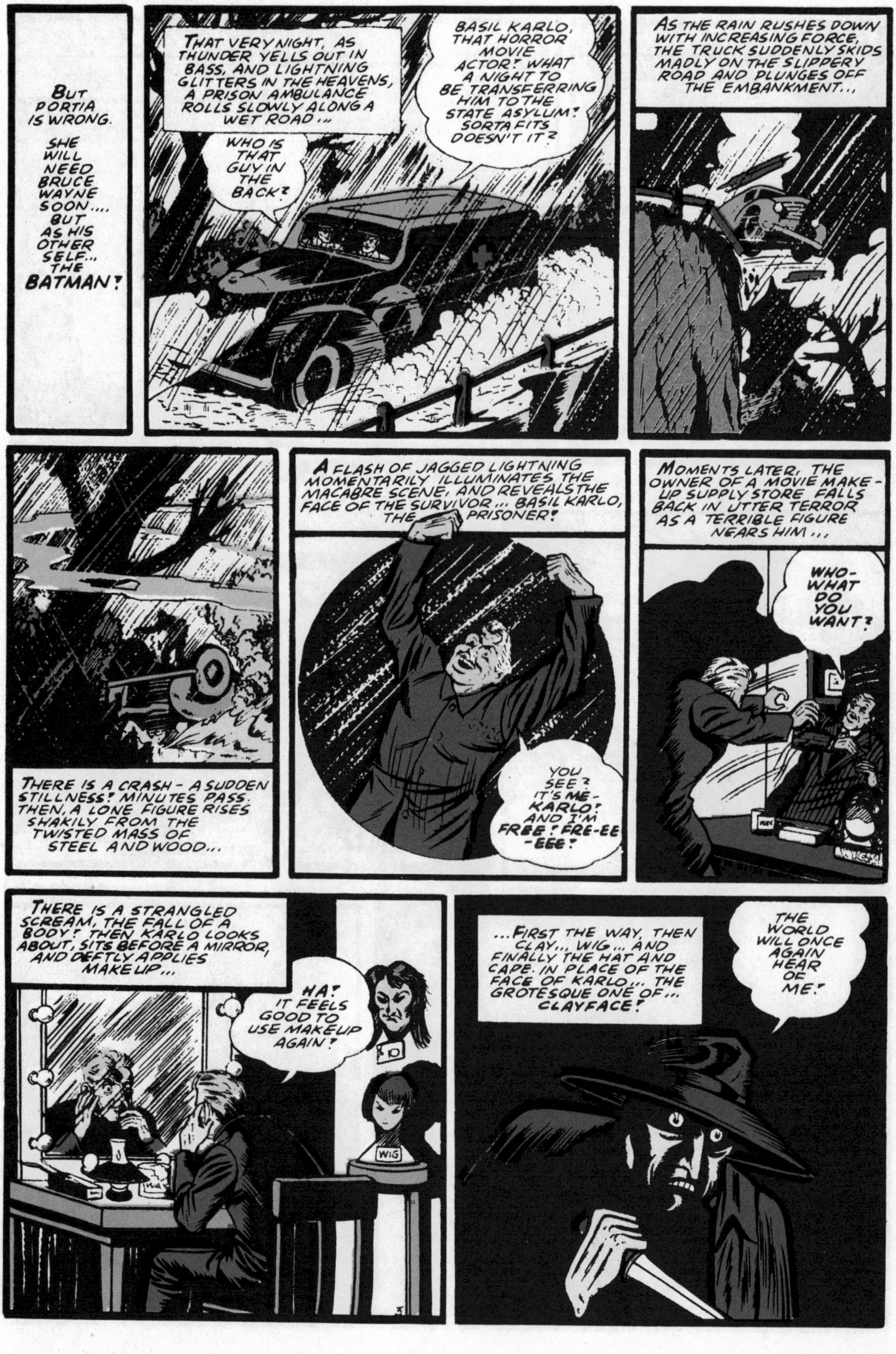
BUT PORTIA IS WRONG. SHE WILL NEED BRUCE WAYNE SOON.... BUT AS HIS OTHER SELF... THE BATMAN!
THAT VERY NIGHT, AS THUNDER YELLS OUT IN BASS, AND LIGHTNING GLITTERS IN THE HEAVENS, A PRISON AMBULANCE ROLLS SLOWLY ALONG A WET ROAD...
WHO IS THAT GUY IN THE BACK?
BASIL KARLO, THAT HORROR MOVIE ACTOR! WHAT A NIGHT TO BE TRANSFERRING HIM TO THE STATE ASYLUM! SORTA FITS DOESN'T IT?
AS THE RAIN RUSHES DOWN WITH INCREASING FORCE, THE TRUCK SUDDENLY SKIDS MADLY ON THE SLIPPERY ROAD AND PLUNGES OFF THE EMBANKMENT...
THERE IS A CRASH - A SUDDEN STILLNESS! MINUTES PASS. THEN, A LONE FIGURE RISES SHAKILY FROM THE TWISTED MASS OF STEEL AND WOOD...
A FLASH OF JAGGED LIGHTNING MOMENTARILY ILLUMINATES THE MACABRE SCENE, AND REVEALS THE FACE OF THE SURVIVOR... BASIL KARLO, THE PRISONER!
YOU SEE? IT'S ME-KARLO! AND I'M FREE! FRE-EE-EEE!
MOMENTS LATER, THE OWNER OF A MOVIE MAKE-UP SUPPLY STORE FALLS BACK IN UTTER TERROR AS A TERRIBLE FIGURE NEARS HIM...
WHO-WHAT DO YOU WANT?
THERE IS A STRANGLED SCREAM, THE FALL OF A BODY! THEN KARLO LOOKS ABOUT, SITS BEFORE A MIRROR, AND DEFTLY APPLIES MAKEUP...
HA! IT FEELS GOOD TO USE MAKEUP AGAIN!
WIG
...FIRST THE WAY, THEN CLAY... WIG... AND FINALLY THE HAT AND CAPE. IN PLACE OF THE FACE OF KARLO... THE GROTESQUE ONE OF... CLAYFACE!
THE WORLD WILL ONCE AGAIN HEAR OF ME!

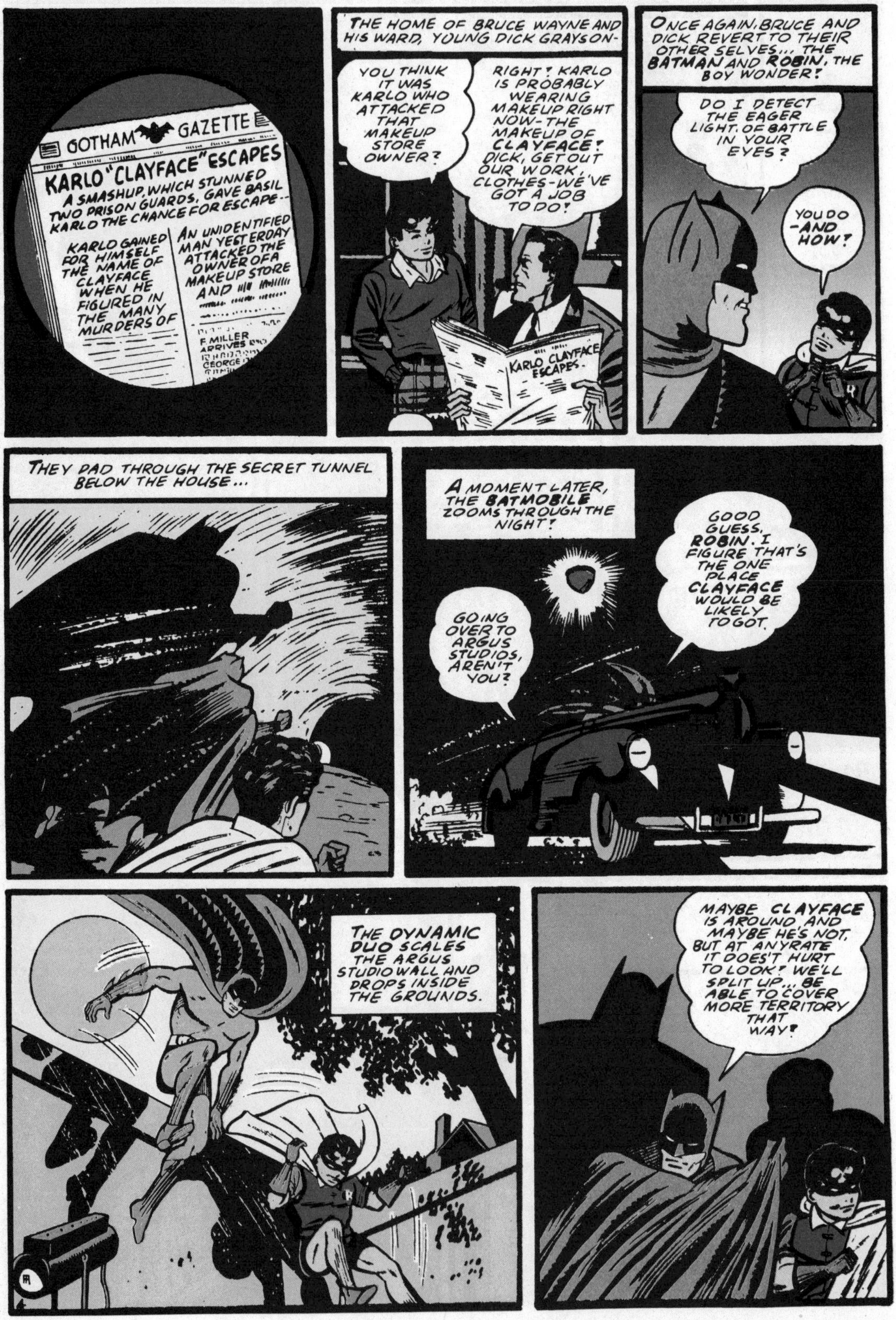
GOTHAM GAZETTE
KARLO "CLAYFACE" ESCAPES
A SMASHUP, WHICH STUNNED TWO PRISON GUARDS, GAVE BASIL KARLO THE CHANCE FOR ESCAPE--
KARLO GAINED FOR HIMSELF THE NAME OF CLAYFACE WHEN HE FIGURED IN THE MANY MURDERS OF
AN UNIDENTIFIED MAN YESTERDAY ATTACKED THE OWNER OF A MAKEUP STORE AND
F. MILLER ARRIVES
THE HOME OF BRUCE WAYNE AND HIS WARD, YOUNG DICK GRAYSON-
YOU THINK IT WAS KARLO WHO ATTACKED THAT MAKEUP STORE OWNER?
RIGHT! KARLO IS PROBABLY WEARING MAKEUP RIGHT NOW-THE MAKEUP OF CLAYFACE! DICK, GET OUT OUR WORK CLOTHES-WE'VE GOT A JOB TO DO!
KARLO CLAYFACE ESCAPES
ONCE AGAIN, BRUCE AND DICK REVERT TO THEIR OTHER SELVES... THE BATMAN AND ROBIN, THE BOY WONDER!
DO I DETECT THE EAGER LIGHT OF BATTLE IN YOUR EYES?
YOU DO -AND HOW!
THEY DAD THROUGH THE SECRET TUNNEL BELOW THE HOUSE...
A MOMENT LATER, THE BATMOBILE ZOOMS THROUGH THE NIGHT!
GOING OVER TO ARGUS STUDIOS, AREN'T YOU?
GOOD GUESS, ROBIN. I FIGURE THAT'S THE ONE PLACE CLAYFACE WOULD BE LIKELY TO GO!
THE DYNAMIC DUO SCALES THE ARGUS STUDIO WALL AND DROPS INSIDE THE GROUNDS.
MAYBE CLAYFACE IS AROUND AND MAYBE HE'S NOT, BUT AT ANYRATE IT DOES'T HURT TO LOOK! WE'LL SPLIT UP... BE ABLE TO COVER MORE TERRITORY THAT WAY!

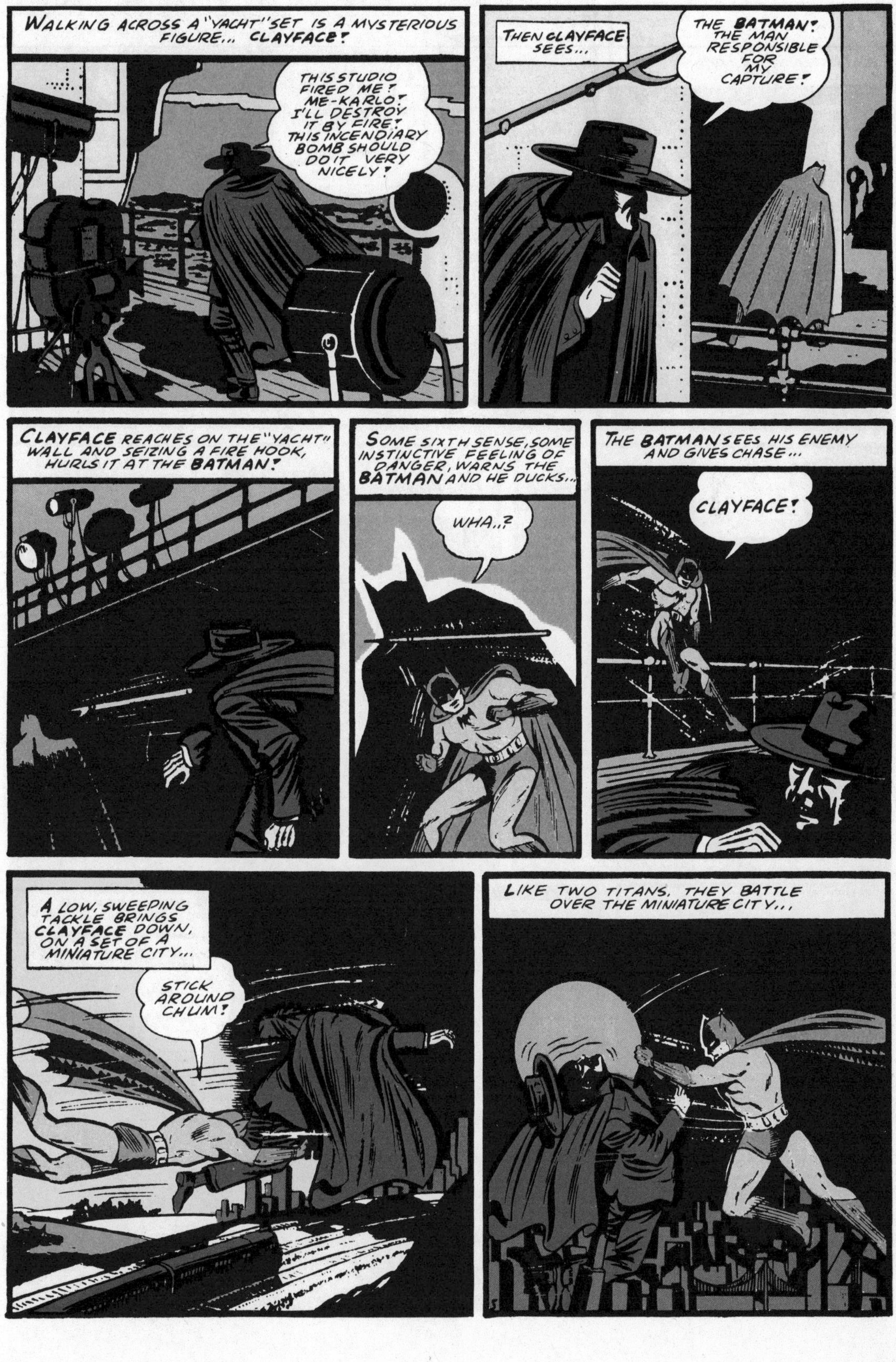
WALKING ACROSS A "YACHT" SET IS A MYSTERIOUS FIGURE... CLAYFACE!
THIS STUDIO FIRED ME! ME-KARLO! I'LL DESTROY IT BY FIRE! THIS INCENDIARY BOMB SHOULD DO IT VERY NICELY!
THEN CLAYFACE SEES...
THE BATMAN! THE MAN RESPONSIBLE FOR MY CAPTURE!
CLAYFACE REACHES ON THE "YACHT" WALL AND SEIZING A FIRE HOOK, HURLS IT AT THE BATMAN!
SOME SIXTH SENSE, SOME INSTINCTIVE FEELING OF DANGER, WARNS THE BATMAN AND HE DUCKS...
WHA..?
THE BATMAN SEES HIS ENEMY AND GIVES CHASE...
CLAYFACE!
A LOW, SWEEPING TACKLE BRINGS CLAYFACE DOWN, ON A SET OF A MINIATURE CITY...
STICK AROUND CHUM!
LIKE TWO TITANS, THEY BATTLE OVER THE MINIATURE CITY...

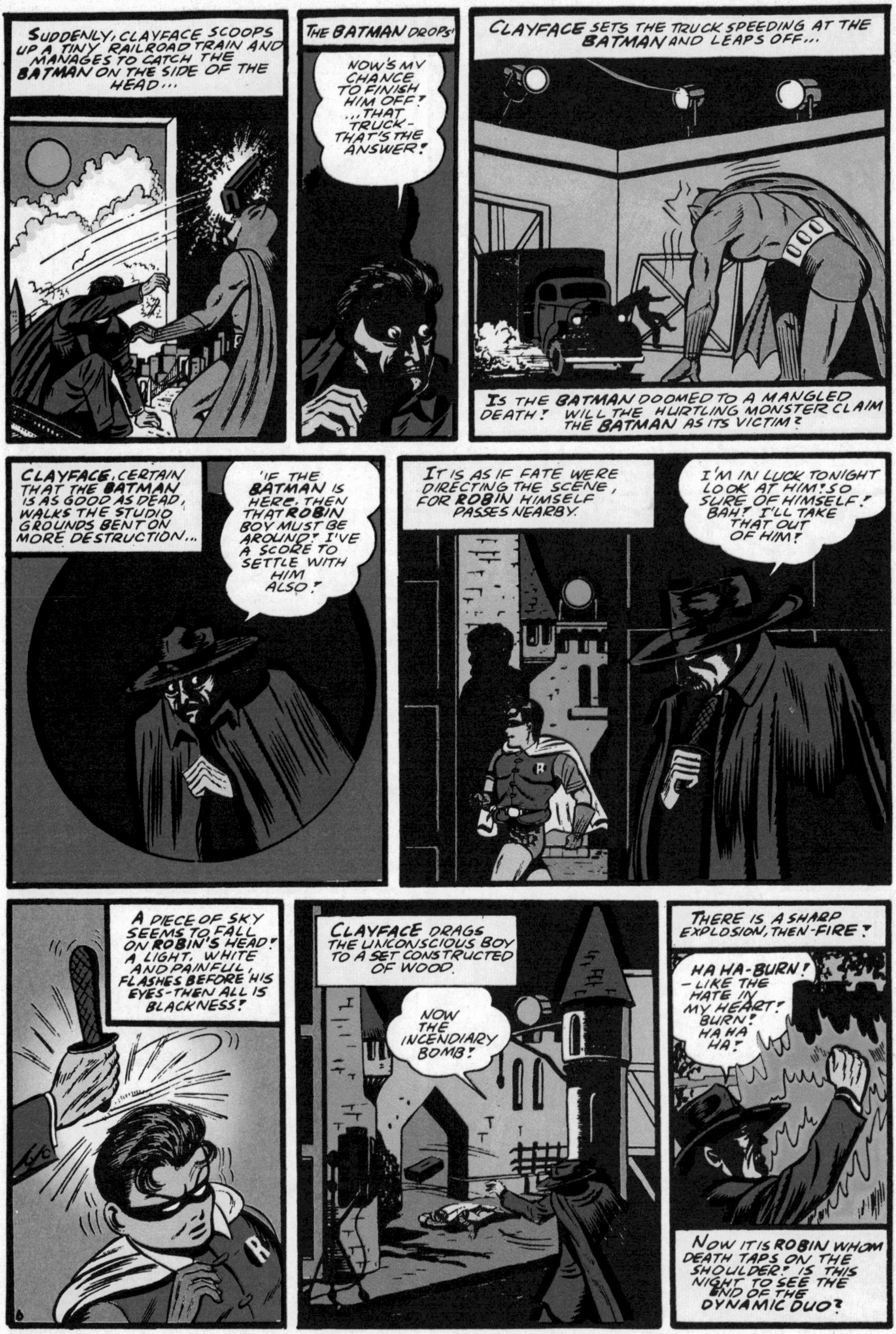
SUDDENLY, CLAYFACE SCOOPS UP A TINY RAILROAD TRAIN AND MANAGES TO CATCH THE BATMAN ON THE SIDE OF THE HEAD...
THE BATMAN DROPS!
NOW'S MY CHANCE TO FINISH HIM OFF! ...THAT TRUCK- THAT'S THE ANSWER!
CLAYFACE SETS THE TRUCK SPEEDING AT THE BATMAN AND LEAPS OFF...
IS THE BATMAN DOOMED TO A MANGLED DEATH! WILL THE HURTLING MONSTER CLAIM THE BATMAN AS ITS VICTIM?
CLAYFACE, CERTAIN THAT THE BATMAN IS AS GOOD AS DEAD, WALKS THE STUDIO GROUNDS BENT ON MORE DESTRUCTION...
'IF THE BATMAN IS HERE, THEN THAT ROBIN BOY MUST BE AROUND! I'VE A SCORE TO SETTLE WITH HIM ALSO!
IT IS AS IF FATE WERE DIRECTING THE SCENE, FOR ROBIN HIMSELF PASSES NEARBY.
I'M IN LUCK TONIGHT LOOK AT HIM! SO SURE OF HIMSELF! BAH! I'LL TAKE THAT OUT OF HIM!
A PIECE OF SKY SEEMS TO FALL ON ROBIN'S HEAD! A LIGHT, WHITE AND PAINFUL, FLASHES BEFORE HIS EYES-THEN ALL IS BLACKNESS!
CLAYFACE DRAGS THE UNCONSCIOUS BOY TO A SET CONSTRUCTED OF WOOD.
NOW THE INCENDIARY BOMB!
THERE IS A SHARP EXPLOSION, THEN-FIRE!
HA HA-BURN! -LIKE THE HATE IN MY HEART! BURN! HA HA HA!
NOW IT IS ROBIN WHOM DEATH TAPS ON THE SHOULDER! IS THIS NIGHT TO SEE THE END OF THE DYNAMIC DUO?

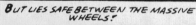

MEANWHILE, WHAT OF THE *DARK KNIGHT?*...AS THE ENGINE OF *DESTRUCTION* ROARS AT HIM, THE *BATMAN* DECIDES UPON *QUICK ACTION*...

GOT TO DO SOMETHING FAST OR I'M A GONER!

THE *BATMAN* DIVES INTO THE PATH OF THE TRUCK!

BUT LIES SAFE BETWEEN THE MASSIVE WHEELS!

THE *BATMAN* HAS MET *CLAYFACE* AND CHECKMATED HIS FIRST MOVE!

MEANWHILE— BACK AT THE FIRE...

IF THERE'S A BOY IN THERE, I'M AFRAID HE'S A GONER!

I TELL YOU I SEEN HIM! IT WAS *CLAYFACE*— AND HE LEFT A KID WITH A COSTUME ON INSIDE!

CLAYFACE!

NOT YET, HE, ISN'T!

BATMAN!

THE *BATMAN* DOUSES HIMSELF WITH WATER...

I'M GOING IN THERE!

HE LASSOES A NEARBY PROJECTION...

YOU CAN'T GO IN THERE— IT'S SHEER SUICIDE!

LISTEN, THE BEST FRIEND I'VE GOT LIES IN THERE- GET OUT OF MY WAY! I'M GOING IN!

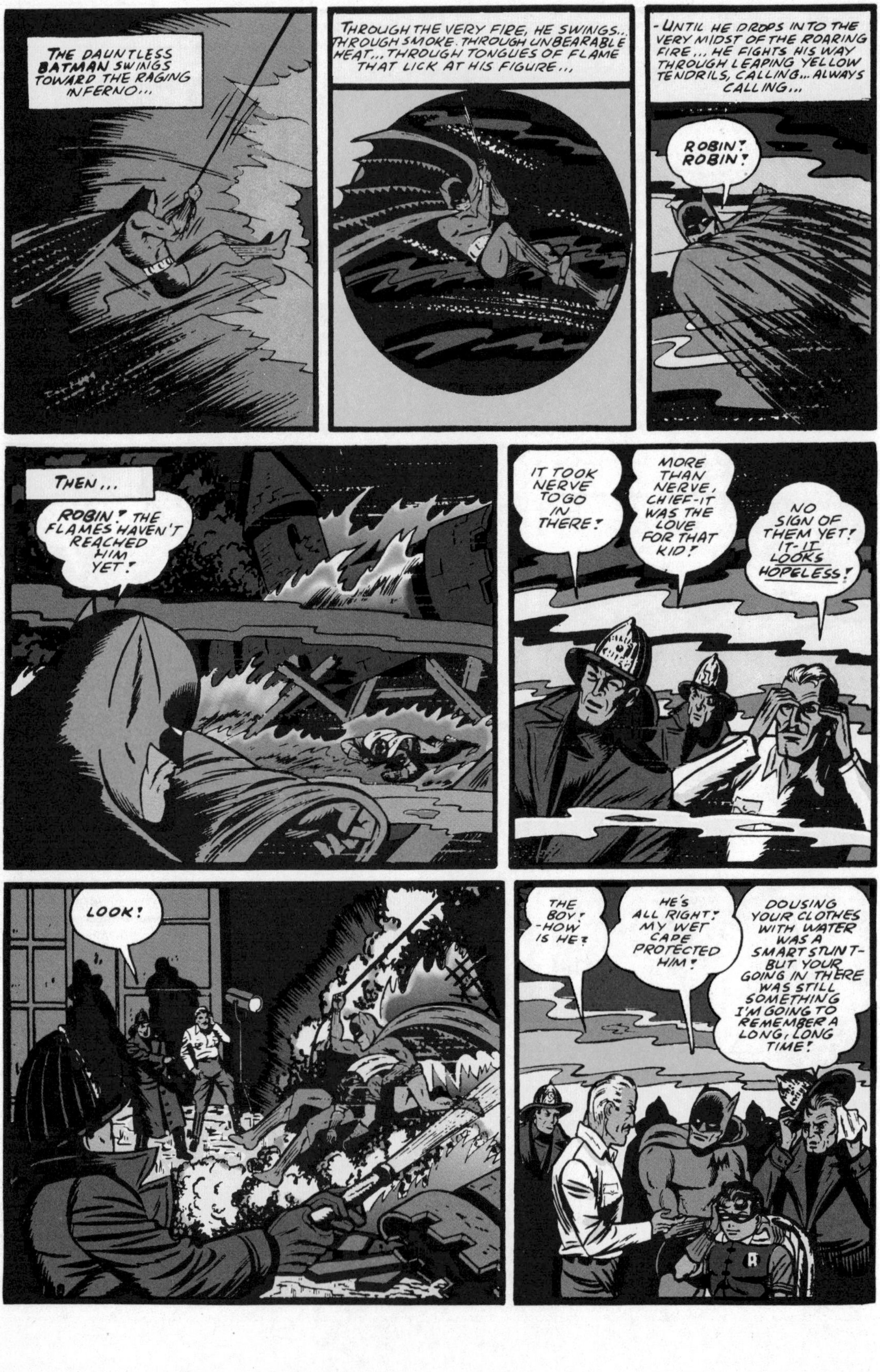
THE DAUNTLESS BATMAN SWINGS TOWARD THE RAGING INFERNO...
THROUGH THE VERY FIRE, HE SWINGS... THROUGH SMOKE. THROUGH UNBEARABLE HEAT... THROUGH TONGUES OF FLAME THAT LICK AT HIS FIGURE...
-UNTIL HE DROPS INTO THE VERY MIDST OF THE ROARING FIRE... HE FIGHTS HIS WAY THROUGH LEAPING YELLOW TENDRILS, CALLING... ALWAYS CALLING...
ROBIN! ROBIN!
THEN...
ROBIN! THE FLAMES HAVEN'T REACHED HIM YET!
IT TOOK NERVE TO GO IN THERE!
MORE THAN NERVE, CHIEF-IT WAS THE LOVE FOR THAT KID!
NO SIGN OF THEM YET! IT-IT LOOKS HOPELESS!
LOOK!
THE BOY! -HOW IS HE?
HE'S ALL RIGHT! MY WET CAPE PROTECTED HIM!
DOUSING YOUR CLOTHES WITH WATER WAS A SMART STUNT- BUT YOUR GOING IN THERE WAS STILL SOMETHING I'M GOING TO REMEMBER A LONG, LONG TIME!

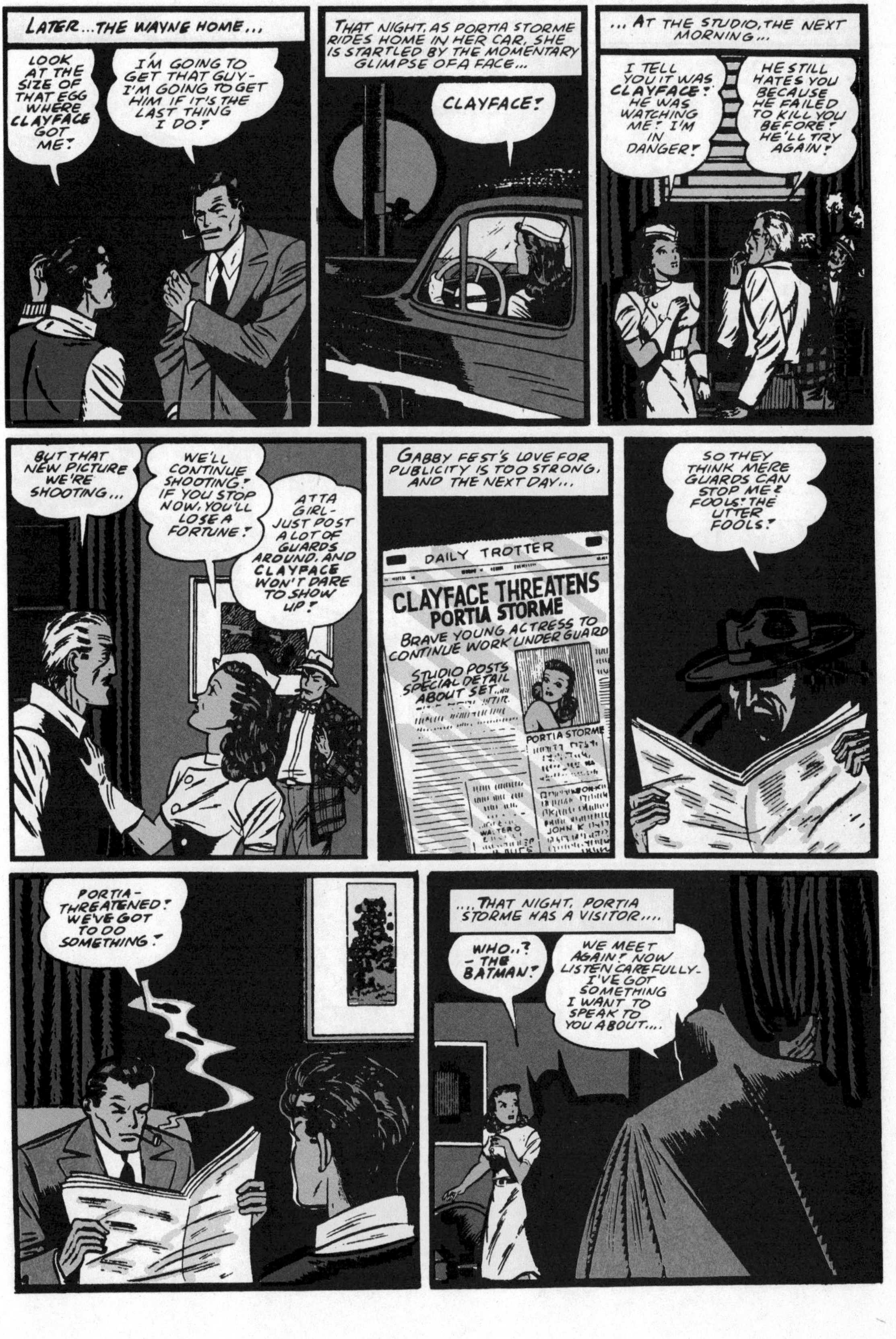
LATER...THE WAYNE HOME...
LOOK AT THE SIZE OF THAT EGG WHERE CLAYFACE GOT ME!
I'M GOING TO GET THAT GUY-- I'M GOING TO GET HIM IF IT'S THE LAST THING I DO!
THAT NIGHT, AS PORTIA STORME RIDES HOME IN HER CAR, SHE IS STARTLED BY THE MOMENTARY GLIMPSE OF A FACE...
CLAYFACE!
...AT THE STUDIO, THE NEXT MORNING...
I TELL YOU IT WAS CLAYFACE! HE WAS WATCHING ME! I'M IN DANGER!
HE STILL HATES YOU BECAUSE HE FAILED TO KILL YOU BEFORE! HE'LL TRY AGAIN!
BUT THAT NEW PICTURE WE'RE SHOOTING...
WE'LL CONTINUE SHOOTING! IF YOU STOP NOW, YOU'LL LOSE A FORTUNE!
ATTA GIRL-- JUST POST A LOT OF GUARDS AROUND, AND CLAYFACE WON'T DARE TO SHOW UP!
GABBY FEST'S LOVE FOR PUBLICITY IS TOO STRONG, AND THE NEXT DAY...
DAILY TROTTER
CLAYFACE THREATENS PORTIA STORME
BRAVE YOUNG ACTRESS TO CONTINUE WORK UNDER GUARD
STUDIO POSTS SPECIAL DETAIL ABOUT SET...
PORTIA STORME
SO THEY THINK MERE GUARDS CAN STOP ME? FOOLS! THE UTTER FOOLS!
PORTIA-- THREATENED! WE'VE GOT TO DO SOMETHING!
...THAT NIGHT, PORTIA STORME HAS A VISITOR....
WHO..? --THE BATMAN!
WE MEET AGAIN! NOW LISTEN CAREFULLY-- I'VE GOT SOMETHING I WANT TO SPEAK TO YOU ABOUT....

EARLY THE NEXT MORNING, A HAND REACHES THROUGH A WINDOW IN THE STUDIO COSTUME DEPARTMENT.

ANOTHER FIGURE JOINS THE MANY EXTRAS THAT STROLL PAST THE GUARDS ONTO THE SET...

NOW DON'T WORRY ABOUT A THING, PORTIA— WITH ALL THE POLICE I'VE GOT POSTED, CLAYFACE WON'T DARE TO SHOW UP!

...I'LL TRY NOT TO, MR. BENTLEY... BUT I HAVE A QUEER FEELING THAT HE WILL.

SUDDENLY, TWO MANTLED FORMS RACE TOWARD THE GUARDED SET....THEY ARE THE BATMAN AND ROBIN!

LET US THROUGH! PORTIA STORME IS IN TERRIBLE DANGER!

YEAH— FROM MASKED GUYS LIKE YOU!

LET'S GRAB 'EM, BOYS!

OKAY, BUDDY— YOU ASKED FOR IT!

I SAID, WE'RE GOING THROUGH!

...AND HE'S NOT KIDDING!

I REPEAT, GENTLEMEN— WE'RE GOING THROUGH!

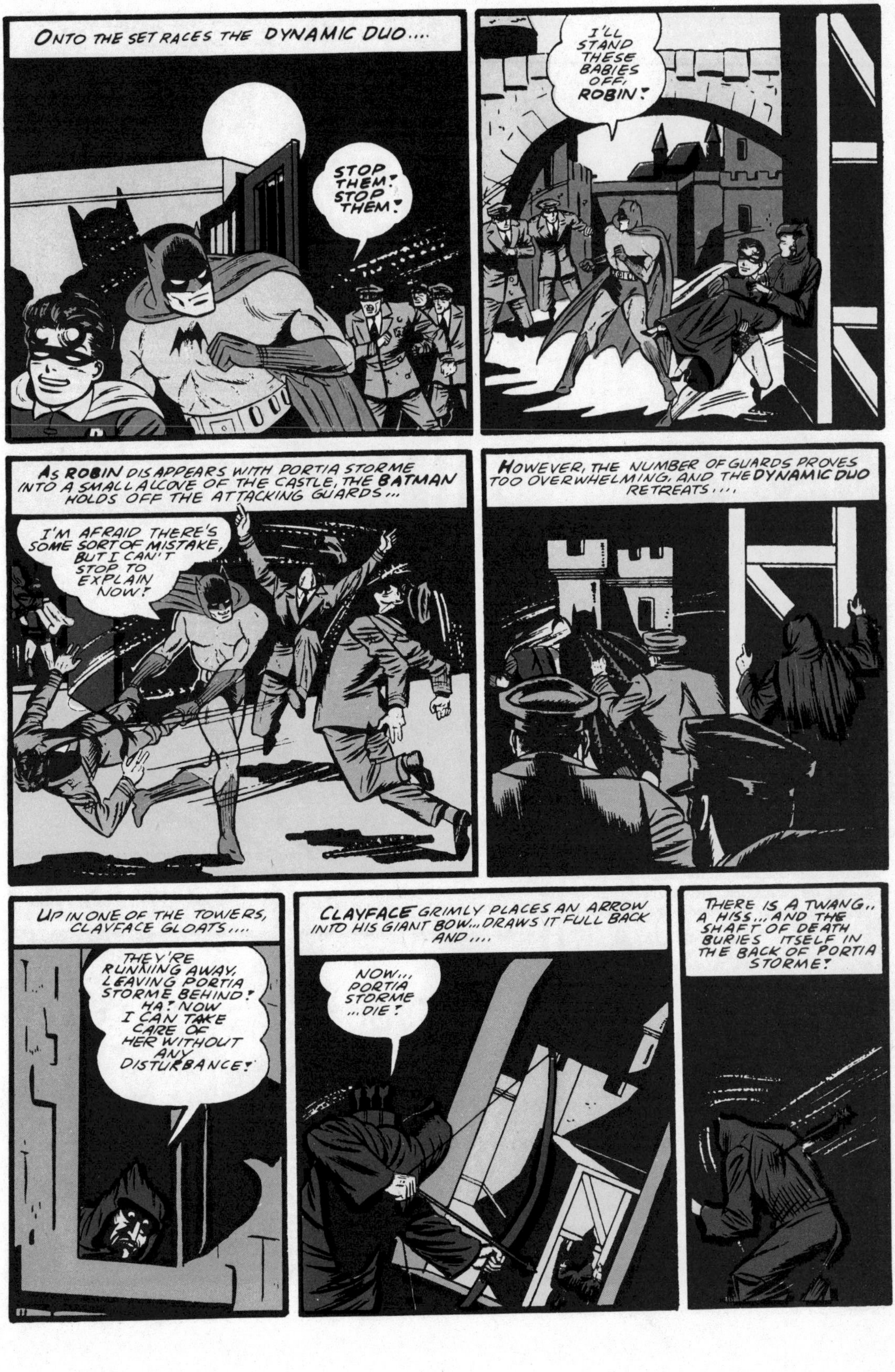
ONTO THE SET RACES THE DYNAMIC DUO....
STOP THEM! STOP THEM!
I'LL STAND THESE BABIES OFF, ROBIN!
AS ROBIN DISAPPEARS WITH PORTIA STORME INTO A SMALL ALCOVE OF THE CASTLE, THE BATMAN HOLDS OFF THE ATTACKING GUARDS...
I'M AFRAID THERE'S SOME SORT OF MISTAKE, BUT I CAN'T STOP TO EXPLAIN NOW!
HOWEVER, THE NUMBER OF GUARDS PROVES TOO OVERWHELMING, AND THE DYNAMIC DUO RETREATS....
UP IN ONE OF THE TOWERS, CLAYFACE GLOATS....
THEY'RE RUNNING AWAY, LEAVING PORTIA STORME BEHIND! HA! NOW I CAN TAKE CARE OF HER WITHOUT ANY DISTURBANCE!
CLAYFACE GRIMLY PLACES AN ARROW INTO HIS GIANT BOW...DRAWS IT FULL BACK AND....
NOW... PORTIA STORME ...DIE!
THERE IS A TWANG.. A HISS...AND THE SHAFT OF DEATH BURIES ITSELF IN THE BACK OF PORTIA STORME!

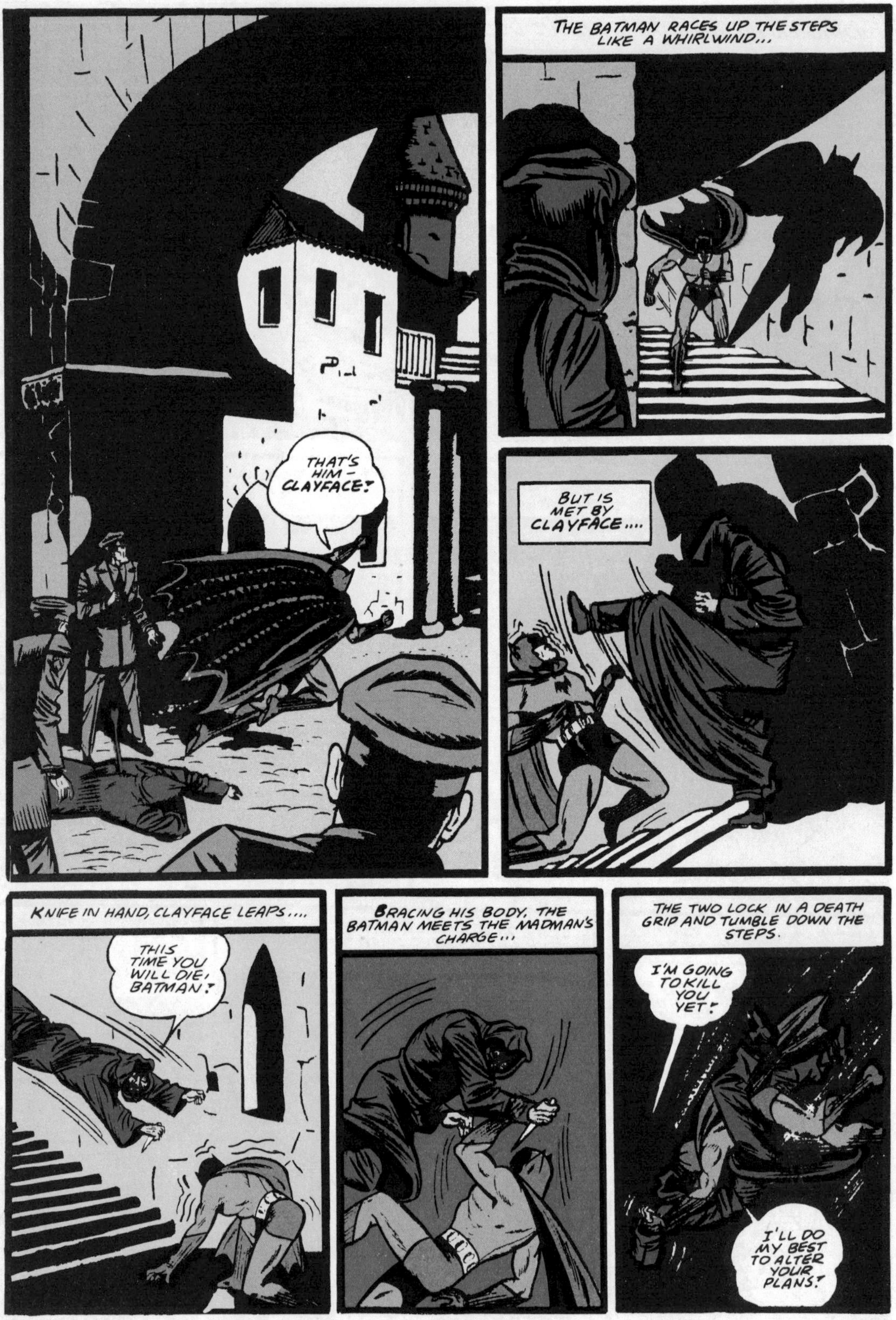
THAT'S HIM— CLAYFACE!
THE BATMAN RACES UP THE STEPS LIKE A WHIRLWIND...
BUT IS MET BY CLAYFACE....
KNIFE IN HAND, CLAYFACE LEAPS....
THIS TIME YOU WILL DIE, BATMAN!
BRACING HIS BODY, THE BATMAN MEETS THE MADMAN'S CHARGE...
THE TWO LOCK IN A DEATH GRIP AND TUMBLE DOWN THE STEPS.
I'M GOING TO KILL YOU YET!
I'LL DO MY BEST TO ALTER YOUR PLANS!

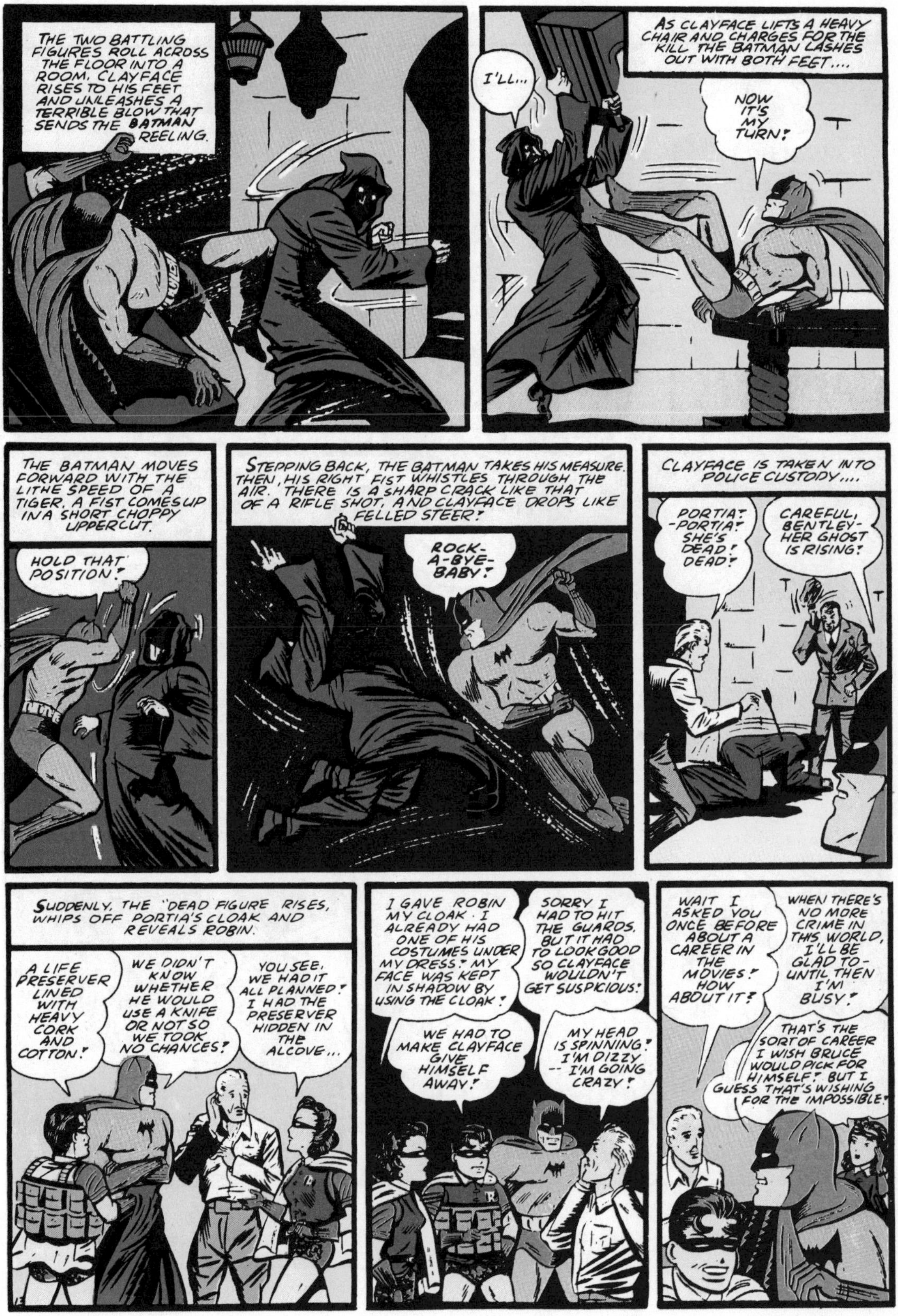

THE TWO BATTLING FIGURES ROLL ACROSS THE FLOOR INTO A ROOM. CLAYFACE RISES TO HIS FEET AND UNLEASHES A TERRIBLE BLOW THAT SENDS THE BATMAN REELING.
AS CLAYFACE LIFTS A HEAVY CHAIR AND CHARGES FOR THE KILL THE BATMAN LASHES OUT WITH BOTH FEET....
I'LL...
NOW IT'S MY TURN!
THE BATMAN MOVES FORWARD WITH THE LITHE SPEED OF A TIGER. A FIST COMES UP IN A SHORT CHOPPY UPPERCUT.
HOLD THAT POSITION!
STEPPING BACK, THE BATMAN TAKES HIS MEASURE. THEN, HIS RIGHT FIST WHISTLES THROUGH THE AIR. THERE IS A SHARP CRACK LIKE THAT OF A RIFLE SHOT, AND CLAYFACE DROPS LIKE FELLED STEER!
ROCK-A-BYE-BABY!
CLAYFACE IS TAKEN INTO POLICE CUSTODY....
PORTIA! -PORTIA! SHE'S DEAD! DEAD!
CAREFUL, BENTLEY-HER GHOST IS RISING!
SUDDENLY, THE "DEAD FIGURE RISES, WHIPS OFF PORTIA'S CLOAK AND REVEALS ROBIN.
A LIFE PRESERVER LINED WITH HEAVY CORK AND COTTON!
WE DIDN'T KNOW WHETHER HE WOULD USE A KNIFE OR NOT SO WE TOOK NO CHANCES!
YOU SEE, WE HAD IT ALL PLANNED! I HAD THE PRESERVER HIDDEN IN THE ALCOVE...
I GAVE ROBIN MY CLOAK. I ALREADY HAD ONE OF HIS COSTUMES UNDER MY DRESS! MY FACE WAS KEPT IN SHADOW BY USING THE CLOAK!
SORRY I HAD TO HIT THE GUARDS, BUT IT HAD TO LOOK GOOD SO CLAYFACE WOULDN'T GET SUSPICIOUS!
WE HAD TO MAKE CLAYFACE GIVE HIMSELF AWAY!
MY HEAD IS SPINNING! I'M DIZZY -- I'M GOING CRAZY!
WAIT I ASKED YOU ONCE BEFORE ABOUT A CAREER IN THE MOVIES! HOW ABOUT IT?
WHEN THERE'S NO MORE CRIME IN THIS WORLD, I'LL BE GLAD TO-UNTIL THEN I'M BUSY!
THAT'S THE SORT OF CAREER I WISH BRUCE WOULD PICK FOR HIMSELF! BUT I GUESS THAT'S WISHING FOR THE IMPOSSIBLE!

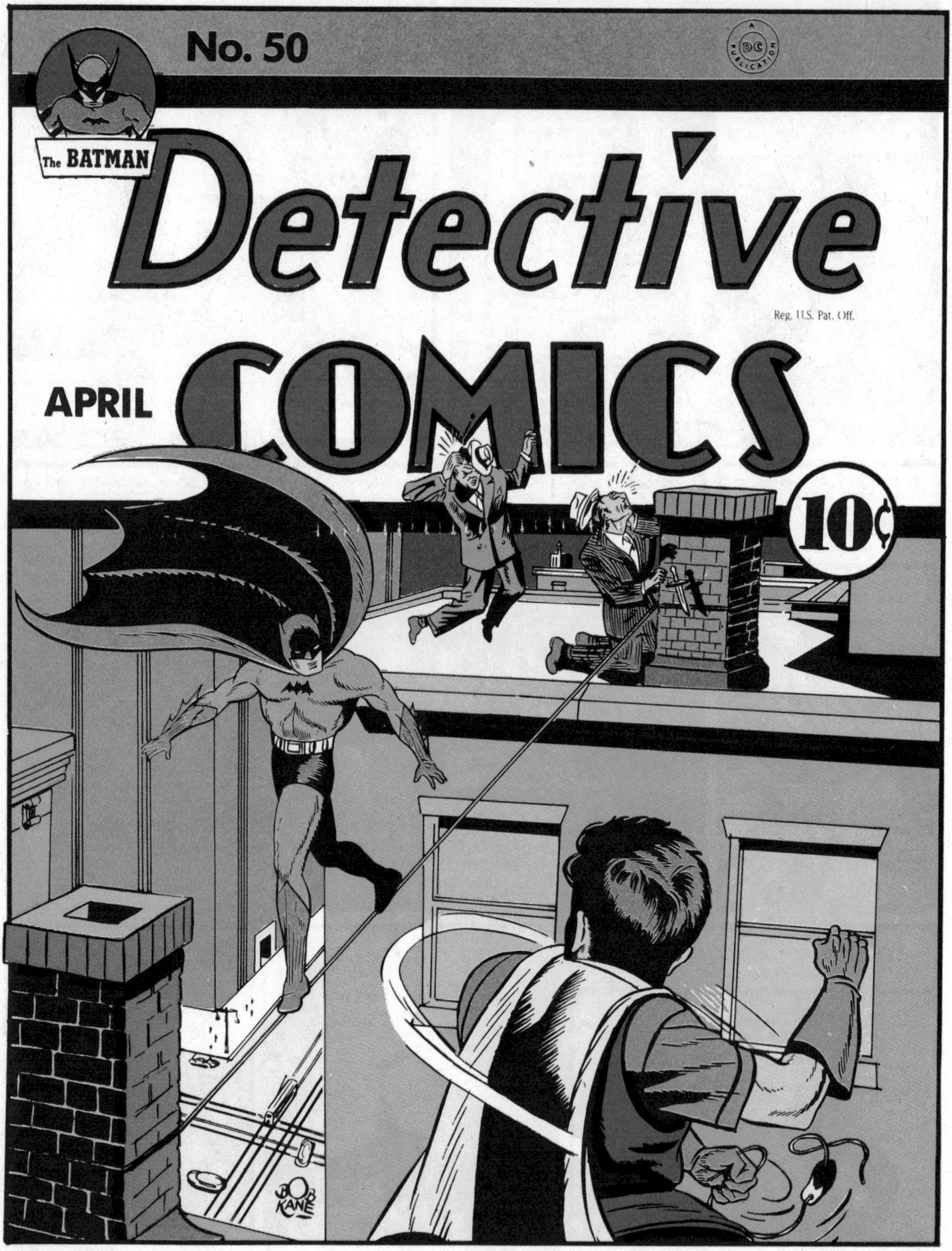
No. 50
A DC PUBLICATION
The BATMAN
Detective
Reg. U.S. Pat. Off.
APRIL
COMICS
10¢
BOB KANE

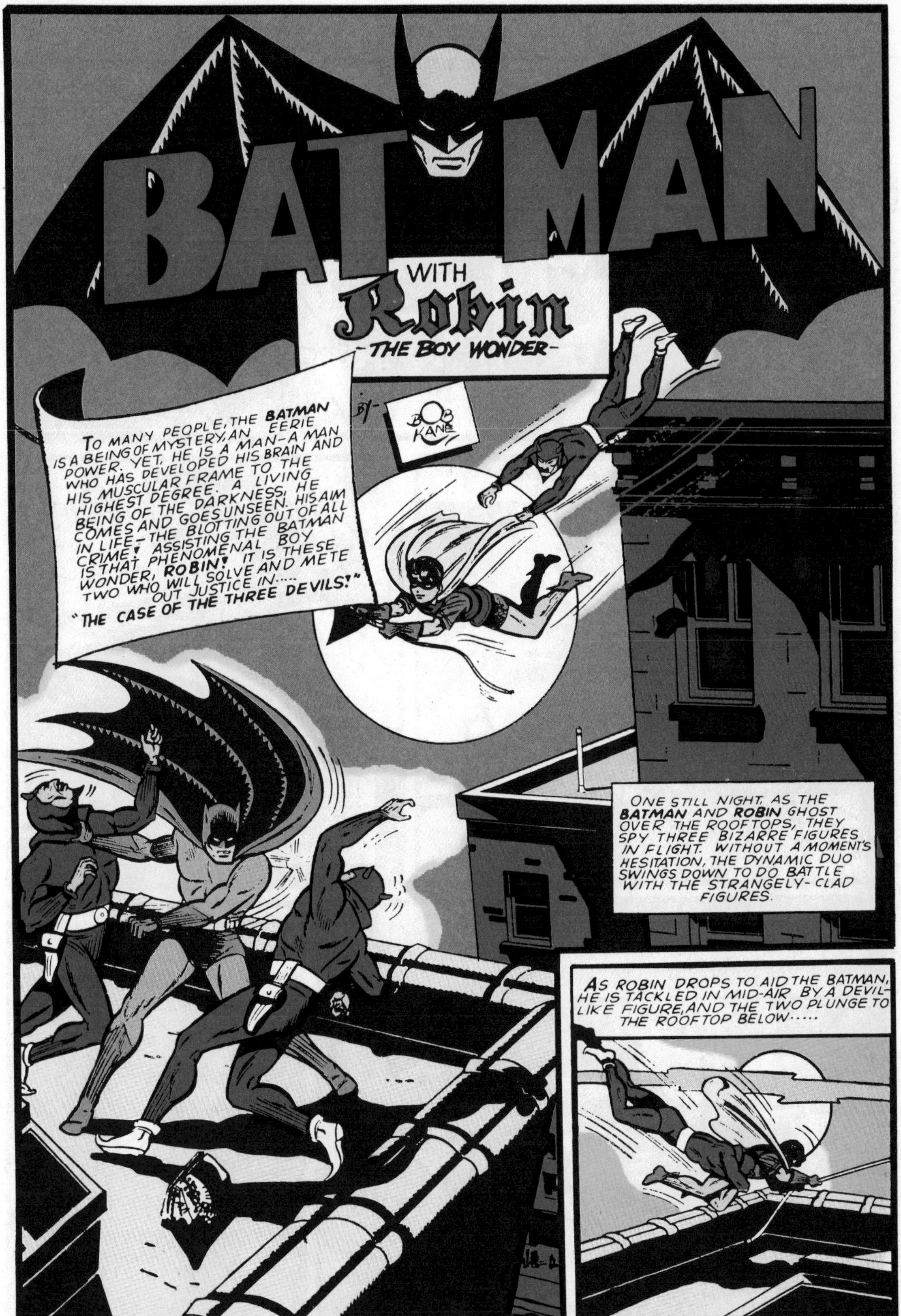
BATMAN
WITH
Robin
-THE BOY WONDER-
BY-
BOB KANE
TO MANY PEOPLE, THE BATMAN IS A BEING OF MYSTERY, AN EERIE POWER. YET, HE IS A MAN—A MAN WHO HAS DEVELOPED HIS BRAIN AND HIS MUSCULAR FRAME TO THE HIGHEST DEGREE. A LIVING BEING OF THE DARKNESS, HE COMES AND GOES UNSEEN. HIS AIM IN LIFE—THE BLOTTING OUT OF ALL CRIME! ASSISTING THE BATMAN IS THAT PHENOMENAL BOY WONDER, ROBIN! IT IS THESE TWO WHO WILL SOLVE AND METE OUT JUSTICE IN.....
"THE CASE OF THE THREE DEVILS!"
ONE STILL NIGHT, AS THE BATMAN AND ROBIN GHOST OVER THE ROOFTOPS, THEY SPY THREE BIZARRE FIGURES IN FLIGHT. WITHOUT A MOMENT'S HESITATION, THE DYNAMIC DUO SWINGS DOWN TO DO BATTLE WITH THE STRANGELY-CLAD FIGURES.
AS ROBIN DROPS TO AID THE BATMAN, HE IS TACKLED IN MID-AIR BY A DEVIL-LIKE FIGURE, AND THE TWO PLUNGE TO THE ROOFTOP BELOW.....

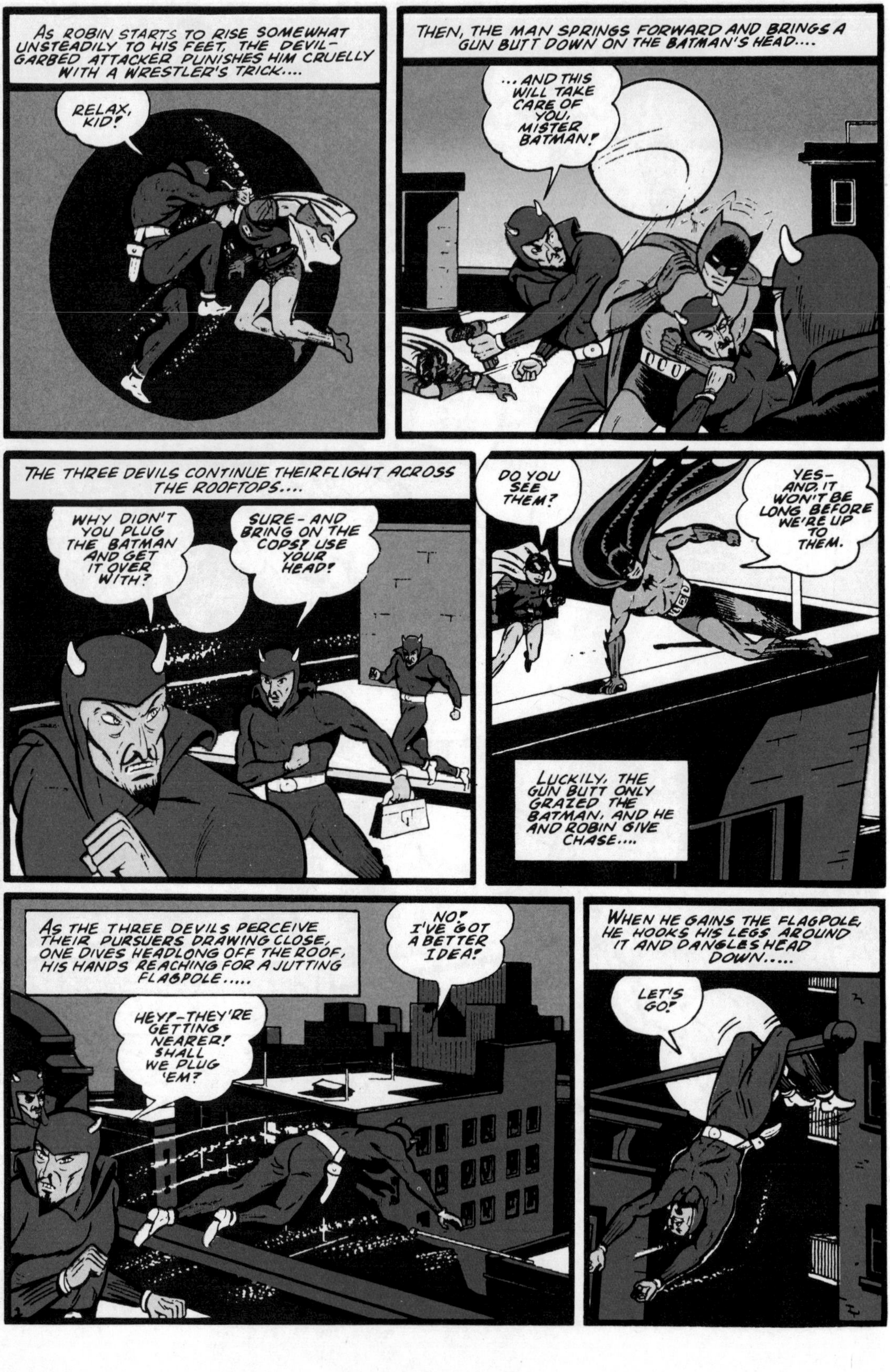
AS ROBIN STARTS TO RISE SOMEWHAT UNSTEADILY TO HIS FEET, THE DEVIL-GARBED ATTACKER PUNISHES HIM CRUELLY WITH A WRESTLER'S TRICK....
RELAX, KID!
THEN, THE MAN SPRINGS FORWARD AND BRINGS A GUN BUTT DOWN ON THE BATMAN'S HEAD....
...AND THIS WILL TAKE CARE OF YOU, MISTER BATMAN!
THE THREE DEVILS CONTINUE THEIR FLIGHT ACROSS THE ROOFTOPS....
WHY DIDN'T YOU PLUG THE BATMAN AND GET IT OVER WITH?
SURE- AND BRING ON THE COPS? USE YOUR HEAD!
DO YOU SEE THEM?
YES- AND, IT WON'T BE LONG BEFORE WE'RE UP TO THEM.
LUCKILY, THE GUN BUTT ONLY GRAZED THE BATMAN, AND HE AND ROBIN GIVE CHASE....
AS THE THREE DEVILS PERCEIVE THEIR PURSUERS DRAWING CLOSE, ONE DIVES HEADLONG OFF THE ROOF, HIS HANDS REACHING FOR A JUTTING FLAGPOLE.....
HEY!-THEY'RE GETTING NEARER! SHALL WE PLUG 'EM?
NO! I'VE GOT A BETTER IDEA!
WHEN HE GAINS THE FLAGPOLE, HE HOOKS HIS LEGS AROUND IT AND DANGLES HEAD DOWN.....
LET'S GO!

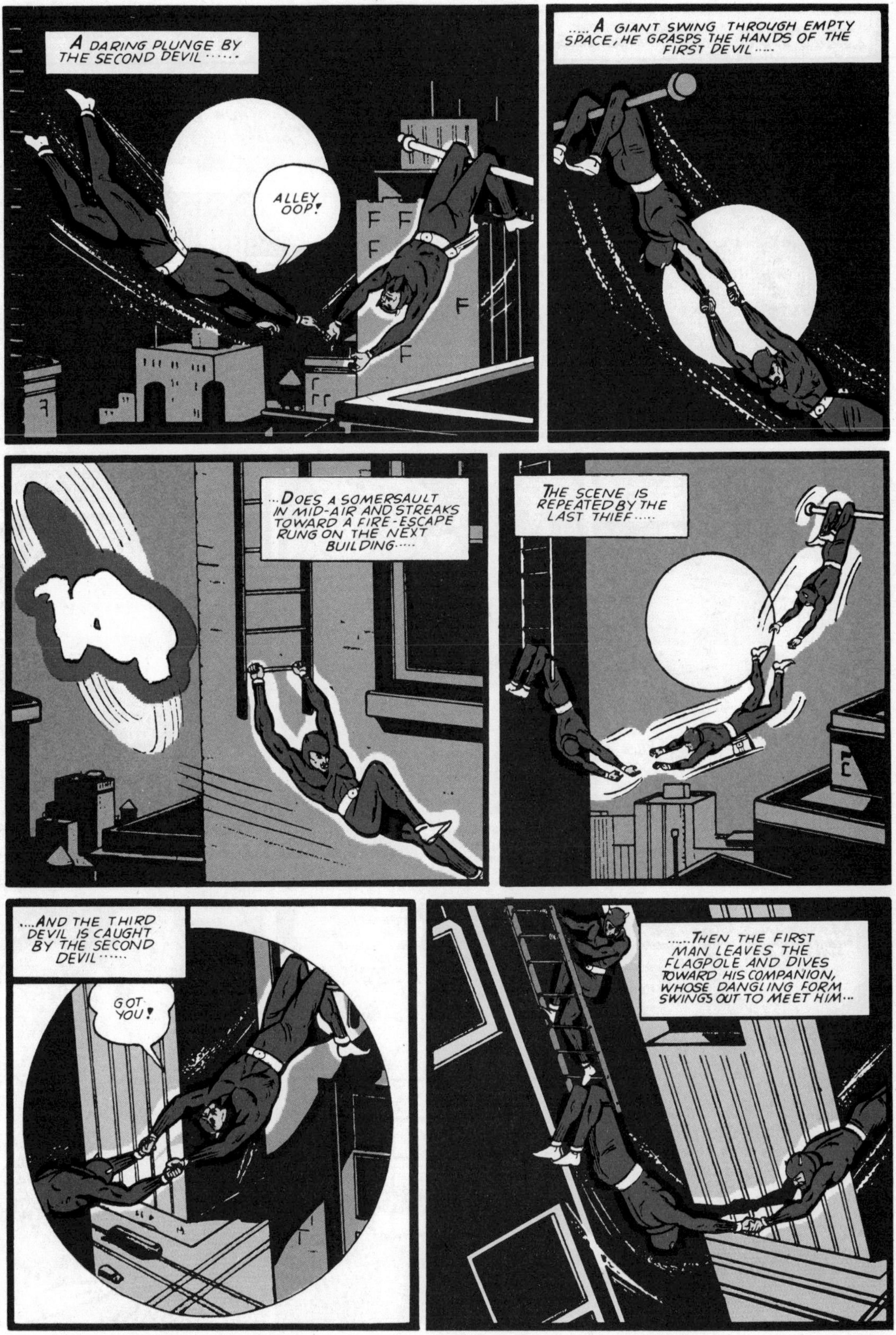
A DARING PLUNGE BY THE SECOND DEVIL......
ALLEY OOP!
.....A GIANT SWING THROUGH EMPTY SPACE, HE GRASPS THE HANDS OF THE FIRST DEVIL.....
...DOES A SOMERSAULT IN MID-AIR AND STREAKS TOWARD A FIRE-ESCAPE RUNG ON THE NEXT BUILDING.....
THE SCENE IS REPEATED BY THE LAST THIEF.....
....AND THE THIRD DEVIL IS CAUGHT BY THE SECOND DEVIL......
GOT YOU!
......THEN THE FIRST MAN LEAVES THE FLAGPOLE AND DIVES TOWARD HIS COMPANION, WHOSE DANGLING FORM SWINGS OUT TO MEET HIM...

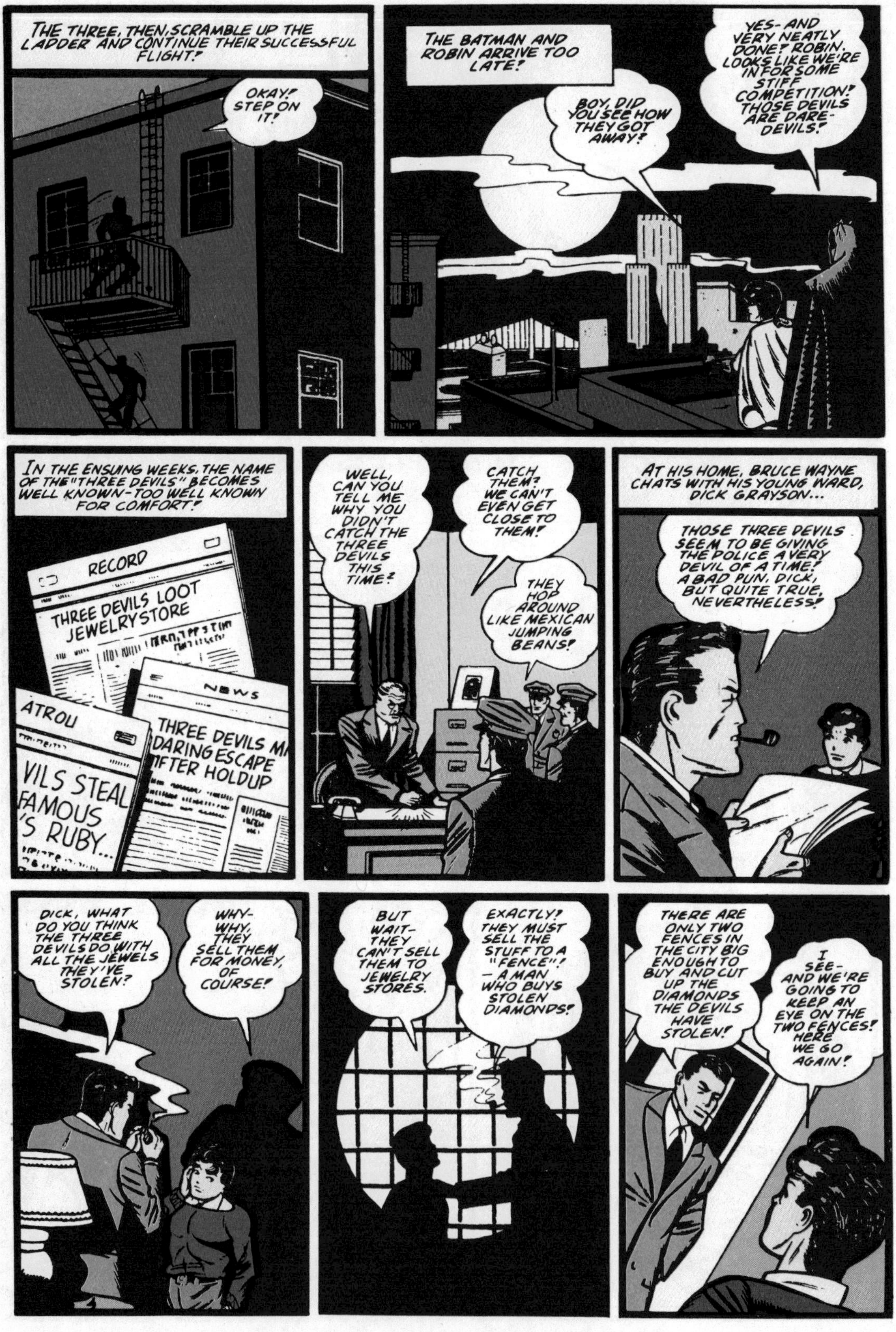
THE THREE, THEN, SCRAMBLE UP THE LADDER AND CONTINUE THEIR SUCCESSFUL FLIGHT!
OKAY! STEP ON IT!
THE BATMAN AND ROBIN ARRIVE TOO LATE!
BOY, DID YOU SEE HOW THEY GOT AWAY?
YES- AND VERY NEATLY DONE! ROBIN. LOOKS LIKE WE'RE IN FOR SOME STIFF COMPETITION! THOSE DEVILS ARE DARE-DEVILS!
IN THE ENSUING WEEKS, THE NAME OF THE "THREE DEVILS" BECOMES WELL KNOWN-TOO WELL KNOWN FOR COMFORT!
RECORD
THREE DEVILS LOOT JEWELRYSTORE
NEWS
THREE DEVILS M
DARING ESCAPE
IFTER HOLDUP
ATROU
VILS STEAL
FAMOUS
'S RUBY...
WELL, CAN YOU TELL ME WHY YOU DIDN'T CATCH THE THREE DEVILS THIS TIME?
CATCH THEM? WE CAN'T EVEN GET CLOSE TO THEM!
THEY HOP AROUND LIKE MEXICAN JUMPING BEANS!
AT HIS HOME, BRUCE WAYNE CHATS WITH HIS YOUNG WARD, DICK GRAYSON...
THOSE THREE DEVILS SEEM TO BE GIVING THE POLICE A VERY DEVIL OF A TIME! A BAD PUN, DICK, BUT QUITE TRUE, NEVERTHELESS!
DICK, WHAT DO YOU THINK THE THREE DEVILS DO WITH ALL THE JEWELS THEY'VE STOLEN?
WHY- WHY, THEY SELL THEM FOR MONEY, OF COURSE!
BUT WAIT- THEY CAN'T SELL THEM TO JEWELRY STORES.
EXACTLY! THEY MUST SELL THE STUFF TO A "FENCE"! - A MAN WHO BUYS STOLEN DIAMONDS!
THERE ARE ONLY TWO FENCES IN THE CITY BIG ENOUGH TO BUY AND CUT UP THE DIAMONDS THE DEVILS HAVE STOLEN!
I SEE- AND WE'RE GOING TO KEEP AN EYE ON THE TWO FENCES! HERE WE GO AGAIN!

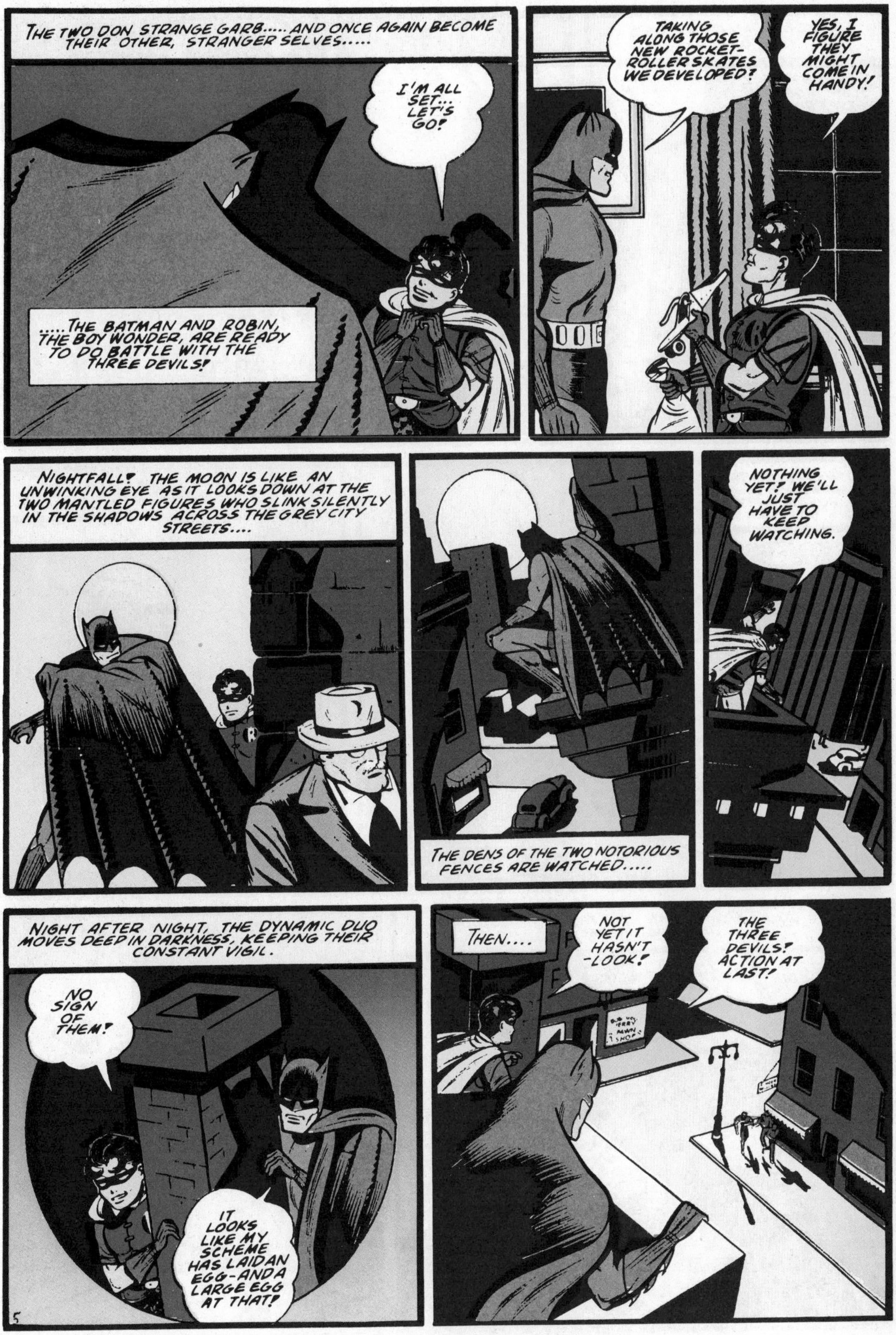
THE TWO DON STRANGE GARB..... AND ONCE AGAIN BECOME THEIR OTHER, STRANGER SELVES.....
I'M ALL SET... LET'S GO!
.....THE BATMAN AND ROBIN, THE BOY WONDER, ARE READY TO DO BATTLE WITH THE THREE DEVILS!
TAKING ALONG THOSE NEW ROCKET-ROLLER SKATES WE DEVELOPED?
YES, I FIGURE THEY MIGHT COME IN HANDY!
NIGHTFALL! THE MOON IS LIKE AN UNWINKING EYE AS IT LOOKS DOWN AT THE TWO MANTLED FIGURES WHO SLINK SILENTLY IN THE SHADOWS ACROSS THE GREY CITY STREETS....
THE DENS OF THE TWO NOTORIOUS FENCES ARE WATCHED.....
NOTHING YET! WE'LL JUST HAVE TO KEEP WATCHING.
NIGHT AFTER NIGHT, THE DYNAMIC DUO MOVES DEEP IN DARKNESS, KEEPING THEIR CONSTANT VIGIL.
NO SIGN OF THEM!
IT LOOKS LIKE MY SCHEME HAS LAID AN EGG-AND A LARGE EGG AT THAT!
5
THEN....
NOT YET IT HASN'T -LOOK!
THE THREE DEVILS! ACTION AT LAST!

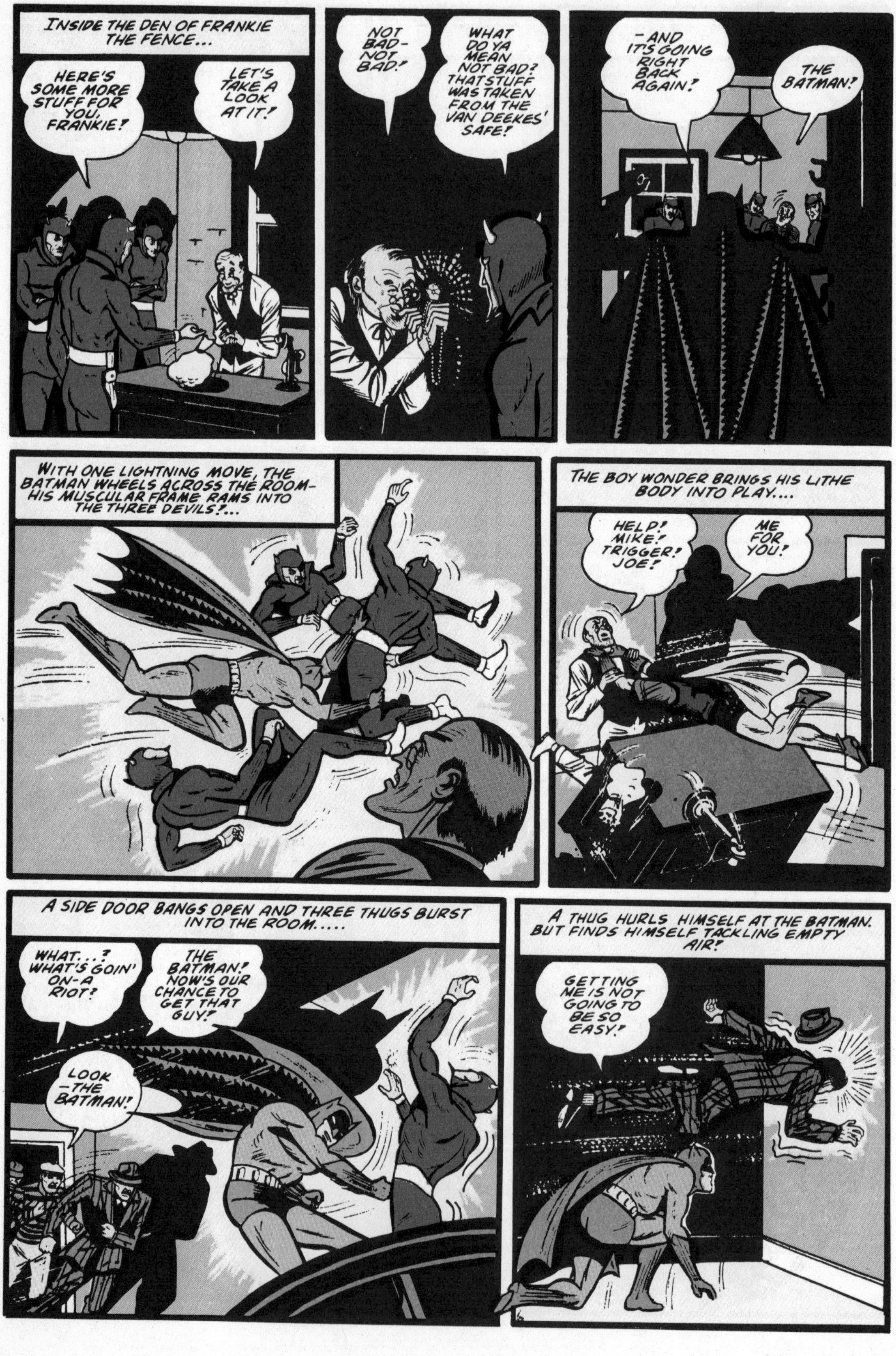

INSIDE THE DEN OF FRANKIE THE FENCE...
HERE'S SOME MORE STUFF FOR YOU, FRANKIE!
LET'S TAKE A LOOK AT IT!
NOT BAD- NOT BAD!
WHAT DO YA MEAN NOT BAD? THAT STUFF WAS TAKEN FROM THE VAN DEEKES' SAFE!
-AND IT'S GOING RIGHT BACK AGAIN!
THE BATMAN!
WITH ONE LIGHTNING MOVE, THE BATMAN WHEELS ACROSS THE ROOM- HIS MUSCULAR FRAME RAMS INTO THE THREE DEVILS!...
THE BOY WONDER BRINGS HIS LITHE BODY INTO PLAY....
HELP! MIKE! TRIGGER! JOE!
ME FOR YOU!
A SIDE DOOR BANGS OPEN AND THREE THUGS BURST INTO THE ROOM.....
WHAT...? WHAT'S GOIN' ON-A RIOT?
THE BATMAN! NOW'S OUR CHANCE TO GET THAT GUY!
LOOK -THE BATMAN!
A THUG HURLS HIMSELF AT THE BATMAN. BUT FINDS HIMSELF TACKLING EMPTY AIR!
GETTING ME IS NOT GOING TO BE SO EASY!

THAT'S WHAT I WANT! OOPS... PARDON ME!

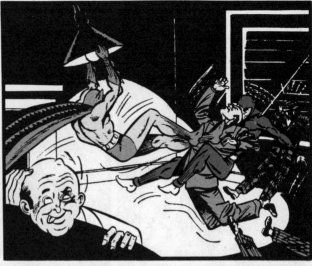

THE BATMAN AND ROBIN HOLD THEIR OWN AGAINST ODDS!

NICE LITTLE RIOT WE STARTED, EH, ROBIN?

IT'S NOT SO BAD!

I'D BE SAFER FIGHTING A TIGER THAN THE BATMAN, WOW!?

FRANKIE WHIPS OUT A GLEAMING KNIFE, AND CIRCLING BEHIND THE BATMAN, RAISES IT ALOFT FOR THE PLUNGE.....

AWK!

BONK!

CRIME DOES NOT PAY! by Rodmann Krueger

I DON'T KNOW HOW THIS BOOK GOT MIXED UP IN YOUR PLACE, BUT IT'S A CINCH YOU NEVER READ IT!

TRIGGER GETS DESPERATE AND LIVES UP TO HIS NAME.... AVOIDING THE WHINING BULLETS, THE BATMAN GRAZES HIS HEAD ON THE EDGE OF THE TABLE!

I'LL STOP YA!

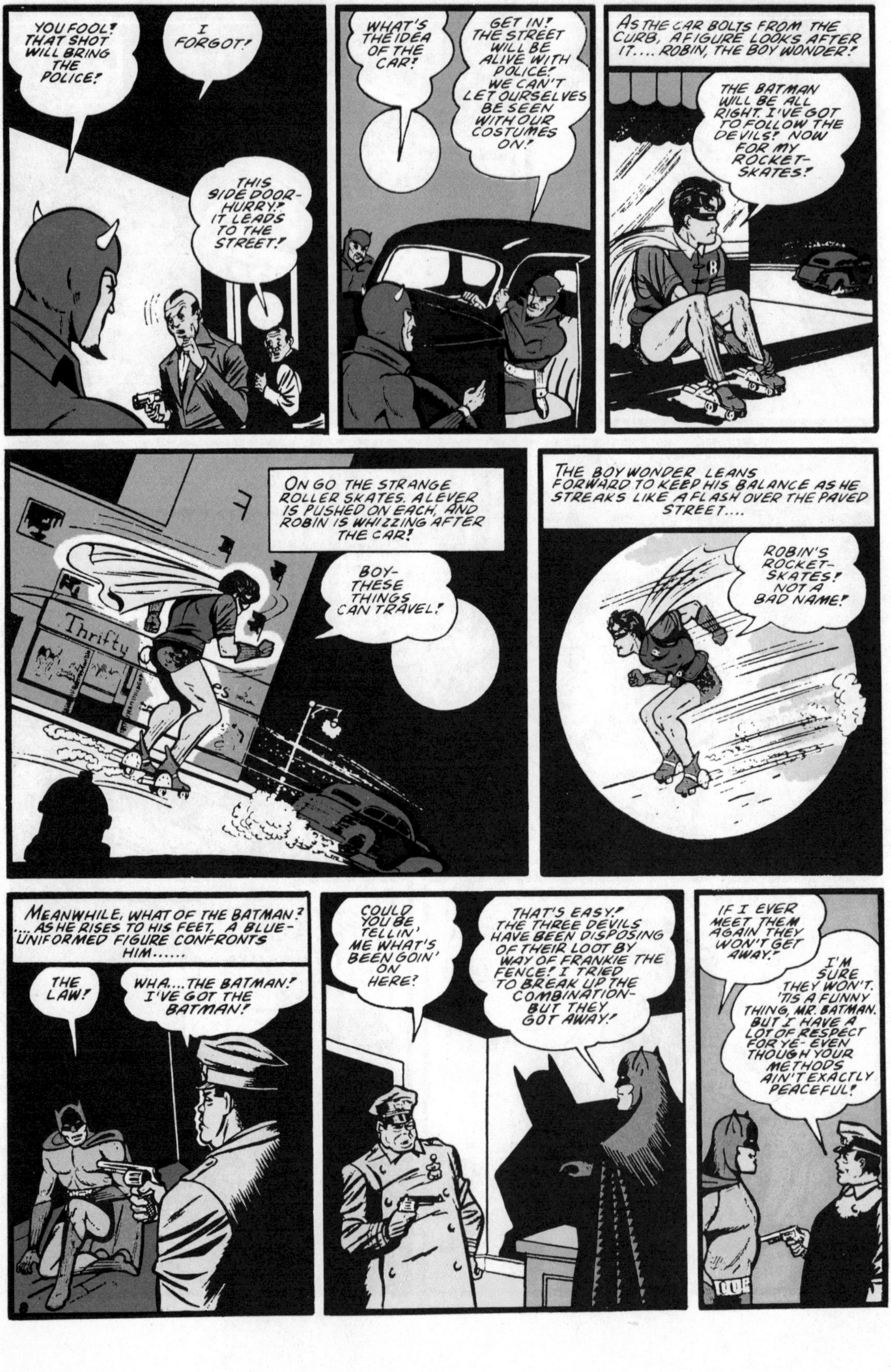
YOU FOOL! THAT SHOT WILL BRING THE POLICE!
I FORGOT!
THIS SIDE DOOR-HURRY! IT LEADS TO THE STREET!
WHAT'S THE IDEA OF THE CAR?
GET IN! THE STREET WILL BE ALIVE WITH POLICE! WE CAN'T LET OURSELVES BE SEEN WITH OUR COSTUMES ON!
AS THE CAR BOLTS FROM THE CURB, A FIGURE LOOKS AFTER IT.... ROBIN, THE BOY WONDER!
THE BATMAN WILL BE ALL RIGHT. I'VE GOT TO FOLLOW THE DEVILS! NOW FOR MY ROCKET-SKATES!
ON GO THE STRANGE ROLLER SKATES. A LEVER IS PUSHED ON EACH, AND ROBIN IS WHIZZING AFTER THE CAR!
BOY-THESE THINGS CAN TRAVEL!
Thrifty
THE BOY WONDER LEANS FORWARD TO KEEP HIS BALANCE AS HE STREAKS LIKE A FLASH OVER THE PAVED STREET....
ROBIN'S ROCKET-SKATES! NOT A BAD NAME!
MEANWHILE, WHAT OF THE BATMAN? ....AS HE RISES TO HIS FEET, A BLUE-UNIFORMED FIGURE CONFRONTS HIM......
THE LAW!
WHA....THE BATMAN! I'VE GOT THE BATMAN!
COULD YOU BE TELLIN' ME WHAT'S BEEN GOIN' ON HERE?
THAT'S EASY! THE THREE DEVILS HAVE BEEN DISPOSING OF THEIR LOOT BY WAY OF FRANKIE THE FENCE! I TRIED TO BREAK UP THE COMBINATION-BUT THEY GOT AWAY!
IF I EVER MEET THEM AGAIN THEY WON'T GET AWAY!
I'M SURE THEY WON'T. 'TIS A FUNNY THING, MR. BATMAN. BUT I HAVE A LOT OF RESPECT FOR YE- EVEN THOUGH YOUR METHODS AIN'T EXACTLY PEACEFUL!

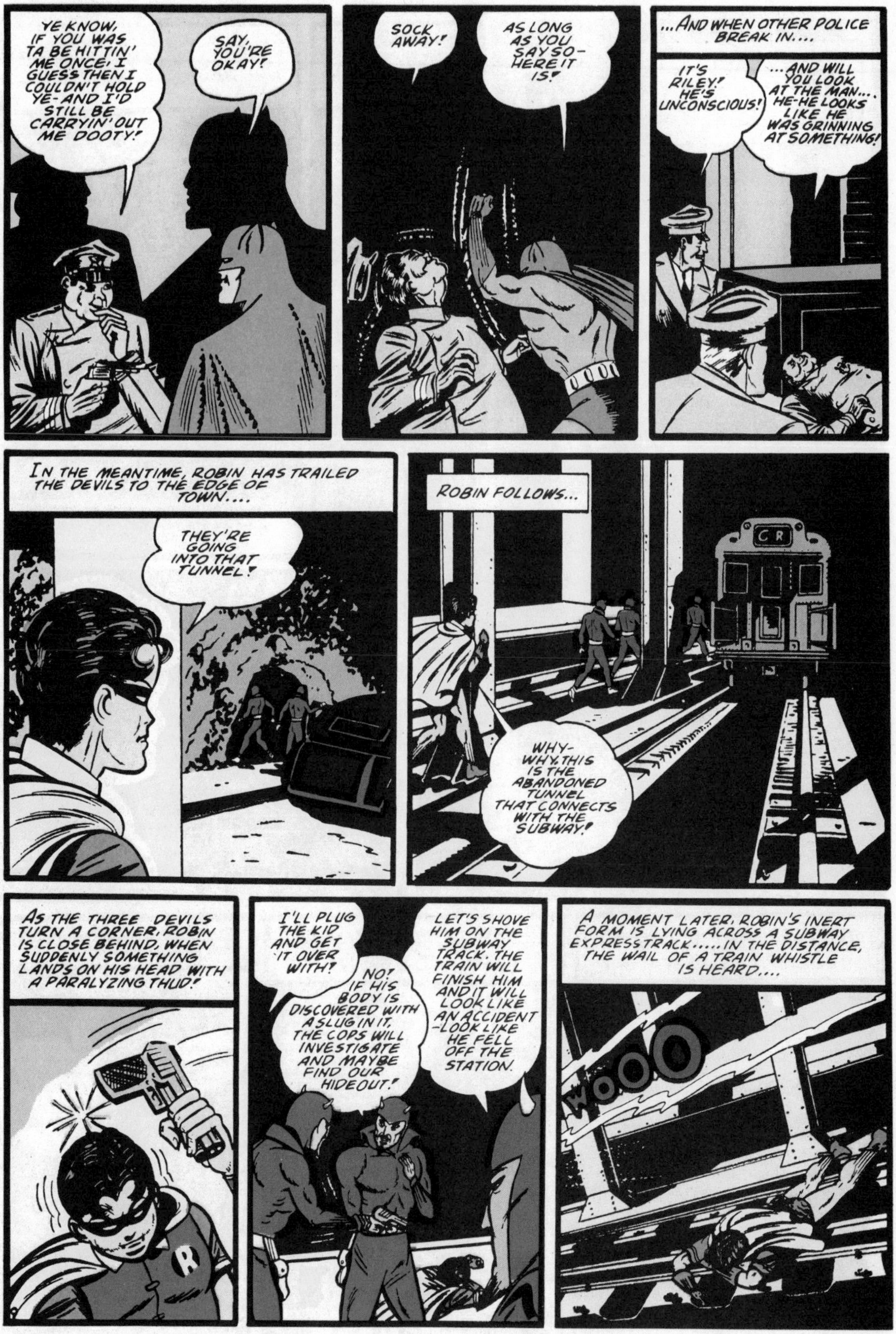
YE KNOW, IF YOU WAS TA BE HITTIN' ME ONCE, I GUESS THEN I COULDN'T HOLD YE-AND I'D STILL BE CARRYIN' OUT ME DOOTY!
SAY, YOU'RE OKAY!
SOCK AWAY!
AS LONG AS YOU SAY SO-HERE IT IS!
...AND WHEN OTHER POLICE BREAK IN....
IT'S RILEY! HE'S UNCONSCIOUS!
...AND WILL YOU LOOK AT THE MAN.... HE-HE LOOKS LIKE HE WAS GRINNING AT SOMETHING!
IN THE MEANTIME, ROBIN HAS TRAILED THE DEVILS TO THE EDGE OF TOWN....
THEY'RE GOING INTO THAT TUNNEL!
ROBIN FOLLOWS...
WHY-WHY, THIS IS THE ABANDONED TUNNEL THAT CONNECTS WITH THE SUBWAY!
AS THE THREE DEVILS TURN A CORNER, ROBIN IS CLOSE BEHIND, WHEN SUDDENLY SOMETHING LANDS ON HIS HEAD WITH A PARALYZING THUD!
I'LL PLUG THE KID AND GET IT OVER WITH!
NO! IF HIS BODY IS DISCOVERED WITH A SLUG IN IT, THE COPS WILL INVESTIGATE AND MAYBE FIND OUR HIDEOUT!
LET'S SHOVE HIM ON THE SUBWAY TRACK. THE TRAIN WILL FINISH HIM AND IT WILL LOOK LIKE AN ACCIDENT -LOOK LIKE HE FELL OFF THE STATION.
A MOMENT LATER, ROBIN'S INERT FORM IS LYING ACROSS A SUBWAY EXPRESS TRACK.....IN THE DISTANCE, THE WAIL OF A TRAIN WHISTLE IS HEARD....
WOOOO

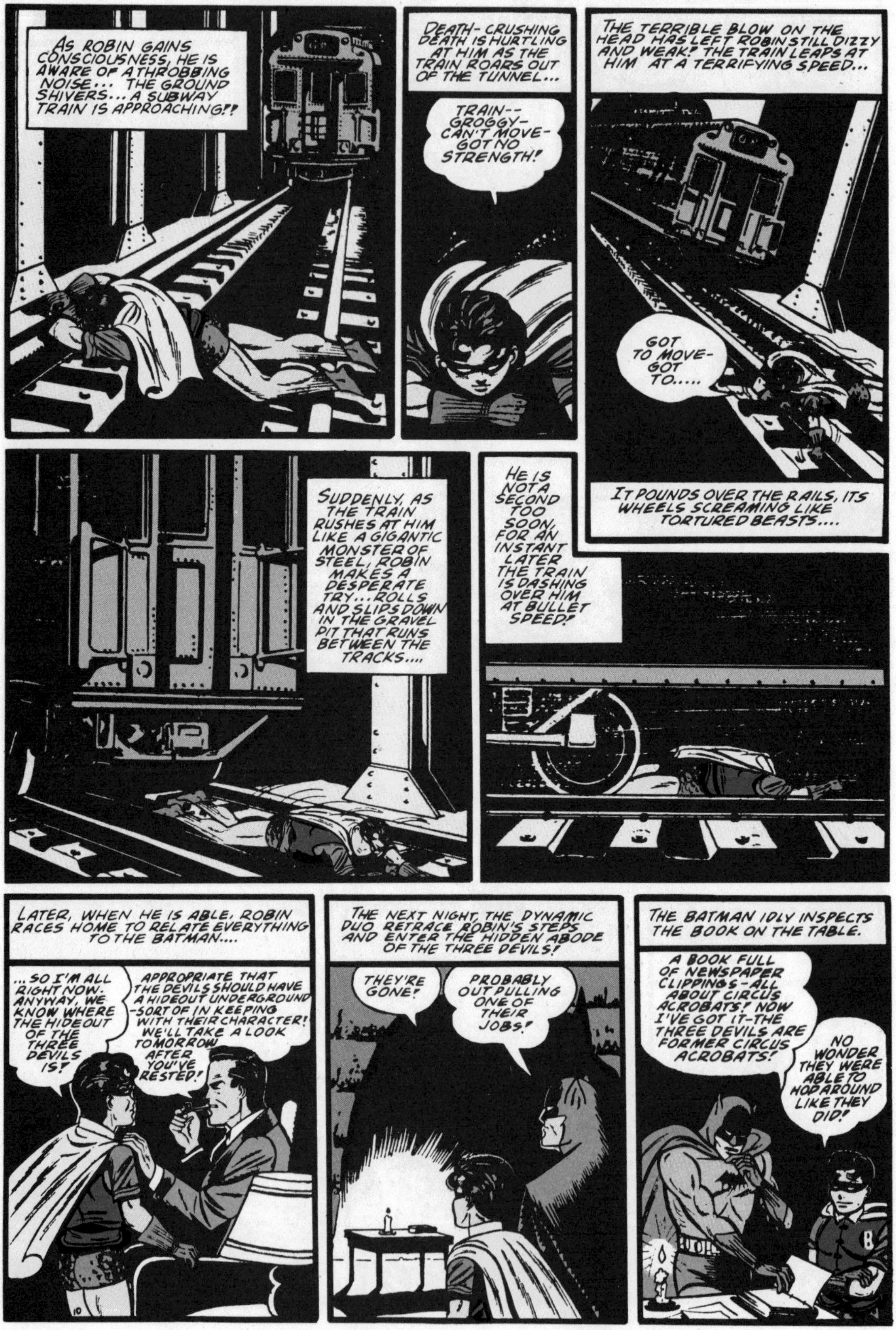
AS ROBIN GAINS CONSCIOUSNESS, HE IS AWARE OF A THROBBING NOISE... THE GROUND SHIVERS... A SUBWAY TRAIN IS APPROACHING!?!
DEATH- CRUSHING DEATH IS HURTLING AT HIM AS THE TRAIN ROARS OUT OF THE TUNNEL...
TRAIN-- GROGGY- CAN'T MOVE- GOT NO STRENGTH!
THE TERRIBLE BLOW ON THE HEAD HAS LEFT ROBIN STILL DIZZY AND WEAK! THE TRAIN LEAPS AT HIM AT A TERRIFYING SPEED...
GOT TO MOVE- GOT TO.....
IT POUNDS OVER THE RAILS, ITS WHEELS SCREAMING LIKE TORTURED BEASTS....
SUDDENLY, AS THE TRAIN RUSHES AT HIM LIKE A GIGANTIC MONSTER OF STEEL, ROBIN MAKES A DESPERATE TRY... ROLLS AND SLIPS DOWN IN THE GRAVEL PIT THAT RUNS BETWEEN THE TRACKS....
HE IS NOT A SECOND TOO SOON, FOR AN INSTANT LATER THE TRAIN IS DASHING OVER HIM AT BULLET SPEED!
LATER, WHEN HE IS ABLE, ROBIN RACES HOME TO RELATE EVERYTHING TO THE BATMAN....
...SO I'M ALL RIGHT NOW- ANYWAY, WE KNOW WHERE THE HIDEOUT OF THE THREE DEVILS IS!
APPROPRIATE THAT THE DEVILS SHOULD HAVE A HIDEOUT UNDERGROUND -SORT OF IN KEEPING WITH THEIR CHARACTER! WE'LL TAKE A LOOK TOMORROW AFTER YOU'VE RESTED!
10
THE NEXT NIGHT, THE DYNAMIC DUO RETRACE ROBIN'S STEPS AND ENTER THE HIDDEN ABODE OF THE THREE DEVILS!
THEY'RE GONE!
PROBABLY OUT PULLING ONE OF THEIR JOBS!
THE BATMAN IDLY INSPECTS THE BOOK ON THE TABLE.
A BOOK FULL OF NEWSPAPER CLIPPINGS - ALL ABOUT CIRCUS ACROBATS! NOW I'VE GOT IT- THE THREE DEVILS ARE FORMER CIRCUS ACROBATS!
NO WONDER THEY WERE ABLE TO HOP AROUND LIKE THEY DID!

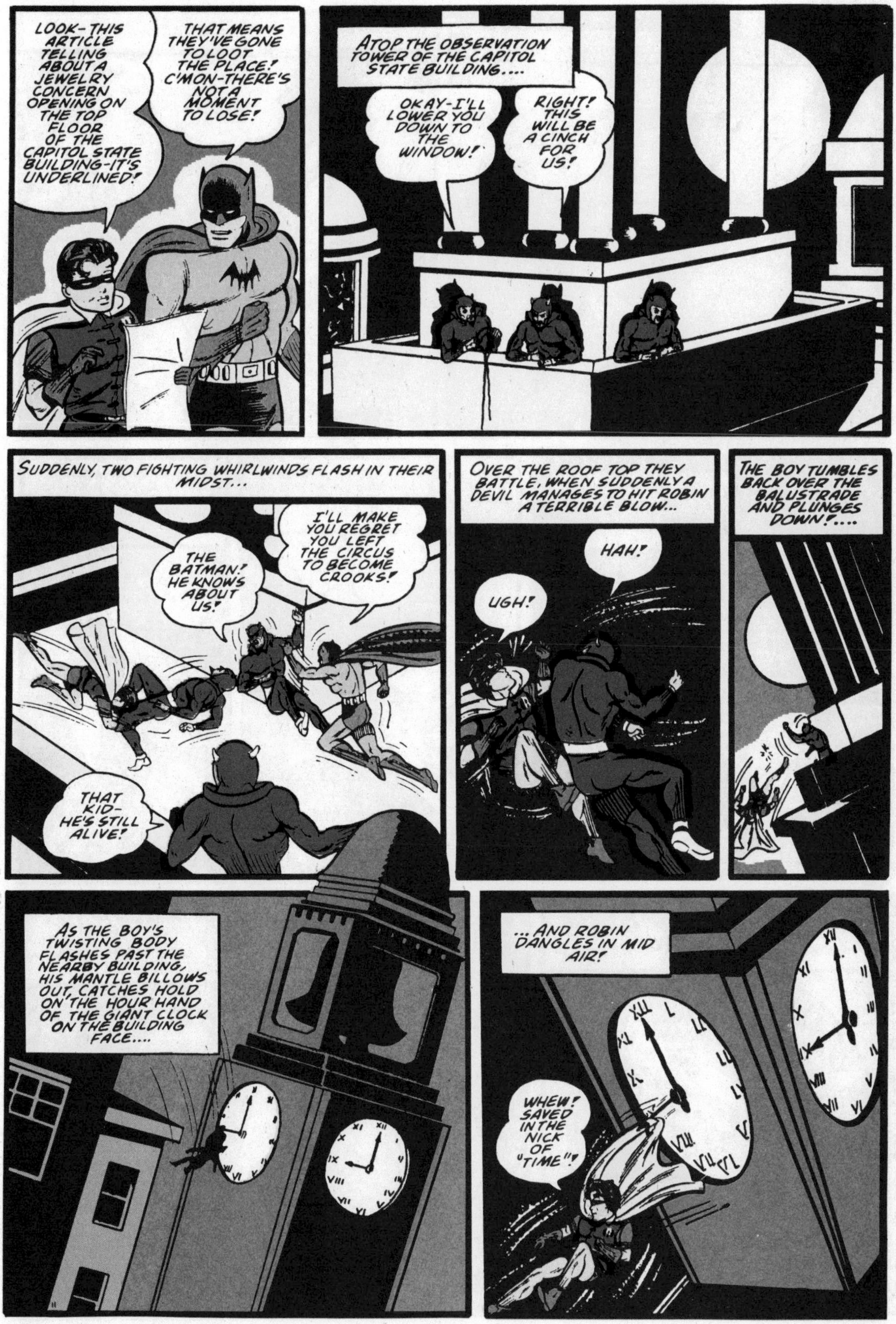
LOOK-THIS ARTICLE TELLING ABOUT A JEWELRY CONCERN OPENING ON THE TOP FLOOR OF THE CAPITOL STATE BUILDING-IT'S UNDERLINED!
THAT MEANS THEY'VE GONE TO LOOT THE PLACE! C'MON-THERE'S NOT A MOMENT TO LOSE!
ATOP THE OBSERVATION TOWER OF THE CAPITOL STATE BUILDING....
OKAY-I'LL LOWER YOU DOWN TO THE WINDOW!
RIGHT! THIS WILL BE A CINCH FOR US!
SUDDENLY, TWO FIGHTING WHIRLWINDS FLASH IN THEIR MIDST...
THE BATMAN! HE KNOWS ABOUT US!
I'LL MAKE YOU REGRET YOU LEFT THE CIRCUS TO BECOME CROOKS!
THAT KID- HE'S STILL ALIVE!
OVER THE ROOF TOP THEY BATTLE, WHEN SUDDENLY A DEVIL MANAGES TO HIT ROBIN A TERRIBLE BLOW...
HAH!
UGH!
THE BOY TUMBLES BACK OVER THE BALUSTRADE AND PLUNGES DOWN!....
AS THE BOY'S TWISTING BODY FLASHES PAST THE NEARBY BUILDING, HIS MANTLE BILLOWS OUT, CATCHES HOLD ON THE HOUR HAND OF THE GIANT CLOCK ON THE BUILDING FACE....
...AND ROBIN DANGLES IN MID AIR!
WHEW! SAVED IN THE NICK OF "TIME"!

THE BATMAN MAKES A DESPERATE LEAP FOR THE BELFRY TOWER....

THAT CAPE WON'T STAND THE STRAIN VERY LONG! I'VE GOT TO HELP! THAT BELFRY TOWER... I MAY BE ABLE TO REACH HIM FROM THERE!

THE THREE DEVILS SPRING AFTER THE BATMAN!

HE'S THE ONLY ONE WHO KNOWS WHO WE ARE!

WE'VE GOT TO KILL HIM TO PROTECT OURSELVES!

HIGH UP ON THE BELL TOWER CROSS-BEAMS, THERE IS A TITANIC STRUGGLE...

MEANWHILE, AS ROBIN DANGLES PERILOUSLY IN SPACE, A MURDEROUS DEVIL LEVELS A GUN AT HIS HELPLESS FIGURE...

NOW'S MY CHANCE TO GET THAT KID - I CAN'T MISS...

A CREAKING BOARD WARNS ROBIN, WHOSE HAND DARTS IN HIS JERKIN AND PRODUCES THE SLING-SHOT!

NOT A SECOND TO LOSE...

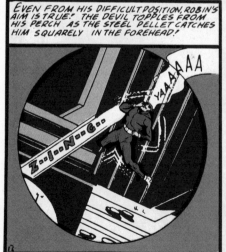

EVEN FROM HIS DIFFICULT POSITION, ROBIN'S AIM IS TRUE! THE DEVIL TOPPLES FROM HIS PERCH AS THE STEEL PELLET CATCHES HIM SQUARELY IN THE FOREHEAD!

YAAAAAA

Z-I-N-G

SUDDENLY, THE CLOCK INDICATES NINE O'CLOCK! UP IN THE BELFRY, MACHINERY SETS THE BELL IN MOTION TO TOLL THE HOUR...

THE HOUR - NOW'S MY CHANCE!

THE BATMAN SPRINGS...

AS THE BATMAN CATCHES THE CLAPPER, THE BELL SWINGS OUT...

RING! RING!

RING OUT, WILD BELLS!

RING!

...THEN AS IT SWINGS BACK AGAIN INTO THE BELFRY, THE BATMAN LASHES OUT WITH BOTH FEET!

...AND, HERE'S WHERE I RING THE BELL WITH YOU FELLOWS!

...THE MURDERING DEVILS TOPPLE TO THE FLOOR BELOW!

WITH THE AID OF HIS SILK ROPE, THE BATMAN RESCUES ROBIN!

LATER...

WHEW! I'VE HAD ENOUGH EXCITEMENT TO DO ME FOR A LONG TIME!

THOSE DEVILS DID GIVE US A BIT OF TROUBLE, DIDN'T THEY?

LIKE A LOT OF OTHER PEOPLE, THEY THOUGHT THEY COULD PICK UP WEALTH THE EASY WAY. THEY SHOULD HAVE REALIZED THAT'S THE HARDEST WAY — WHICH ONCE AGAIN PROVES THAT CRIME DOESN'T PAY!

THEY WOULD HAVE BEEN MUCH BETTER OFF IF THEY HAD STAYED WITH THE CIRCUS.

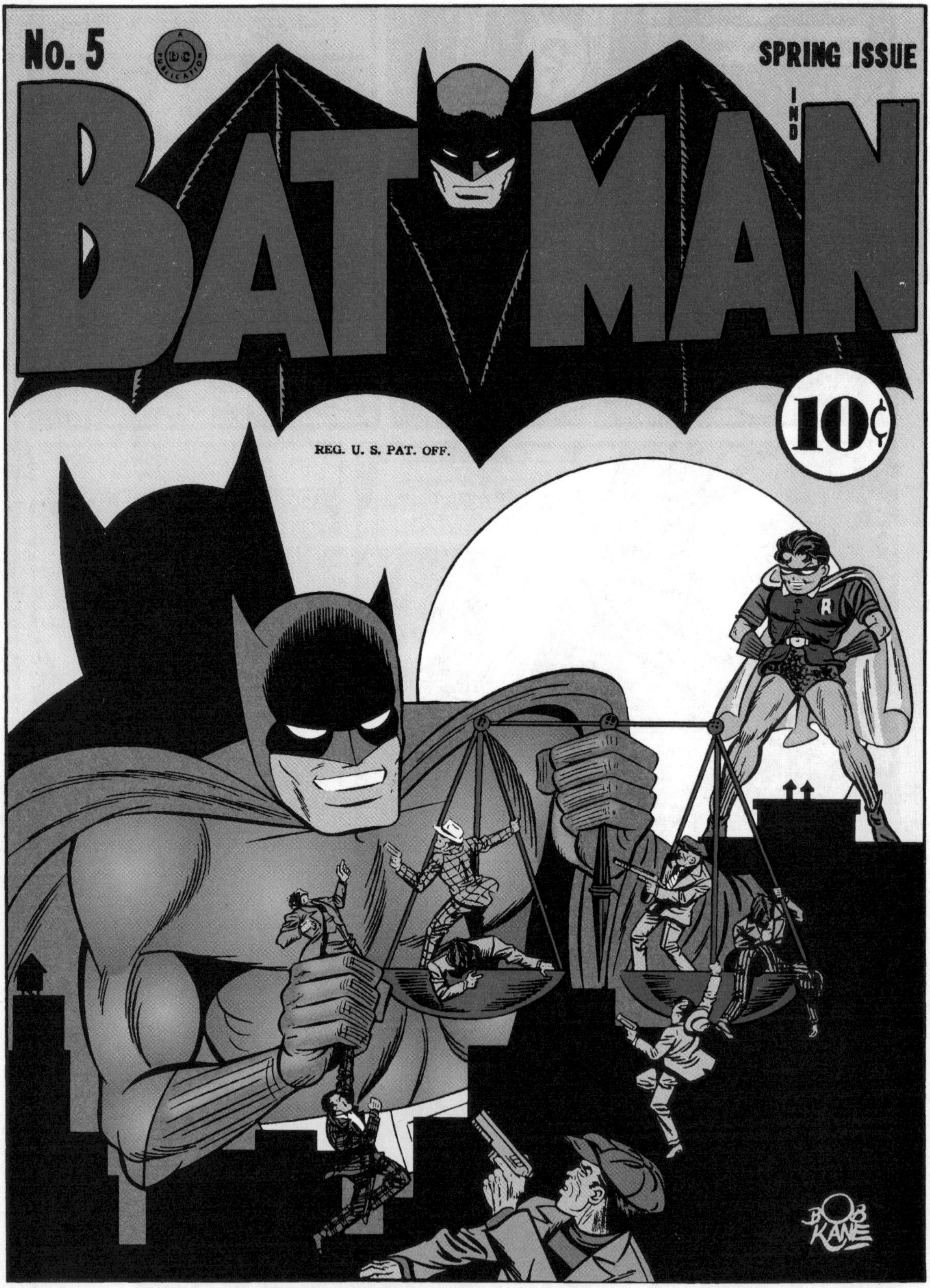
No. 5
A DC PUBLICATION
SPRING ISSUE
IND
BATMAN
10¢
REG. U. S. PAT. OFF.
R
BOB KANE

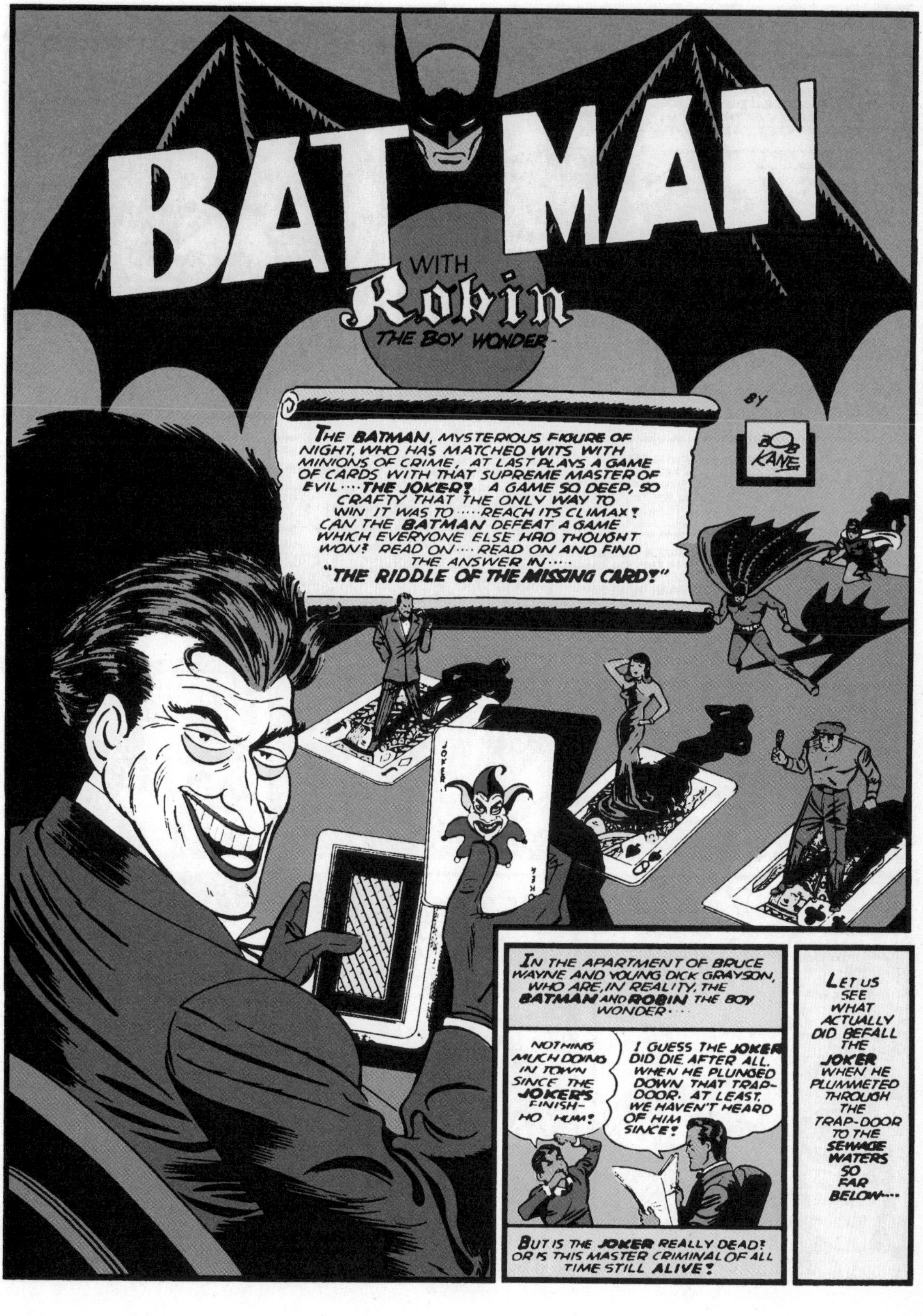
BATMAN
WITH Robin THE BOY WONDER
BY BOB KANE
THE BATMAN, MYSTERIOUS FIGURE OF NIGHT, WHO HAS MATCHED WITS WITH MINIONS OF CRIME, AT LAST PLAYS A GAME OF CARDS WITH THAT SUPREME MASTER OF EVIL.... THE JOKER! A GAME SO DEEP, SO CRAFTY THAT THE ONLY WAY TO WIN IT WAS TO..... REACH ITS CLIMAX! CAN THE BATMAN DEFEAT A GAME WHICH EVERYONE ELSE HAD THOUGHT WON? READ ON.... READ ON AND FIND THE ANSWER IN.....
"THE RIDDLE OF THE MISSING CARD!"
JOKER
IN THE APARTMENT OF BRUCE WAYNE AND YOUNG DICK GRAYSON, WHO ARE, IN REALITY, THE BATMAN AND ROBIN THE BOY WONDER...
NOTHING MUCH DOING IN TOWN SINCE THE JOKER'S FINISH— HO HUM!
I GUESS THE JOKER DID DIE AFTER ALL. WHEN HE PLUNGED DOWN THAT TRAP-DOOR. AT LEAST, WE HAVEN'T HEARD OF HIM SINCE!
BUT IS THE JOKER REALLY DEAD? OR IS THIS MASTER CRIMINAL OF ALL TIME STILL ALIVE!
LET US SEE WHAT ACTUALLY DID BEFALL THE JOKER WHEN HE PLUMMETED THROUGH THE TRAP-DOOR TO THE SEWAGE WATERS SO FAR BELOW....

A CLINGING FOG HANGS LIKE A PALL OVER THE WATERFRONT. A SMALL BOAT LOOMS IN THE FOG AND RIDES STEALTHILY ON THE BLACK WATER THAT LAPS GENTLY AT THE DOCK-POSTS. A VOICE CALLS OUT...

HE-LP... HE-LP....

LISTEN... SOMEONE IN TROUBLE!

SO WHAT? WE CAN'T STOP TO PICK HIM UP.

HEY.... YOU GONE CRAZY? PUT OUT THAT LIGHT! THE COPS WILL SEE US!

SHUT UP... CAN'T YOU SEE WHO IT IS? IT'S THE JOKER!

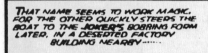

THAT NAME SEEMS TO WORK MAGIC, FOR THE OTHER QUICKLY STEERS THE BOAT TO THE JOKER'S BOBBING FORM LATER, IN A DESERTED FACTORY BUILDING NEARBY——

HOW COME YOU WERE FLOATING AROUND THE WATER AT THIS TIME OF NIGHT?

..HAD A TUSSLE WITH THE BATMAN—FELL DOWN TO SEWAGE WATER... KEPT SWIMMING THROUGH THE PIPE TILL I FOUND WHERE IT EMPTIES INTO THE BAY.... EXHAUSTED.... THEN YOU FOUND ME!

AFTER THE JOKER HAS REGAINED SOME OF HIS STRENGTH...

I'M CURIOUS TO KNOW WHY YOU HESITATED TO PICK ME UP AT FIRST.. HIDING SOMETHING FROM THE POLICE?

YOU GUESSED IT. WE HAD A STEWARD HIDE SOME DIAMONDS ON AN INCOMING STEAMER..

..AND THEN WE SMUGGLE THEM IN! BUT THE DIAMOND SMUGGLING BUSINESS IS PRETTY WELL SHOT--WHAT WITH THE WAR GOIN' ON?

WHY DID YOU CHANGE YOUR MIND ABOUT PICKING ME UP AFTER YOU SAW WHO I WAS?

WE THINK MAYBE YOU CAN FIGURE OUT A NEW RACKET FOR US

WE NEED A NEW RACKET. YOU'RE A GUY WITH BRAINS.

I'LL INTRODUCE US. I'M QUEENIE. THIS IS DIAMOND JACK DEEGAN.. AND THE BIG LUG IS CLUBSY

DEY CALLS ME DATS ON ACCOUNTA I AM AN EXPORT AT CONKIN' GUYS OVER DA BEAN!

I'VE JUST HAD A DROLL THOUGHT. I'M THE JOKER... WE HAVE BLACK-HAIRED QUEENIE....THE BLACK QUEEN....DIAMOND JACK--THE JACK OF DIAMONDS....

...AND CLUBSY, HERE THE KING OF CLUBS! FOUR CARDS-- FOUR CARDS ABOUT TO PLAY A GAME OF CHANCE WITH THE POLICE!

I DON'T LIKE TO PLAY WID DE COPS. YA CAN'T CHEAT WID DEM. DE LAST TIME I PLAYED RUMMY WID SERGEANT CASEY. HE....

SHUT UP, CLUBSY!

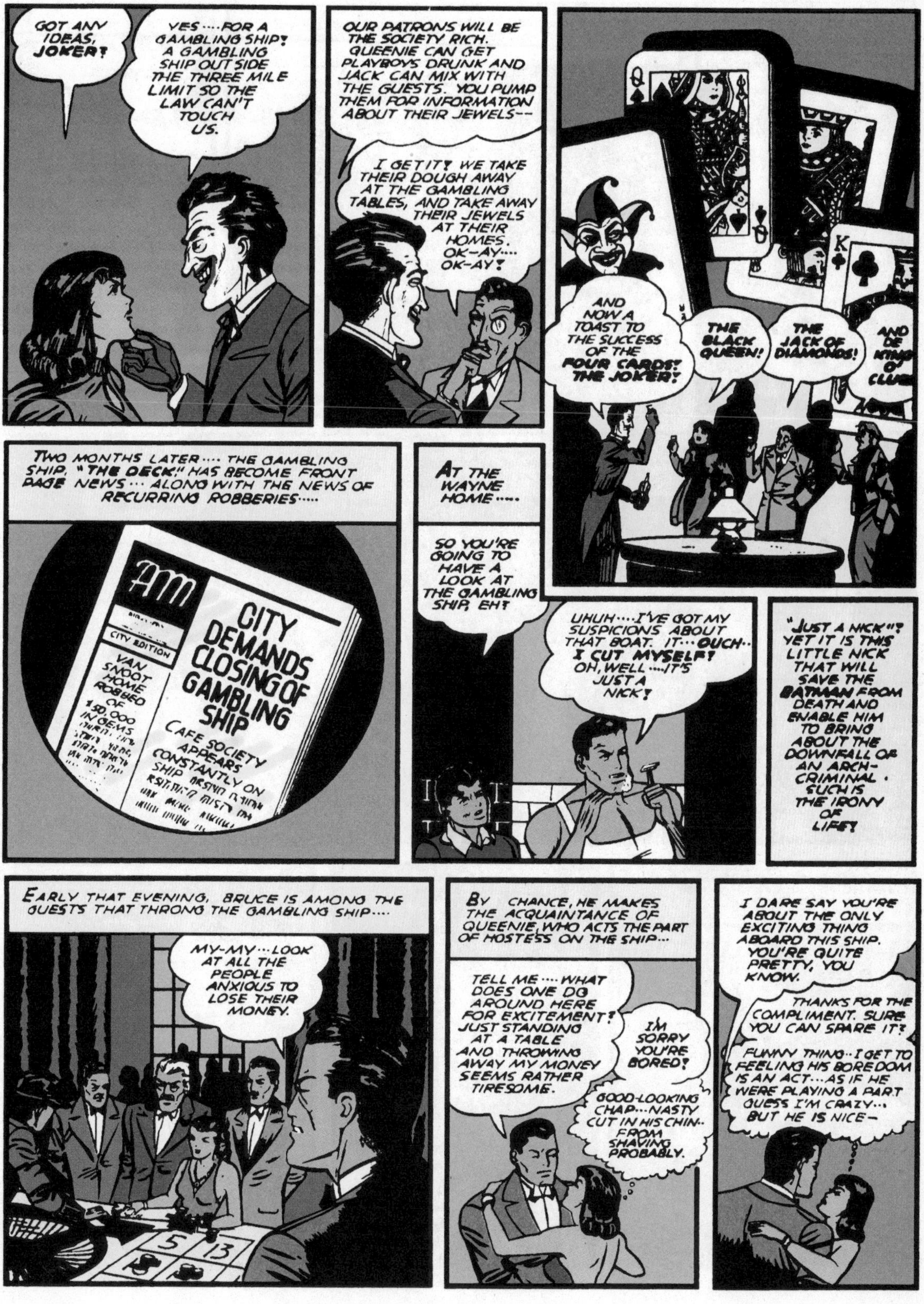
GOT ANY IDEAS, JOKER?
YES....FOR A GAMBLING SHIP! A GAMBLING SHIP OUT SIDE THE THREE MILE LIMIT SO THE LAW CAN'T TOUCH US.
OUR PATRONS WILL BE THE SOCIETY RICH. QUEENIE CAN GET PLAYBOYS DRUNK AND JACK CAN MIX WITH THE GUESTS. YOU PUMP THEM FOR INFORMATION ABOUT THEIR JEWELS--
I GET IT! WE TAKE THEIR DOUGH AWAY AT THE GAMBLING TABLES, AND TAKE AWAY THEIR JEWELS AT THEIR HOMES. OK-AY.... OK-AY!
AND NOW A TOAST TO THE SUCCESS OF THE FOUR CARDS! THE JOKER!
THE BLACK QUEEN!
THE JACK OF DIAMONDS!
TWO MONTHS LATER.... THE GAMBLING SHIP, "THE DECK!" HAS BECOME FRONT PAGE NEWS... ALONG WITH THE NEWS OF RECURRING ROBBERIES.....
CITY EDITION
VAN SNOOT HOME ROBBED OF 150,000 IN GEMS
CITY DEMANDS CLOSING OF GAMBLING SHIP
CAFE SOCIETY APPEARS CONSTANTLY ON SHIP
AT THE WAYNE HOME.....
SO YOU'RE GOING TO HAVE A LOOK AT THE GAMBLING SHIP, EH?
UHUH....I'VE GOT MY SUSPICIONS ABOUT THAT BOAT. IT... OUCH.. I CUT MYSELF! OH, WELL....IT'S JUST A NICK!
"JUST A NICK"? YET IT IS THIS LITTLE NICK THAT WILL SAVE THE BATMAN FROM DEATH AND ENABLE HIM TO BRING ABOUT THE DOWNFALL OF AN ARCH-CRIMINAL. SUCH IS THE IRONY OF LIFE!
EARLY THAT EVENING, BRUCE IS AMONG THE GUESTS THAT THRONG THE GAMBLING SHIP....
MY-MY...LOOK AT ALL THE PEOPLE ANXIOUS TO LOSE THEIR MONEY.
5 13
BY CHANCE, HE MAKES THE ACQUAINTANCE OF QUEENIE, WHO ACTS THE PART OF HOSTESS ON THE SHIP...
TELL ME....WHAT DOES ONE DO AROUND HERE FOR EXCITEMENT? JUST STANDING AT A TABLE AND THROWING AWAY MY MONEY SEEMS RATHER TIRESOME.
I'M SORRY YOU'RE BORED!
GOOD-LOOKING CHAP...NASTY CUT IN HIS CHIN.. FROM SHAVING PROBABLY.
I DARE SAY YOU'RE ABOUT THE ONLY EXCITING THING ABOARD THIS SHIP. YOU'RE QUITE PRETTY, YOU KNOW.
THANKS FOR THE COMPLIMENT. SURE YOU CAN SPARE IT?
FUNNY THING..I GET TO FEELING HIS BOREDOM IS AN ACT...AS IF HE WERE PLAYING A PART. GUESS I'M CRAZY... BUT HE IS NICE-

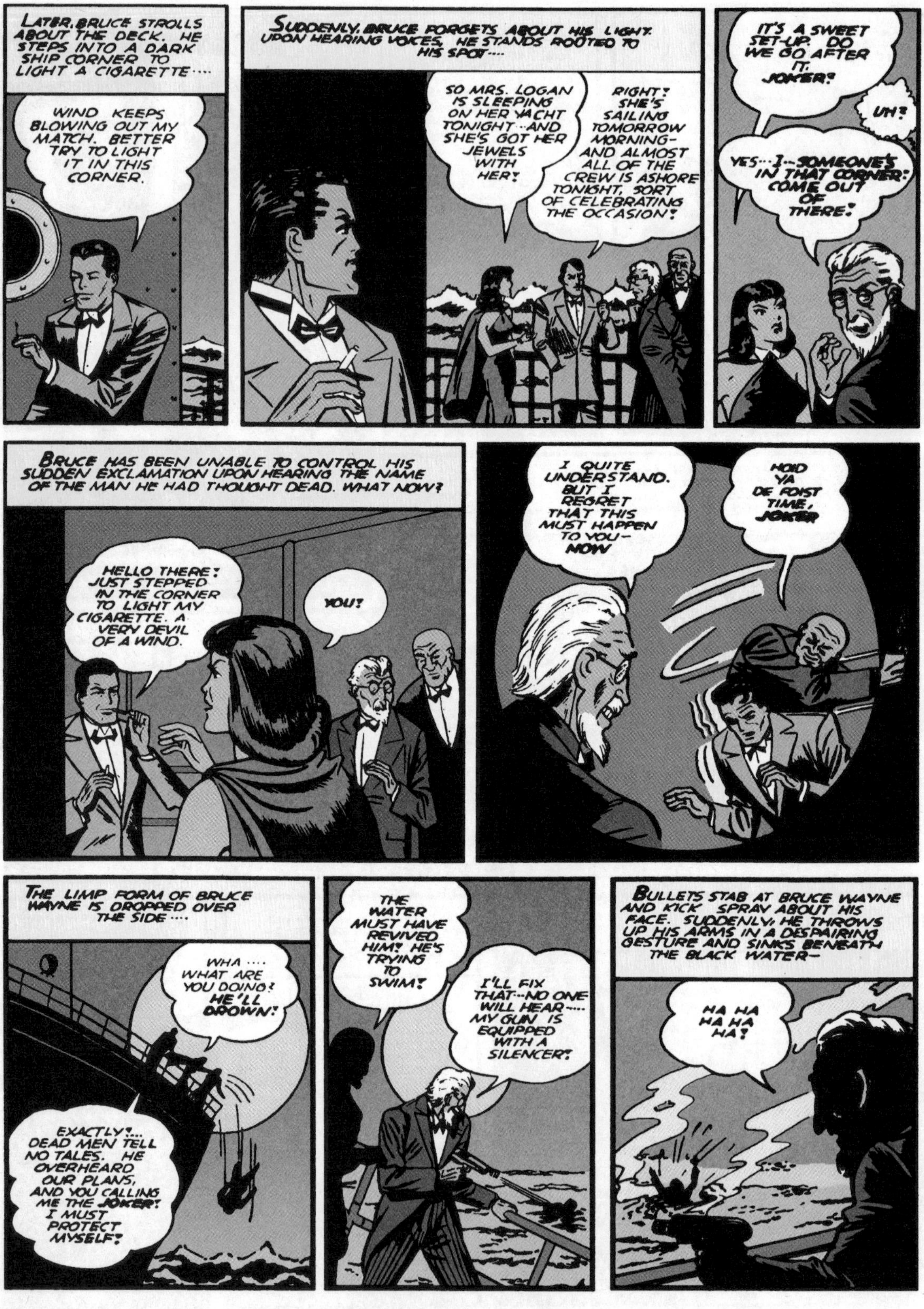
LATER, BRUCE STROLLS ABOUT THE DECK. HE STEPS INTO A DARK SHIP CORNER TO LIGHT A CIGARETTE....
WIND KEEPS BLOWING OUT MY MATCH. BETTER TRY TO LIGHT IT IN THIS CORNER.
SUDDENLY, BRUCE FORGETS ABOUT HIS LIGHT UPON HEARING VOICES. HE STANDS ROOTED TO HIS SPOT....
SO MRS. LOGAN IS SLEEPING ON HER YACHT TONIGHT--AND SHE'S GOT HER JEWELS WITH HER!
RIGHT! SHE'S SAILING TOMORROW MORNING-AND ALMOST ALL OF THE CREW IS ASHORE TONIGHT, SORT OF CELEBRATING THE OCCASION!
IT'S A SWEET SET-UP. DO WE GO AFTER IT, JOKER?
UH?
YES--I--SOMEONE'S IN THAT CORNER! COME OUT OF THERE!
BRUCE HAS BEEN UNABLE TO CONTROL HIS SUDDEN EXCLAMATION UPON HEARING THE NAME OF THE MAN HE HAD THOUGHT DEAD. WHAT NOW?
HELLO THERE! JUST STEPPED IN THE CORNER TO LIGHT MY CIGARETTE. A VERY DEVIL OF A WIND.
YOU!
I QUITE UNDERSTAND. BUT I REGRET THAT THIS MUST HAPPEN TO YOU-NOW
HOID YA DE FOIST TIME, JOKER
THE LIMP FORM OF BRUCE WAYNE IS DROPPED OVER THE SIDE....
WHA.... WHAT ARE YOU DOING? HE'LL DROWN!
EXACTLY!... DEAD MEN TELL NO TALES. HE OVERHEARD OUR PLANS, AND YOU CALLING ME THE JOKER! I MUST PROTECT MYSELF!
THE WATER MUST HAVE REVIVED HIM! HE'S TRYING TO SWIM!
I'LL FIX THAT--NO ONE WILL HEAR---- MY GUN IS EQUIPPED WITH A SILENCER!
BULLETS STAB AT BRUCE WAYNE AND KICK SPRAY ABOUT HIS FACE. SUDDENLY, HE THROWS UP HIS ARMS IN A DESPAIRING GESTURE AND SINKS BENEATH THE BLACK WATER-
HA HA HA HA HA!

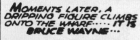

MOMENTS LATER, A DRIPPING FIGURE CLIMBS ONTO THE WHARF..... *IT IS BRUCE WAYNE*...

GOOD THING I HAD PRESENCE OF MIND TO PRETEND I WAS HIT. NOW HOME...AND SOME DRY CLOTHES!

AFTER ACQUAINTING YOUNG DICK WITH THE FACTS, HE AND THE BOY DON STRANGE GARB TO BECOME THE *BATMAN* AND *ROBIN, THE BOY WONDER*....

THEY RACE THROUGH A SECRET TUNNEL THAT RUNS UNDER THE WAYNE HOME....

....TO A BARN HOUSING A SUPER-CHARGED CAR. THE *BATMAN* STEPS ON THE THROTTLE AND THE *BATMOBILE* LEAPS AWAY AND OUT INTO THE NIGHT!

IT RACES THROUGH THE STREETS LIKE A RUNAWAY COMET AND FINALLY SKIDS TO A HALT BEFORE THE LOGAN YACHT.....

WE MAY BE TOO LATE!

JUST IN TIME, I SEE!

THE BATMAN?

GREETINGS, JOKER! NICE TO SEE YOU AGAIN!

UGH!

BRING THAT POP-GUN BACK TO THE TOY COUNTER!

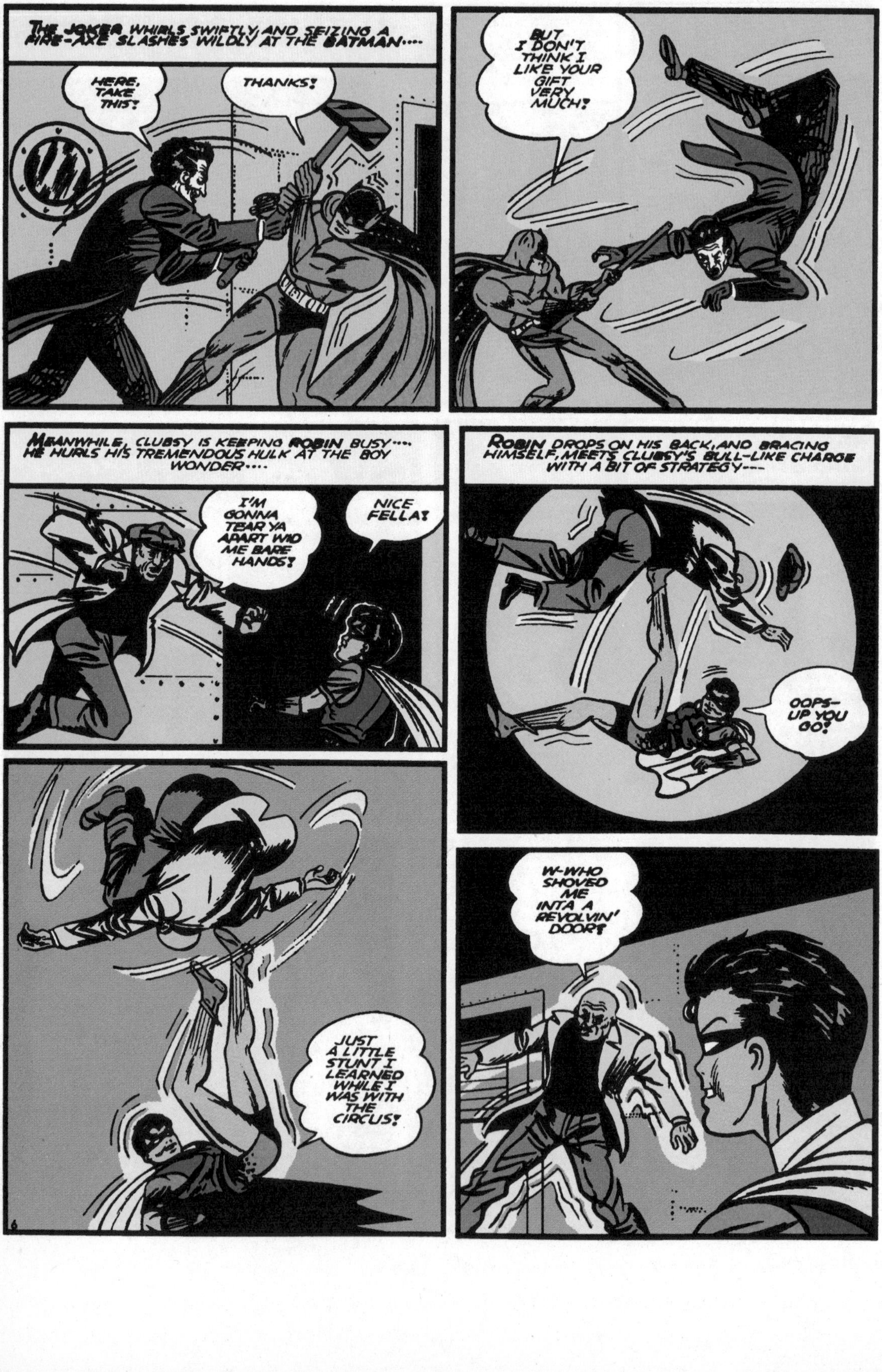
THE JOKER WHIRLS SWIFTLY, AND SEIZING A FIRE-AXE SLASHES WILDLY AT THE BATMAN....
HERE, TAKE THIS!
THANKS!
BUT I DON'T THINK I LIKE YOUR GIFT VERY MUCH!
MEANWHILE, CLUBSY IS KEEPING ROBIN BUSY.... HE HURLS HIS TREMENDOUS HULK AT THE BOY WONDER....
I'M GONNA TEAR YA APART WID ME BARE HANDS!
NICE FELLA!
ROBIN DROPS ON HIS BACK, AND BRACING HIMSELF, MEETS CLUBSY'S BULL-LIKE CHARGE WITH A BIT OF STRATEGY---
OOPS-- UP YOU GO!
JUST A LITTLE STUNT I LEARNED WHILE I WAS WITH THE CIRCUS!
6
W-WHO SHOVED ME INTA A REVOLVIN' DOOR?

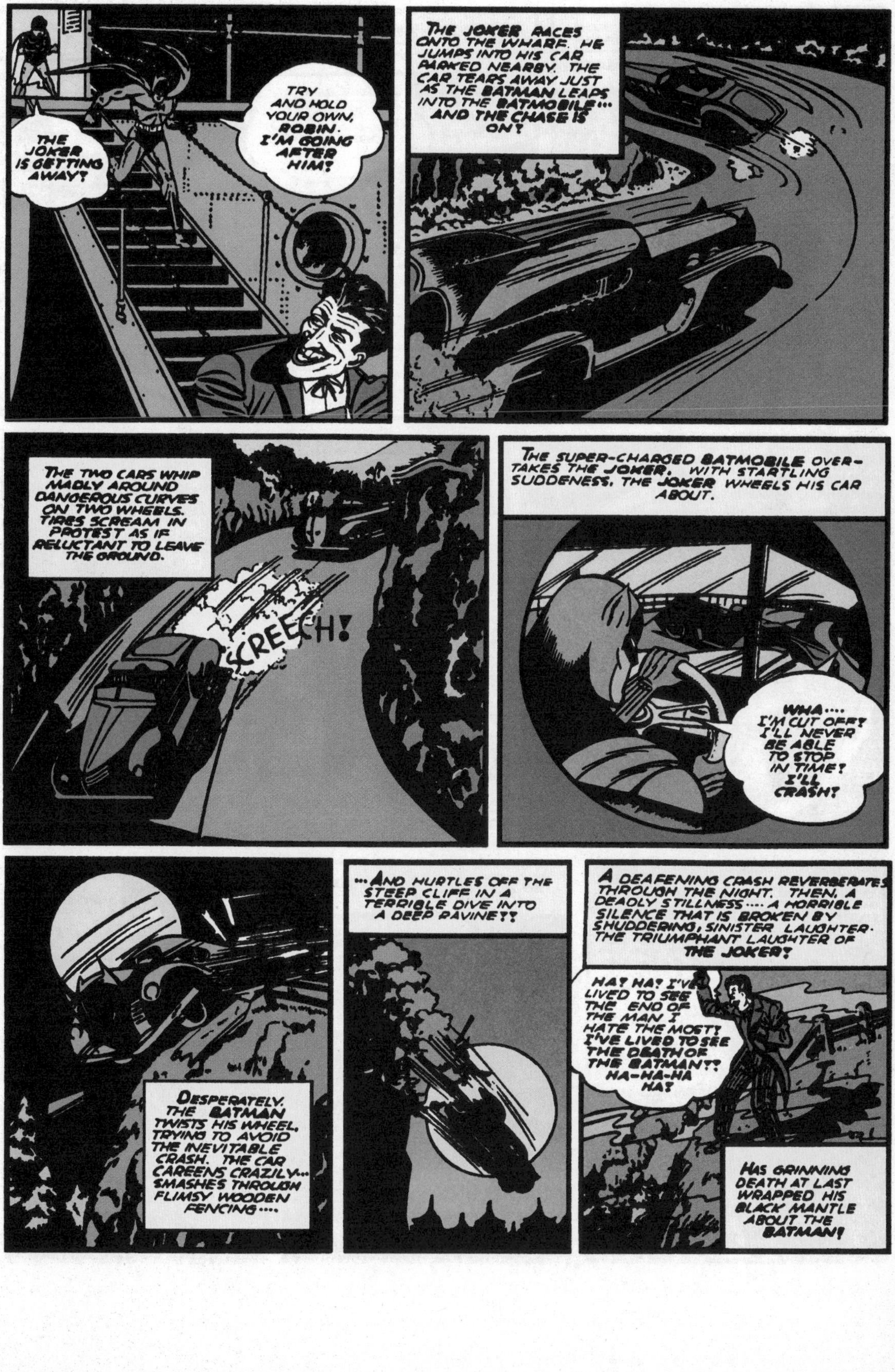
THE JOKER IS GETTING AWAY!
TRY AND HOLD YOUR OWN, ROBIN. I'M GOING AFTER HIM!
THE JOKER RACES ONTO THE WHARF. HE JUMPS INTO HIS CAR PARKED NEARBY. THE CAR TEARS AWAY JUST AS THE BATMAN LEAPS INTO THE BATMOBILE... AND THE CHASE IS ON!
THE TWO CARS WHIP MADLY AROUND DANGEROUS CURVES ON TWO WHEELS. TIRES SCREAM IN PROTEST AS IF RELUCTANT TO LEAVE THE GROUND.
SCREECH!
THE SUPER-CHARGED BATMOBILE OVER-TAKES THE JOKER. WITH STARTLING SUDDENESS, THE JOKER WHEELS HIS CAR ABOUT.
WHA.... I'M CUT OFF! I'LL NEVER BE ABLE TO STOP IN TIME! I'LL CRASH!
DESPERATELY, THE BATMAN TWISTS HIS WHEEL, TRYING TO AVOID THE INEVITABLE CRASH. THE CAR CAREENS CRAZILY... SMASHES THROUGH FLIMSY WOODEN FENCING....
...AND HURTLES OFF THE STEEP CLIFF IN A TERRIBLE DIVE INTO A DEEP RAVINE!!
A DEAFENING CRASH REVERBERATES THROUGH THE NIGHT. THEN, A DEADLY STILLNESS.... A HORRIBLE SILENCE THAT IS BROKEN BY SHUDDERING, SINISTER LAUGHTER. THE TRIUMPHANT LAUGHTER OF THE JOKER!
HA! HA! I'VE LIVED TO SEE THE END OF THE MAN I HATE THE MOST! I'VE LIVED TO SEE THE DEATH OF THE BATMAN!! HA-HA-HA HA!
HAS GRINNING DEATH AT LAST WRAPPED HIS BLACK MANTLE ABOUT THE BATMAN!

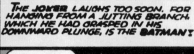

THE JOKER LAUGHS TOO SOON, FOR HANGING FROM A JUTTING BRANCH, WHICH HE HAD GRASPED IN HIS DOWNWARD PLUNGE, IS THE BATMAN!

STEPPED OUT JUST IN TIME---

MEANWHILE, ROBIN, TOO, HAS HIS TROUBLES. AS HE STEPS BACK TO AVOID DIAMOND JACK'S GUN, CLUBSY WRAPS HIS HUGE ARMS ABOUT HIM---

THAT BRAT IS TOUGHER TO HANDLE THAN A DOZEN COPS!

DAT'S FINE! GOTCHA!

UH!

HOLD HIM? HAH! THIS'LL QUIET HIM FOR AWHILE!

WHEN THE JOKER ARRIVES BACK ON THE GAMBLING SHIP---

HELLO! YOU BACK? WHAT HAPPENED?

I--ROBIN-- THIS HAS BEEN A FORTUNATE DAY FOR ME, THE BATMAN AND ROBIN-- BOTH IN ONE DAY!

WE WERE GOING OVER HIM FOR ANY SECRET WEAPONS AN' LOOK WHAT WE FOUND.... A WIRELESS... BUILT IN HIS BELT-BUCKLE.

SO THAT'S HOW THEY CONTACT EACH OTHER! NOW I CAN TELL FOR SURE WHETHER THE BATMAN IS REALLY DEAD.....

BATMAN-- DEAD?

ROBIN'S BELT IS REMOVED BY THE JOKER AND----

IF HE ANSWERS THIS CALL....

WHA-- MY WIRELESS? MUST BE ROBIN!

YES, ROBIN-- WHAT IS IT?

BATMAN-- ALIVE! I KNEW IT! I FELT IT!

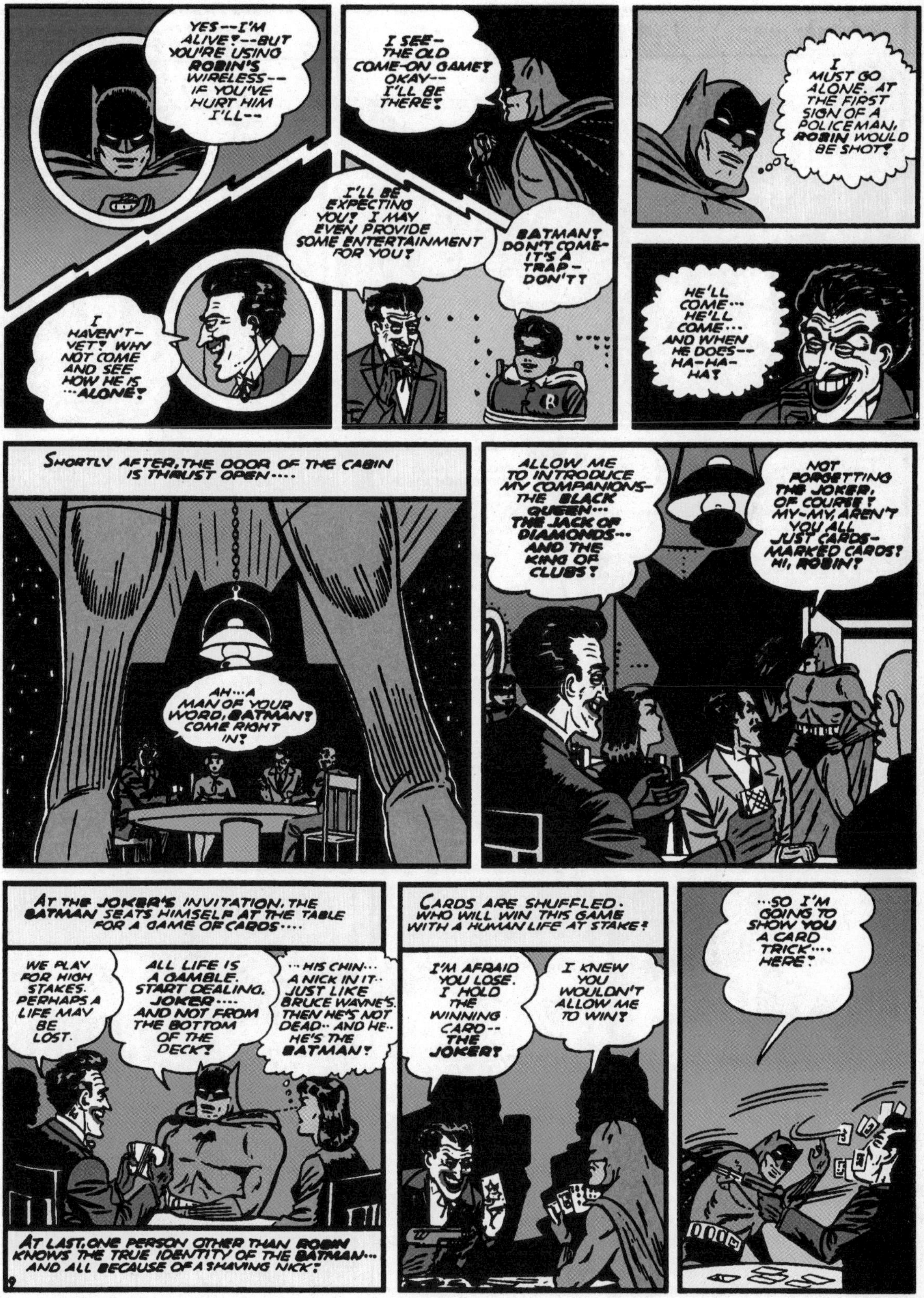
YES--I'M ALIVE!--BUT YOU'RE USING ROBIN'S WIRELESS--IF YOU'VE HURT HIM I'LL--
I SEE--THE OLD COME-ON GAME! OKAY--I'LL BE THERE!
I MUST GO ALONE. AT THE FIRST SIGN OF A POLICEMAN, ROBIN WOULD BE SHOT!
I HAVEN'T--YET! WHY NOT COME AND SEE HOW HE IS ...ALONE!
I'LL BE EXPECTING YOU! I MAY EVEN PROVIDE SOME ENTERTAINMENT FOR YOU!
BATMAN! DON'T COME--IT'S A TRAP--DON'T!
HE'LL COME... HE'LL COME... AND WHEN HE DOES--HA-HA-HA!
SHORTLY AFTER, THE DOOR OF THE CABIN IS THRUST OPEN....
AH...A MAN OF YOUR WORD, BATMAN! COME RIGHT IN!
ALLOW ME TO INTRODUCE MY COMPANIONS--THE BLACK QUEEN... THE JACK OF DIAMONDS... AND THE KING OF CLUBS!
NOT FORGETTING THE JOKER, OF COURSE! MY-MY, AREN'T YOU ALL JUST CARDS--MARKED CARDS! HI, ROBIN!
AT THE JOKER'S INVITATION, THE BATMAN SEATS HIMSELF AT THE TABLE FOR A GAME OF CARDS....
WE PLAY FOR HIGH STAKES. PERHAPS A LIFE MAY BE LOST.
ALL LIFE IS A GAMBLE. START DEALING, JOKER.... AND NOT FROM THE BOTTOM OF THE DECK!
...HIS CHIN... A NICK IN IT.. JUST LIKE BRUCE WAYNE'S. THEN HE'S NOT DEAD.. AND HE.. HE'S THE BATMAN!
AT LAST, ONE PERSON OTHER THAN ROBIN KNOWS THE TRUE IDENTITY OF THE BATMAN... AND ALL BECAUSE OF A SHAVING NICK!
CARDS ARE SHUFFLED. WHO WILL WIN THIS GAME WITH A HUMAN LIFE AT STAKE?
I'M AFRAID YOU LOSE. I HOLD THE WINNING CARD--THE JOKER!
I KNEW YOU WOULDN'T ALLOW ME TO WIN!
...SO I'M GOING TO SHOW YOU A CARD TRICK.... HERE!

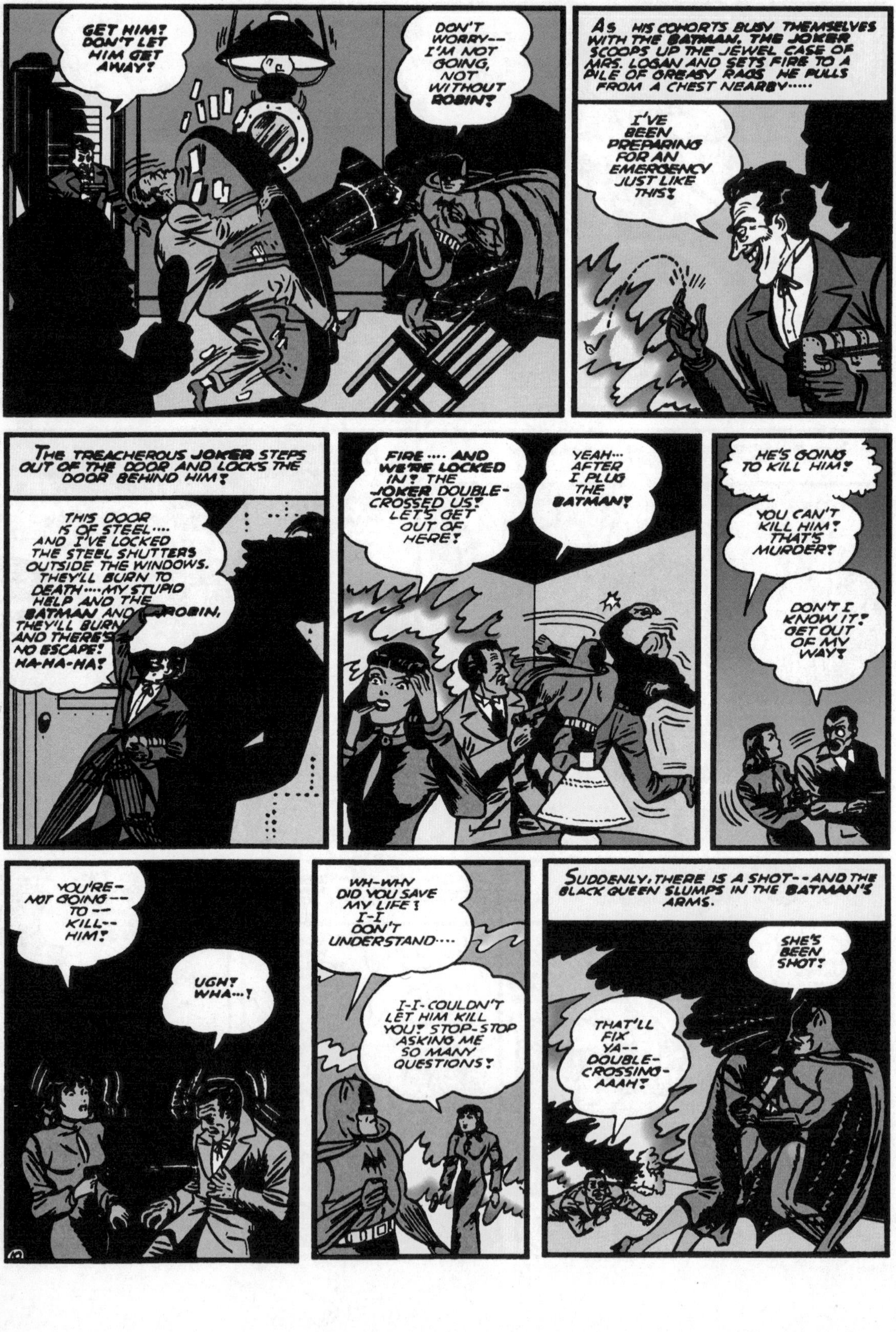
GET HIM! DON'T LET HIM GET AWAY!
DON'T WORRY-- I'M NOT GOING, NOT WITHOUT ROBIN!
AS HIS COHORTS BUSY THEMSELVES WITH THE BATMAN, THE JOKER SCOOPS UP THE JEWEL CASE OF MRS. LOGAN AND SETS FIRE TO A PILE OF GREASY RAGS HE PULLS FROM A CHEST NEARBY.....
I'VE BEEN PREPARING FOR AN EMERGENCY JUST LIKE THIS!
THE TREACHEROUS JOKER STEPS OUT OF THE DOOR AND LOCKS THE DOOR BEHIND HIM!
THIS DOOR IS OF STEEL.... AND I'VE LOCKED THE STEEL SHUTTERS OUTSIDE THE WINDOWS. THEY'LL BURN TO DEATH....MY STUPID HELP AND THE BATMAN AND ROBIN. THEY'LL BURN AND THERE'S NO ESCAPE! HA-HA-HA!
FIRE.... AND WE'RE LOCKED IN! THE JOKER DOUBLE-CROSSED US! LET'S GET OUT OF HERE!
YEAH... AFTER I PLUG THE BATMAN!
HE'S GOING TO KILL HIM!
YOU CAN'T KILL HIM! THAT'S MURDER!
DON'T I KNOW IT! GET OUT OF MY WAY!
YOU'RE-NOT GOING-- TO-- KILL-- HIM!
UGH! WHA...!
WH-WHY DID YOU SAVE MY LIFE! I-I DON'T UNDERSTAND....
I-I-COULDN'T LET HIM KILL YOU! STOP-STOP ASKING ME SO MANY QUESTIONS!
SUDDENLY, THERE IS A SHOT--AND THE BLACK QUEEN SLUMPS IN THE BATMAN'S ARMS.
SHE'S BEEN SHOT!
THAT'LL FIX YA-- DOUBLE-CROSSING-AAAH!

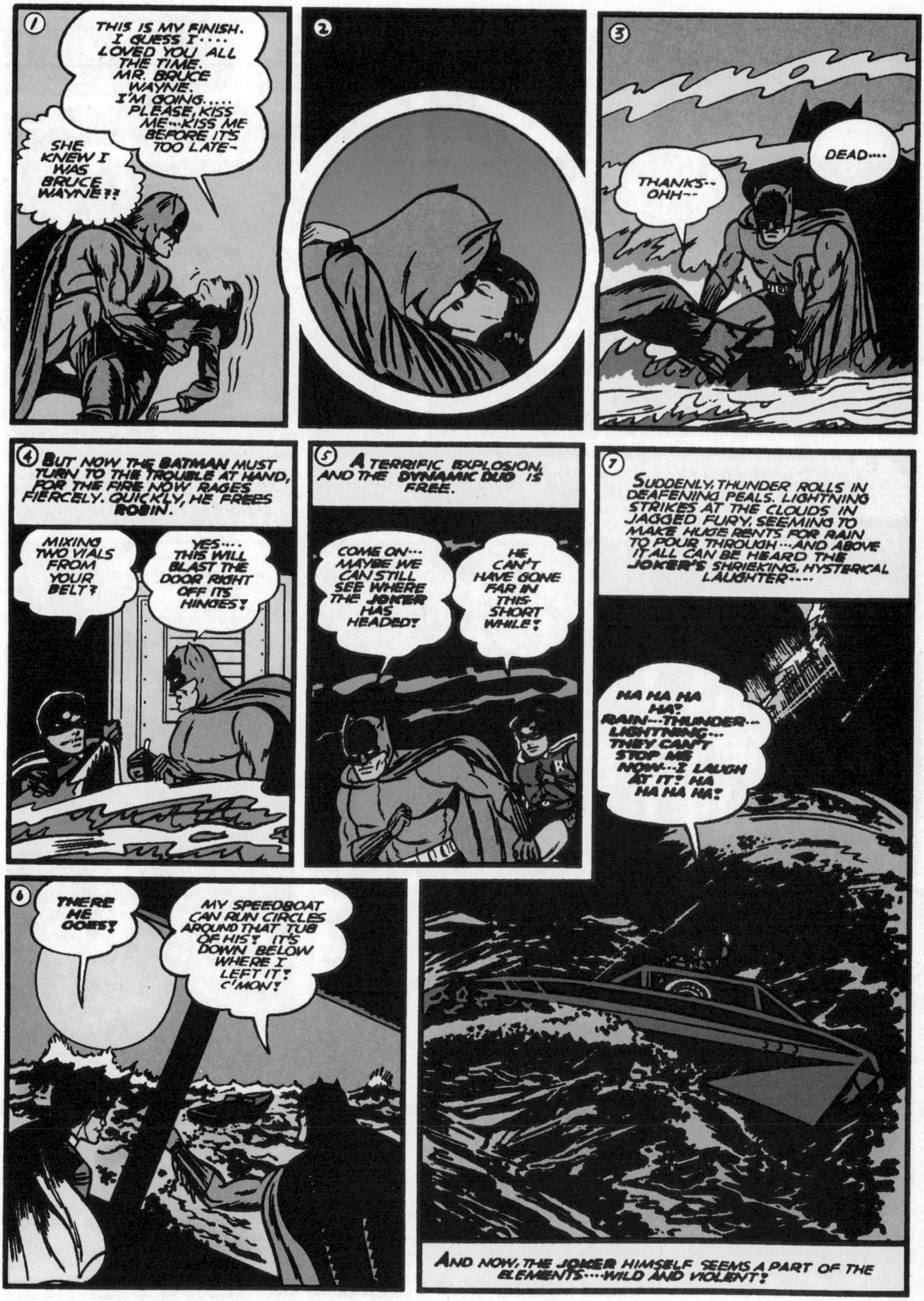

THIS IS MY FINISH. I GUESS I.... LOVED YOU ALL THE TIME. MR. BRUCE WAYNE. I'M GOING..... PLEASE, KISS ME--KISS ME BEFORE IT'S TOO LATE-
SHE KNEW I WAS BRUCE WAYNE??
THANKS-- OHH--
DEAD....
BUT NOW THE BATMAN MUST TURN TO THE TROUBLE AT HAND, FOR THE FIRE NOW RAGES FIERCELY. QUICKLY, HE FREES ROBIN.
MIXING TWO VIALS FROM YOUR BELT?
YES.... THIS WILL BLAST THE DOOR RIGHT OFF ITS HINGES!
A TERRIFIC EXPLOSION, AND THE DYNAMIC DUO IS FREE.
COME ON--- MAYBE WE CAN STILL SEE WHERE THE JOKER HAS HEADED!
HE CAN'T HAVE GONE FAR IN THIS SHORT WHILE!
THERE HE GOES!
MY SPEEDBOAT CAN RUN CIRCLES AROUND THAT TUB OF HIS! IT'S DOWN BELOW WHERE I LEFT IT! C'MON!
SUDDENLY, THUNDER ROLLS IN DEAFENING PEALS. LIGHTNING STRIKES AT THE CLOUDS IN JAGGED FURY, SEEMING TO MAKE HUGE RENTS FOR RAIN TO POUR THROUGH...AND ABOVE IT ALL CAN BE HEARD THE JOKER'S SHRIEKING, HYSTERICAL LAUGHTER----
HA HA HA HA! RAIN---THUNDER--- LIGHTNING--- THEY CAN'T STOP ME NOW--I LAUGH AT IT! HA HA HA HA!
AND NOW, THE JOKER HIMSELF SEEMS A PART OF THE ELEMENTS....WILD AND VIOLENT!

1 THE JOKER BECOMES AWARE OF THE BATMAN'S SPEEDBOAT CUTTING THROUGH THE WATER, SHORTENING HIS LEAD....

BLAST THEM... I'VE GOT TO FIND A PLACE WHERE I CAN HOLD THEM OFF. THAT LIGHTHOUSE... JUST THE SPOT! HA HA HA!

2 THERE HE GOES...TOWARDS THAT LIGHTHOUSE!

...AND THAT'S JUST WHERE WE'RE GOING!

3 THE LIGHTHOUSE KEEPER FALLS PREY TO THE MADMAN'S WRATH---

WHO?

HA HA HA! FOOL! GET OUT OF MY WAY!

4 BUT THE BATMAN ARRIVES ON THE SCENE. IN ONE BURST OF SPEED, HE IS AFTER THE JOKER ---CHASING HIM UP THE WINDING, LIGHTHOUSE STAIRCASE...

HI, PAL-- YOU DIDN'T REALLY THINK YOU COULD LOSE ME THAT EASY, DID YOU?

7 WITH QUICK PRESENCE OF MIND, THE BATMAN REACHES OUT IN ONE DESPERATE TRY.....AND MANAGES TO MAKE GOOD HIS CLUTCH FOR SAFETY!

YOU WON'T HOLD ON THAT RAIL TOO LONG... HA-HA-HA-HA AFTER I CRUSH YOUR FINGER TIPS. HA-HA HA!

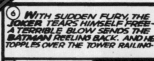

5 UP THE TWISTING STAIRS THEY RACE, UNTIL THEY REACH THE WINDSWEPT TOWER. A SINGLE BOUND BRINGS THE BATMAN TO GRIPS WITH THE GRIM JESTER!

WE'RE PLAYING THE SAME GAME, JOKER.. BUT NOT WITH CARDS THIS TIME

6 WITH SUDDEN FURY, THE JOKER TEARS HIMSELF FREE- A TERRIBLE BLOW SENDS THE BATMAN REELING BACK. AND HE TOPPLES OVER THE TOWER RAILING...

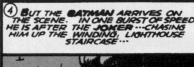

HA-HA THE JOKER WILL STILL WIN IN ANY GAME! HA-HA!

CAN THE JOKER SEND THE BATMAN PLUNGING TO A WATERY GRAVE?

12

138

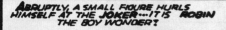

ABRUPTLY, A SMALL FIGURE HURLS HIMSELF AT THE *JOKER* ....IT IS *ROBIN THE BOY WONDER!*

YOU FORGOT ABOUT ME!

YOU!

ENRAGED, THE KILLER-CLOWN CATAPULTS TOWARD THE BOY WONDER.....BUT ROBIN SUDDENLY DROPS TO ONE KNEE...

I'LL ATTEND TO YOU FIRST!

BROTHER, ARE YOU DUE FOR A SURPRISE!

UP-- AND OVER!

AS THE JOKER'S HURTLING BODY LOOMS ABOVE HIM, ROBIN QUICKLY THRUSTS UP HIS HANDS...BRACES HIMSELF...AND WITH ONE SWIFT MOVEMENT, THROWS THE MADMAN OVER HIS HEAD!

OUT INTO EMPTY SPACE FLIES THE *JOKER* ...AND DOWN, DOWN HE PLUNGES, HIS BODY TWISTING AND TURNING .....

...DOWN INTO THE GREEDY WATERS THAT SWALLOW UP HIS HURTLING FORM!

THIS IS ONE GAME THE *JOKER* LOST!

...AND HE LOST BECAUSE HE LOST TRACK OF ONE CARD....BUT NEVER MIND THAT...LET'S RETURN THESE JEWELS!

LATER THAT EVENING.....

WHAT DID YOU MEAN WHEN YOU SAID THE *JOKER* LOST BECAUSE HE DIDN'T KEEP TRACK OF ONE CARD?

I MEAN THE FOUR CARDS! THERE SHOULD HAVE BEEN FIVE! HE HAD THE KING OF CLUBS...THE JACK OF DIAMONDS...THE BLACK QUEEN OF SPADES... AND, OF COURSE, THE *JOKER.* HE FORGOT ONE CARD.

...HE FORGOT ABOUT HEARTS......AND THERE WAS A HEART.... THE HEART OF THAT GIRL WHO DIED BACK THERE. HE DIDN'T COUNT ON THAT...AND THAT DEFEATED HIM!

BUT IS THE *JOKER* REALLY DEFEATED? OR DOES HE STILL LIVE TO HOLD A HIDDEN TRICK? ONLY THE STORM-LASHED, TURBULENT SEA CAN ANSWER THAT QUESTION!

BO KANE

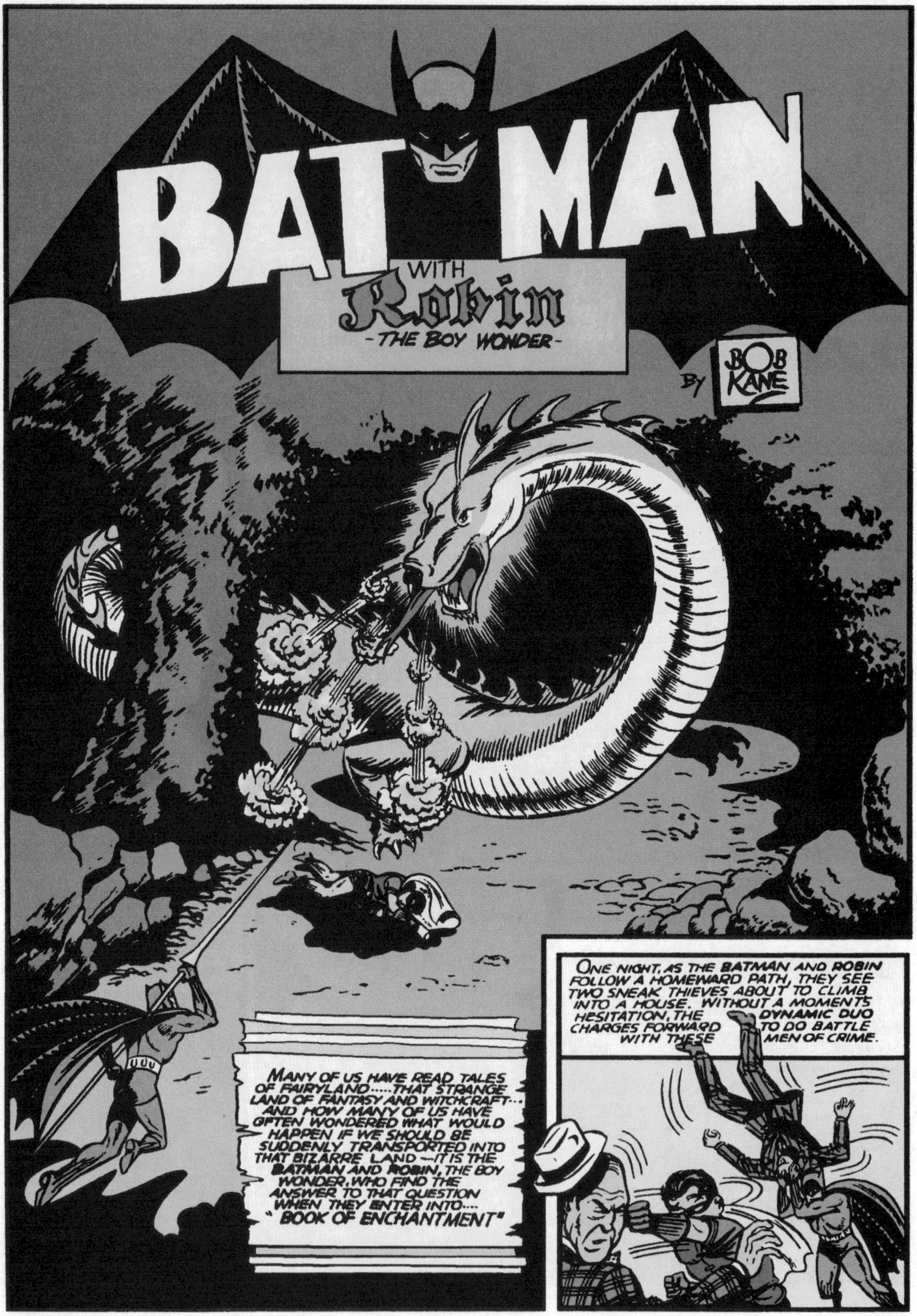
BATMAN
WITH Robin
-THE BOY WONDER-
BY BOB KANE
MANY OF US HAVE READ TALES OF FAIRYLAND.....THAT STRANGE LAND OF FANTASY AND WITCHCRAFT... AND HOW MANY OF US HAVE OFTEN WONDERED WHAT WOULD HAPPEN IF WE SHOULD BE SUDDENLY TRANSPORTED INTO THAT BIZARRE LAND -- IT IS THE BATMAN AND ROBIN, THE BOY WONDER, WHO FIND THE ANSWER TO THAT QUESTION WHEN THEY ENTER INTO.... "BOOK OF ENCHANTMENT"
ONE NIGHT, AS THE BATMAN AND ROBIN FOLLOW A HOMEWARD PATH, THEY SEE TWO SNEAK THIEVES ABOUT TO CLIMB INTO A HOUSE. WITHOUT A MOMENTS HESITATION, THE DYNAMIC DUO CHARGES FORWARD TO DO BATTLE WITH THESE MEN OF CRIME.

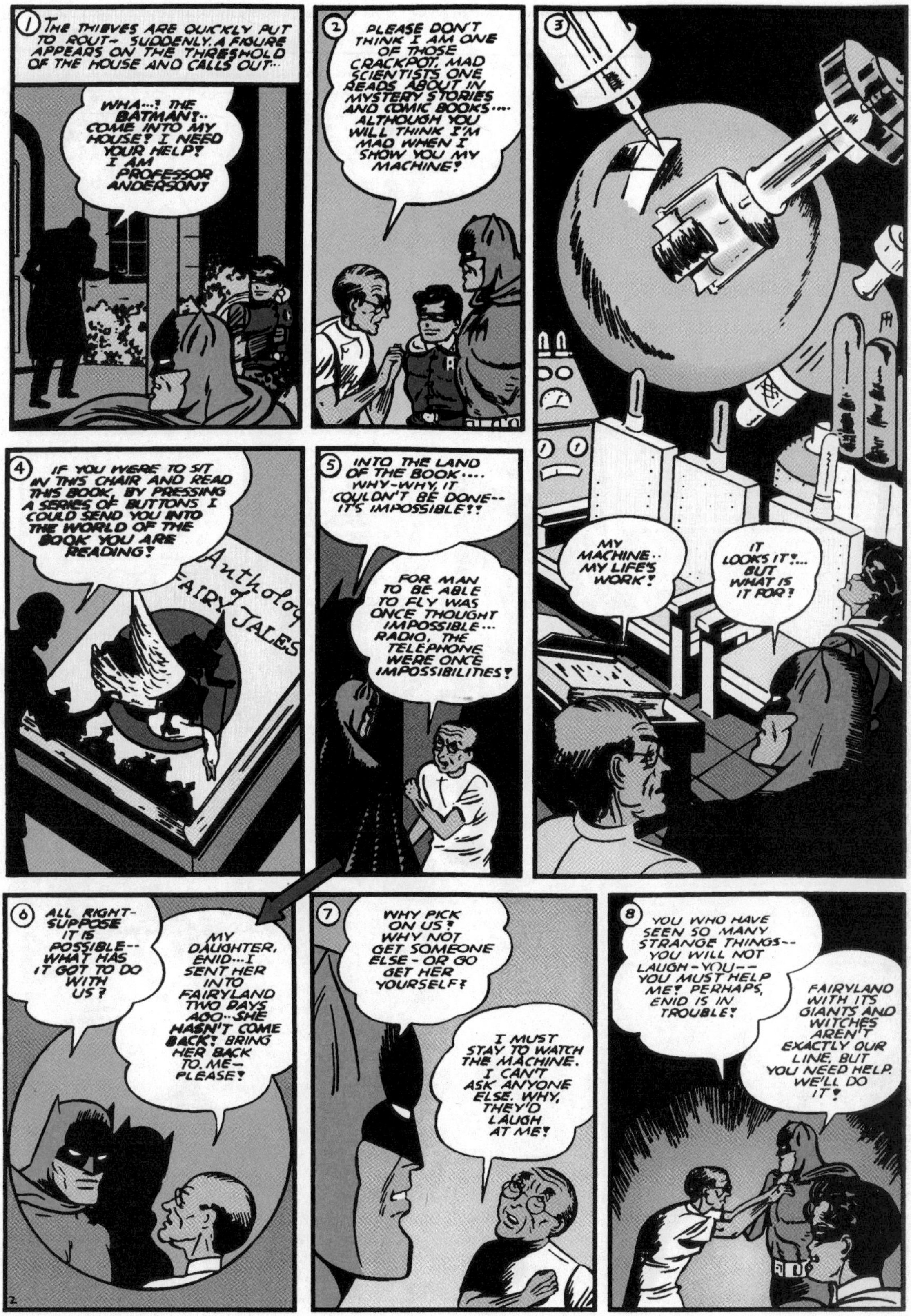

THE THIEVES ARE QUICKLY PUT TO ROUT-- SUDDENLY A FIGURE APPEARS ON THE THRESHOLD OF THE HOUSE AND CALLS OUT...
WHA...? THE BATMAN?.. COME INTO MY HOUSE? I NEED YOUR HELP? I AM PROFESSOR ANDERSON!
PLEASE DON'T THINK I AM ONE OF THOSE CRACKPOT, MAD SCIENTISTS ONE READS ABOUT IN MYSTERY STORIES AND COMIC BOOKS.... ALTHOUGH YOU WILL THINK I'M MAD WHEN I SHOW YOU MY MACHINE!
MY MACHINE.. MY LIFE'S WORK!
IT LOOKS IT!... BUT WHAT IS IT FOR?
IF YOU WERE TO SIT IN THIS CHAIR AND READ THIS BOOK, BY PRESSING A SERIES OF BUTTONS I COULD SEND YOU INTO THE WORLD OF THE BOOK YOU ARE READING!
Anthology of FAIRY TALES
INTO THE LAND OF THE BOOK.... WHY-WHY, IT COULDN'T BE DONE-- IT'S IMPOSSIBLE!!
FOR MAN TO BE ABLE TO FLY WAS ONCE THOUGHT IMPOSSIBLE... RADIO, THE TELEPHONE WERE ONCE IMPOSSIBILITIES!
ALL RIGHT-SUPPOSE IT IS POSSIBLE-- WHAT HAS IT GOT TO DO WITH US?
MY DAUGHTER, ENID...I SENT HER INTO FAIRYLAND TWO DAYS AGO--SHE HASN'T COME BACK! BRING HER BACK TO ME-PLEASE!
WHY PICK ON US? WHY NOT GET SOMEONE ELSE - OR GO GET HER YOURSELF?
I MUST STAY TO WATCH THE MACHINE. I CAN'T ASK ANYONE ELSE. WHY, THEY'D LAUGH AT ME!
YOU WHO HAVE SEEN SO MANY STRANGE THINGS-- YOU WILL NOT LAUGH-YOU-- YOU MUST HELP ME! PERHAPS, ENID IS IN TROUBLE!
FAIRYLAND WITH ITS GIANTS AND WITCHES AREN'T EXACTLY OUR LINE, BUT YOU NEED HELP. WE'LL DO IT!

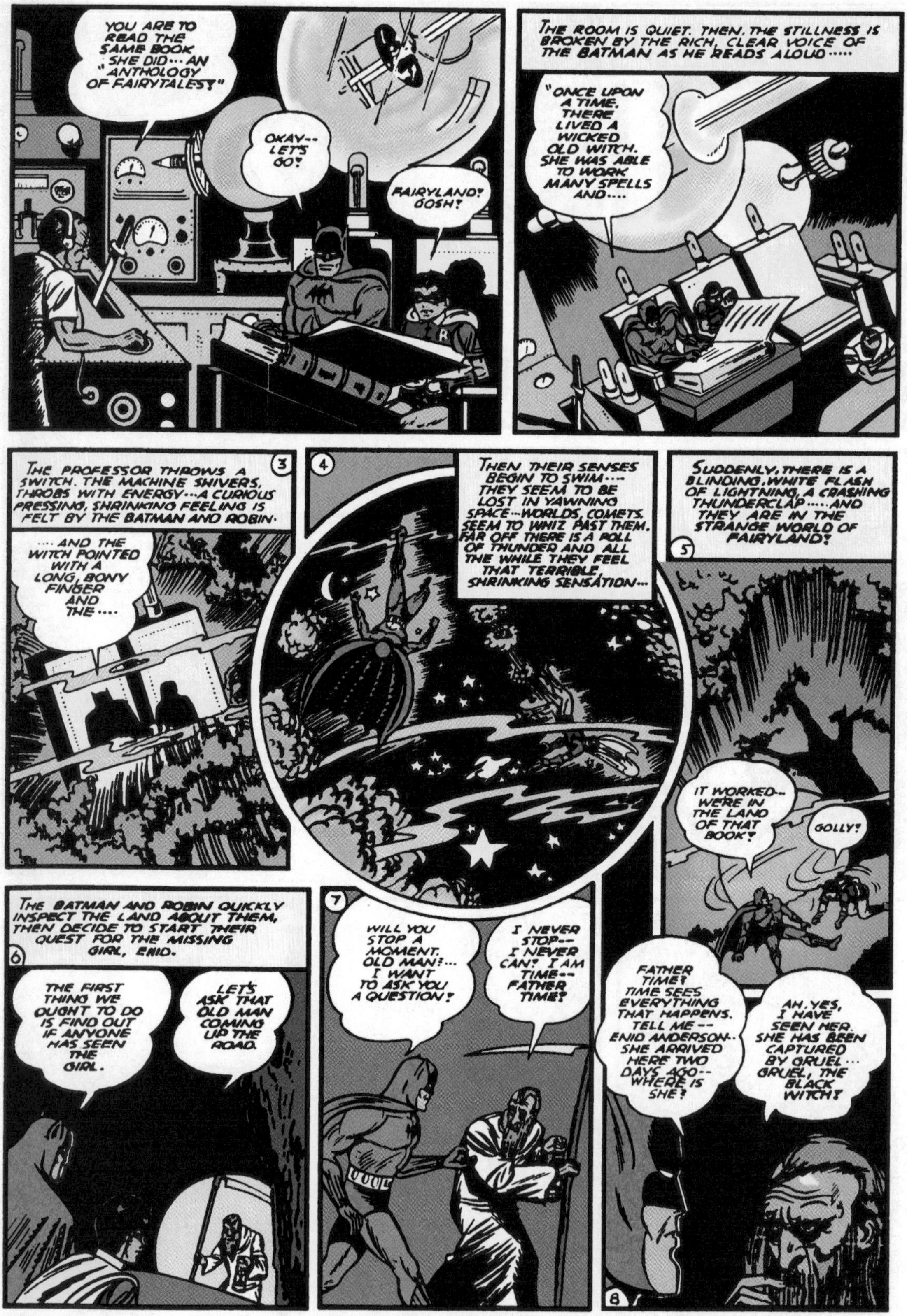
YOU ARE TO READ THE SAME BOOK SHE DID... AN "ANTHOLOGY OF FAIRYTALES!"
OKAY-- LET'S GO!
FAIRYLAND! GOSH!
THE ROOM IS QUIET. THEN, THE STILLNESS IS BROKEN BY THE RICH, CLEAR VOICE OF THE BATMAN AS HE READS ALOUD.....
"ONCE UPON A TIME, THERE LIVED A WICKED OLD WITCH. SHE WAS ABLE TO WORK MANY SPELLS AND....
THE PROFESSOR THROWS A SWITCH. THE MACHINE SHIVERS, THROBS WITH ENERGY...A CURIOUS PRESSING, SHRINKING FEELING IS FELT BY THE BATMAN AND ROBIN.
...AND THE WITCH POINTED WITH A LONG, BONY FINGER AND THE....
THEN THEIR SENSES BEGIN TO SWIM.... THEY SEEM TO BE LOST IN YAWNING SPACE--WORLDS, COMETS, SEEM TO WHIZ PAST THEM. FAR OFF THERE IS A ROLL OF THUNDER AND ALL THE WHILE THEY FEEL THAT TERRIBLE SHRINKING SENSATION...
SUDDENLY, THERE IS A BLINDING, WHITE FLASH OF LIGHTNING, A CRASHING THUNDERCLAP.....AND THEY ARE IN THE STRANGE WORLD OF FAIRYLAND!
IT WORKED-- WE'RE IN THE LAND OF THAT BOOK!
GOLLY!
THE BATMAN AND ROBIN QUICKLY INSPECT THE LAND ABOUT THEM, THEN DECIDE TO START THEIR QUEST FOR THE MISSING GIRL, ENID.
THE FIRST THING WE OUGHT TO DO IS FIND OUT IF ANYONE HAS SEEN THE GIRL.
LET'S ASK THAT OLD MAN COMING UP THE ROAD.
WILL YOU STOP A MOMENT, OLD MAN?... I WANT TO ASK YOU A QUESTION!
I NEVER STOP-- I NEVER CAN! I AM TIME-- FATHER TIME!
FATHER TIME? TIME SEES EVERYTHING THAT HAPPENS. TELL ME -- ENID ANDERSON-- SHE ARRIVED HERE TWO DAYS AGO-- WHERE IS SHE?
AH, YES, I HAVE SEEN HER. SHE HAS BEEN CAPTURED BY GRUEL... GRUEL, THE BLACK WITCH!

THE BLACK WITCH?

YES-- AND YOU MUST RESCUE THE GIRL BEFORE THIS DAY ENDS. ANYONE WHO REMAINS IN FAIRYLAND FOR THREE DAYS IS COMPELLED TO REMAIN HERE FOREVER!!

YOU HAVE TILL SUNDOWN TO TAKE HER BACK TO YOUR OWN LAND. ELSE SHE MAY NEVER LEAVE.... REMEMBER-- SUNDOWN?!

LOOKS LIKE WE HAVE A MAN-SIZED JOB ON OUR HANDS.

YES, AND WHAT'S THAT UP THERE IN THE SKY?

FRAMED AGAINST THE SKY IS A WEIRD SIGHT.... A WITCH ON A BROOMSTICK?

THERE THEY ARE-- HEE HEE!

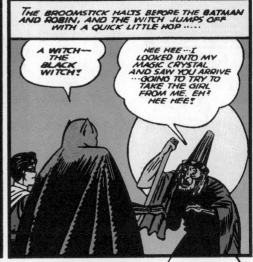

THE BROOMSTICK HALTS BEFORE THE BATMAN AND ROBIN, AND THE WITCH JUMPS OFF WITH A QUICK LITTLE HOP .....

A WITCH-- THE BLACK WITCH!

HEE HEE...I LOOKED INTO MY MAGIC CRYSTAL AND SAW YOU ARRIVE ...GOING TO TRY TO TAKE THE GIRL FROM ME. EH? HEE HEE!

LET US SEE HOW YOUR MIGHT SHALL AVAIL AGAINST MY MAGIC. IF YOU WOULD FIGHT... HERE -- FIGHT TWO OF MY SERVANTS--

A PUFF OF SMOKE. IT CLEARS SLOWLY, AND IN ITS PLACE STAND TWO STRANGE LOOKING CREATURES....

HERE ARE TWO OPPONENTS FOR YOU-- BURN-- THE MAN OF FIRE... AND FREEZE-- THE MAN OF ICE! HEE HEE!

WITH THE EMBRACE OF EITHER OF THEIR OPPONENTS MEANING DEATH, THE BATMAN AND ROBIN FACE A SUPREME TEST...CAN THEY WIN?

DEFEAT THEM--IF YOU CAN'T HEE HEE HEE!

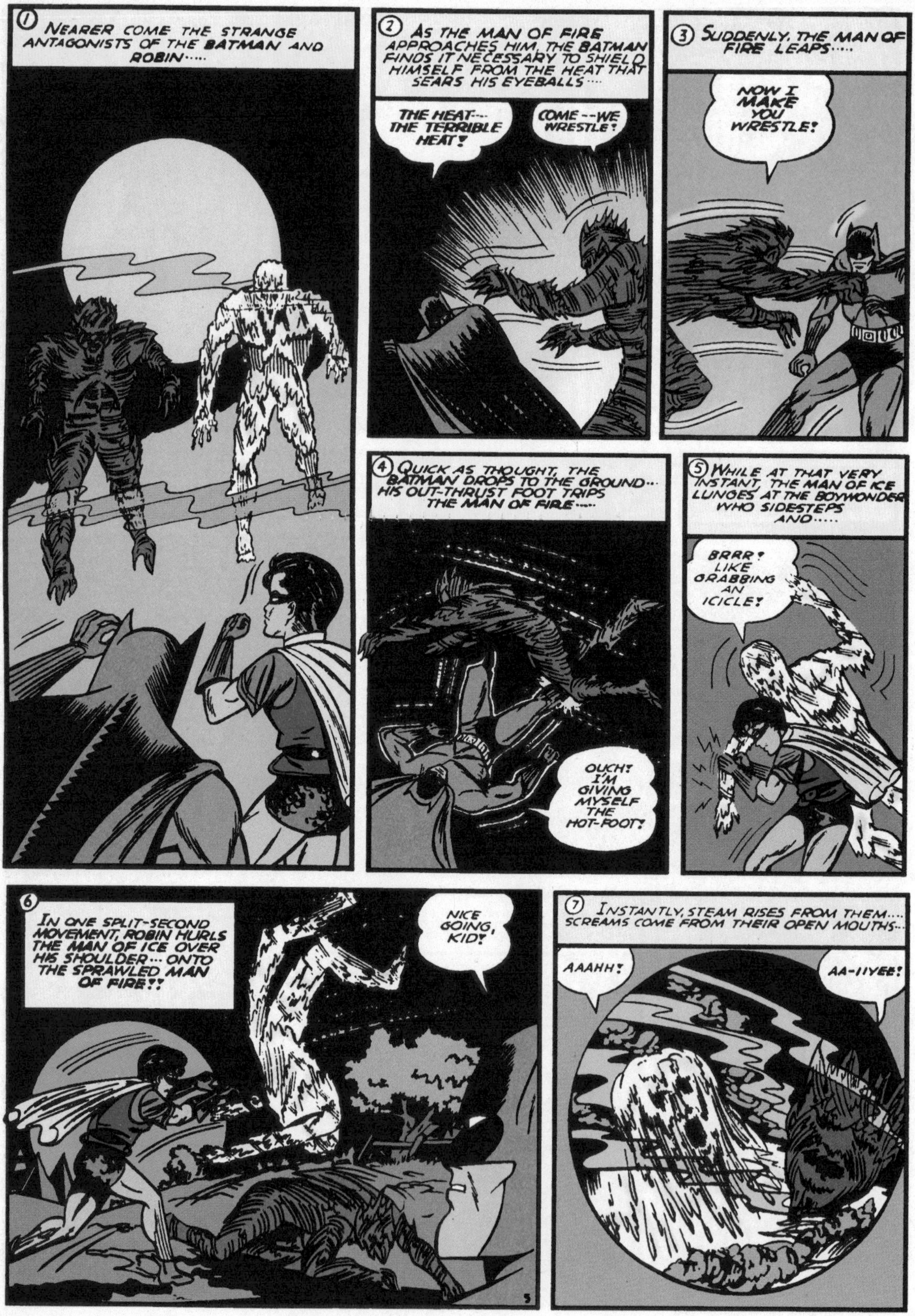
1 NEARER COME THE STRANGE ANTAGONISTS OF THE BATMAN AND ROBIN.....
2 AS THE MAN OF FIRE APPROACHES HIM, THE BATMAN FINDS IT NECESSARY TO SHIELD HIMSELF FROM THE HEAT THAT SEARS HIS EYEBALLS....
THE HEAT--- THE TERRIBLE HEAT!
COME --WE WRESTLE!
3 SUDDENLY, THE MAN OF FIRE LEAPS.....
NOW I MAKE YOU WRESTLE!
4 QUICK AS THOUGHT, THE BATMAN DROPS TO THE GROUND... HIS OUT-THRUST FOOT TRIPS THE MAN OF FIRE.....
OUCH! I'M GIVING MYSELF THE HOT-FOOT!
5 WHILE AT THAT VERY INSTANT, THE MAN OF ICE LUNGES AT THE BOYWONDER WHO SIDESTEPS AND.....
BRRR! LIKE GRABBING AN ICICLE!
6 IN ONE SPLIT-SECOND MOVEMENT, ROBIN HURLS THE MAN OF ICE OVER HIS SHOULDER... ONTO THE SPRAWLED MAN OF FIRE!!
NICE GOING, KID!
7 INSTANTLY, STEAM RISES FROM THEM.... SCREAMS COME FROM THEIR OPEN MOUTHS...
AAAHH!
AA-IIYEE!

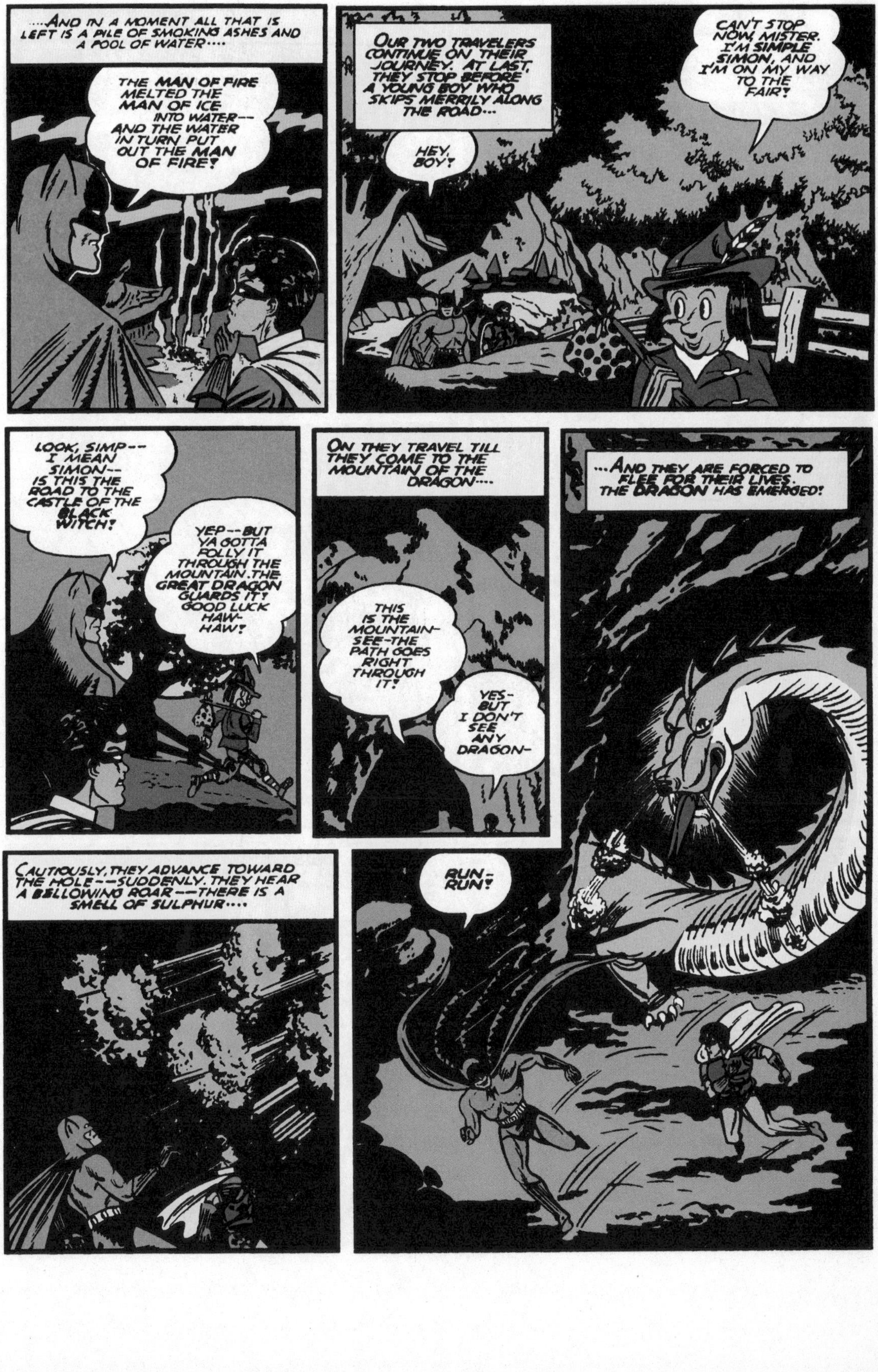
....AND IN A MOMENT ALL THAT IS LEFT IS A PILE OF SMOKING ASHES AND A POOL OF WATER....
THE MAN OF FIRE MELTED THE MAN OF ICE INTO WATER-- AND THE WATER IN TURN PUT OUT THE MAN OF FIRE!
OUR TWO TRAVELERS CONTINUE ON THEIR JOURNEY. AT LAST, THEY STOP BEFORE A YOUNG BOY WHO SKIPS MERRILY ALONG THE ROAD...
HEY, BOY!
CAN'T STOP NOW, MISTER. I'M SIMPLE SIMON, AND I'M ON MY WAY TO THE FAIR!
LOOK, SIMP-- I MEAN SIMON-- IS THIS THE ROAD TO THE CASTLE OF THE BLACK WITCH?
YEP--BUT YA GOTTA FOLLY IT THROUGH THE MOUNTAIN. THE GREAT DRAGON GUARDS IT! GOOD LUCK HAW-HAW!
ON THEY TRAVEL TILL THEY COME TO THE MOUNTAIN OF THE DRAGON....
THIS IS THE MOUNTAIN-SEE-THE PATH GOES RIGHT THROUGH IT!
YES-BUT I DON'T SEE ANY DRAGON-
CAUTIOUSLY, THEY ADVANCE TOWARD THE HOLE--SUDDENLY, THEY HEAR A BELLOWING ROAR--THERE IS A SMELL OF SULPHUR....
...AND THEY ARE FORCED TO FLEE FOR THEIR LIVES. THE DRAGON HAS EMERGED!
RUN-RUN!

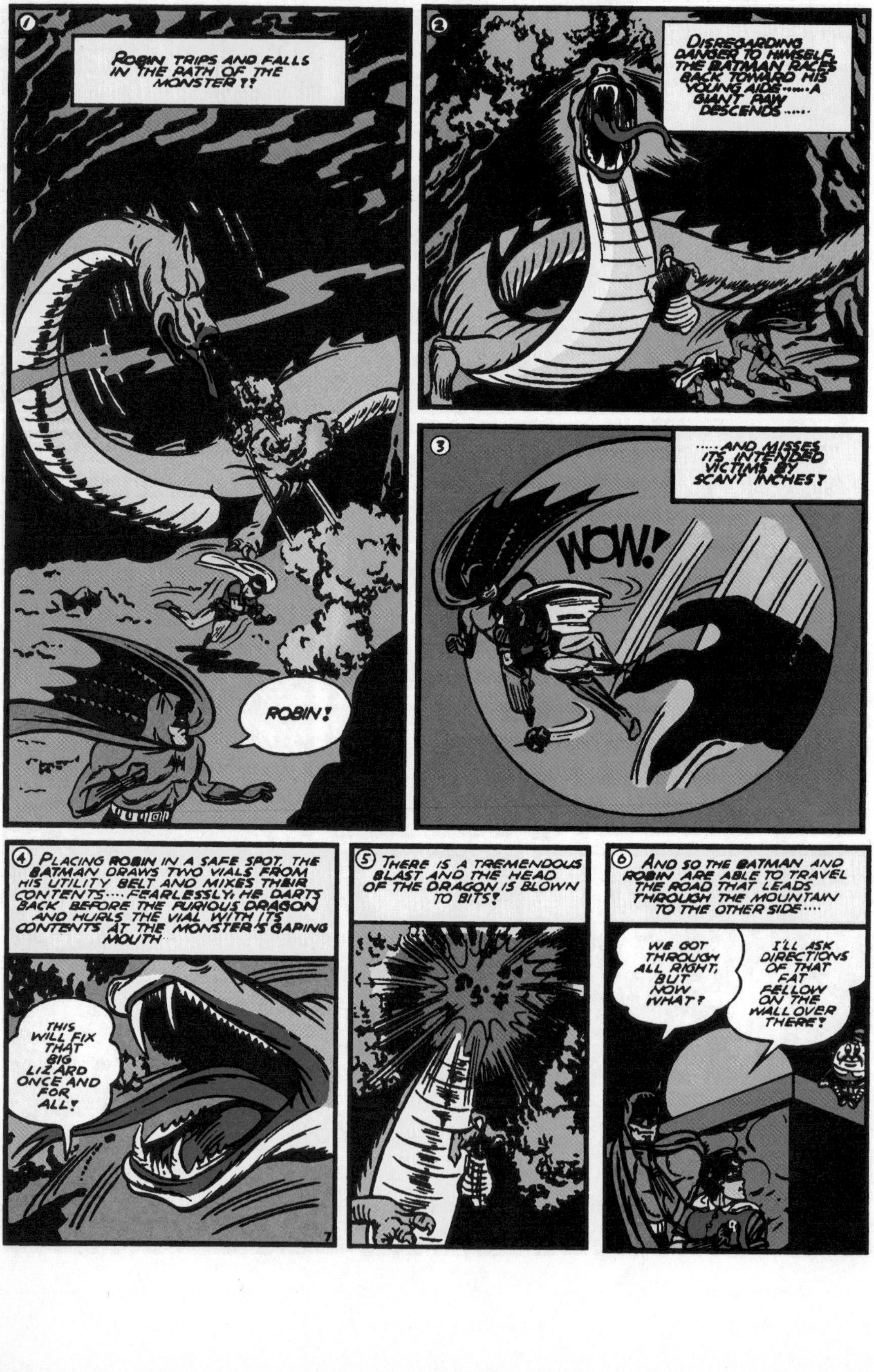

ROBIN TRIPS AND FALLS IN THE PATH OF THE MONSTER!!
ROBIN!
DISREGARDING DANGER TO HIMSELF, THE BATMAN RACES BACK TOWARD HIS YOUNG AIDE......A GIANT PAW DESCENDS......
.....AND MISSES ITS INTENDED VICTIMS BY SCANT INCHES!
WOW!
PLACING ROBIN IN A SAFE SPOT, THE BATMAN DRAWS TWO VIALS FROM HIS UTILITY BELT AND MIXES THEIR CONTENTS.... FEARLESSLY, HE DARTS BACK BEFORE THE FURIOUS DRAGON AND HURLS THE VIAL WITH ITS CONTENTS AT THE MONSTER'S GAPING MOUTH
THIS WILL FIX THAT BIG LIZARD ONCE AND FOR ALL!
THERE IS A TREMENDOUS BLAST AND THE HEAD OF THE DRAGON IS BLOWN TO BITS!
AND SO THE BATMAN AND ROBIN ARE ABLE TO TRAVEL THE ROAD THAT LEADS THROUGH THE MOUNTAIN TO THE OTHER SIDE....
WE GOT THROUGH ALL RIGHT, BUT NOW WHAT?
I'LL ASK DIRECTIONS OF THAT FAT FELLOW ON THE WALL OVER THERE!

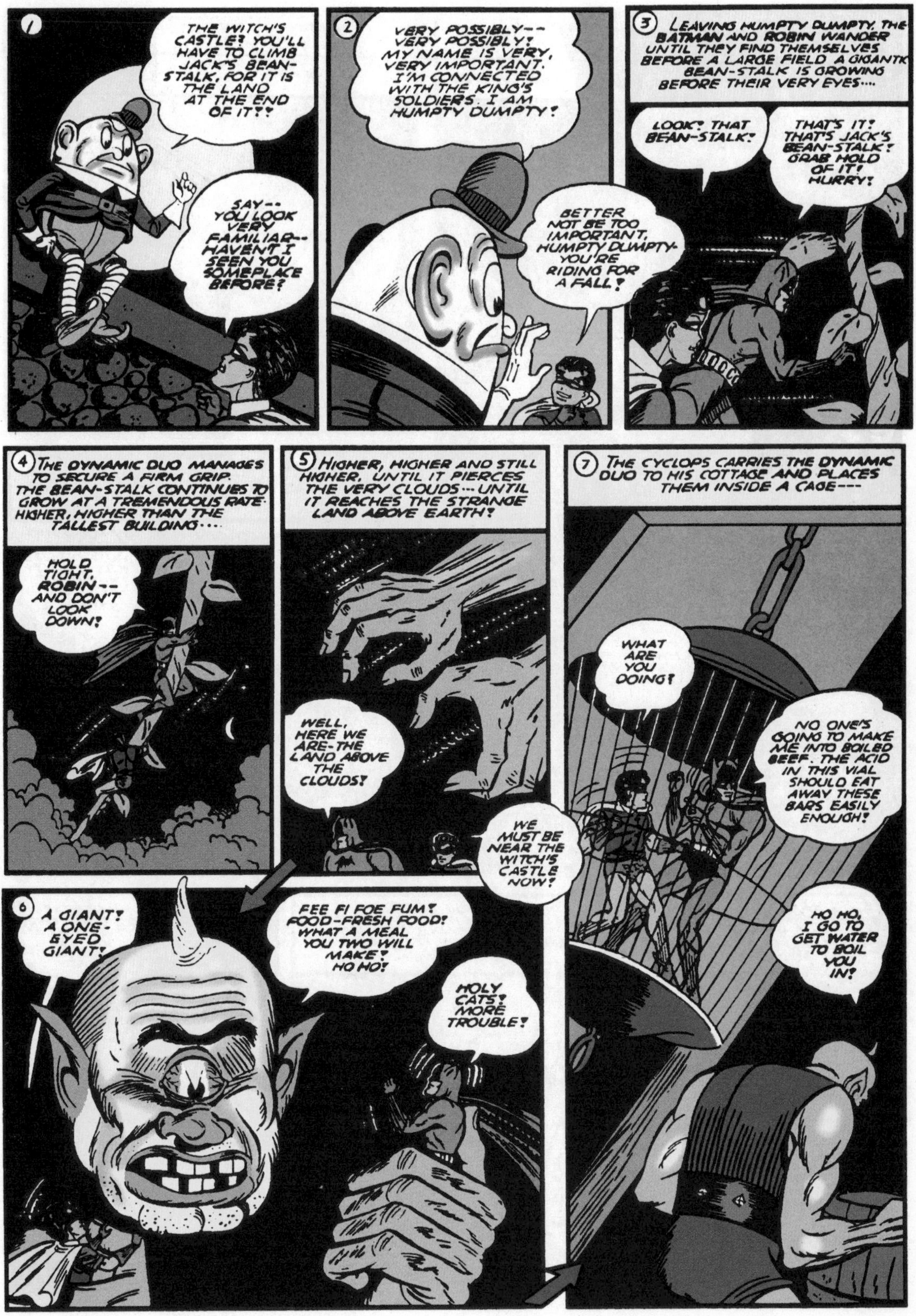
THE WITCH'S CASTLE? YOU'LL HAVE TO CLIMB JACK'S BEAN-STALK, FOR IT IS THE LAND AT THE END OF IT!!
SAY-- YOU LOOK VERY FAMILIAR-- HAVEN'T I SEEN YOU SOMEPLACE BEFORE?
VERY POSSIBLY-- VERY POSSIBLY! MY NAME IS VERY, VERY IMPORTANT. I'M CONNECTED WITH THE KING'S SOLDIERS. I AM HUMPTY DUMPTY!
BETTER NOT BE TOO IMPORTANT, HUMPTY DUMPTY- YOU'RE RIDING FOR A FALL!
LEAVING HUMPTY DUMPTY, THE BATMAN AND ROBIN WANDER UNTIL THEY FIND THEMSELVES BEFORE A LARGE FIELD A GIGANTIC BEAN-STALK IS GROWING BEFORE THEIR VERY EYES....
LOOK! THAT BEAN-STALK!
THAT'S IT! THAT'S JACK'S BEAN-STALK! GRAB HOLD OF IT! HURRY!
THE DYNAMIC DUO MANAGES TO SECURE A FIRM GRIP. THE BEAN-STALK CONTINUES TO GROW AT A TREMENDOUS RATE- HIGHER, HIGHER THAN THE TALLEST BUILDING....
HOLD TIGHT, ROBIN-- AND DON'T LOOK DOWN!
HIGHER, HIGHER AND STILL HIGHER, UNTIL IT PIERCES THE VERY CLOUDS--- UNTIL IT REACHES THE STRANGE LAND ABOVE EARTH!
WELL, HERE WE ARE-THE LAND ABOVE THE CLOUDS!
WE MUST BE NEAR THE WITCH'S CASTLE NOW!
A GIANT! A ONE-EYED GIANT!
FEE FI FOE FUM! FOOD-FRESH FOOD! WHAT A MEAL YOU TWO WILL MAKE! HO HO!
HOLY CATS! MORE TROUBLE!
THE CYCLOPS CARRIES THE DYNAMIC DUO TO HIS COTTAGE AND PLACES THEM INSIDE A CAGE---
WHAT ARE YOU DOING?
NO ONE'S GOING TO MAKE ME INTO BOILED BEEF. THE ACID IN THIS VIAL SHOULD EAT AWAY THESE BARS EASILY ENOUGH!
HO HO, I GO TO GET WATER TO BOIL YOU IN!

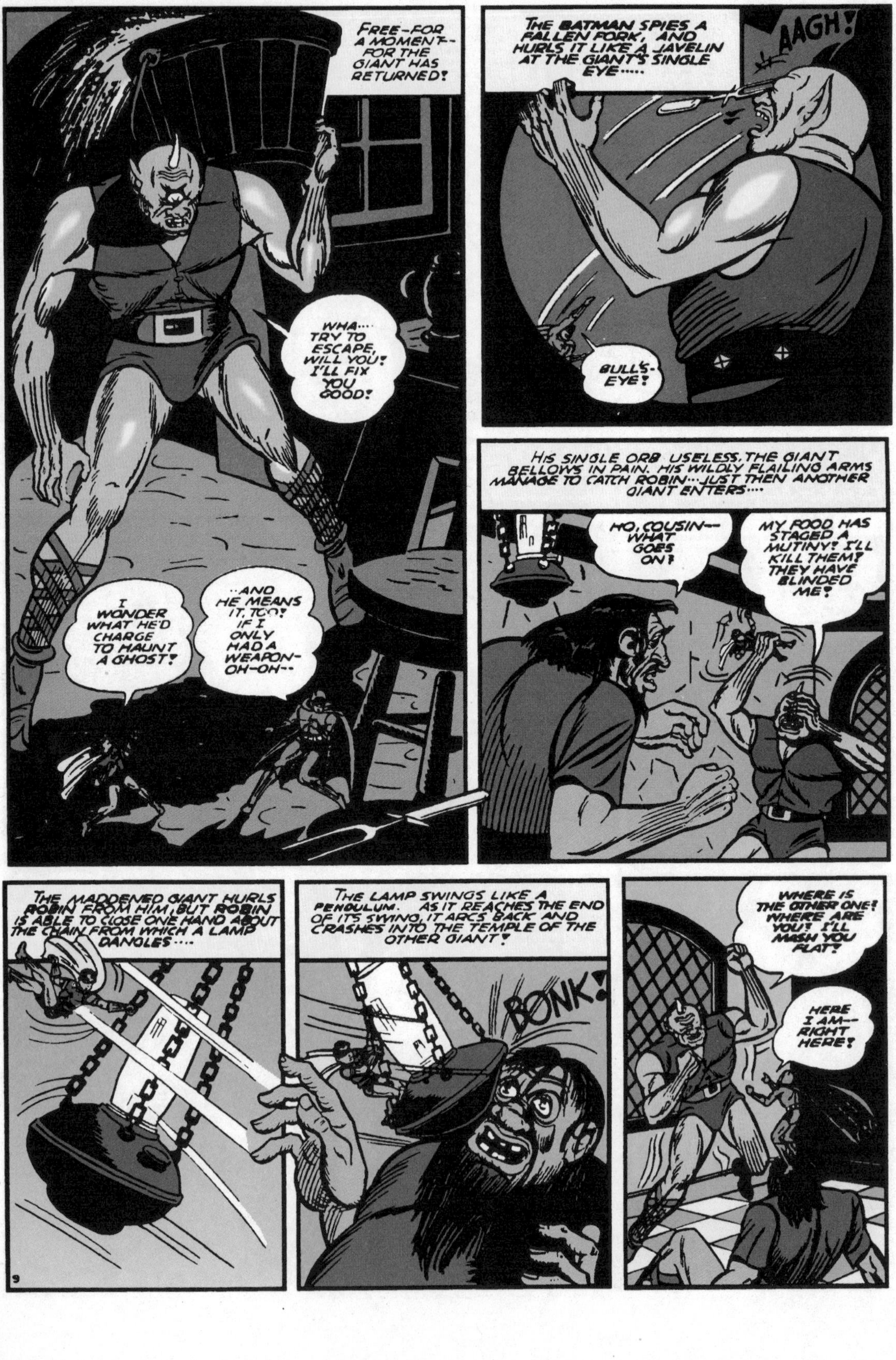
FREE—FOR A MOMENT—FOR THE GIANT HAS RETURNED!
WHA.... TRY TO ESCAPE, WILL YOU! I'LL FIX YOU GOOD!
I WONDER WHAT HE'D CHARGE TO HAUNT A GHOST!
...AND HE MEANS IT, TOO! IF I ONLY HAD A WEAPON—OH-OH--
THE BATMAN SPIES A FALLEN FORK, AND HURLS IT LIKE A JAVELIN AT THE GIANT'S SINGLE EYE.....
AAGH!
BULL'S-EYE!
HIS SINGLE ORB USELESS, THE GIANT BELLOWS IN PAIN. HIS WILDLY FLAILING ARMS MANAGE TO CATCH ROBIN... JUST THEN ANOTHER GIANT ENTERS....
HO, COUSIN-- WHAT GOES ON?
MY FOOD HAS STAGED A MUTINY! I'LL KILL THEM! THEY HAVE BLINDED ME!
THE MADDENED GIANT HURLS ROBIN FROM HIM, BUT ROBIN IS ABLE TO CLOSE ONE HAND ABOUT THE CHAIN FROM WHICH A LAMP DANGLES....
9
THE LAMP SWINGS LIKE A PENDULUM. AS IT REACHES THE END OF ITS SWING, IT ARCS BACK AND CRASHES INTO THE TEMPLE OF THE OTHER GIANT!
BONK!
WHERE IS THE OTHER ONE! WHERE ARE YOU! I'LL MASH YOU FLAT!
HERE I AM—RIGHT HERE!

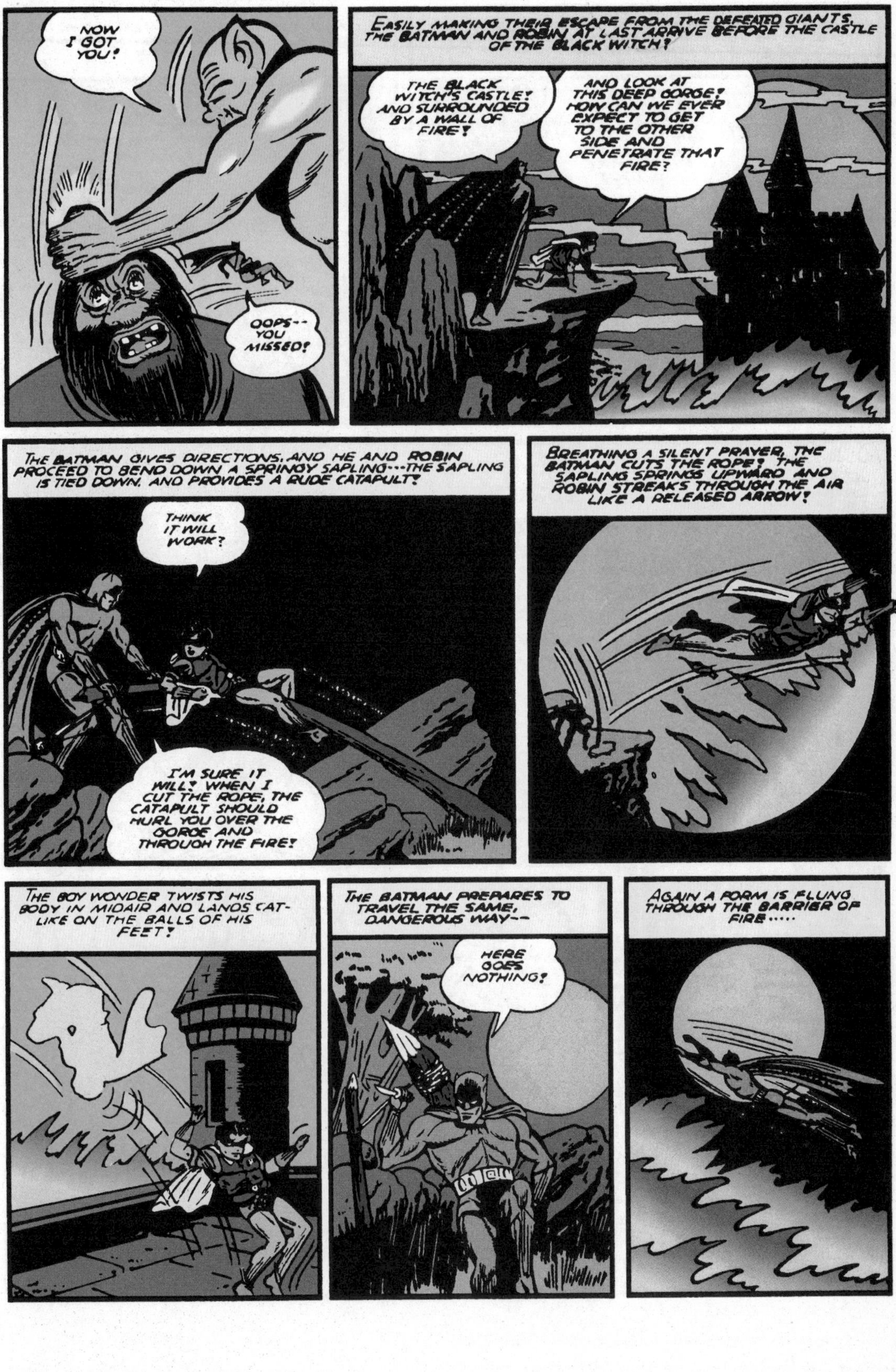
NOW I GOT YOU!
OOPS-- YOU MISSED!
EASILY MAKING THEIR ESCAPE FROM THE DEFEATED GIANTS, THE BATMAN AND ROBIN AT LAST ARRIVE BEFORE THE CASTLE OF THE BLACK WITCH!
THE BLACK WITCH'S CASTLE! AND SURROUNDED BY A WALL OF FIRE!
AND LOOK AT THIS DEEP GORGE! HOW CAN WE EVER EXPECT TO GET TO THE OTHER SIDE AND PENETRATE THAT FIRE?
THE BATMAN GIVES DIRECTIONS, AND HE AND ROBIN PROCEED TO BEND DOWN A SPRINGY SAPLING---THE SAPLING IS TIED DOWN, AND PROVIDES A RUDE CATAPULT!
THINK IT WILL WORK?
I'M SURE IT WILL! WHEN I CUT THE ROPE, THE CATAPULT SHOULD HURL YOU OVER THE GORGE AND THROUGH THE FIRE!
BREATHING A SILENT PRAYER, THE BATMAN CUTS THE ROPE! THE SAPLING SPRINGS UPWARD AND ROBIN STREAKS THROUGH THE AIR LIKE A RELEASED ARROW!
THE BOY WONDER TWISTS HIS BODY IN MIDAIR AND LANDS CAT-LIKE ON THE BALLS OF HIS FEET!
THE BATMAN PREPARES TO TRAVEL THE SAME, DANGEROUS WAY--
HERE GOES NOTHING!
AGAIN A FORM IS FLUNG THROUGH THE BARRIER OF FIRE.....

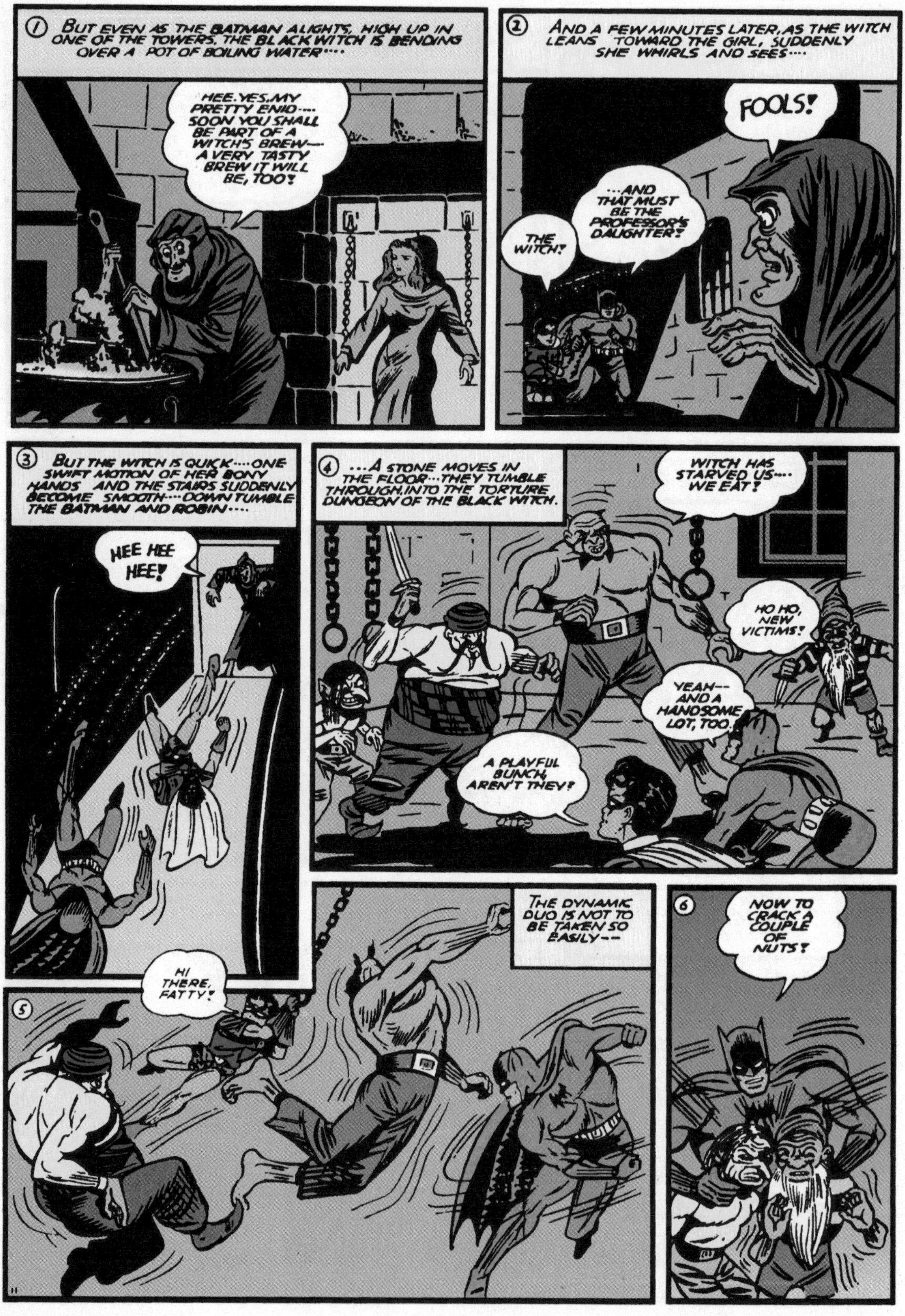
1
BUT EVEN AS THE BATMAN ALIGHTS, HIGH UP IN ONE OF THE TOWERS, THE BLACK WITCH IS BENDING OVER A POT OF BOILING WATER....
HEE. YES. MY PRETTY ENID.... SOON YOU SHALL BE PART OF A WITCH'S BREW--- A VERY TASTY BREW IT WILL BE, TOO!
2
AND A FEW MINUTES LATER, AS THE WITCH LEANS TOWARD THE GIRL, SUDDENLY SHE WHIRLS AND SEES....
FOOLS!
THE WITCH!
...AND THAT MUST BE THE PROFESSOR'S DAUGHTER!
3
BUT THE WITCH IS QUICK....ONE SWIFT MOTION OF HER BONY HANDS AND THE STAIRS SUDDENLY BECOME SMOOTH....DOWN TUMBLE THE BATMAN AND ROBIN....
HEE HEE HEE!
4
...A STONE MOVES IN THE FLOOR...THEY TUMBLE THROUGH, INTO THE TORTURE DUNGEON OF THE BLACK WITCH.
WITCH HAS STARVED US.... WE EAT!
HO HO, NEW VICTIMS!
YEAH-- AND A HANDSOME LOT, TOO.
A PLAYFUL BUNCH, AREN'T THEY?
THE DYNAMIC DUO IS NOT TO BE TAKEN SO EASILY--
5
HI THERE, FATTY!
6
NOW TO CRACK A COUPLE OF NUTS!

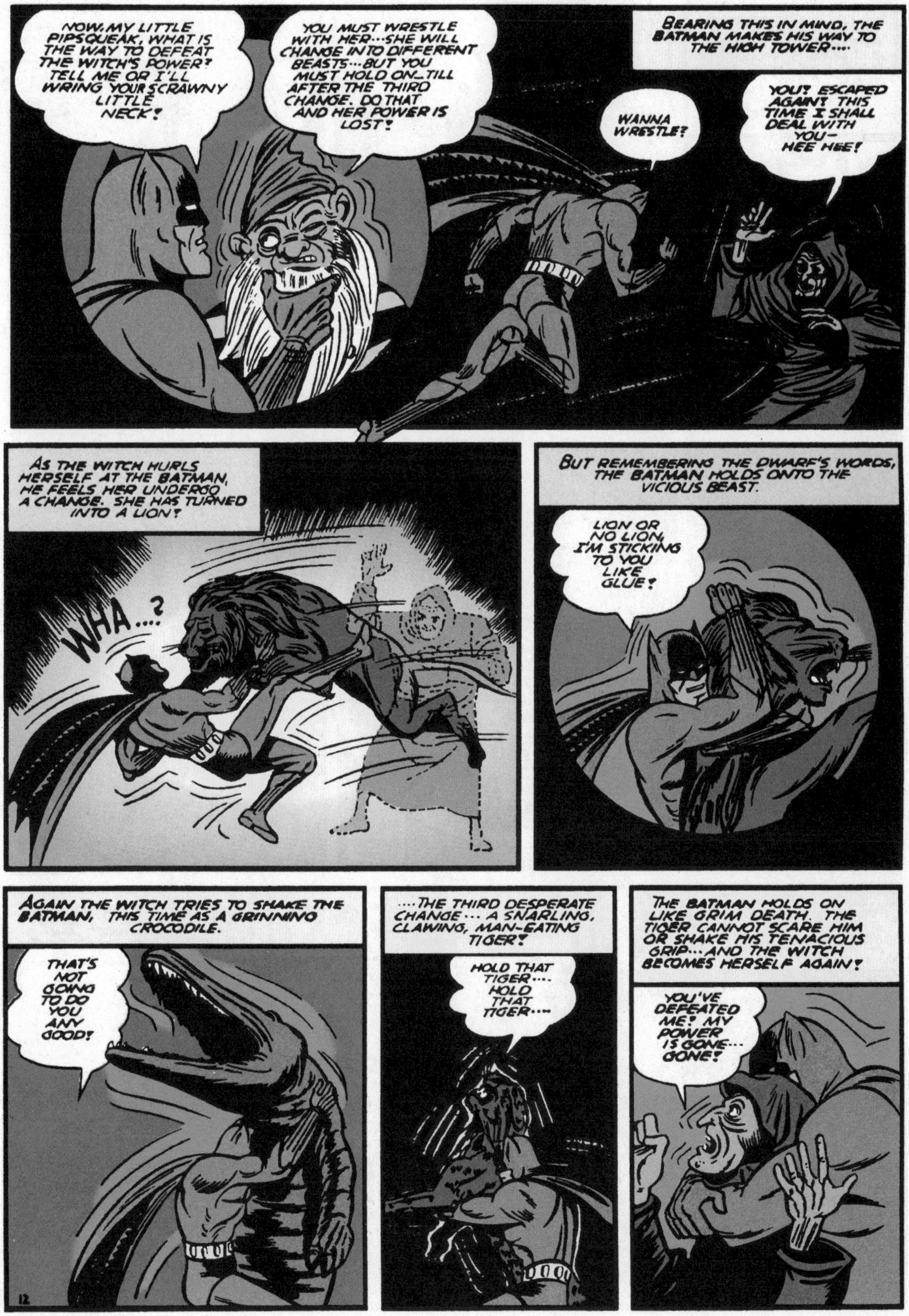

NOW, MY LITTLE PIPSQUEAK, WHAT IS THE WAY TO DEFEAT THE WITCH'S POWER? TELL ME OR I'LL WRING YOUR SCRAWNY LITTLE NECK!
YOU MUST WRESTLE WITH HER...SHE WILL CHANGE INTO DIFFERENT BEASTS...BUT YOU MUST HOLD ON_TILL AFTER THE THIRD CHANGE. DO THAT AND HER POWER IS LOST!
BEARING THIS IN MIND, THE BATMAN MAKES HIS WAY TO THE HIGH TOWER....
WANNA WRESTLE?
YOU! ESCAPED AGAIN! THIS TIME I SHALL DEAL WITH YOU– HEE HEE!
AS THE WITCH HURLS HERSELF AT THE BATMAN, HE FEELS HER UNDERGO A CHANGE. SHE HAS TURNED INTO A LION!
WHA...?
BUT REMEMBERING THE DWARF'S WORDS, THE BATMAN HOLDS ONTO THE VICIOUS BEAST.
LION OR NO LION, I'M STICKING TO YOU LIKE GLUE!
AGAIN THE WITCH TRIES TO SHAKE THE BATMAN, THIS TIME AS A GRINNING CROCODILE.
THAT'S NOT GOING TO DO YOU ANY GOOD!
12
....THE THIRD DESPERATE CHANGE... A SNARLING, CLAWING, MAN-EATING TIGER!
HOLD THAT TIGER.... HOLD THAT TIGER....
THE BATMAN HOLDS ON LIKE GRIM DEATH. THE TIGER CANNOT SCARE HIM OR SHAKE HIS TENACIOUS GRIP... AND THE WITCH BECOMES HERSELF AGAIN!
YOU'VE DEFEATED ME! MY POWER IS GONE... GONE!

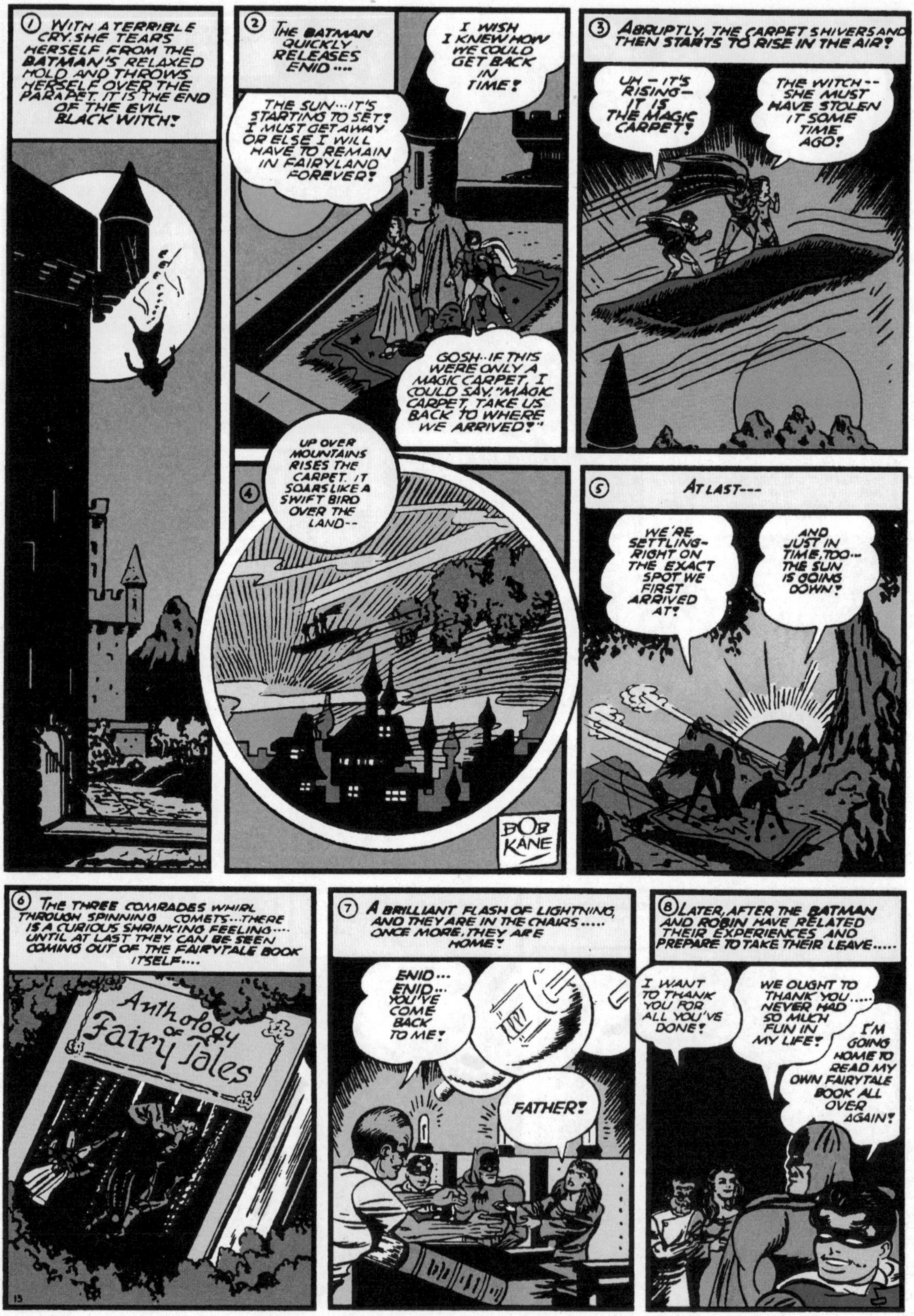
WITH A TERRIBLE CRY, SHE TEARS HERSELF FROM THE BATMAN'S RELAXED HOLD AND THROWS HERSELF OVER THE PARAPET. IT IS THE END OF THE EVIL BLACK WITCH!
THE BATMAN QUICKLY RELEASES ENID....
I WISH I KNEW HOW WE COULD GET BACK IN TIME!
THE SUN...IT'S STARTING TO SET! I MUST GET AWAY OR ELSE I WILL HAVE TO REMAIN IN FAIRYLAND FOREVER!
GOSH..IF THIS WERE ONLY A MAGIC CARPET, I COULD SAY, "MAGIC CARPET, TAKE US BACK TO WHERE WE ARRIVED!"
ABRUPTLY, THE CARPET SHIVERS AND THEN STARTS TO RISE IN THE AIR!
UH - IT'S RISING - IT IS THE MAGIC CARPET!
THE WITCH -- SHE MUST HAVE STOLEN IT SOME TIME AGO!
UP OVER MOUNTAINS RISES THE CARPET. IT SOARS LIKE A SWIFT BIRD OVER THE LAND--
BOB KANE
AT LAST---
WE'RE SETTLING RIGHT ON THE EXACT SPOT WE FIRST ARRIVED AT!
AND JUST IN TIME, TOO-- THE SUN IS GOING DOWN!
THE THREE COMRADES WHIRL THROUGH SPINNING COMETS...THERE IS A CURIOUS SHRINKING FEELING.... UNTIL AT LAST THEY CAN BE SEEN COMING OUT OF THE FAIRYTALE BOOK ITSELF....
Anthology of Fairy Tales
A BRILLIANT FLASH OF LIGHTNING, AND THEY ARE IN THE CHAIRS..... ONCE MORE, THEY ARE HOME!
ENID... ENID... YOU'VE COME BACK TO ME!
FATHER!
LATER, AFTER THE BATMAN AND ROBIN HAVE RELATED THEIR EXPERIENCES AND PREPARE TO TAKE THEIR LEAVE.....
I WANT TO THANK YOU FOR ALL YOU'VE DONE!
WE OUGHT TO THANK YOU..... NEVER HAD SO MUCH FUN IN MY LIFE!
I'M GOING HOME TO READ MY OWN FAIRYTALE BOOK ALL OVER AGAIN!

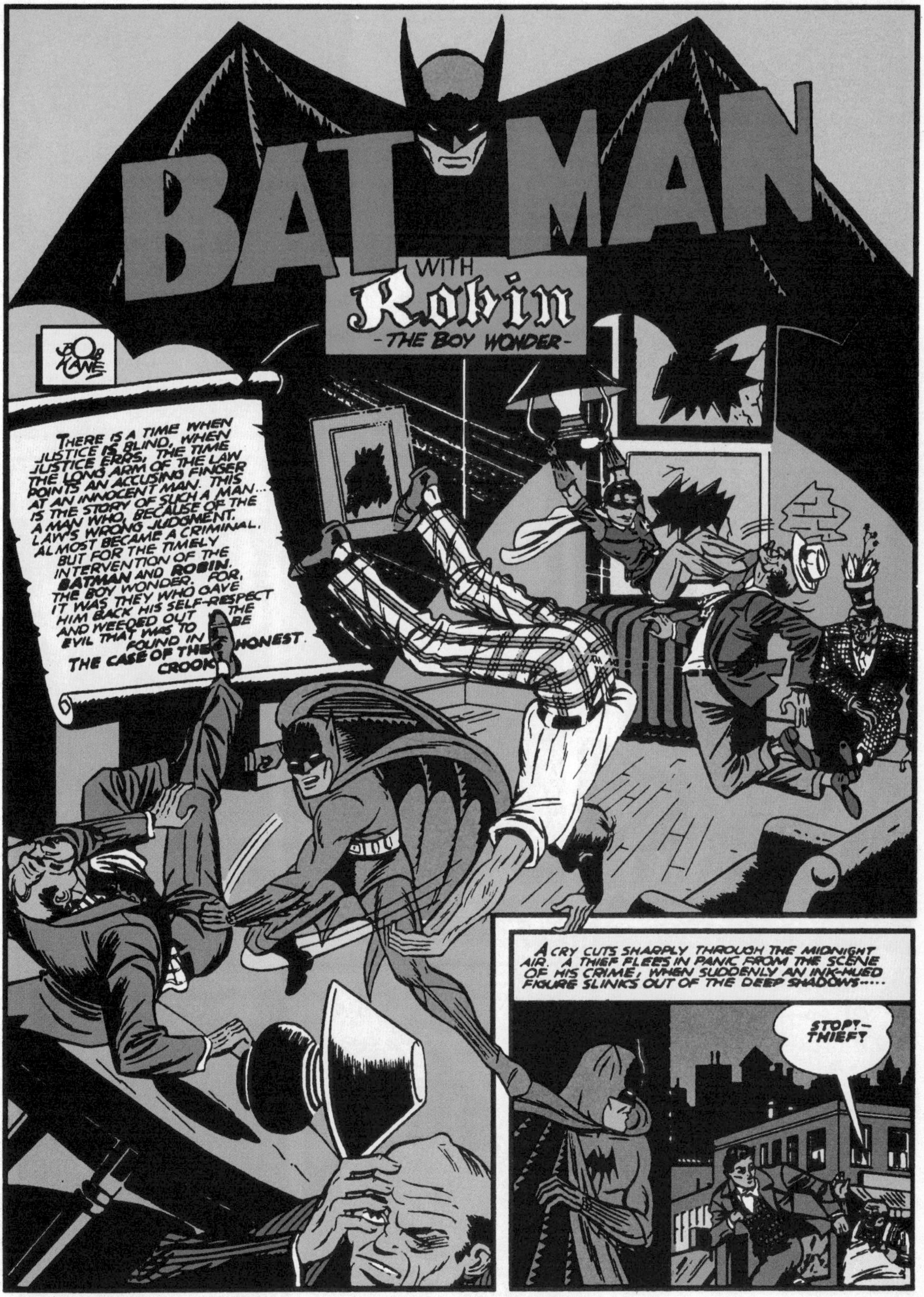
BATMAN
WITH Robin
-THE BOY WONDER-
BOB KANE
THERE IS A TIME WHEN JUSTICE IS BLIND, WHEN JUSTICE ERRS, THE TIME THE LONG ARM OF THE LAW POINTS AN ACCUSING FINGER AT AN INNOCENT MAN. THIS IS THE STORY OF SUCH A MAN... A MAN WHO, BECAUSE OF THE LAW'S WRONG JUDGMENT, ALMOST BECAME A CRIMINAL, BUT FOR THE TIMELY INTERVENTION OF THE BATMAN AND ROBIN, THE BOY WONDER. FOR, IT WAS THEY WHO GAVE HIM BACK HIS SELF-RESPECT AND WEEDED OUT THE EVIL THAT WAS TO BE FOUND IN
THE CASE OF THE HONEST CROOK
A CRY CUTS SHARPLY THROUGH THE MIDNIGHT AIR. A THIEF FLEES IN PANIC FROM THE SCENE OF HIS CRIME, WHEN SUDDENLY AN INK-HUED FIGURE SLINKS OUT OF THE DEEP SHADOWS.....
STOP!— THIEF!

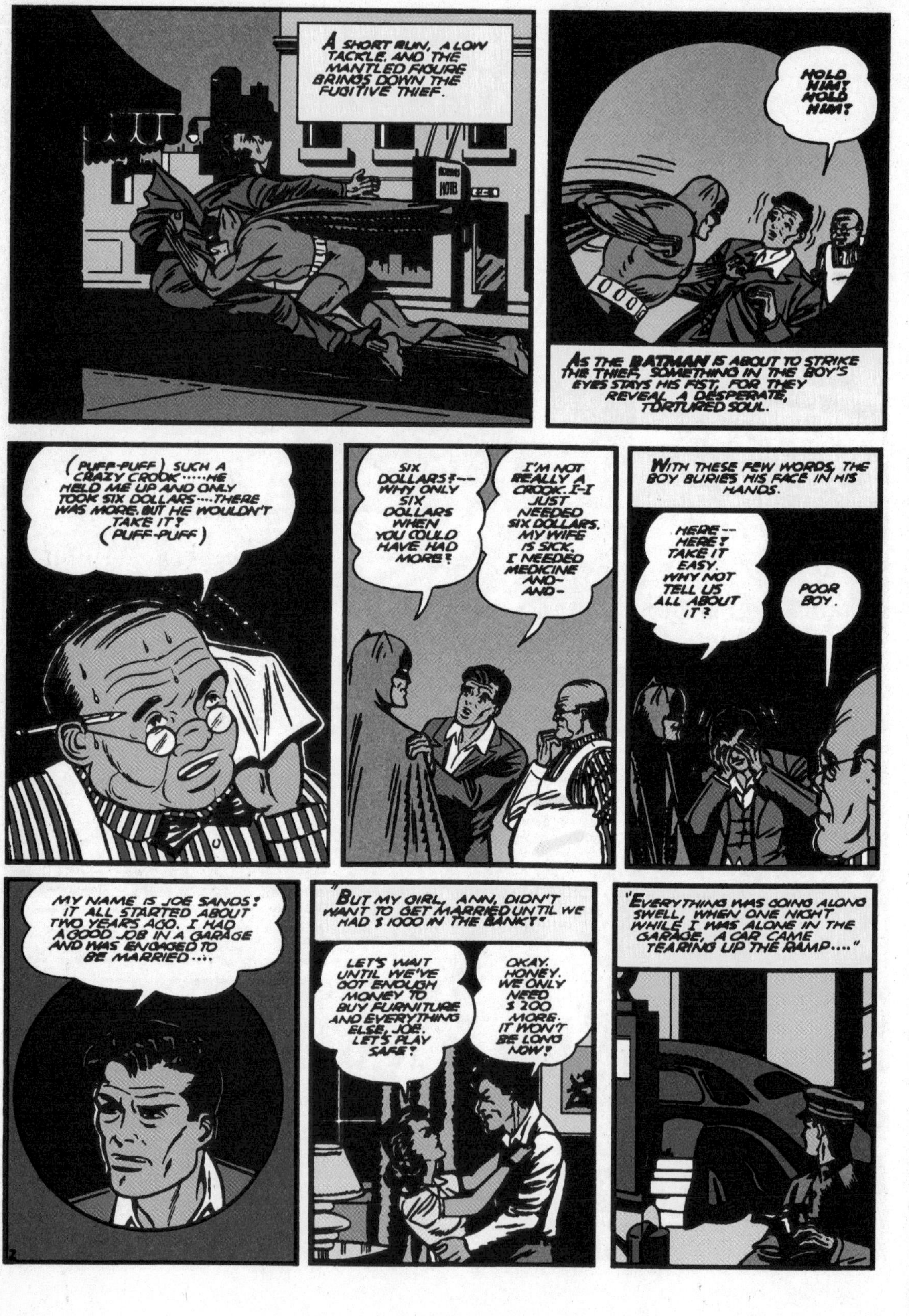
A SHORT RUN, A LOW TACKLE, AND THE MANTLED FIGURE BRINGS DOWN THE FUGITIVE THIEF.
HOLD HIM! HOLD HIM!
AS THE BATMAN IS ABOUT TO STRIKE THE THIEF, SOMETHING IN THE BOY'S EYES STAYS HIS FIST, FOR THEY REVEAL A DESPERATE, TORTURED SOUL.
(PUFF-PUFF) SUCH A CRAZY CROOK.....HE HELD ME UP AND ONLY TOOK SIX DOLLARS....THERE WAS MORE, BUT HE WOULDN'T TAKE IT! (PUFF-PUFF)
SIX DOLLARS?-- WHY ONLY SIX DOLLARS WHEN YOU COULD HAVE HAD MORE?
I'M NOT REALLY A CROOK. I-I JUST NEEDED SIX DOLLARS. MY WIFE IS SICK. I NEEDED MEDICINE AND-AND-
WITH THESE FEW WORDS, THE BOY BURIES HIS FACE IN HIS HANDS.
HERE-- HERE! TAKE IT EASY. WHY NOT TELL US ALL ABOUT IT?
POOR BOY.
MY NAME IS JOE SANOS! IT ALL STARTED ABOUT TWO YEARS AGO. I HAD A GOOD JOB IN A GARAGE AND WAS ENGAGED TO BE MARRIED....
"BUT MY GIRL, ANN, DIDN'T WANT TO GET MARRIED UNTIL WE HAD $1000 IN THE BANK!"
LET'S WAIT UNTIL WE'VE GOT ENOUGH MONEY TO BUY FURNITURE AND EVERYTHING ELSE, JOE. LET'S PLAY SAFE!
OKAY, HONEY. WE ONLY NEED $200 MORE. IT WON'T BE LONG NOW!
"EVERYTHING WAS GOING ALONG SWELL, WHEN ONE NIGHT WHILE I WAS ALONE IN THE GARAGE, A CAR CAME TEARING UP THE RAMP...."

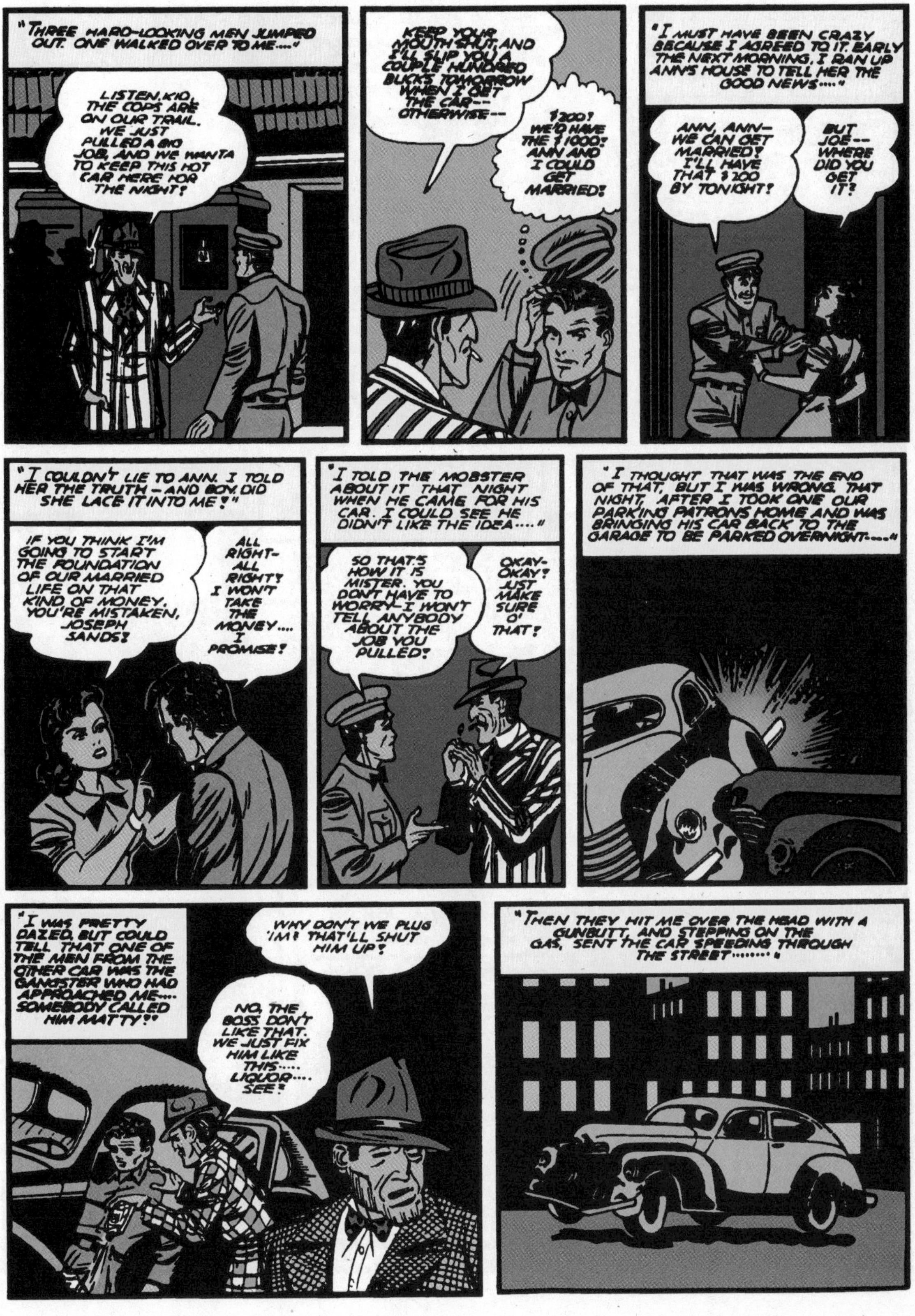
"THREE HARD-LOOKING MEN JUMPED OUT. ONE WALKED OVER TO ME...."
LISTEN, KID, THE COPS ARE ON OUR TRAIL. WE JUST PULLED A BIG JOB, AND WE WANTA TO KEEP THIS HOT CAR HERE FOR THE NIGHT!
KEEP YOUR MOUTH SHUT, AND I'LL SLIP YOU A COUPLE HUNDRED BUCKS TOMORROW WHEN I GET THE CAR-- OTHERWISE--
$200! WE'D HAVE THE $1000! ANN AND I COULD GET MARRIED!
"I MUST HAVE BEEN CRAZY BECAUSE I AGREED TO IT. EARLY THE NEXT MORNING, I RAN UP ANN'S HOUSE TO TELL HER THE GOOD NEWS...."
ANN, ANN-- WE CAN GET MARRIED! I'LL HAVE THAT $200 BY TONIGHT!
BUT JOE-- WHERE DID YOU GET IT?
"I COULDN'T LIE TO ANN. I TOLD HER THE TRUTH -- AND BOY, DID SHE LACE IT INTO ME!"
IF YOU THINK I'M GOING TO START THE FOUNDATION OF OUR MARRIED LIFE ON THAT KIND OF MONEY, YOU'RE MISTAKEN, JOSEPH SANDS!
ALL RIGHT-- ALL RIGHT! I WON'T TAKE THE MONEY.... I PROMISE!
"I TOLD THE MOBSTER ABOUT IT THAT NIGHT WHEN HE CAME FOR HIS CAR. I COULD SEE HE DIDN'T LIKE THE IDEA...."
SO THAT'S HOW IT IS MISTER. YOU DON'T HAVE TO WORRY-- I WON'T TELL ANYBODY ABOUT THE JOB YOU PULLED!
OKAY-- OKAY! JUST MAKE SURE O' THAT!
"I THOUGHT THAT WAS THE END OF THAT, BUT I WAS WRONG. THAT NIGHT, AFTER I TOOK ONE OUR PARKING PATRONS HOME AND WAS BRINGING HIS CAR BACK TO THE GARAGE TO BE PARKED OVERNIGHT...."
"I WAS PRETTY DAZED, BUT COULD TELL THAT ONE OF THE MEN FROM THE OTHER CAR WAS THE GANGSTER WHO HAD APPROACHED ME.... SOMEBODY CALLED HIM MATTY!"
WHY DON'T WE PLUG 'IM! THAT'LL SHUT HIM UP!
NO, THE BOSS DON'T LIKE THAT. WE JUST FIX HIM LIKE THIS..... LIQUOR.... SEE?
"THEN THEY HIT ME OVER THE HEAD WITH A GUNBUTT, AND STEPPING ON THE GAS, SENT THE CAR SPEEDING THROUGH THE STREET........"

"I WAS STILL UNCONSCIOUS, AND WITH NOBODY STEERING IT, THE CAR SWERVED AND CRASHED INTO A STORE..."

CRASH!

VIC'S BA

"A COP PULLED ME OUT OF THE WRECK."

DRUNK-- DRUNK AS A LORD!

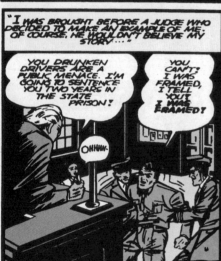

"I WAS BROUGHT BEFORE A JUDGE WHO DECIDED TO MAKE AN EXAMPLE OF ME. OF COURSE, HE WOULDN'T BELIEVE MY STORY..."

YOU DRUNKEN DRIVERS ARE A PUBLIC MENACE. I'M GOING TO SENTENCE YOU TWO YEARS IN THE STATE PRISON!

YOU CAN'T! I WAS FRAMED, I TELL YOU! I WAS FRAMED!

OHHH--

"ANN WAS WAITING FOR ME WHEN I GOT OUT. I WAS BROKE. THEY HAD TAKEN MY SAVINGS TO PAY FOR THE DAMAGES TO THE STORE AND THE CAR."

THE FIRST THING I'M GOING TO DO IS GET THAT GANGSTER WHO FRAMED ME TO GET ME OUT OF THE WAY!

NO-NO! THEY'LL KILL YOU! JOE, IF YOU FORGET ABOUT HIM-- I'LL MARRY YOU TODAY! PLEASE-- FOR ME!

"A SWELL GIRL, ANN. I AGREED, AND WE WERE MARRIED AS SOON AS I GOT MYSELF A JOB."

...DO YOU, ANN DAVIS, TAKE THIS MAN TO.....

"I GUESS WE THOUGHT ALL OUR TROUBLES WERE OVER THEN, BUT WE WERE WRONG. ONE DAY, MY BOSS CALLED ME INTO HIS OFFICE....."

I'VE JUST LEARNED YOU HAVE A PRISON RECORD. WE CAN'T ALLOW THAT IN THIS COMPANY. YOU'RE DISCHARGED.

"--AND IT WAS THE SAME WITH EVERY OTHER JOB. AS SOON AS THEY FOUND OUT I WAS ONCE IN JAIL ---"

ARUMPH! IN VIEW OF YOUR PAST RECORD-- ARUMPH--

YEAH-- I KNOW-- I'M FIRED!

"....IT GOT SO I COULDN'T HOLD ANY JOB. WE WERE ALMOST FLAT BROKE THE DAY ANN FELL SICK---"

SHE'LL BE ALL RIGHT, DOC-- SHE'LL BE ALL RIGHT!

GET THIS PRESCRIPTION FILLED AND BUY THESE MEDICINES. THAT'LL DO IT!

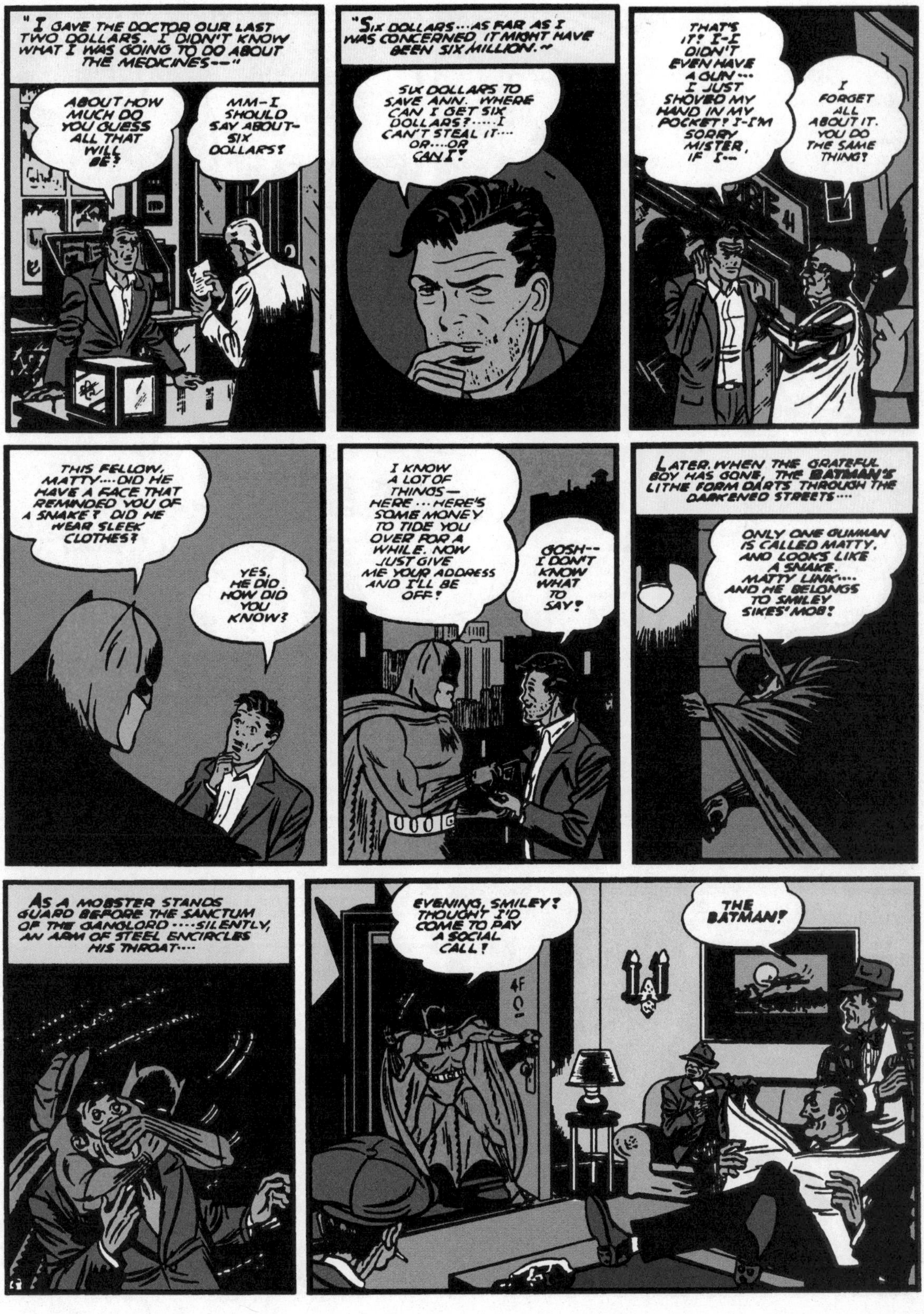
"I GAVE THE DOCTOR OUR LAST TWO DOLLARS. I DIDN'T KNOW WHAT I WAS GOING TO DO ABOUT THE MEDICINES--"
ABOUT HOW MUCH DO YOU GUESS ALL THAT WILL BE?
MM-I SHOULD SAY ABOUT- SIX DOLLARS!
"SIX DOLLARS... AS FAR AS I WAS CONCERNED, IT MIGHT HAVE BEEN SIX MILLION."
SIX DOLLARS TO SAVE ANN. WHERE CAN I GET SIX DOLLARS?.....I CAN'T STEAL IT.... OR....OR CAN I?
THAT'S IT! I-I DIDN'T EVEN HAVE A GUN... I JUST SHOVED MY HAND IN MY POCKET! I-I'M SORRY MISTER, IF I--
I FORGET ALL ABOUT IT. YOU DO THE SAME THING!
THIS FELLOW, MATTY....DID HE HAVE A FACE THAT REMINDED YOU OF A SNAKE? DID HE WEAR SLEEK CLOTHES?
YES, HE DID. HOW DID YOU KNOW?
I KNOW A LOT OF THINGS— HERE...HERE'S SOME MONEY TO TIDE YOU OVER FOR A WHILE. NOW JUST GIVE ME YOUR ADDRESS AND I'LL BE OFF!
GOSH-- I DON'T KNOW WHAT TO SAY!
LATER, WHEN THE GRATEFUL BOY HAS GONE, THE BATMAN'S LITHE FORM DARTS THROUGH THE DARKENED STREETS....
ONLY ONE GUNMAN IS CALLED MATTY, AND LOOKS LIKE A SNAKE. MATTY LINK.... AND HE BELONGS TO SMILEY SIKES' MOB!
AS A MOBSTER STANDS GUARD BEFORE THE SANCTUM OF THE GANGLORD....SILENTLY, AN ARM OF STEEL ENCIRCLES HIS THROAT....
EVENING, SMILEY! THOUGHT I'D COME TO PAY A SOCIAL CALL!
THE BATMAN!

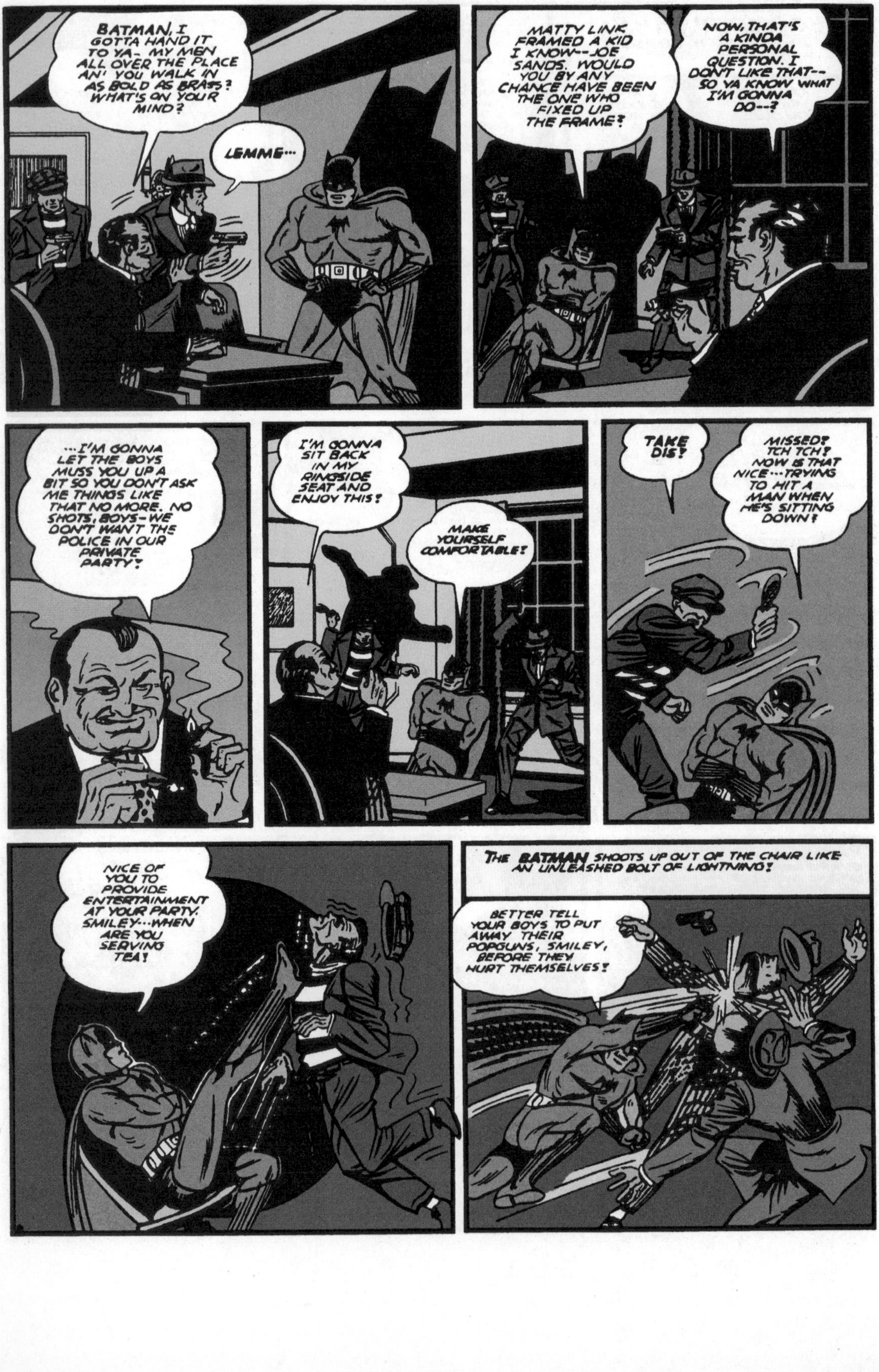
BATMAN, I GOTTA HAND IT TO YA- MY MEN ALL OVER THE PLACE AN' YOU WALK IN AS BOLD AS BRASS? WHAT'S ON YOUR MIND?
LEMME...
MATTY LINK FRAMED A KID I KNOW--JOE SANDS. WOULD YOU BY ANY CHANCE HAVE BEEN THE ONE WHO FIXED UP THE FRAME?
NOW, THAT'S A KINDA PERSONAL QUESTION. I DON'T LIKE THAT-- SO YA KNOW WHAT I'M GONNA DO--?
...I'M GONNA LET THE BOYS MUSS YOU UP A BIT SO YOU DON'T ASK ME THINGS LIKE THAT NO MORE. NO SHOTS, BOYS-WE DON'T WANT THE POLICE IN OUR PRIVATE PARTY!
I'M GONNA SIT BACK IN MY RINGSIDE SEAT AND ENJOY THIS!
MAKE YOURSELF COMFORTABLE!
TAKE DIS!
MISSED? TCH TCH! NOW IS THAT NICE...TRYING TO HIT A MAN WHEN HE'S SITTING DOWN?
NICE OF YOU TO PROVIDE ENTERTAINMENT AT YOUR PARTY, SMILEY...WHEN ARE YOU SERVING TEA!
THE BATMAN SHOOTS UP OUT OF THE CHAIR LIKE AN UNLEASHED BOLT OF LIGHTNING!
BETTER TELL YOUR BOYS TO PUT AWAY THEIR POPGUNS, SMILEY, BEFORE THEY HURT THEMSELVES!

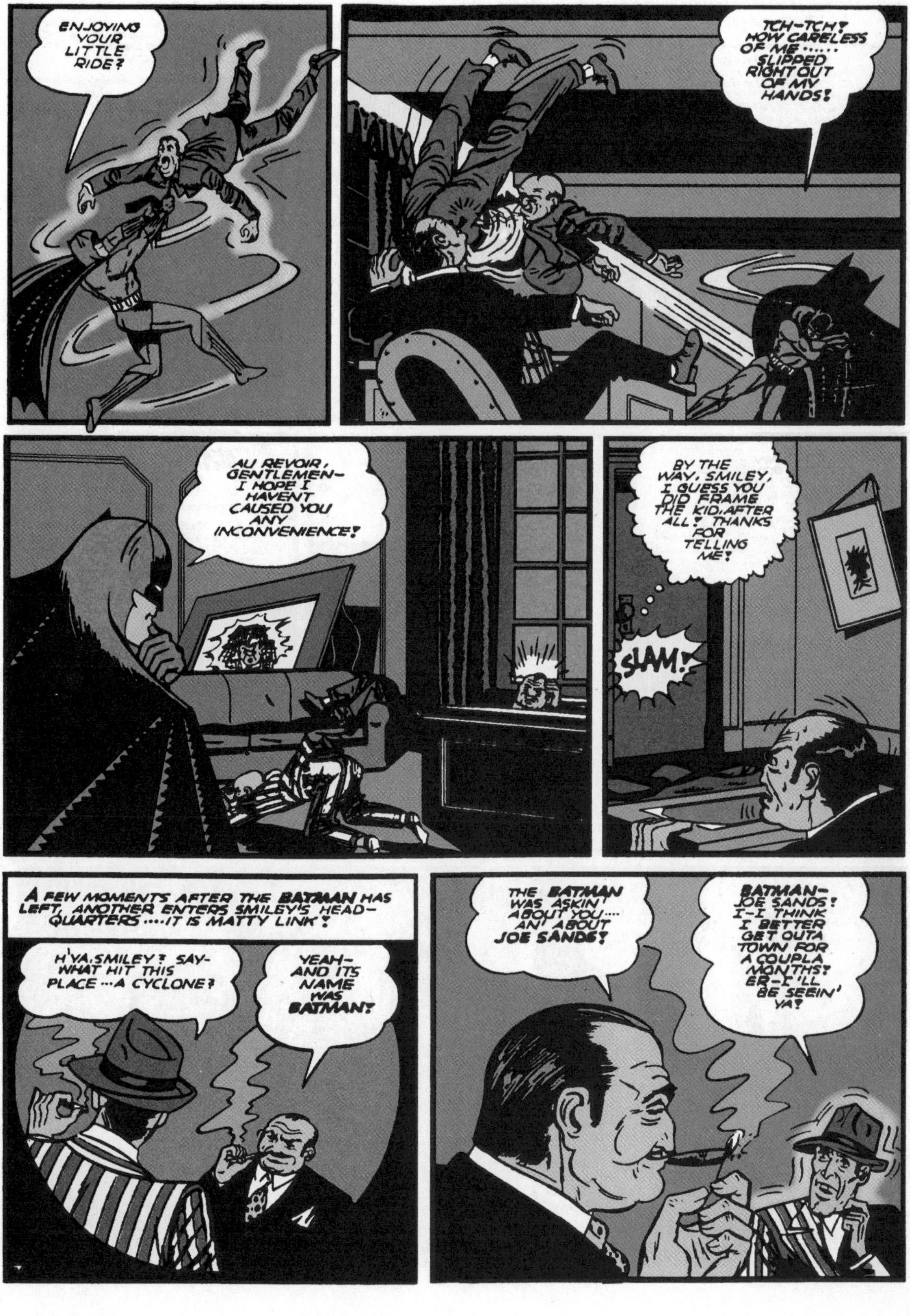
ENJOYING YOUR LITTLE RIDE?
TCH-TCH! HOW CARELESS OF ME...... SLIPPED RIGHT OUT OF MY HANDS!
AU REVOIR, GENTLEMEN- I HOPE I HAVENT CAUSED YOU ANY INCONVENIENCE!
BY THE WAY, SMILEY, I GUESS YOU DID FRAME THE KID AFTER ALL! THANKS FOR TELLING ME!
SLAM!
A FEW MOMENTS AFTER THE BATMAN HAS LEFT, ANOTHER ENTERS SMILEY'S HEAD-QUARTERS....IT IS MATTY LINK!
H'YA, SMILEY? SAY- WHAT HIT THIS PLACE...A CYCLONE?
YEAH- AND ITS NAME WAS BATMAN!
THE BATMAN WAS ASKIN' ABOUT YOU.... AN' ABOUT JOE SANDS!
BATMAN- JOE SANDS! I-I THINK I BETTER GET OUTA TOWN FOR A COUPLA MONTHS! ER-I'LL BE SEEIN' YA!

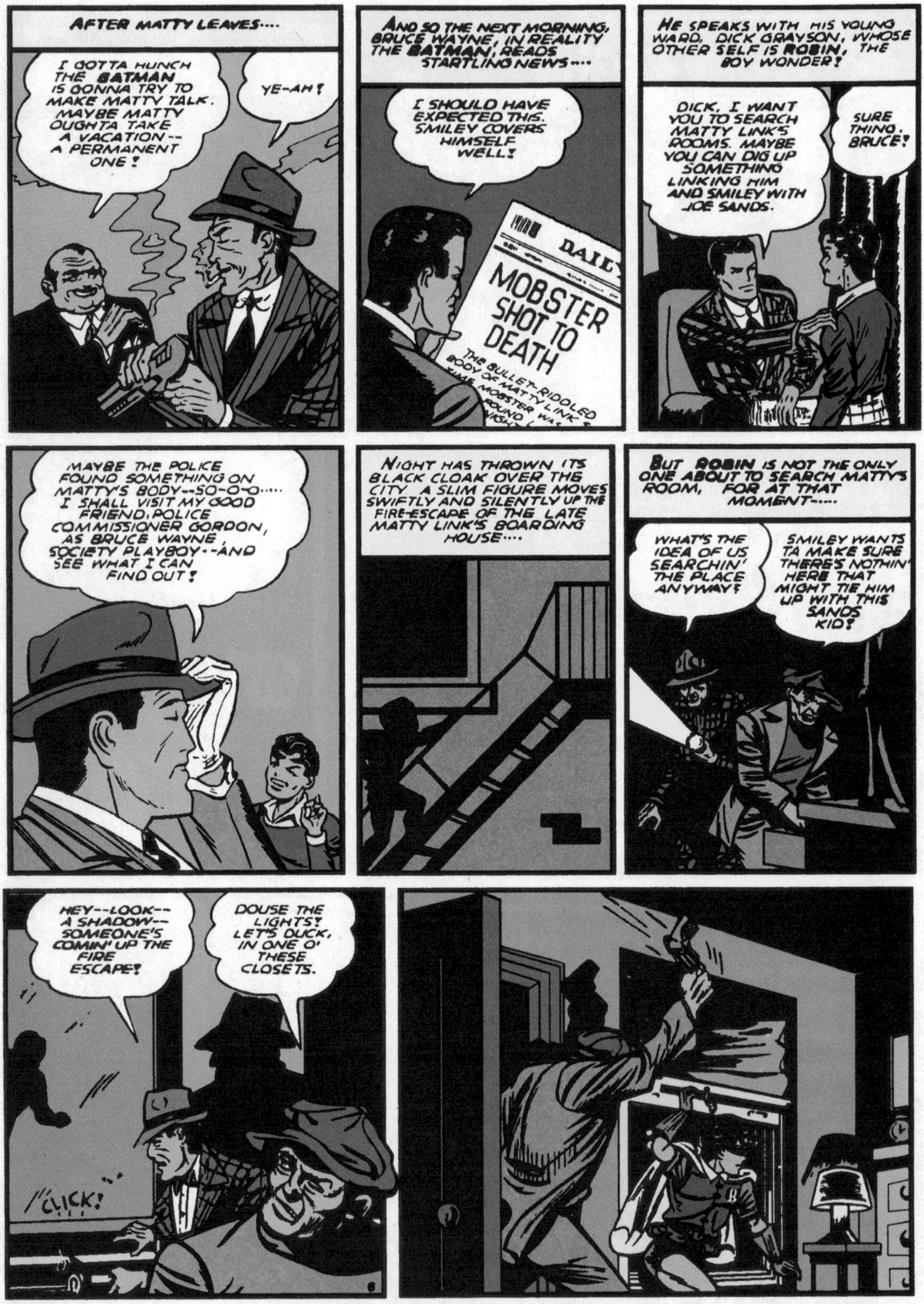
AFTER MATTY LEAVES....
I GOTTA HUNCH THE BATMAN IS GONNA TRY TO MAKE MATTY TALK. MAYBE MATTY OUGHTA TAKE A VACATION-- A PERMANENT ONE!
YE-AH!
AND SO THE NEXT MORNING, BRUCE WAYNE, IN REALITY THE BATMAN, READS STARTLING NEWS....
I SHOULD HAVE EXPECTED THIS. SMILEY COVERS HIMSELF WELL!
MOBSTER SHOT TO DEATH
THE BULLET-RIDDLED BODY OF MATTY LINK
HE SPEAKS WITH HIS YOUNG WARD, DICK GRAYSON, WHOSE OTHER SELF IS ROBIN, THE BOY WONDER!
DICK, I WANT YOU TO SEARCH MATTY LINK'S ROOMS. MAYBE YOU CAN DIG UP SOMETHING LINKING HIM AND SMILEY WITH JOE SANDS.
SURE THING, BRUCE!
MAYBE THE POLICE FOUND SOMETHING ON MATTY'S BODY--SO-O-O..... I SHALL VISIT MY GOOD FRIEND, POLICE COMMISSIONER GORDON, AS BRUCE WAYNE, SOCIETY PLAYBOY--AND SEE WHAT I CAN FIND OUT!
NIGHT HAS THROWN ITS BLACK CLOAK OVER THE CITY. A SLIM FIGURE MOVES SWIFTLY AND SILENTLY UP THE FIRE-ESCAPE OF THE LATE MATTY LINK'S BOARDING HOUSE....
BUT ROBIN IS NOT THE ONLY ONE ABOUT TO SEARCH MATTY'S ROOM, FOR AT THAT MOMENT-----
WHAT'S THE IDEA OF US SEARCHIN' THE PLACE ANYWAY?
SMILEY WANTS TA MAKE SURE THERE'S NOTHIN' HERE THAT MIGHT TIE HIM UP WITH THIS SANDS KID!
HEY--LOOK-- A SHADOW-- SOMEONE'S COMIN' UP THE FIRE ESCAPE!
DOUSE THE LIGHTS! LET'S DUCK, IN ONE O' THESE CLOSETS.
CLICK!

THE SANDS OF TIME DROP SLOWLY. BRUCE HAS ALREADY REACHED HOME AND WAITS IMPATIENTLY FOR *ROBIN'S* RETURN.

IT'S LATE... HE SHOULD HAVE BEEN BACK HOURS AGO...

HASTILY, HE DONS HIS COSTUME. AN INSTANT LATER, HE SENDS THE WEIRD *BATMOBILE* STREAKING THROUGH THE CITY STREETS--

SOMETHING'S HAPPENED TO HIM-- I FEEL IT!

MOMENTS LATER, THE *BATMAN* STOPS BEFORE THE DOOR OF MATTY'S ROOM.....

THE STRANGEST FEELING JUST CAME OVER ME. I--I SEEM TO DREAD OPENING THIS DOOR--

A TOUCH OF THE KNOB, AND THE DOOR SLOWLY SWINGS OPEN. LIGHT FROM THE HALL LAMP ILLUMINATES A SMALL, STILL FIGURE ON THE FLOOR!

ROBIN?

HIS HEAD... ALL BLOODY.... HE'S BEEN CLUBBED... CLUBBED TO DEATH! ROBIN'S DEAD?!

THE *BATMAN*, MAN WHO HAS FACED A THOUSAND DANGERS, MAN OF STRENGTH AND WILL-POWER, NOW BENDS HIS HEAD AND WEEPS. ANGUISHED SOBS ARE TORN FROM HIM!

SLOWLY, HIS GREAT FRAME STRAIGHTENS. SMALL VEINS STAND OUT ON HIS FEATURES. MUSCLES CORD IN HIS THROAT. HIS EYES BECOME FIRES, HIS MOUTH A KNIFE-EDGED LINE--

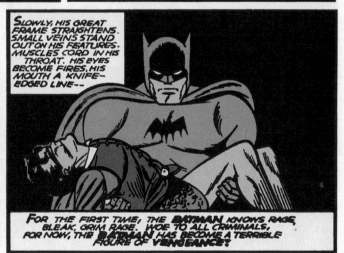

FOR THE FIRST TIME, THE *BATMAN* KNOWS RAGE, BLEAK, GRIM RAGE. WOE TO ALL CRIMINALS, FOR NOW, THE *BATMAN* HAS BECOME A TERRIBLE HOUR OF *VENGEANCE!*

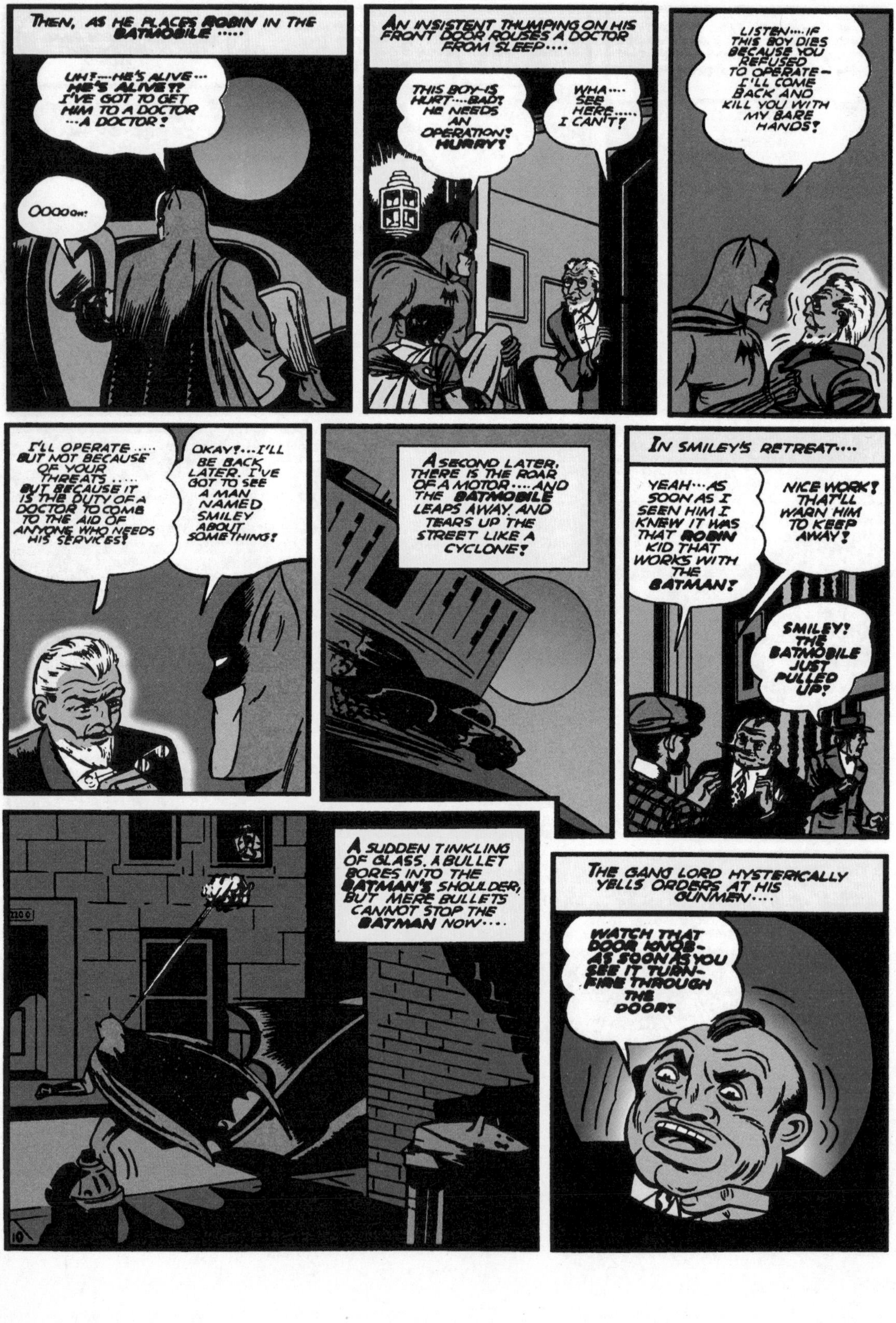
THEN, AS HE PLACES ROBIN IN THE BATMOBILE.....
UH?---HE'S ALIVE--- HE'S ALIVE!? I'VE GOT TO GET HIM TO A DOCTOR ---A DOCTOR!
OOOOOH!
AN INSISTENT THUMPING ON HIS FRONT DOOR ROUSES A DOCTOR FROM SLEEP....
THIS BOY-IS HURT....BAD! HE NEEDS AN OPERATION! HURRY!
WHA.... SEE HERE..... I CAN'T!
LISTEN....IF THIS BOY DIES BECAUSE YOU REFUSED TO OPERATE- I'LL COME BACK AND KILL YOU WITH MY BARE HANDS!
I'LL OPERATE..... BUT NOT BECAUSE OF YOUR THREATS..... BUT BECAUSE IT IS THE DUTY OF A DOCTOR TO COME TO THE AID OF ANYONE WHO NEEDS HIS SERVICES!
OKAY!...I'LL BE BACK LATER. I'VE GOT TO SEE A MAN NAMED SMILEY ABOUT SOMETHING!
A SECOND LATER, THERE IS THE ROAR OF A MOTOR....AND THE BATMOBILE LEAPS AWAY AND TEARS UP THE STREET LIKE A CYCLONE!
IN SMILEY'S RETREAT....
YEAH...AS SOON AS I SEEN HIM I KNEW IT WAS THAT ROBIN KID THAT WORKS WITH THE BATMAN!
NICE WORK! THAT'LL WARN HIM TO KEEP AWAY!
SMILEY! THE BATMOBILE JUST PULLED UP!
A SUDDEN TINKLING OF GLASS. A BULLET BORES INTO THE BATMAN'S SHOULDER, BUT MERE BULLETS CANNOT STOP THE BATMAN NOW....
THE GANG LORD HYSTERICALLY YELLS ORDERS AT HIS GUNMEN....
WATCH THAT DOOR KNOB- AS SOON AS YOU SEE IT TURN- FIRE THROUGH THE DOOR!

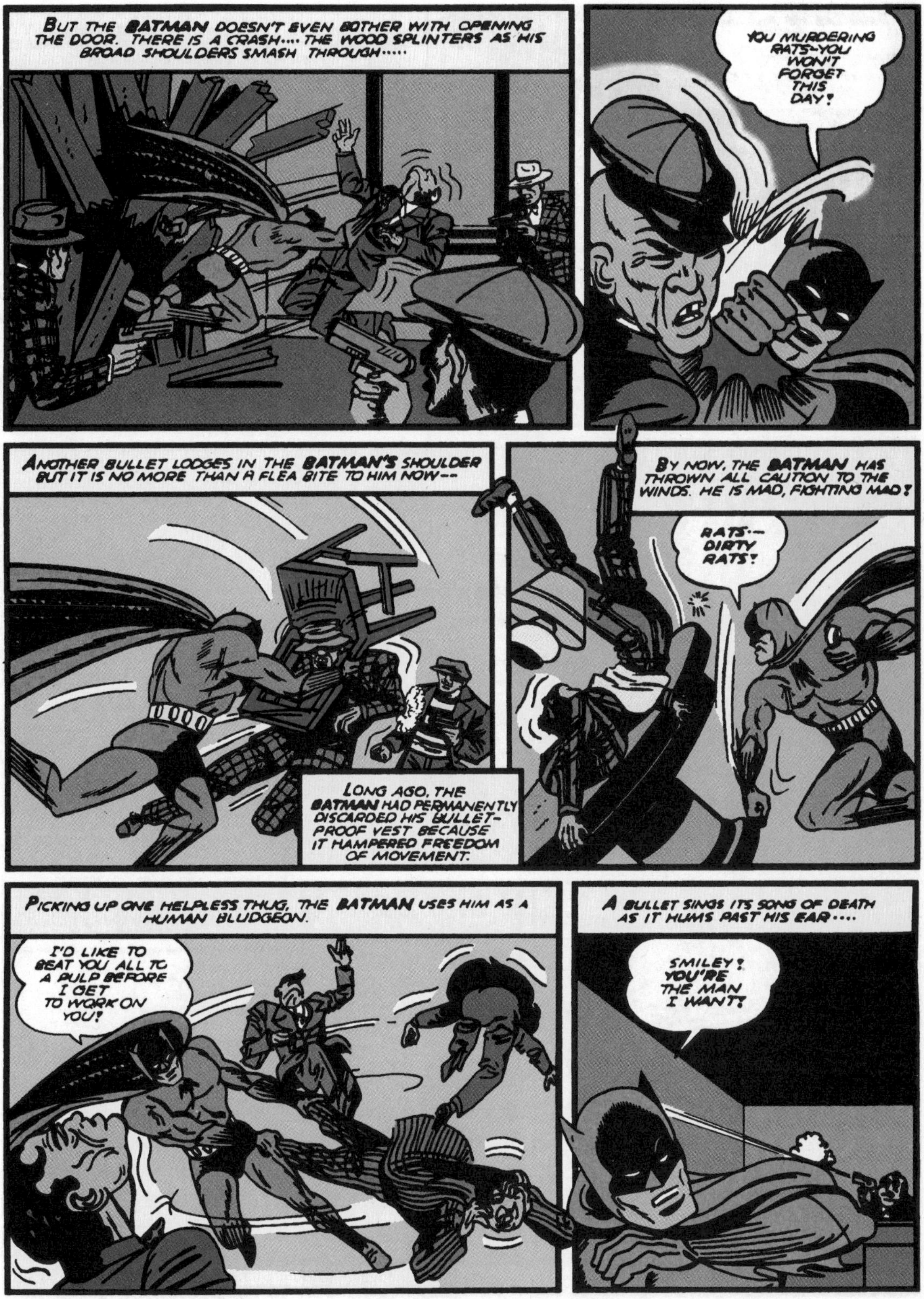
BUT THE BATMAN DOESN'T EVEN BOTHER WITH OPENING THE DOOR. THERE IS A CRASH.... THE WOOD SPLINTERS AS HIS BROAD SHOULDERS SMASH THROUGH.....
YOU MURDERING RATS-YOU WON'T FORGET THIS DAY!
ANOTHER BULLET LODGES IN THE BATMAN'S SHOULDER BUT IT IS NO MORE THAN A FLEA BITE TO HIM NOW--
LONG AGO, THE BATMAN HAD PERMANENTLY DISCARDED HIS BULLET-PROOF VEST BECAUSE IT HAMPERED FREEDOM OF MOVEMENT.
BY NOW, THE BATMAN HAS THROWN ALL CAUTION TO THE WINDS. HE IS MAD, FIGHTING MAD!
RATS--DIRTY RATS!
PICKING UP ONE HELPLESS THUG, THE BATMAN USES HIM AS A HUMAN BLUDGEON.
I'D LIKE TO BEAT YOU ALL TO A PULP BEFORE I GET TO WORK ON YOU!
A BULLET SINGS ITS SONG OF DEATH AS IT HUMS PAST HIS EAR....
SMILEY! YOU'RE THE MAN I WANT!

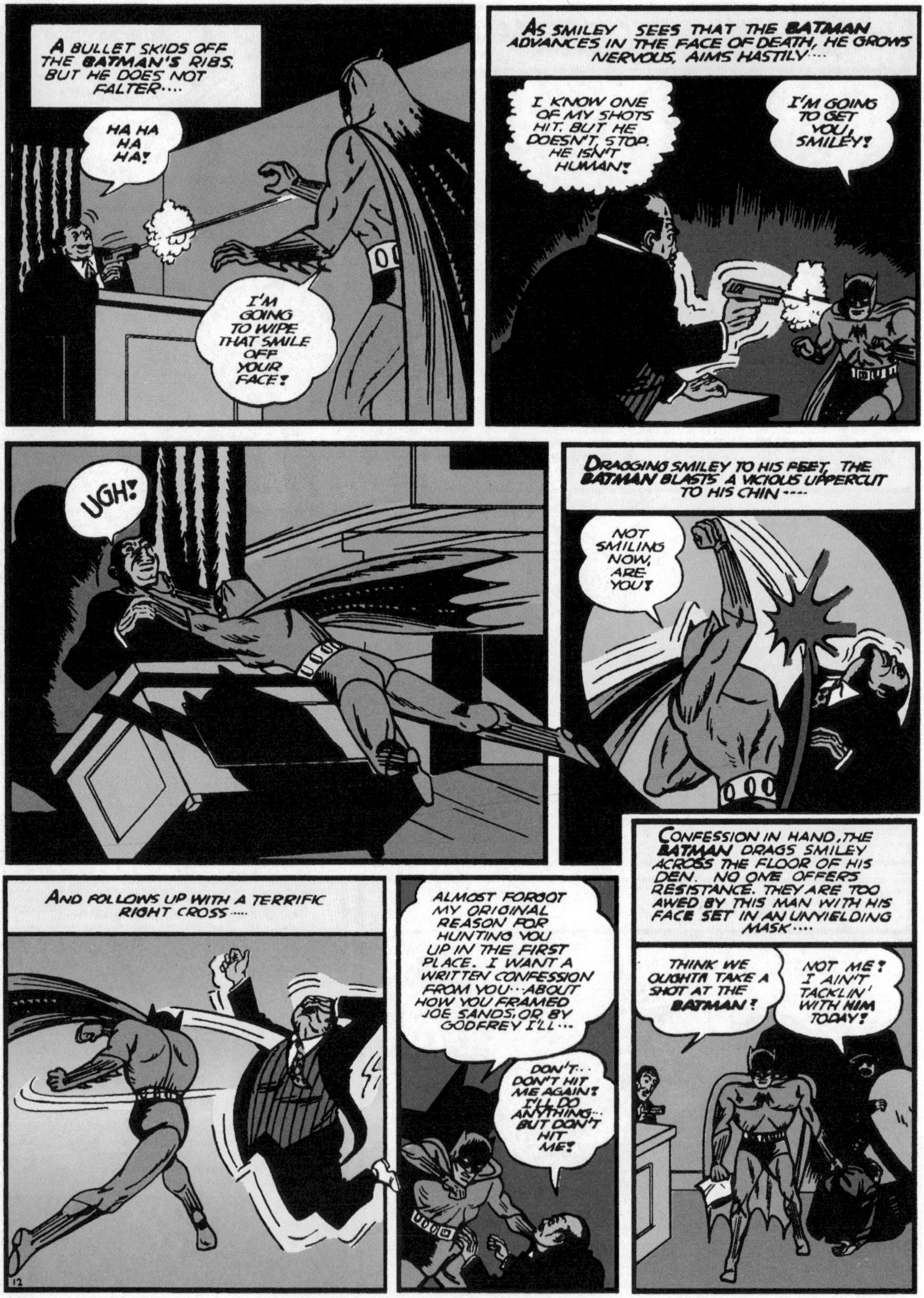
A BULLET SKIDS OFF THE BATMAN'S RIBS, BUT HE DOES NOT FALTER....
HA HA HA HA!
I'M GOING TO WIPE THAT SMILE OFF YOUR FACE!
AS SMILEY SEES THAT THE BATMAN ADVANCES IN THE FACE OF DEATH, HE GROWS NERVOUS, AIMS HASTILY....
I KNOW ONE OF MY SHOTS HIT, BUT HE DOESN'T STOP. HE ISN'T HUMAN!
I'M GOING TO GET YOU, SMILEY!
UGH!
DRAGGING SMILEY TO HIS FEET, THE BATMAN BLASTS A VICIOUS UPPERCUT TO HIS CHIN....
NOT SMILING NOW, ARE YOU?
AND FOLLOWS UP WITH A TERRIFIC RIGHT CROSS.....
12
ALMOST FORGOT MY ORIGINAL REASON FOR HUNTING YOU UP IN THE FIRST PLACE. I WANT A WRITTEN CONFESSION FROM YOU...ABOUT HOW YOU FRAMED JOE SANDS, OR BY GODFREY I'LL...
DON'T.. DON'T HIT ME AGAIN! I'LL DO ANYTHING... BUT DON'T HIT ME!
CONFESSION IN HAND, THE BATMAN DRAGS SMILEY ACROSS THE FLOOR OF HIS DEN. NO ONE OFFERS RESISTANCE. THEY ARE TOO AWED BY THIS MAN WITH HIS FACE SET IN AN UNYIELDING MASK....
THINK WE OUGHTA TAKE A SHOT AT THE BATMAN?
NOT ME! I AIN'T TACKLIN' WITH HIM TODAY!

HERE....HERE'S SMILEY....AND HERE'S SOMETHING YOU MIGHT BE INTERESTED IN.... A CONFESSION!

THE POLICE ARE TOO ASTOUNDED TO EVEN HALT THE MASKED FIGURE....

DID--DID YOU SEE HIS FACE?

YEAH! THAT'S THE FIRST TIME I EVER SAW IT LOOK LIKE THAT! IT--IT WAS TERRIBLE....LIKE A DEMON'S!

A FEW MOMENTS LATER....

HOW IS HE.. HOW IS ROBIN?

HE'LL BE ALL RIGHT, HE'LL LIVE!

I--I---I THINK I'M GOING TO BE A SISSY AND FAINT, DOC....SORRY!

"SISSY, AND FAINT!" I DON'T KNOW HOW HE KEPT GOING THE WAY HE DID....WITH THREE BULLETS IN HIM! AMAZING....AMAZING....

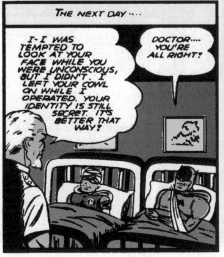

THE NEXT DAY....

I--I WAS TEMPTED TO LOOK AT YOUR FACE WHILE YOU WERE UNCONSCIOUS, BUT I DIDN'T. I LEFT YOUR COWL ON WHILE I OPERATED. YOUR IDENTITY IS STILL SECRET. IT'S BETTER THAT WAY!

DOCTOR.....YOU'RE ALL RIGHT!

BY THE WAY.....THOSE PEOPLE YOU WANTED ME TO GET IN TOUCH WITH ARE WAITING OUTSIDE!

THANKS TO YOU, MY NAME IS CLEARED NOW AND ANN WILL BE ALL RIGHT!

...AND ME, I GAVE HIM A JOB IN MY STORE! HE IS A NICE BOY!

ALL'S WELL THAT ENDS WELL, EH, ROBIN!

BOB KANE

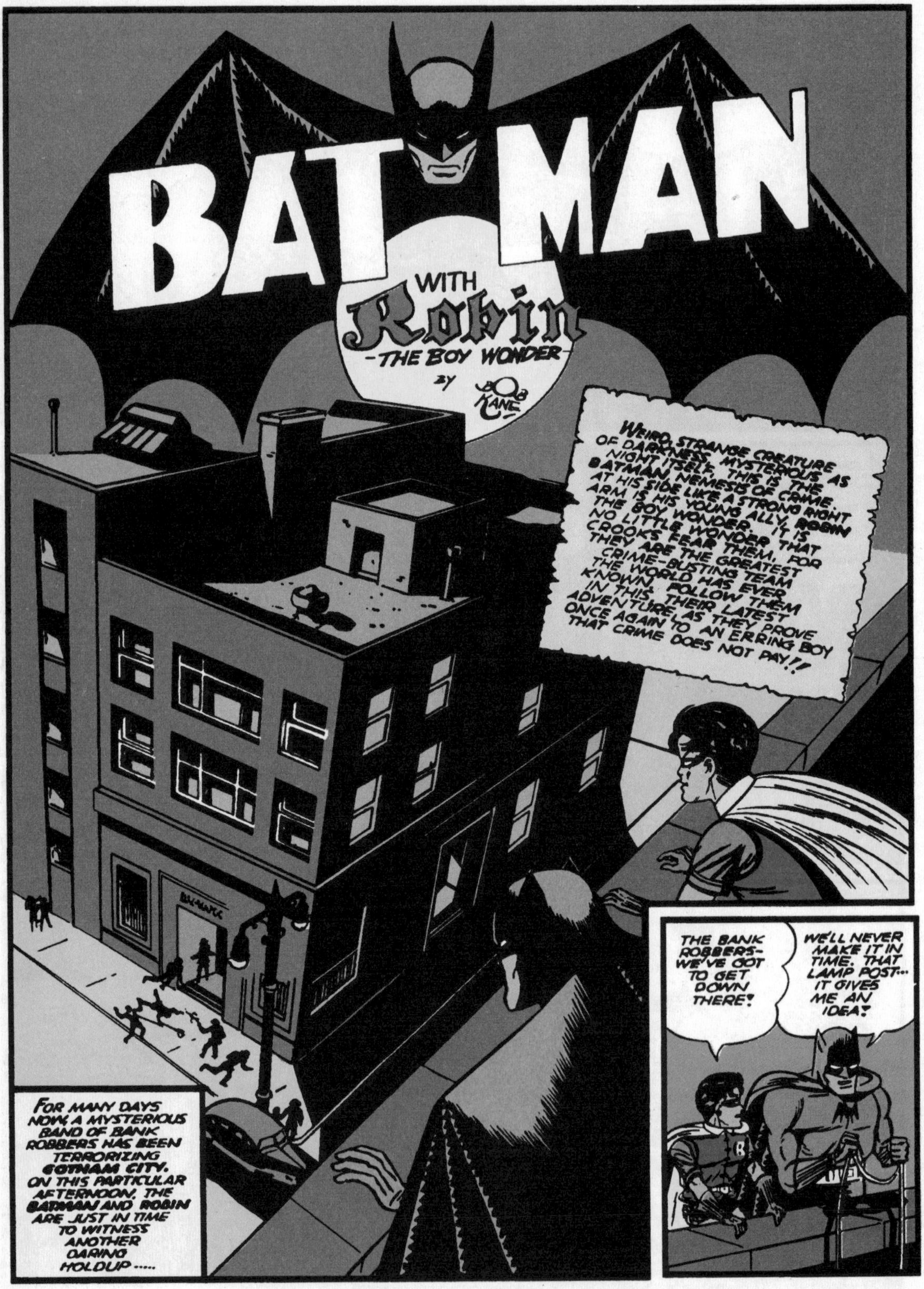
BAT MAN
WITH Robin
-THE BOY WONDER-
BY BOB KANE
WEIRD, STRANGE CREATURE OF DARKNESS, MYSTERIOUS AS NIGHT ITSELF, THIS IS THE BATMAN, NEMESIS OF CRIME. AT HIS SIDE LIKE A STRONG RIGHT ARM IS HIS YOUNG ALLY, ROBIN THE BOY WONDER. IT IS NO LITTLE WONDER THAT CROOKS FEAR THEM, FOR THEY ARE THE GREATEST CRIME-BUSTING TEAM THE WORLD HAS EVER KNOWN. FOLLOW THEM IN THIS, THEIR LATEST ADVENTURE, AS THEY PROVE ONCE AGAIN TO AN ERRING BOY THAT CRIME DOES NOT PAY!!
FOR MANY DAYS NOW, A MYSTERIOUS BAND OF BANK ROBBERS HAS BEEN TERRORIZING GOTHAM CITY. ON THIS PARTICULAR AFTERNOON, THE BATMAN AND ROBIN ARE JUST IN TIME TO WITNESS ANOTHER DARING HOLDUP.....
THE BANK ROBBERS- WE'VE GOT TO GET DOWN THERE!
WE'LL NEVER MAKE IT IN TIME. THAT LAMP POST... IT GIVES ME AN IDEA!

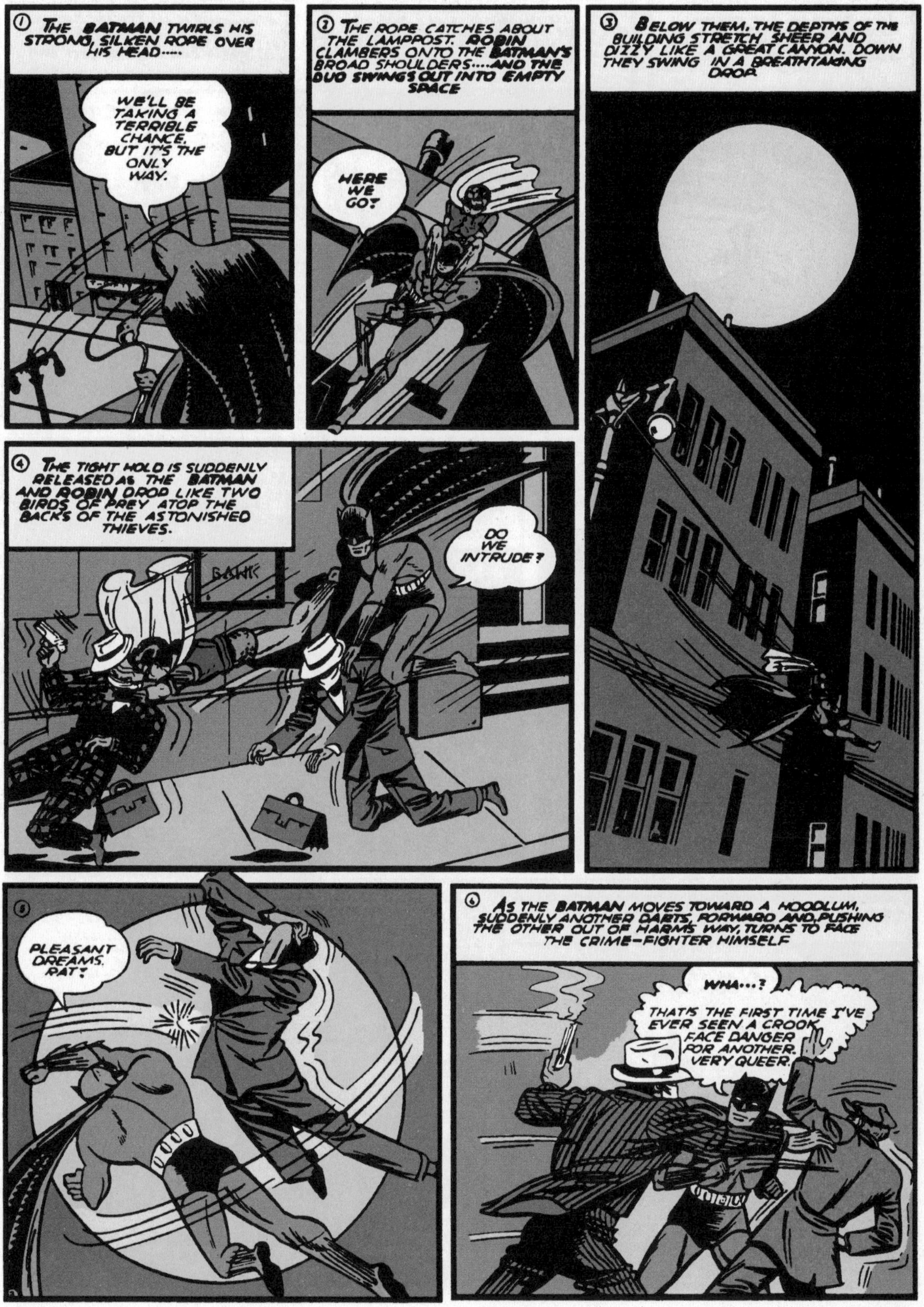
1 THE BATMAN TWIRLS HIS STRONG, SILKEN ROPE OVER HIS HEAD.....
WE'LL BE TAKING A TERRIBLE CHANCE. BUT IT'S THE ONLY WAY.
2 THE ROPE CATCHES ABOUT THE LAMPPOST. ROBIN CLAMBERS ONTO THE BATMAN'S BROAD SHOULDERS....AND THE DUO SWINGS OUT INTO EMPTY SPACE
HERE WE GO!
3 BELOW THEM, THE DEPTHS OF THE BUILDING STRETCH SHEER AND DIZZY LIKE A GREAT CANYON. DOWN THEY SWING IN A BREATHTAKING DROP.
4 THE TIGHT HOLD IS SUDDENLY RELEASED AS THE BATMAN AND ROBIN DROP LIKE TWO BIRDS OF PREY ATOP THE BACKS OF THE ASTONISHED THIEVES.
BANK
DO WE INTRUDE?
5
PLEASANT DREAMS, RAT!
6 AS THE BATMAN MOVES TOWARD A HOODLUM, SUDDENLY ANOTHER DARTS, FORWARD AND, PUSHING THE OTHER OUT OF HARM'S WAY, TURNS TO FACE THE CRIME-FIGHTER HIMSELF
WHA...?
THAT'S THE FIRST TIME I'VE EVER SEEN A CROOK FACE DANGER FOR ANOTHER. VERY QUEER.

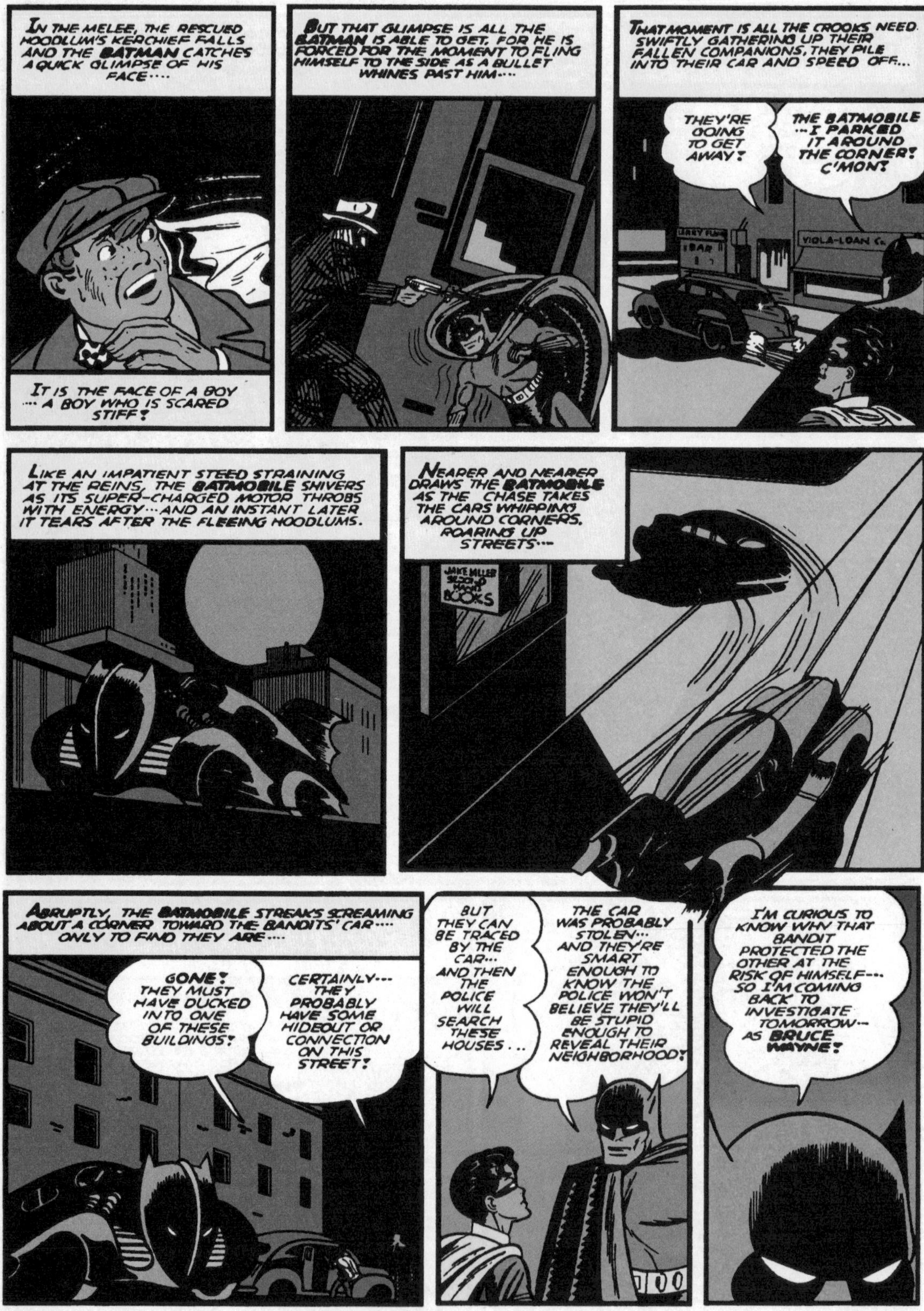
IN THE MELEE, THE RESCUED HOODLUM'S KERCHIEF FALLS AND THE BATMAN CATCHES A QUICK GLIMPSE OF HIS FACE....
IT IS THE FACE OF A BOY ... A BOY WHO IS SCARED STIFF!
BUT THAT GLIMPSE IS ALL THE BATMAN IS ABLE TO GET, FOR HE IS FORCED FOR THE MOMENT TO FLING HIMSELF TO THE SIDE AS A BULLET WHINES PAST HIM....
THAT MOMENT IS ALL THE CROOKS NEED. SWIFTLY GATHERING UP THEIR FALLEN COMPANIONS, THEY PILE INTO THEIR CAR AND SPEED OFF...
THEY'RE GOING TO GET AWAY!
THE BATMOBILE ...I PARKED IT AROUND THE CORNER! C'MON!
BAR
VIOLA-LOAN Co.
LIKE AN IMPATIENT STEED STRAINING AT THE REINS, THE BATMOBILE SHIVERS AS ITS SUPER-CHARGED MOTOR THROBS WITH ENERGY... AND AN INSTANT LATER IT TEARS AFTER THE FLEEING HOODLUMS.
NEARER AND NEARER DRAWS THE BATMOBILE AS THE CHASE TAKES THE CARS WHIPPING AROUND CORNERS, ROARING UP STREETS...
JAKE MILLER
BOOKS
ABRUPTLY, THE BATMOBILE STREAKS SCREAMING ABOUT A CORNER TOWARD THE BANDITS' CAR.... ONLY TO FIND THEY ARE....
GONE! THEY MUST HAVE DUCKED INTO ONE OF THESE BUILDINGS!
CERTAINLY--- THEY PROBABLY HAVE SOME HIDEOUT OR CONNECTION ON THIS STREET!
BUT THEY CAN BE TRACED BY THE CAR... AND THEN THE POLICE WILL SEARCH THESE HOUSES...
THE CAR WAS PROBABLY STOLEN... AND THEY'RE SMART ENOUGH TO KNOW THE POLICE WON'T BELIEVE THEY'LL BE STUPID ENOUGH TO REVEAL THEIR NEIGHBORHOOD!
I'M CURIOUS TO KNOW WHY THAT BANDIT PROTECTED THE OTHER AT THE RISK OF HIMSELF--- SO I'M COMING BACK TO INVESTIGATE TOMORROW-- AS BRUCE WAYNE!

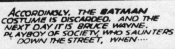

ACCORDINGLY, THE BATMAN COSTUME IS DISCARDED, AND THE NEXT DAY IT IS BRUCE WAYNE, PLAYBOY OF SOCIETY, WHO SAUNTERS DOWN THE STREET, WHEN....

OOF!

UGH!

YOU BIG APE...WHY DON'T YOU LOOK---BRUCE.... BRUCE WAYNE?

LINDA PAGE? WELL, WELL! I HAVEN'T SEEN YOU IN A DOG'S AGE. THE WHOLE CROWD HAS BEEN ASKING ABOUT YOU?

TELL THE CROWD I WOKE UP ONE DAY TO REALIZE THERE ARE MORE IMPORTANT THINGS THAN CAFE SOCIETY-SO-O-O....I'VE MOVED OUT AND BECOME A NURSE!

A NURSE? YOU...YOU GAVE UP A PLACE IN SOCIETY TO WORK FOR A LIVING? IT'S...IT'S STUPID!

YOU'RE THE ONE WHO'S STUPID---WASTING YOUR LIFE AS THE GREAT SOCIETY PLAYBOY. YOU'VE GOT TALENT. IF YOU WANTED TO YOU--

AH-AH! DON'T TRY TO REFORM ME. I'M HAVING TOO GOOD A TIME TO KILL MYSELF WITH WORK!

IT'S NO USE TALKING TO YOU-- C'MON- AT LEAST, YOU CAN WALK ME HOME.

SURE- I WANT TO SEE THIS LITTLE FLAT OF YOURS- "WOIKING GOIL."

ARMY & NAVY STORE

AS THEY NEAR LINDA'S MODEST APARTMENT BUILDING....

HELLO, MRS. GROGAN. WHAT'S WRONG? YOU LOOK WORRIED.

IT'S MY BOY, TOMMY-- IF ONLY HIS FATHER WERE ALIVE, HE'D PUT A STOP TO HIS RUNNING AROUND.

TOMMY-BOY GIVING HER TROUBLE?

TOMMY IS REALLY A GOOD KID AT HEART, BUT LATELY HE'S BEEN MIXING WITH THE MOB DOWN AT THE POOL PARLOR POOR WOMAN.... I FEEL SORRY FOR HER!

TOMMY HAS AN OLDER BROTHER, MIKE, WHO IS A GANGSTER. TOMMY IDOLIZES HIS BROTHER MIKE BECAUSE HE'S GOOD TO HIM AND.....

AND HIS MOTHER IS AFRAID HE'LL FOLLOW IN MIKE'S FOOTSTEPS. THE USUAL STORY!

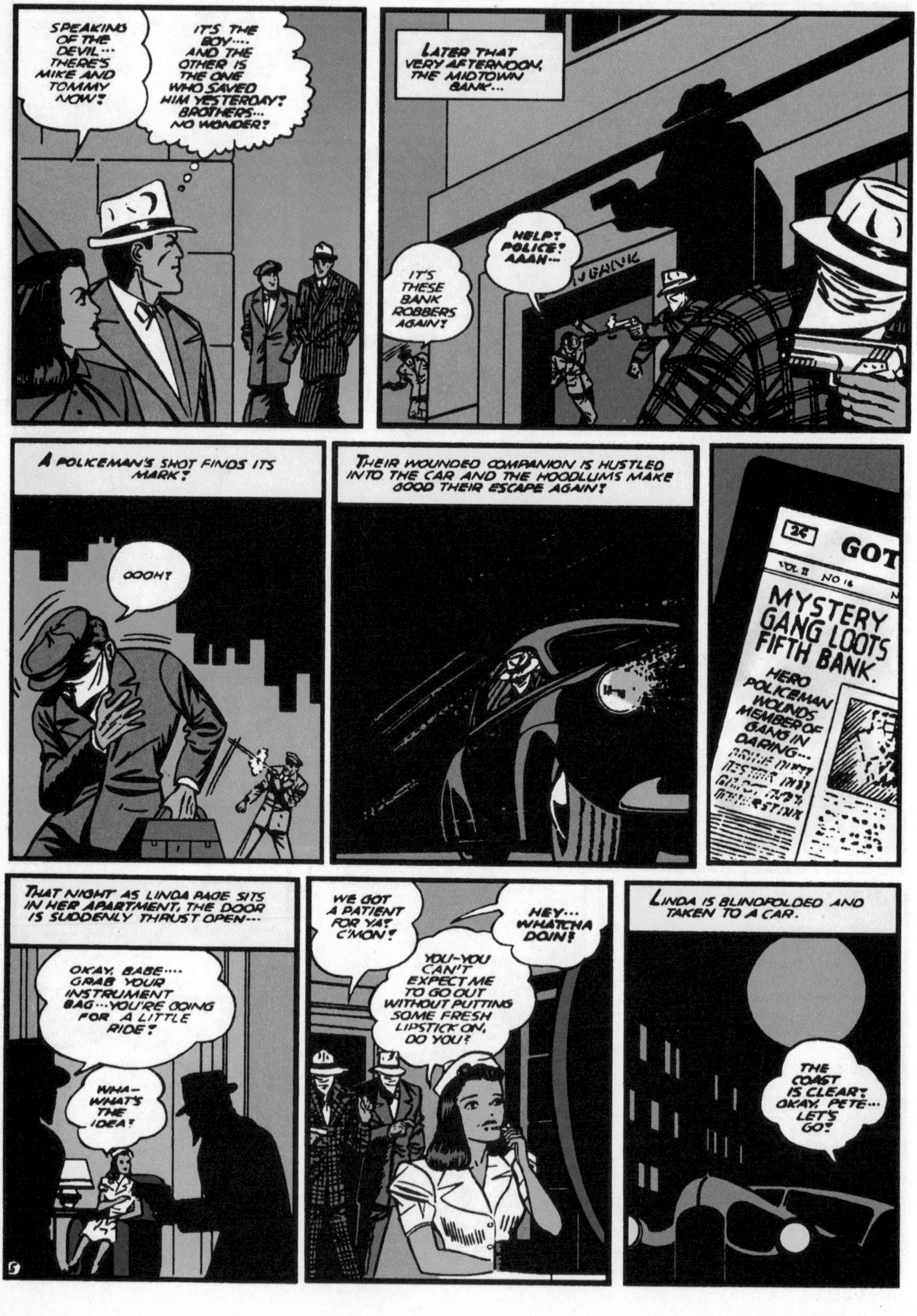
SPEAKING OF THE DEVIL... THERE'S MIKE AND TOMMY NOW!
IT'S THE BOY.... AND THE OTHER IS THE ONE WHO SAVED HIM YESTERDAY! BROTHERS... NO WONDER!
LATER THAT VERY AFTERNOON, THE MIDTOWN BANK...
HELP! POLICE! AAAH---
IT'S THESE BANK ROBBERS AGAIN!
A POLICEMAN'S SHOT FINDS ITS MARK!
OOOH!
THEIR WOUNDED COMPANION IS HUSTLED INTO THE CAR AND THE HOODLUMS MAKE GOOD THEIR ESCAPE AGAIN!
2¢
GOT
MYSTERY GANG LOOTS FIFTH BANK.
HERO POLICEMAN WOUNDS MEMBER OF GANG IN DARING...
THAT NIGHT AS LINDA PAGE SITS IN HER APARTMENT, THE DOOR IS SUDDENLY THRUST OPEN---
OKAY, BABE.... GRAB YOUR INSTRUMENT BAG...YOU'RE GOING FOR A LITTLE RIDE!
WHA-WHAT'S THE IDEA?
WE GOT A PATIENT FOR YA! C'MON!
HEY... WHATCHA DOIN!
YOU-YOU CAN'T EXPECT ME TO GO OUT WITHOUT PUTTING SOME FRESH LIPSTICK ON, DO YOU?
LINDA IS BLINDFOLDED AND TAKEN TO A CAR.
THE COAST IS CLEAR! OKAY, PETE... LET'S GO!

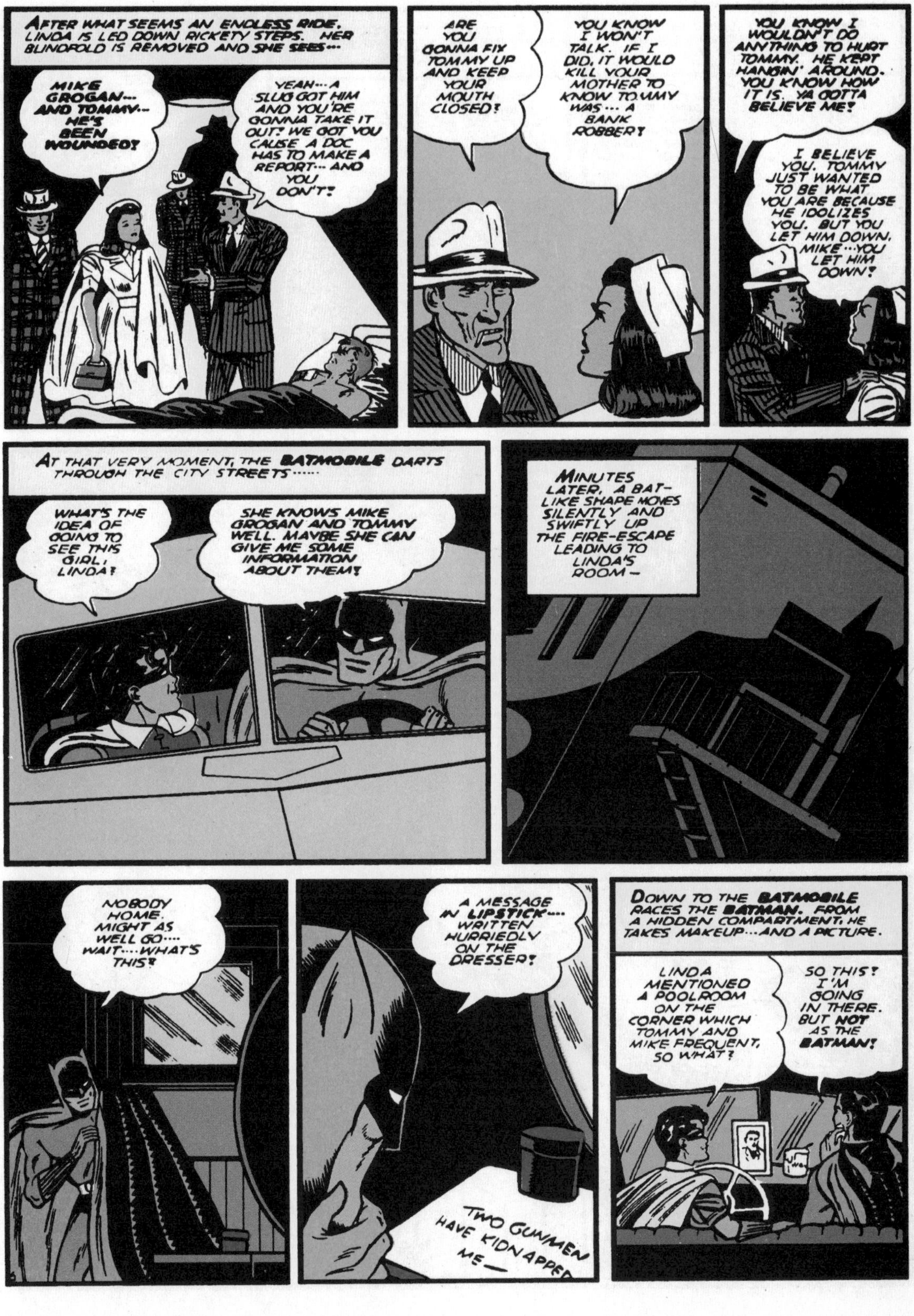
AFTER WHAT SEEMS AN ENDLESS RIDE, LINDA IS LED DOWN RICKETY STEPS. HER BLINDFOLD IS REMOVED AND SHE SEES---
MIKE GROGAN--- AND TOMMY-- HE'S BEEN WOUNDED!
YEAH--- A SLUG GOT HIM AND YOU'RE GONNA TAKE IT OUT! WE GOT YOU CAUSE A DOC HAS TO MAKE A REPORT--- AND YOU DON'T!
ARE YOU GONNA FIX TOMMY UP AND KEEP YOUR MOUTH CLOSED?
YOU KNOW I WON'T TALK. IF I DID, IT WOULD KILL YOUR MOTHER TO KNOW TOMMY WAS--- A BANK ROBBER!
YOU KNOW I WOULDN'T DO ANYTHING TO HURT TOMMY. HE KEPT HANGIN' AROUND. YOU KNOW HOW IT IS. YA GOTTA BELIEVE ME!
I BELIEVE YOU. TOMMY JUST WANTED TO BE WHAT YOU ARE BECAUSE HE IDOLIZES YOU. BUT YOU LET HIM DOWN, MIKE---YOU LET HIM DOWN!
AT THAT VERY MOMENT, THE BATMOBILE DARTS THROUGH THE CITY STREETS......
WHAT'S THE IDEA OF GOING TO SEE THIS GIRL, LINDA?
SHE KNOWS MIKE GROGAN AND TOMMY WELL. MAYBE SHE CAN GIVE ME SOME INFORMATION ABOUT THEM!
MINUTES LATER, A BAT-LIKE SHAPE MOVES SILENTLY AND SWIFTLY UP THE FIRE-ESCAPE LEADING TO LINDA'S ROOM-
NOBODY HOME. MIGHT AS WELL GO---- WAIT----WHAT'S THIS?
A MESSAGE IN LIPSTICK---- WRITTEN HURRIEDLY ON THE DRESSER!
TWO GUNMEN HAVE KIDNAPPED ME—
DOWN TO THE BATMOBILE RACES THE BATMAN. FROM A HIDDEN COMPARTMENT, HE TAKES MAKEUP---AND A PICTURE.
LINDA MENTIONED A POOLROOM ON THE CORNER WHICH TOMMY AND MIKE FREQUENT, SO WHAT?
SO THIS? I'M GOING IN THERE. BUT NOT AS THE BATMAN!

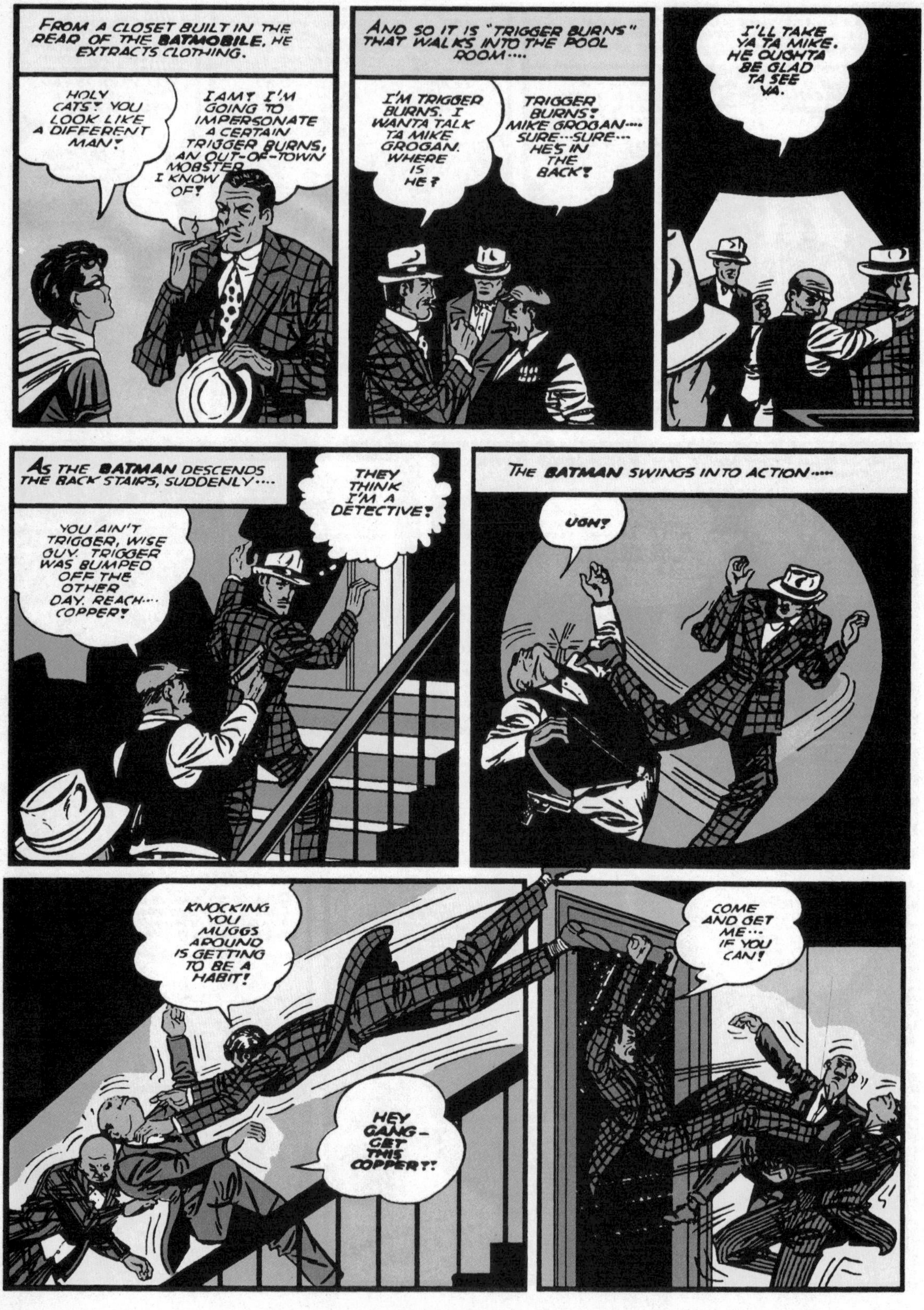

FROM A CLOSET BUILT IN THE REAR OF THE BATMOBILE, HE EXTRACTS CLOTHING.
HOLY CATS! YOU LOOK LIKE A DIFFERENT MAN!
I AM! I'M GOING TO IMPERSONATE A CERTAIN TRIGGER BURNS, AN OUT-OF-TOWN MOBSTER I KNOW OF!
AND SO IT IS "TRIGGER BURNS" THAT WALKS INTO THE POOL ROOM....
I'M TRIGGER BURNS. I WANTA TALK TA MIKE GROGAN. WHERE IS HE?
TRIGGER BURNS! MIKE GROGAN.... SURE...SURE... HE'S IN THE BACK!
I'LL TAKE YA TA MIKE. HE OUGHTA BE GLAD TA SEE YA.
AS THE BATMAN DESCENDS THE BACK STAIRS, SUDDENLY....
YOU AIN'T TRIGGER, WISE GUY. TRIGGER WAS BUMPED OFF THE OTHER DAY. REACH.... COPPER!
THEY THINK I'M A DETECTIVE!
THE BATMAN SWINGS INTO ACTION.....
UGH!
KNOCKING YOU MUGGS AROUND IS GETTING TO BE A HABIT!
HEY GANG-GET THIS COPPER!!
COME AND GET ME... IF YOU CAN!

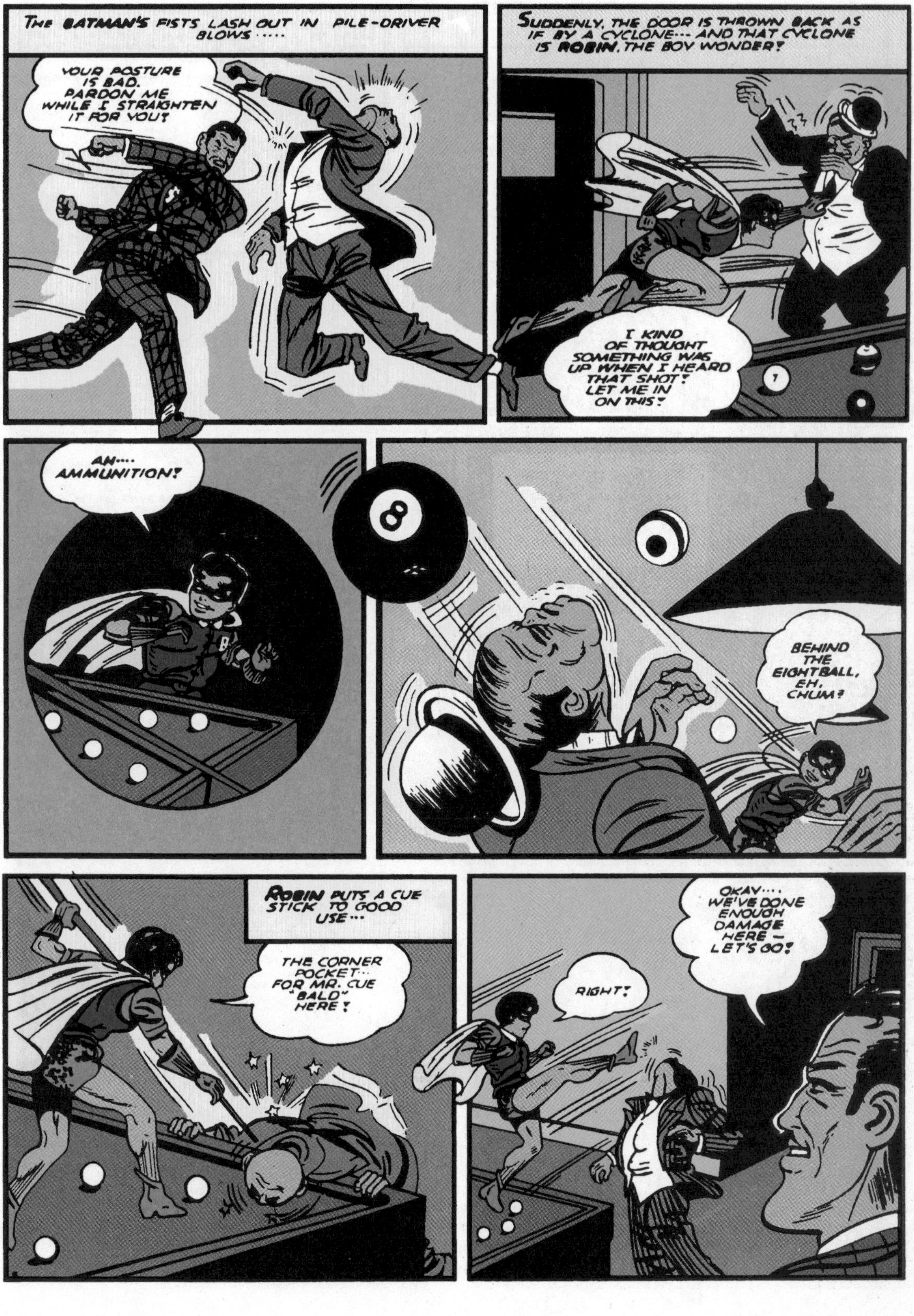

THE BATMAN'S FISTS LASH OUT IN PILE-DRIVER BLOWS.....
YOUR POSTURE IS BAD. PARDON ME WHILE I STRAIGHTEN IT FOR YOU!
SUDDENLY, THE DOOR IS THROWN BACK AS IF BY A CYCLONE--- AND THAT CYCLONE IS ROBIN, THE BOY WONDER!
I KIND OF THOUGHT SOMETHING WAS UP WHEN I HEARD THAT SHOT! LET ME IN ON THIS!
AH.... AMMUNITION!
BEHIND THE EIGHTBALL, EH, CHUM?
ROBIN PUTS A CUE STICK TO GOOD USE...
THE CORNER POCKET... FOR MR. CUE "BALD" HERE!
OKAY.... WE'VE DONE ENOUGH DAMAGE HERE — LET'S GO!
RIGHT!

AFTER THE BATMAN AND ROBIN ARE GONE....

GET THE NUMBER O' THE TRUCK THAT HIT ME?

LISTEN.... THAT DICK WAS AFTER MIKEY! WE GOTTA GET WORD TO 'IM!

I'LL GET TO THE HIDEOUT RIGHT AWAY!

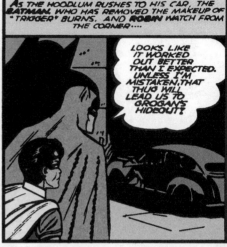

AS THE HOODLUM RUSHES TO HIS CAR, THE BATMAN, WHO HAS REMOVED THE MAKEUP OF "TRIGGER" BURNS, AND ROBIN WATCH FROM THE CORNER....

LOOKS LIKE IT WORKED OUT BETTER THAN I EXPECTED. UNLESS I'M MISTAKEN, THAT THUG WILL LEAD US TO GROGAN'S HIDEOUT!

SHUTTING DOWN THE HEADLIGHTS, THE BATMAN AND ROBIN CAUTIOUSLY FOLLOW THE THUG ...TO THE HIDEOUT ON THE WATERFRONT!

MIKE DOWNSTAIRS!

YEAH? HE'S DOWN WIT DE GANG! ME ... I'M UP HERE WATCHIN' ALL ALONE!

CHEE...DEM SHADOWS GIMME DE CREEPS. THEY GOT SUCH FUNNY SHAPES. DAT ONE LOOKS JUST LIKE A BAT!

BROTHER, YOU WERE NEVER MORE RIGHT IN YOUR WHOLE LIFE!

DOWNSTAIRS....

SURE... THAT COPPER WAS ASKIN' FOR YOU, MIKE.

THEY MUST BE WISE TO US?

YEAH-- WE BETTER ALL SCRAM OUTA HERE. GRAB THE KID AND LET'S GO!

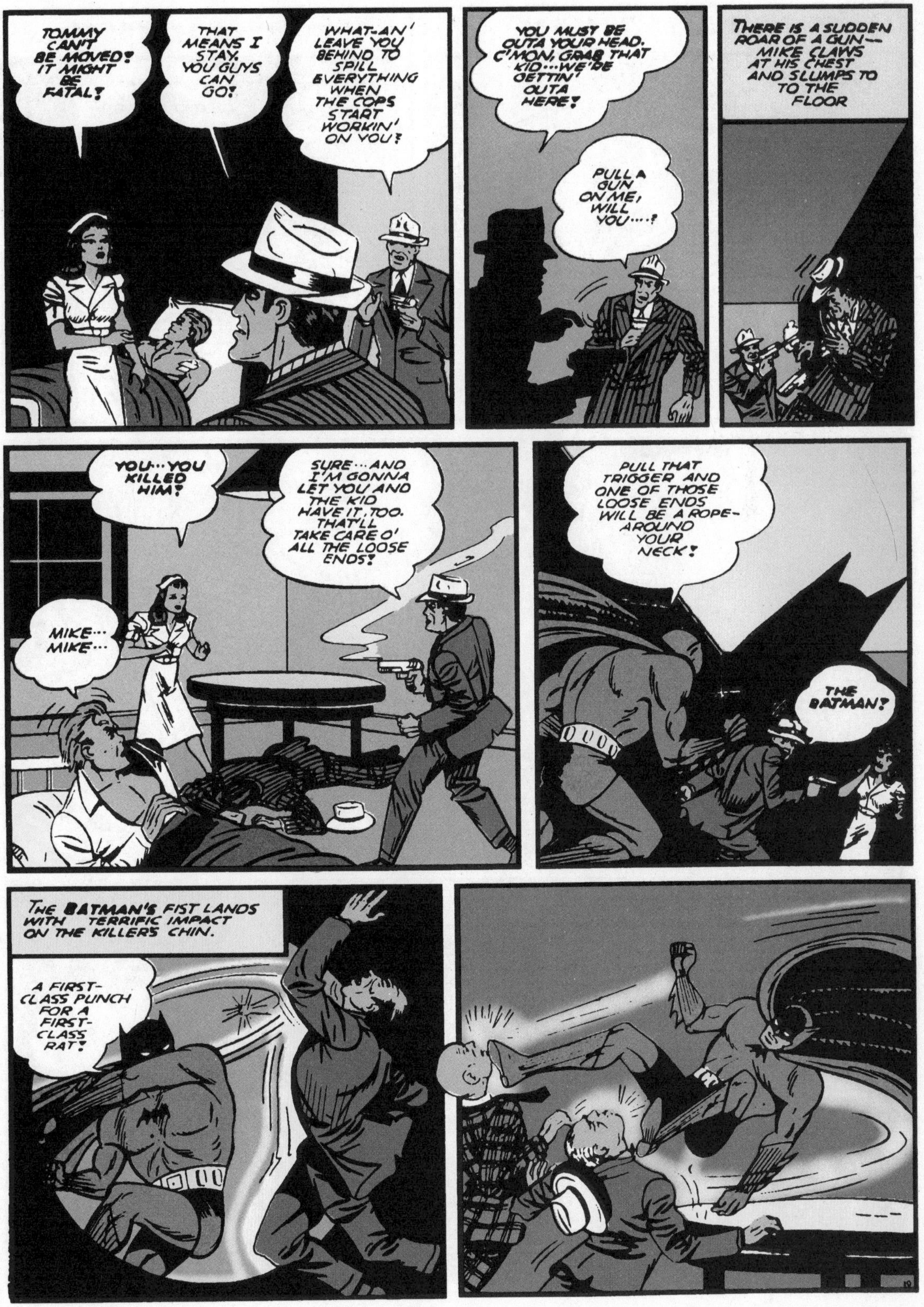

TOMMY CAN'T BE MOVED! IT MIGHT BE FATAL!
THAT MEANS I STAY. YOU GUYS CAN GO!
WHAT-AN' LEAVE YOU BEHIND TO SPILL EVERYTHING WHEN THE COPS START WORKIN' ON YOU!
YOU MUST BE OUTA YOUR HEAD. C'MON, GRAB THAT KID...WE'RE GETTIN' OUTA HERE!
PULL A GUN ON ME, WILL YOU....?
THERE IS A SUDDEN ROAR OF A GUN-- MIKE CLAWS AT HIS CHEST AND SLUMPS TO TO THE FLOOR
YOU...YOU KILLED HIM!
SURE...AND I'M GONNA LET YOU AND THE KID HAVE IT, TOO. THAT'LL TAKE CARE O' ALL THE LOOSE ENDS!
MIKE... MIKE...
PULL THAT TRIGGER AND ONE OF THOSE LOOSE ENDS WILL BE A ROPE-AROUND YOUR NECK!
THE BATMAN!
THE BATMAN'S FIST LANDS WITH TERRIFIC IMPACT ON THE KILLER'S CHIN.
A FIRST-CLASS PUNCH FOR A FIRST-CLASS RAT!

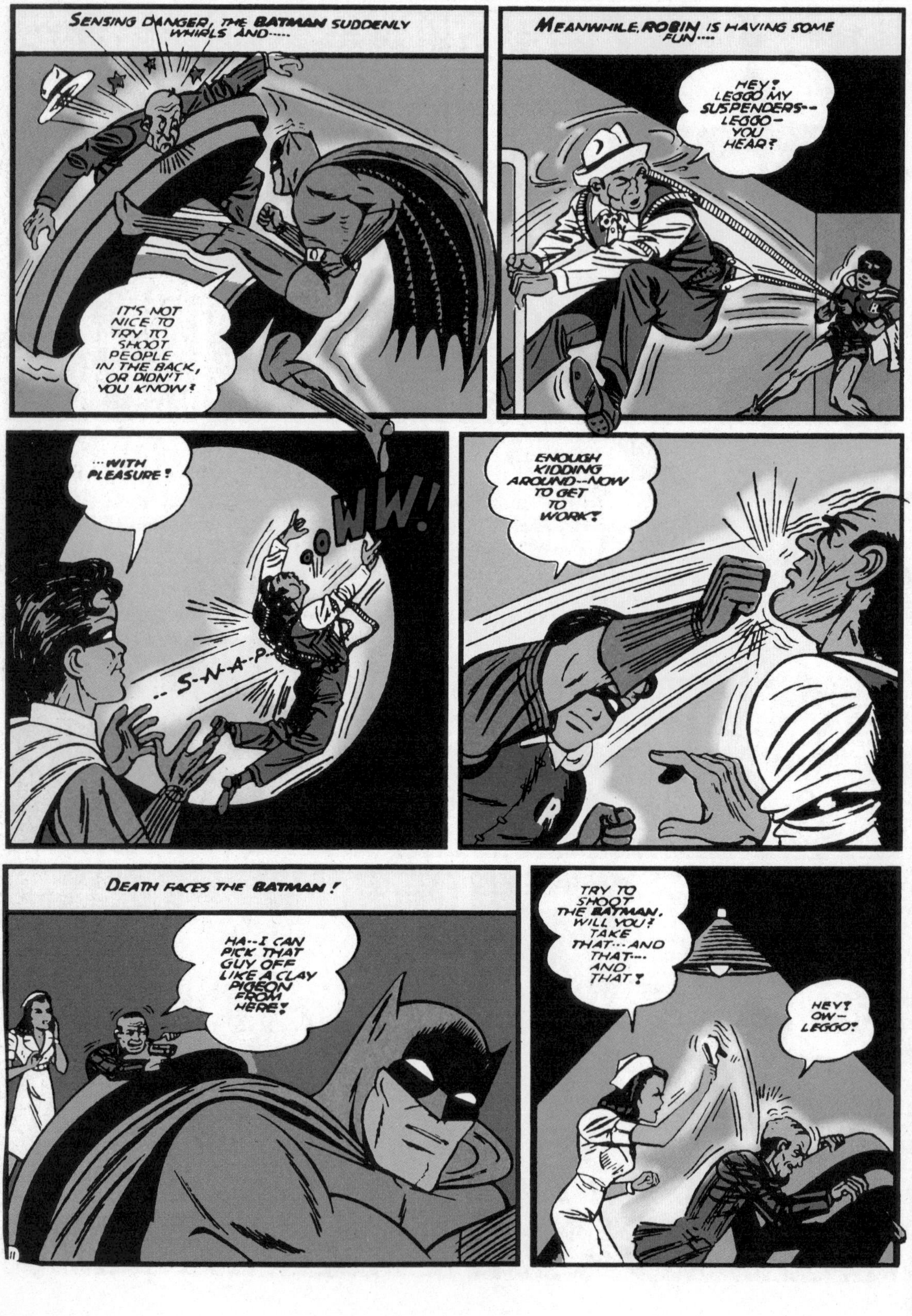

SENSING DANGER, THE BATMAN SUDDENLY WHIRLS AND-----
IT'S NOT NICE TO TRY TO SHOOT PEOPLE IN THE BACK, OR DIDN'T YOU KNOW?
MEANWHILE, ROBIN IS HAVING SOME FUN----
HEY? LEGGO MY SUSPENDERS-- LEGGO- YOU HEAR?
...WITH PLEASURE!
OWW!
-- S-N-A-P--
ENOUGH KIDDING AROUND--NOW TO GET TO WORK?
DEATH FACES THE BATMAN!
HA--I CAN PICK THAT GUY OFF LIKE A CLAY PIGEON FROM HERE?
TRY TO SHOOT THE BATMAN, WILL YOU? TAKE THAT---AND THAT---AND THAT?
HEY? OW- LEGGO?

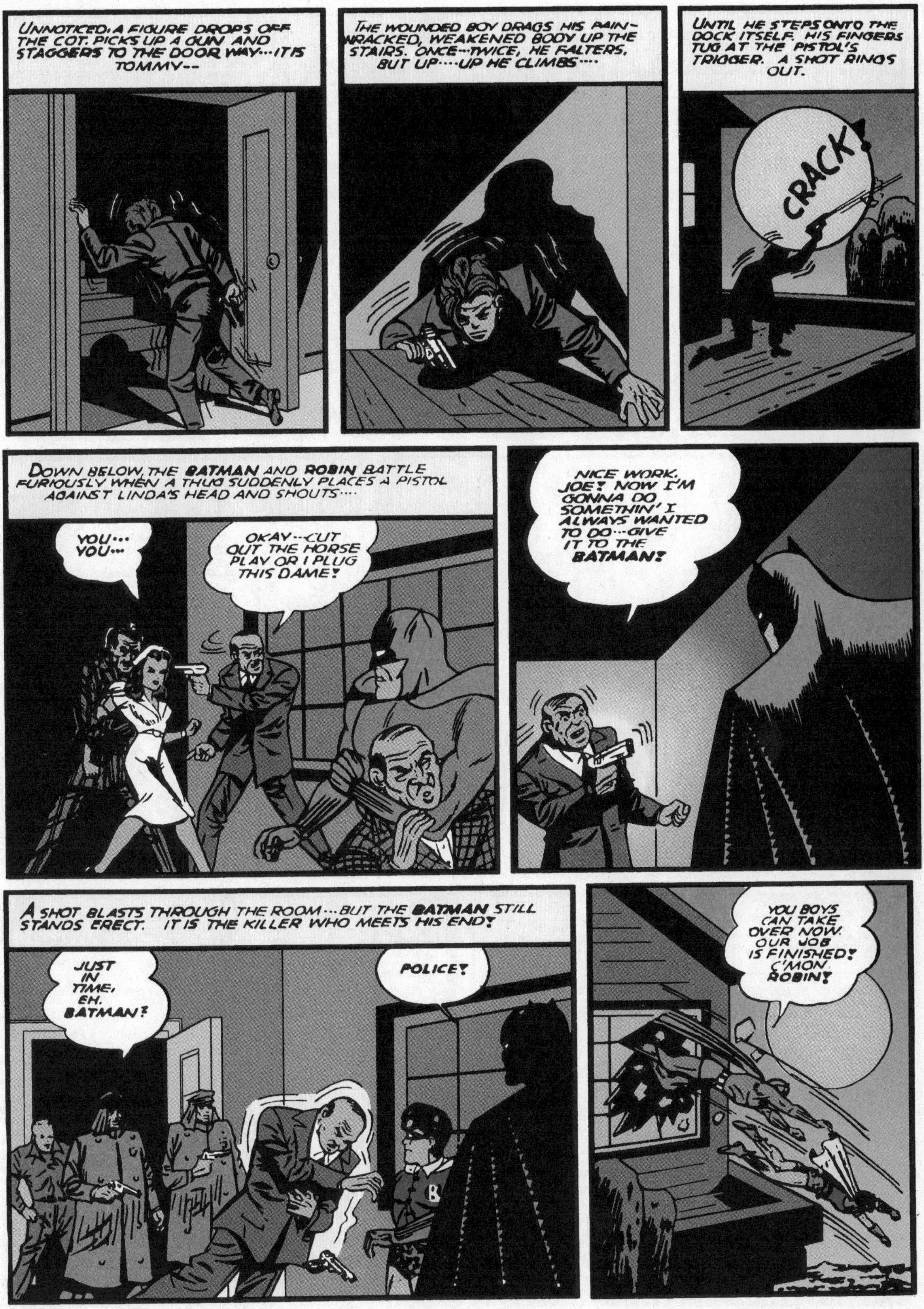
UNNOTICED, A FIGURE DROPS OFF THE COT, PICKS UP A GUN AND STAGGERS TO THE DOOR WAY…IT IS TOMMY--
THE WOUNDED BOY DRAGS HIS PAIN-WRACKED, WEAKENED BODY UP THE STAIRS. ONCE--TWICE, HE FALTERS, BUT UP….UP HE CLIMBS….
UNTIL HE STEPS ONTO THE DOCK ITSELF. HIS FINGERS TUG AT THE PISTOL'S TRIGGER. A SHOT RINGS OUT.
CRACK!
DOWN BELOW, THE BATMAN AND ROBIN BATTLE FURIOUSLY WHEN A THUG SUDDENLY PLACES A PISTOL AGAINST LINDA'S HEAD AND SHOUTS….
YOU… YOU…
OKAY--CUT OUT THE HORSE PLAY OR I PLUG THIS DAME!
NICE WORK, JOE! NOW I'M GONNA DO SOMETHIN' I ALWAYS WANTED TO DO--GIVE IT TO THE BATMAN!
A SHOT BLASTS THROUGH THE ROOM…BUT THE BATMAN STILL STANDS ERECT. IT IS THE KILLER WHO MEETS HIS END!
JUST IN TIME, EH, BATMAN?
POLICE!
YOU BOYS CAN TAKE OVER NOW. OUR JOB IS FINISHED! C'MON, ROBIN!

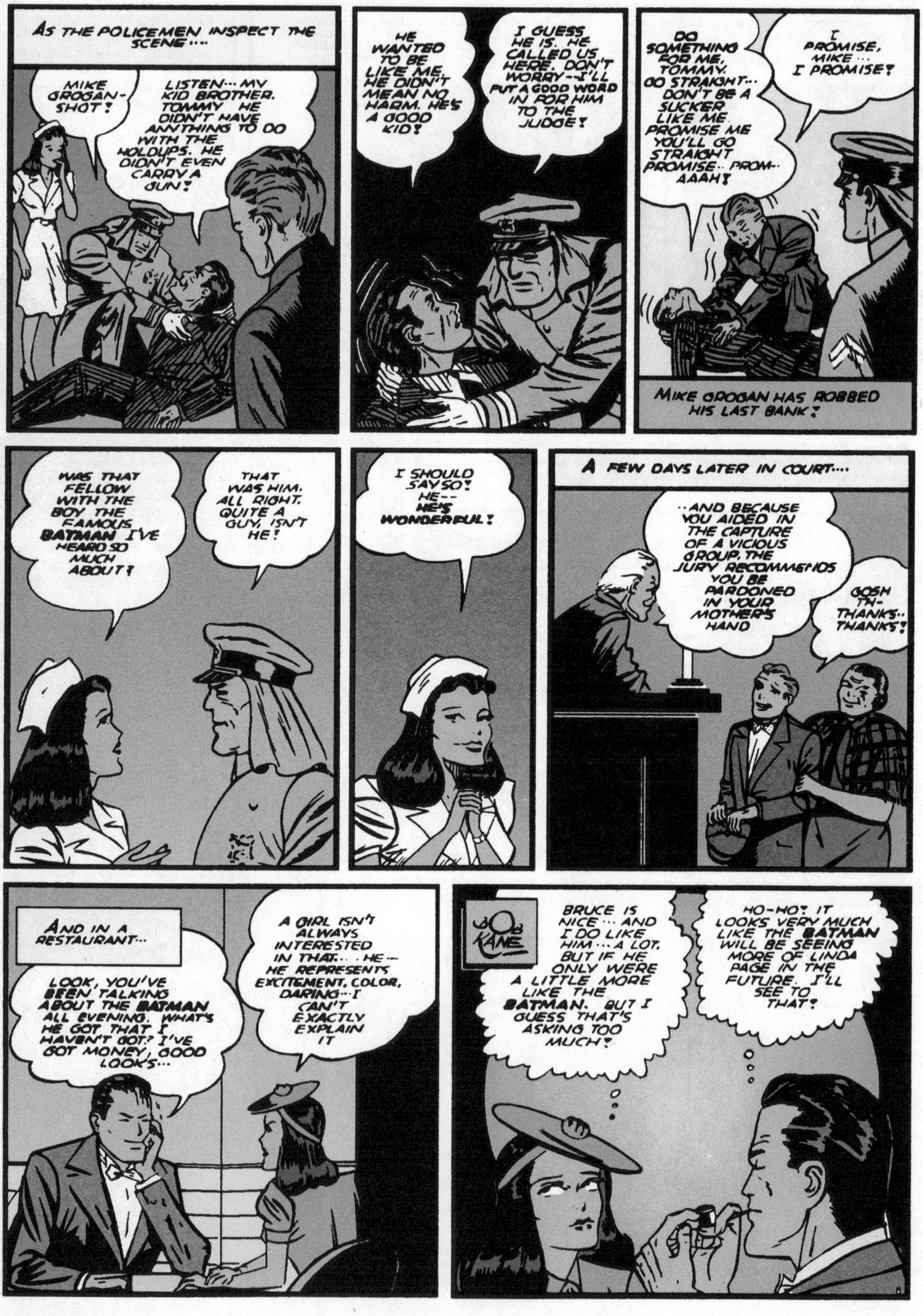
AS THE POLICEMEN INSPECT THE SCENE....
MIKE GROGAN-SHOT!
LISTEN... MY KID BROTHER. TOMMY HE DIDN'T HAVE ANTHING TO DO WITH THE HOLDUPS. HE DIDN'T EVEN CARRY A GUN!
HE WANTED TO BE LIKE ME. HE DIDN'T MEAN NO HARM. HE'S A GOOD KID!
I GUESS HE IS. HE CALLED US HERE. DON'T WORRY--I'LL PUT A GOOD WORD IN FOR HIM TO THE JUDGE!
DO SOMETHING FOR ME, TOMMY. GO STRAIGHT... DON'T BE A SUCKER LIKE ME. PROMISE ME YOU'LL GO STRAIGHT PROMISE.. PROM-- AAAH!
I PROMISE, MIKE... I PROMISE!
MIKE GROGAN HAS ROBBED HIS LAST BANK!
WAS THAT FELLOW WITH THE BOY THE FAMOUS BATMAN I'VE HEARD SO MUCH ABOUT?
THAT WAS HIM, ALL RIGHT. QUITE A GUY, ISN'T HE?
I SHOULD SAY SO! HE-- HE'S WONDERFUL!
A FEW DAYS LATER IN COURT....
..AND BECAUSE YOU AIDED IN THE CAPTURE OF A VICIOUS GROUP, THE JURY RECOMMENDS YOU BE PARDONED IN YOUR MOTHER'S HAND
GOSH TH- THANKS.. THANKS!
AND IN A RESTAURANT...
LOOK, YOU'VE BEEN TALKING ABOUT THE BATMAN ALL EVENING. WHAT'S HE GOT THAT I HAVEN'T GOT? I'VE GOT MONEY, GOOD LOOKS...
A GIRL ISN'T ALWAYS INTERESTED IN THAT... HE-- HE REPRESENTS EXCITEMENT, COLOR, DARING--I CAN'T EXACTLY EXPLAIN IT
BOB KANE
BRUCE IS NICE... AND I DO LIKE HIM... A LOT. BUT IF HE ONLY WERE A LITTLE MORE LIKE THE BATMAN. BUT I GUESS THAT'S ASKING TOO MUCH!
HO-HO! IT LOOKS VERY MUCH LIKE THE BATMAN WILL BE SEEING MORE OF LINDA PAGE IN THE FUTURE. I'LL SEE TO THAT!

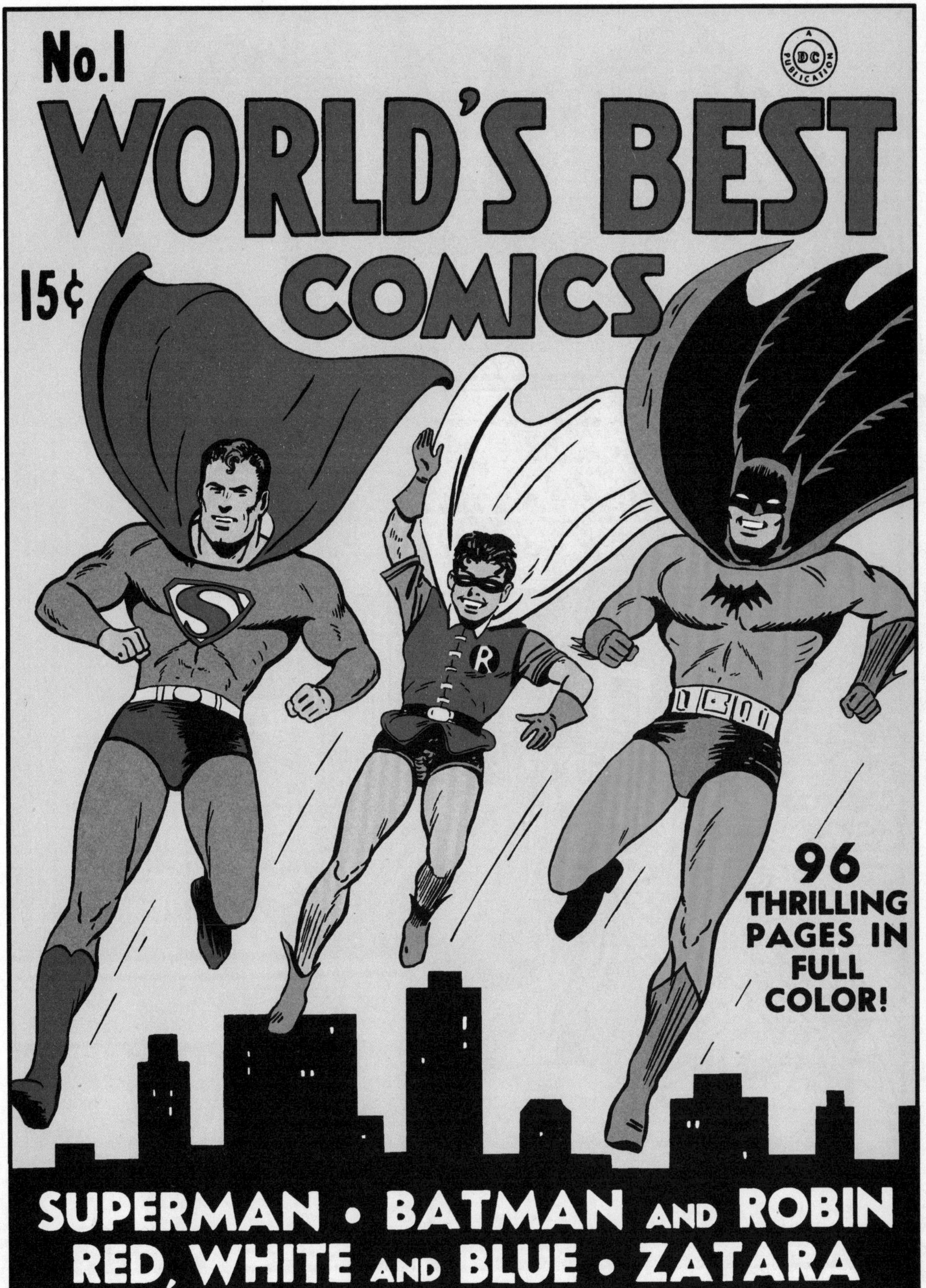

No.1
WORLD'S BEST
COMICS
15¢
A DC PUBLICATION
96 THRILLING PAGES IN FULL COLOR!
SUPERMAN • BATMAN AND ROBIN
RED, WHITE AND BLUE • ZATARA

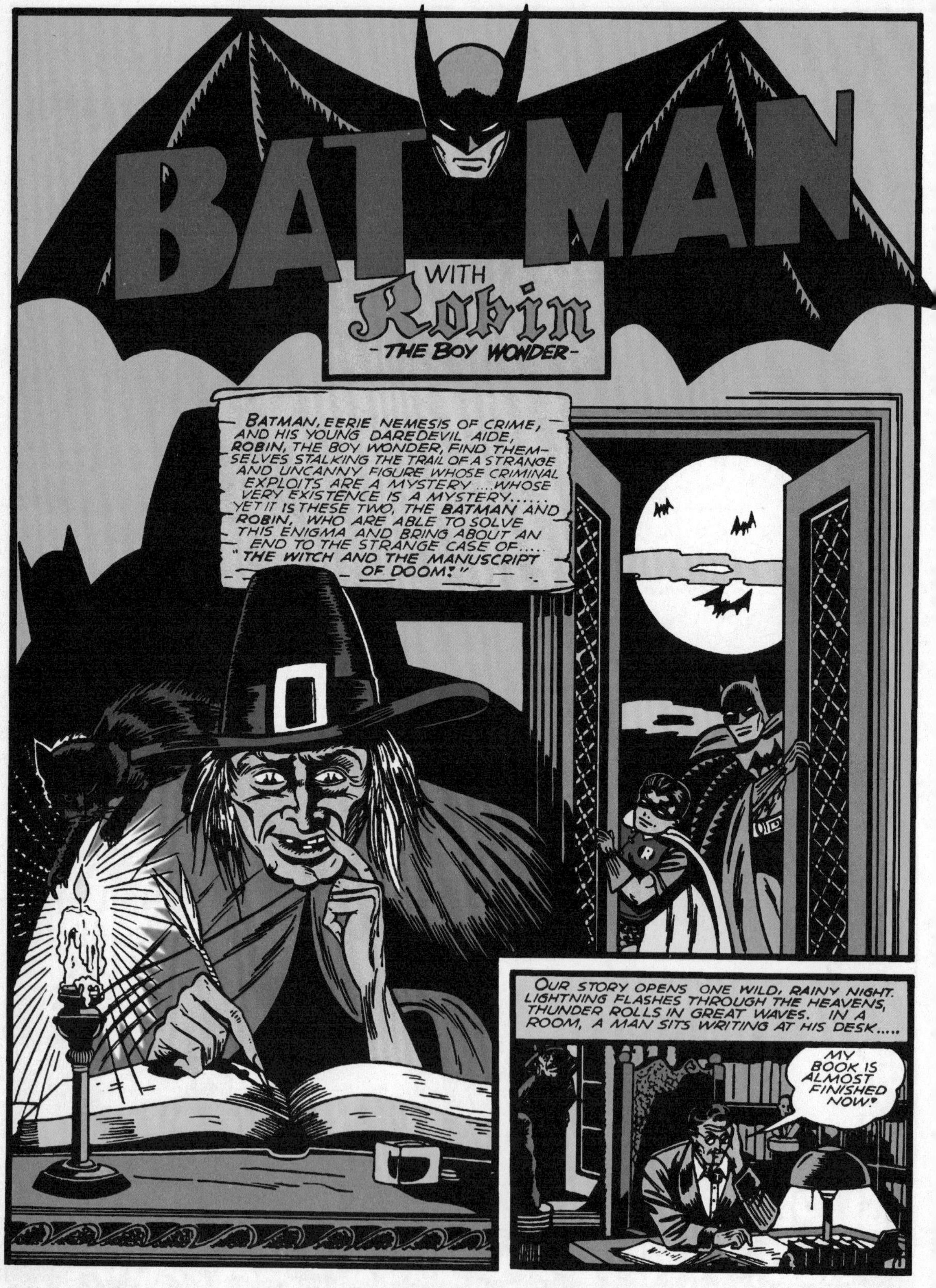
BATMAN
WITH
Robin
-THE BOY WONDER-
BATMAN, EERIE NEMESIS OF CRIME, AND HIS YOUNG DAREDEVIL AIDE, ROBIN, THE BOY WONDER, FIND THEMSELVES STALKING THE TRAIL OF A STRANGE AND UNCANNY FIGURE WHOSE CRIMINAL EXPLOITS ARE A MYSTERY ....WHOSE VERY EXISTENCE IS A MYSTERY...... YET IT IS THESE TWO, THE BATMAN AND ROBIN, WHO ARE ABLE TO SOLVE THIS ENIGMA AND BRING ABOUT AN END TO THE STRANGE CASE OF..... "THE WITCH AND THE MANUSCRIPT OF DOOM!"
OUR STORY OPENS ONE WILD, RAINY NIGHT. LIGHTNING FLASHES THROUGH THE HEAVENS, THUNDER ROLLS IN GREAT WAVES. IN A ROOM, A MAN SITS WRITING AT HIS DESK.....
MY BOOK IS ALMOST FINISHED NOW!

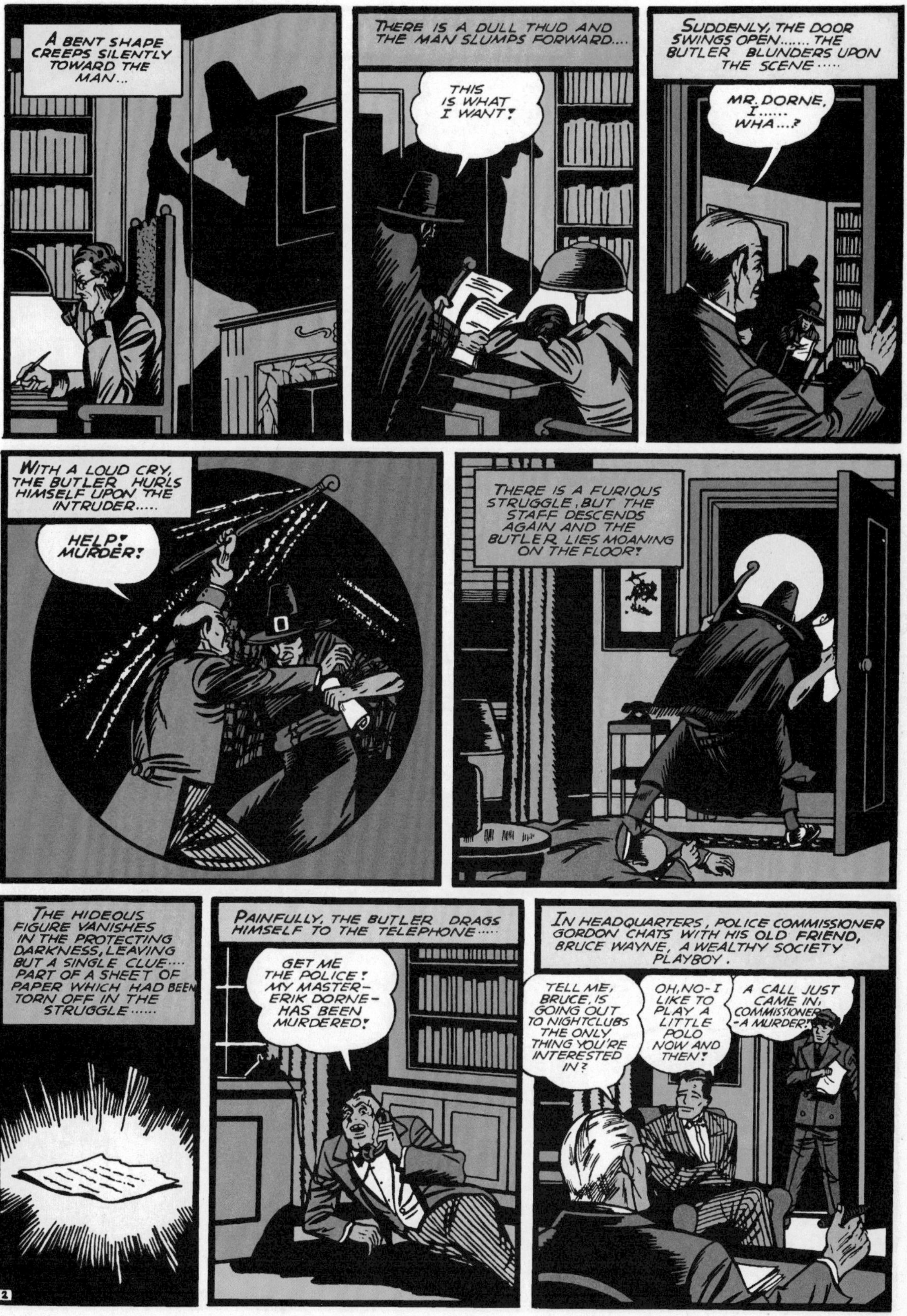
A BENT SHAPE CREEPS SILENTLY TOWARD THE MAN...
THERE IS A DULL THUD AND THE MAN SLUMPS FORWARD....
THIS IS WHAT I WANT!
SUDDENLY, THE DOOR SWINGS OPEN....... THE BUTLER BLUNDERS UPON THE SCENE.....
MR. DORNE, I...... WHA....?
WITH A LOUD CRY, THE BUTLER HURLS HIMSELF UPON THE INTRUDER.....
HELP! MURDER!
THERE IS A FURIOUS STRUGGLE, BUT THE STAFF DESCENDS AGAIN AND THE BUTLER LIES MOANING ON THE FLOOR!
THE HIDEOUS FIGURE VANISHES IN THE PROTECTING DARKNESS, LEAVING BUT A SINGLE CLUE.... PART OF A SHEET OF PAPER WHICH HAD BEEN TORN OFF IN THE STRUGGLE......
2
PAINFULLY, THE BUTLER DRAGS HIMSELF TO THE TELEPHONE.....
GET ME THE POLICE! MY MASTER- ERIK DORNE- HAS BEEN MURDERED!
IN HEADQUARTERS, POLICE COMMISSIONER GORDON CHATS WITH HIS OLD FRIEND, BRUCE WAYNE, A WEALTHY SOCIETY PLAYBOY.
TELL ME, BRUCE, IS GOING OUT TO NIGHTCLUBS THE ONLY THING YOU'RE INTERESTED IN?
OH, NO- I LIKE TO PLAY A LITTLE POLO NOW AND THEN!
A CALL JUST CAME IN, COMMISSIONER -A MURDER!

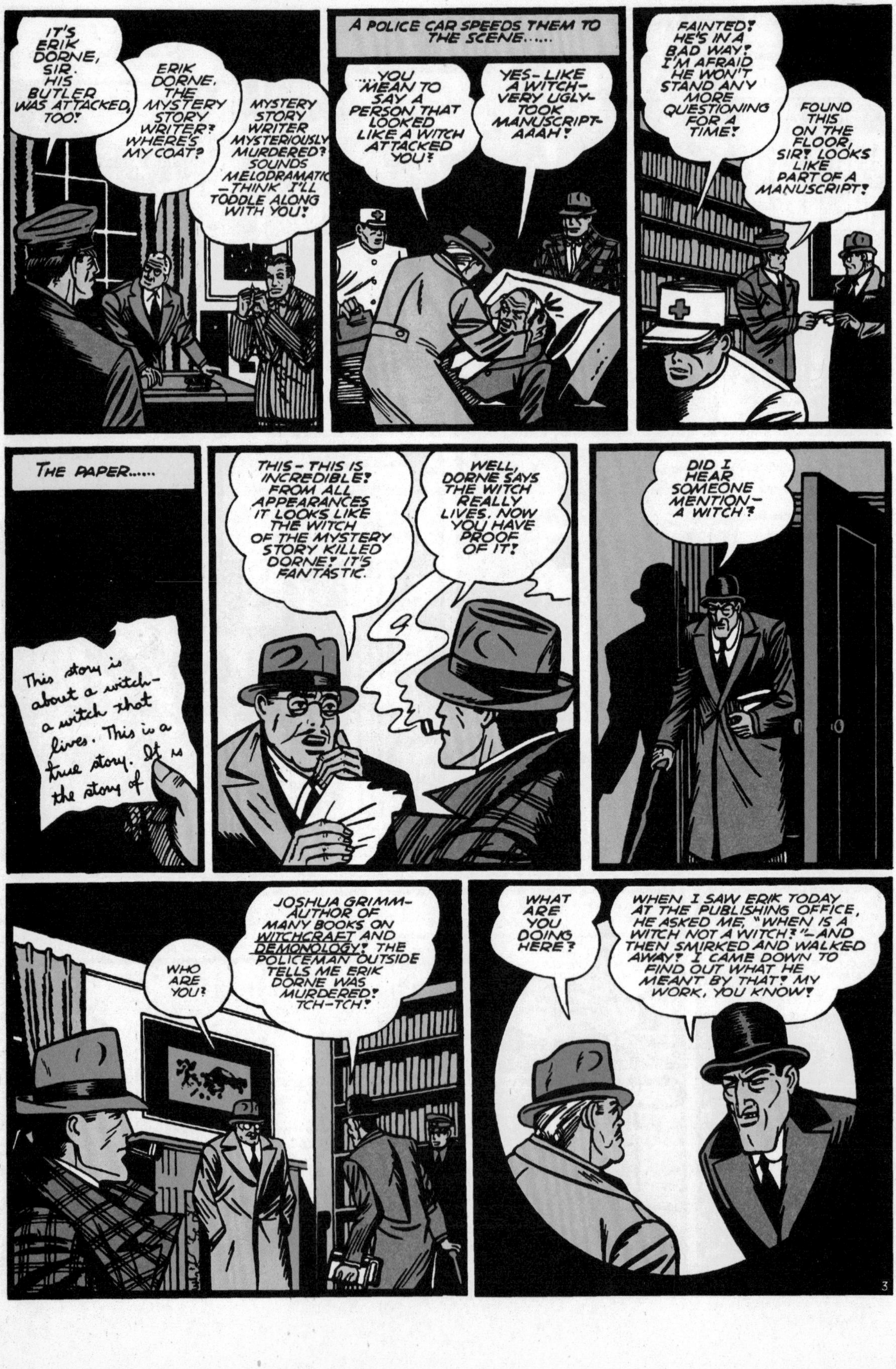
IT'S ERIK DORNE, SIR. HIS BUTLER WAS ATTACKED, TOO!
ERIK DORNE, THE MYSTERY STORY WRITER? WHERE'S MY COAT?
MYSTERY STORY WRITER MYSTERIOUSLY MURDERED? SOUNDS MELODRAMATIC—THINK I'LL TODDLE ALONG WITH YOU!
A POLICE CAR SPEEDS THEM TO THE SCENE......
....YOU MEAN TO SAY A PERSON THAT LOOKED LIKE A WITCH ATTACKED YOU?
YES—LIKE A WITCH—VERY UGLY—TOOK MANUSCRIPT—AAAH!
FAINTED! HE'S IN A BAD WAY! I'M AFRAID HE WON'T STAND ANY MORE QUESTIONING FOR A TIME!
FOUND THIS ON THE FLOOR, SIR! LOOKS LIKE PART OF A MANUSCRIPT!
THE PAPER......
This story is about a witch—a witch that lives. This is a true story. It is the story of
THIS—THIS IS INCREDIBLE! FROM ALL APPEARANCES IT LOOKS LIKE THE WITCH OF THE MYSTERY STORY KILLED DORNE! IT'S FANTASTIC.
WELL, DORNE SAYS THE WITCH REALLY LIVES. NOW YOU HAVE PROOF OF IT!
DID I HEAR SOMEONE MENTION—A WITCH?
WHO ARE YOU?
JOSHUA GRIMM—AUTHOR OF MANY BOOKS ON WITCHCRAFT AND DEMONOLOGY! THE POLICEMAN OUTSIDE TELLS ME ERIK DORNE WAS MURDERED! TCH—TCH!
WHAT ARE YOU DOING HERE?
WHEN I SAW ERIK TODAY AT THE PUBLISHING OFFICE, HE ASKED ME, "WHEN IS A WITCH NOT A WITCH?"—AND THEN SMIRKED AND WALKED AWAY! I CAME DOWN TO FIND OUT WHAT HE MEANT BY THAT! MY WORK, YOU KNOW!
3

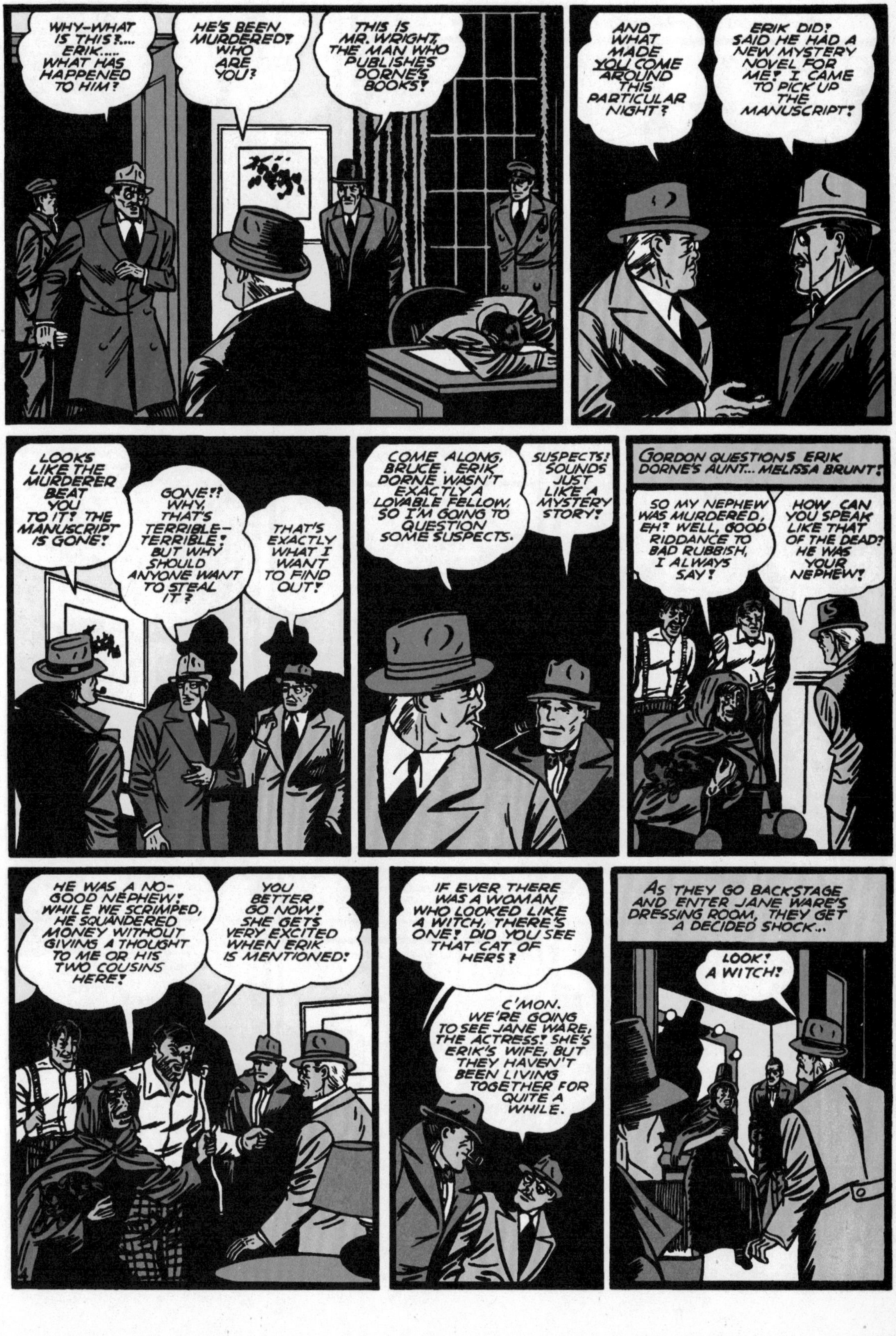

WHY-WHAT IS THIS?.... ERIK..... WHAT HAS HAPPENED TO HIM?
HE'S BEEN MURDERED! WHO ARE YOU?
THIS IS MR. WRIGHT, THE MAN WHO PUBLISHES DORNE'S BOOKS!
AND WHAT MADE YOU COME AROUND THIS PARTICULAR NIGHT?
ERIK DID! SAID HE HAD A NEW MYSTERY NOVEL FOR ME! I CAME TO PICK UP THE MANUSCRIPT!
LOOKS LIKE THE MURDERER BEAT YOU TO IT! THE MANUSCRIPT IS GONE!
GONE!? WHY, THAT'S TERRIBLE-TERRIBLE! BUT WHY SHOULD ANYONE WANT TO STEAL IT?
THAT'S EXACTLY WHAT I WANT TO FIND OUT!
COME ALONG, BRUCE. ERIK DORNE WASN'T EXACTLY A LOVABLE FELLOW, SO I'M GOING TO QUESTION SOME SUSPECTS.
SUSPECTS! SOUNDS JUST LIKE A MYSTERY STORY!
GORDON QUESTIONS ERIK DORNE'S AUNT... MELISSA BRUNT!
SO MY NEPHEW WAS MURDERED, EH? WELL, GOOD RIDDANCE TO BAD RUBBISH, I ALWAYS SAY!
HOW CAN YOU SPEAK LIKE THAT OF THE DEAD? HE WAS YOUR NEPHEW!
HE WAS A NO-GOOD NEPHEW! WHILE WE SCRIMPED, HE SQUANDERED MONEY WITHOUT GIVING A THOUGHT TO ME OR HIS TWO COUSINS HERE!
YOU BETTER GO NOW! SHE GETS VERY EXCITED WHEN ERIK IS MENTIONED!
IF EVER THERE WAS A WOMAN WHO LOOKED LIKE A WITCH, THERE'S ONE! DID YOU SEE THAT CAT OF HERS?
C'MON. WE'RE GOING TO SEE JANE WARE, THE ACTRESS! SHE'S ERIK'S WIFE, BUT THEY HAVEN'T BEEN LIVING TOGETHER FOR QUITE A WHILE.
AS THEY GO BACKSTAGE AND ENTER JANE WARE'S DRESSING ROOM, THEY GET A DECIDED SHOCK...
LOOK! A WITCH!

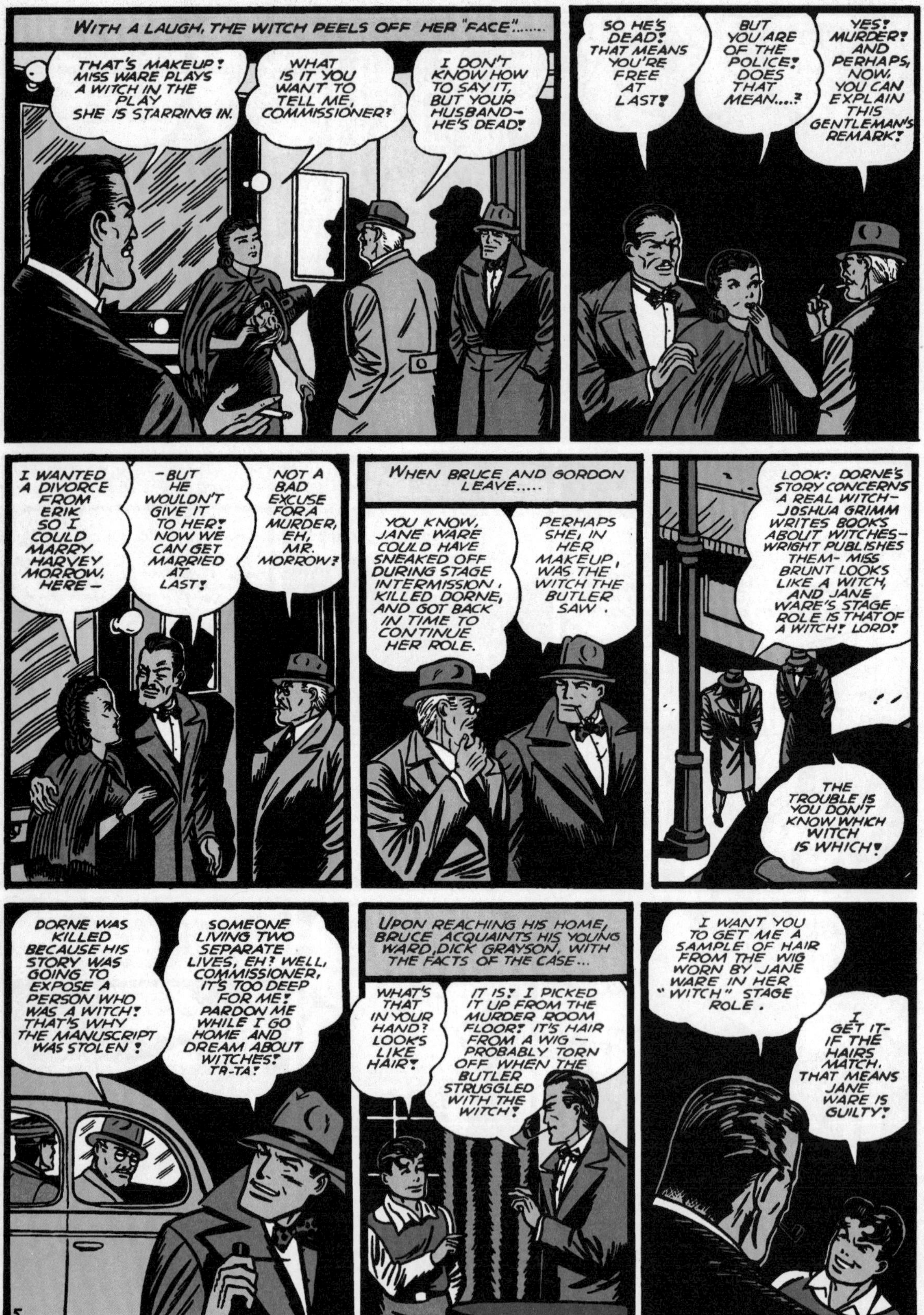

WITH A LAUGH, THE WITCH PEELS OFF HER "FACE"......
THAT'S MAKEUP! MISS WARE PLAYS A WITCH IN THE PLAY SHE IS STARRING IN.
WHAT IS IT YOU WANT TO TELL ME, COMMISSIONER?
I DON'T KNOW HOW TO SAY IT, BUT YOUR HUSBAND-- HE'S DEAD!
SO HE'S DEAD! THAT MEANS YOU'RE FREE AT LAST!
BUT YOU ARE OF THE POLICE! DOES THAT MEAN....?
YES! MURDER! AND PERHAPS, NOW, YOU CAN EXPLAIN THIS GENTLEMAN'S REMARK!
I WANTED A DIVORCE FROM ERIK SO I COULD MARRY HARVEY MORROW, HERE--
--BUT HE WOULDN'T GIVE IT TO HER! NOW WE CAN GET MARRIED AT LAST!
NOT A BAD EXCUSE FOR A MURDER, EH, MR. MORROW?
WHEN BRUCE AND GORDON LEAVE.....
YOU KNOW, JANE WARE COULD HAVE SNEAKED OFF DURING STAGE INTERMISSION, KILLED DORNE, AND GOT BACK IN TIME TO CONTINUE HER ROLE.
PERHAPS SHE, IN HER MAKEUP, WAS THE WITCH THE BUTLER SAW.
LOOK: DORNE'S STORY CONCERNS A REAL WITCH-- JOSHUA GRIMM WRITES BOOKS ABOUT WITCHES-- WRIGHT PUBLISHES THEM-- MISS BRUNT LOOKS LIKE A WITCH, AND JANE WARE'S STAGE ROLE IS THAT OF A WITCH! LORD!
THE TROUBLE IS YOU DON'T KNOW WHICH WITCH IS WHICH!
DORNE WAS KILLED BECAUSE HIS STORY WAS GOING TO EXPOSE A PERSON WHO WAS A WITCH! THAT'S WHY THE MANUSCRIPT WAS STOLEN!
SOMEONE LIVING TWO SEPARATE LIVES, EH? WELL, COMMISSIONER, IT'S TOO DEEP FOR ME! PARDON ME WHILE I GO HOME AND DREAM ABOUT WITCHES! TA-TA!
5
UPON REACHING HIS HOME, BRUCE ACQUAINTS HIS YOUNG WARD, DICK GRAYSON, WITH THE FACTS OF THE CASE...
WHAT'S THAT IN YOUR HAND? LOOKS LIKE HAIR!
IT IS! I PICKED IT UP FROM THE MURDER ROOM FLOOR! IT'S HAIR FROM A WIG -- PROBABLY TORN OFF WHEN THE BUTLER STRUGGLED WITH THE WITCH!
I WANT YOU TO GET ME A SAMPLE OF HAIR FROM THE WIG WORN BY JANE WARE IN HER "WITCH" STAGE ROLE.
I GET IT-- IF THE HAIRS MATCH, THAT MEANS JANE WARE IS GUILTY!

THE NEXT NIGHT, THE TWO DON CLOSE-FITTING COSTUMES, WHICH REVEAL BREATH-TAKING PHYSIQUES OF SYMMETRY....

IF MISS BRUNT KILLED DORNE, THEN SHE MUST HAVE HIDDEN THE MANUSCRIPT! I'M GOING TO LOOK IN HER HOME!

WHEN THE DYNAMIC DUO, THE BATMAN AND ROBIN, INVESTIGATE, EVEN PERFECT CRIMES CAN BE SOLVED!

MOMENTS LATER, A SLIM FIGURE DARTS PAST THE UNWARY STAGE-DOOR WATCHMAN....

THE BOY WONDER MOVES SWIFTLY UP THE STAIRS THAT LEAD TO THE DRESSING ROOMS....

THIS IS THE ROOM! NOW, FOR THAT WIG!

AS ROBIN PULLS HAIRS FROM THE WIG, THE DOOR SUDDENLY SWINGS OPEN....

THE FIRST ACT IS.... WHA...?

A SNEAK THIEF?

MOVING INCREDIBLY SWIFT, ROBIN BOUNDS ACROSS THE ROOM...

SORRY I HAVE TO DO THIS, MISTER!

MPH!

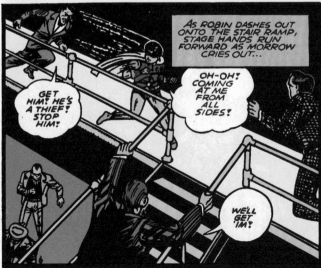

AS ROBIN DASHES OUT ONTO THE STAIR RAMP, STAGE HANDS RUN FORWARD AS MORROW CRIES OUT...

GET HIM! HE'S A THIEF! STOP HIM!

OH-OH! COMING AT ME FROM ALL SIDES!

WE'LL GET 'IM!

ROBIN DECIDES UPON A HEADLONG DIVE INTO SPACE.....

BETTER THIS WAY!

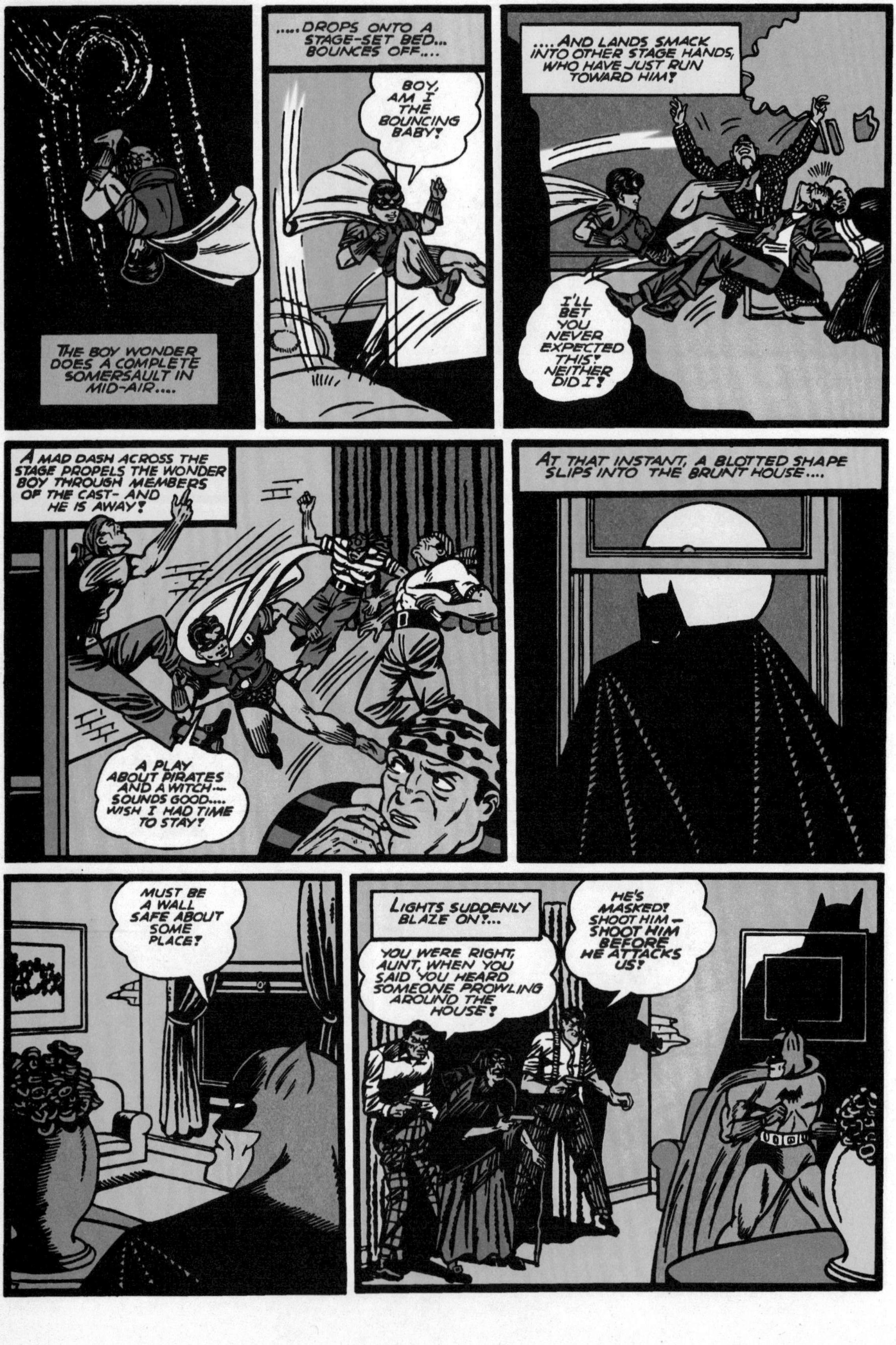
THE BOY WONDER DOES A COMPLETE SOMERSAULT IN MID-AIR....
....DROPS ONTO A STAGE-SET BED... BOUNCES OFF....
BOY, AM I THE BOUNCING BABY!
....AND LANDS SMACK INTO OTHER STAGE HANDS, WHO HAVE JUST RUN TOWARD HIM!
I'LL BET YOU NEVER EXPECTED THIS! NEITHER DID I!
A MAD DASH ACROSS THE STAGE PROPELS THE WONDER BOY THROUGH MEMBERS OF THE CAST- AND HE IS AWAY!
A PLAY ABOUT PIRATES AND A WITCH-- SOUNDS GOOD.... WISH I HAD TIME TO STAY!
AT THAT INSTANT, A BLOTTED SHAPE SLIPS INTO THE BRUNT HOUSE....
MUST BE A WALL SAFE ABOUT SOME PLACE!
LIGHTS SUDDENLY BLAZE ON!...
YOU WERE RIGHT, AUNT, WHEN YOU SAID YOU HEARD SOMEONE PROWLING AROUND THE HOUSE!
HE'S MASKED! SHOOT HIM — SHOOT HIM BEFORE HE ATTACKS US!

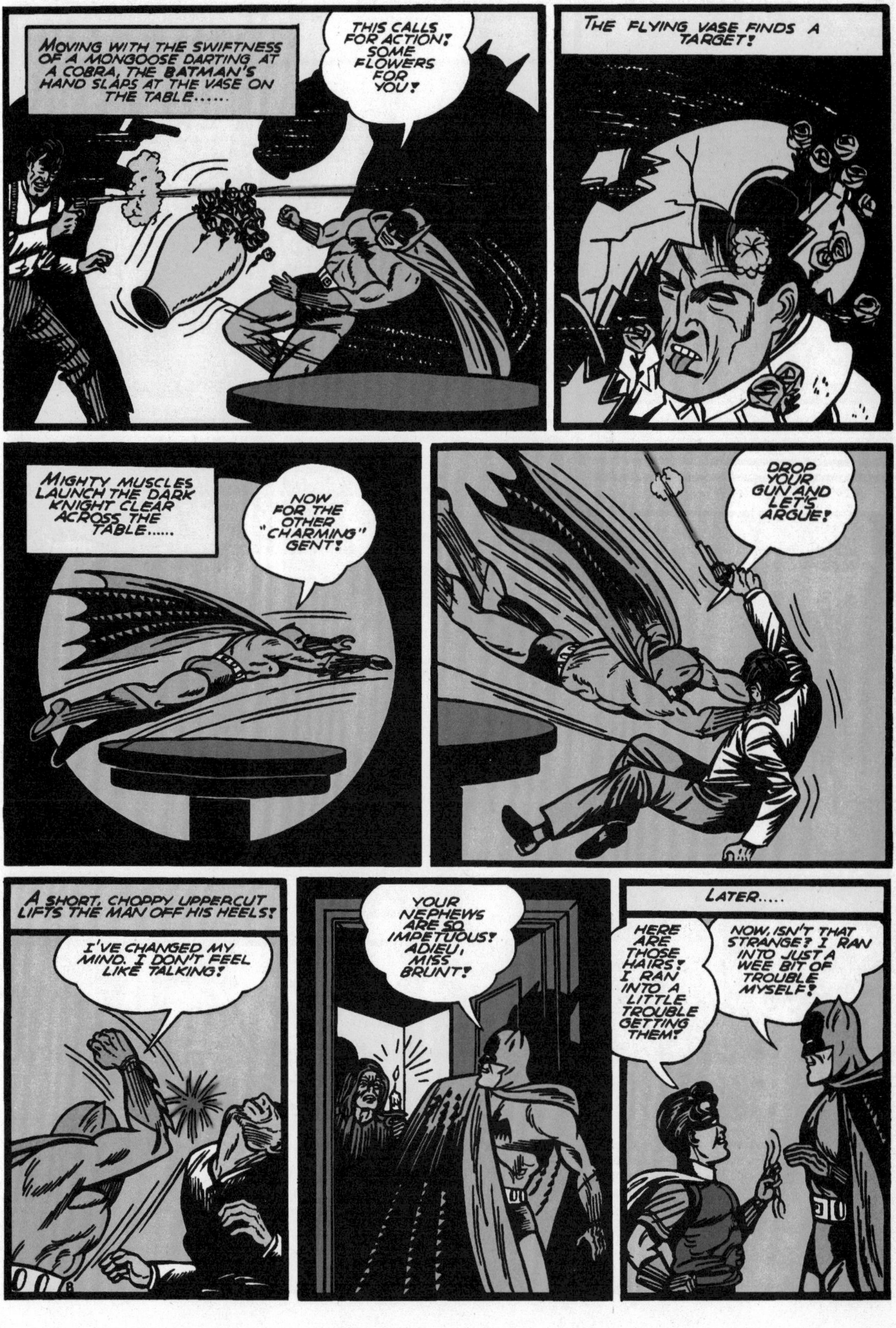
MOVING WITH THE SWIFTNESS OF A MONGOOSE DARTING AT A COBRA, THE BATMAN'S HAND SLAPS AT THE VASE ON THE TABLE......
THIS CALLS FOR ACTION! SOME FLOWERS FOR YOU!
THE FLYING VASE FINDS A TARGET!
MIGHTY MUSCLES LAUNCH THE DARK KNIGHT CLEAR ACROSS THE TABLE......
NOW FOR THE OTHER "CHARMING" GENT!
DROP YOUR GUN AND LET'S ARGUE!
A SHORT, CHOPPY UPPERCUT LIFTS THE MAN OFF HIS HEELS!
I'VE CHANGED MY MIND. I DON'T FEEL LIKE TALKING!
YOUR NEPHEWS ARE SO IMPETUOUS! ADIEU, MISS BRUNT!
LATER.....
HERE ARE THOSE HAIRS! I RAN INTO A LITTLE TROUBLE GETTING THEM!
NOW, ISN'T THAT STRANGE? I RAN INTO JUST A WEE BIT OF TROUBLE MYSELF!

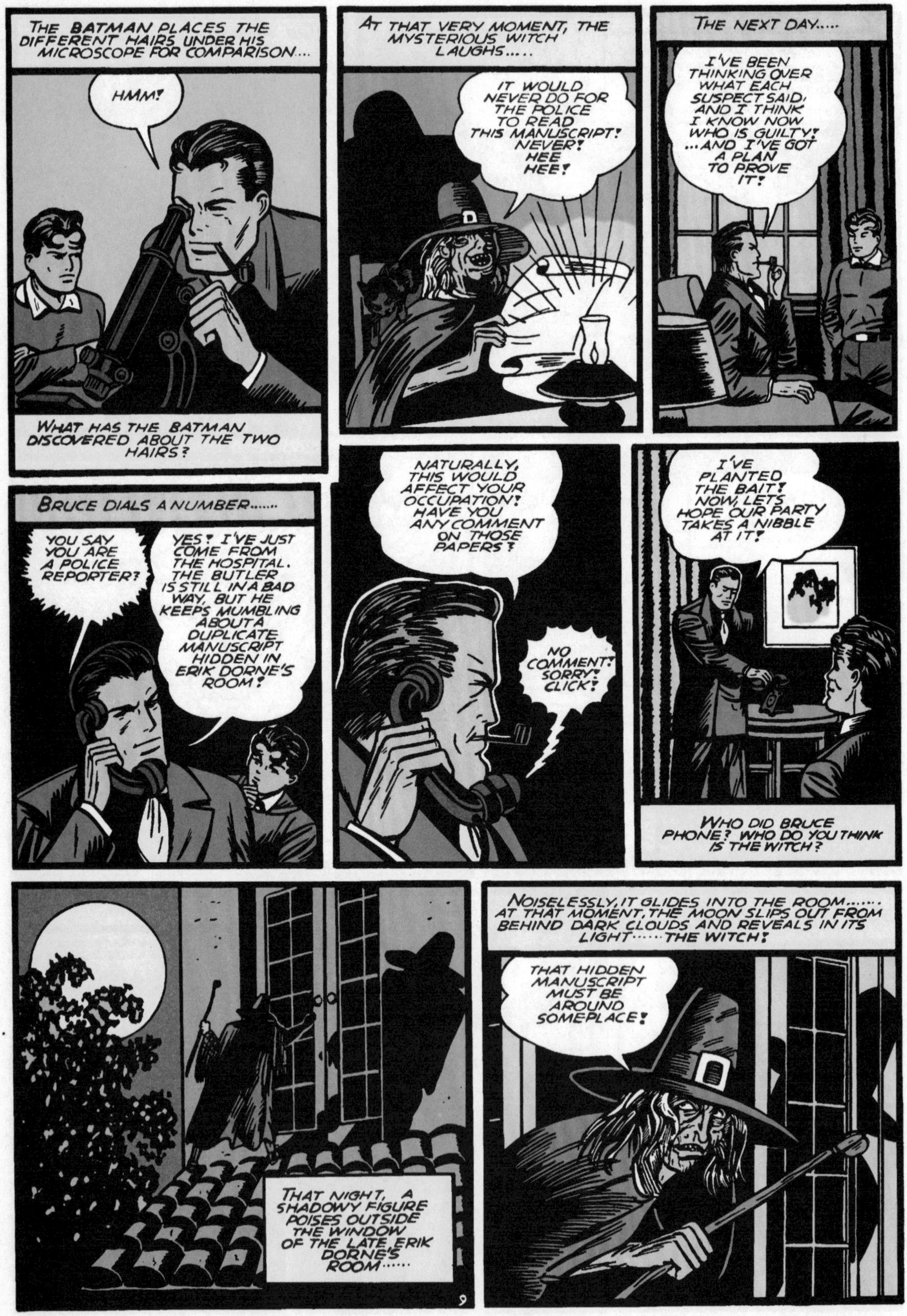
THE BATMAN PLACES THE DIFFERENT HAIRS UNDER HIS MICROSCOPE FOR COMPARISON...
HMM!
WHAT HAS THE BATMAN DISCOVERED ABOUT THE TWO HAIRS?
AT THAT VERY MOMENT, THE MYSTERIOUS WITCH LAUGHS.....
IT WOULD NEVER DO FOR THE POLICE TO READ THIS MANUSCRIPT! NEVER! HEE HEE!
THE NEXT DAY.....
I'VE BEEN THINKING OVER WHAT EACH SUSPECT SAID, AND I THINK I KNOW NOW WHO IS GUILTY! ...AND I'VE GOT A PLAN TO PROVE IT!
BRUCE DIALS A NUMBER......
YOU SAY YOU ARE A POLICE REPORTER?
YES! I'VE JUST COME FROM THE HOSPITAL. THE BUTLER IS STILL IN A BAD WAY, BUT HE KEEPS MUMBLING ABOUT A DUPLICATE MANUSCRIPT HIDDEN IN ERIK DORNE'S ROOM!
NATURALLY, THIS WOULD AFFECT YOUR OCCUPATION! HAVE YOU ANY COMMENT ON THOSE PAPERS?
NO COMMENT! SORRY! CLICK!
I'VE PLANTED THE BAIT! NOW, LETS HOPE OUR PARTY TAKES A NIBBLE AT IT!
WHO DID BRUCE PHONE? WHO DO YOU THINK IS THE WITCH?
THAT NIGHT, A SHADOWY FIGURE POISES OUTSIDE THE WINDOW OF THE LATE ERIK DORNE'S ROOM......
9
NOISELESSLY, IT GLIDES INTO THE ROOM....... AT THAT MOMENT, THE MOON SLIPS OUT FROM BEHIND DARK CLOUDS AND REVEALS IN ITS LIGHT...... THE WITCH!
THAT HIDDEN MANUSCRIPT MUST BE AROUND SOMEPLACE!

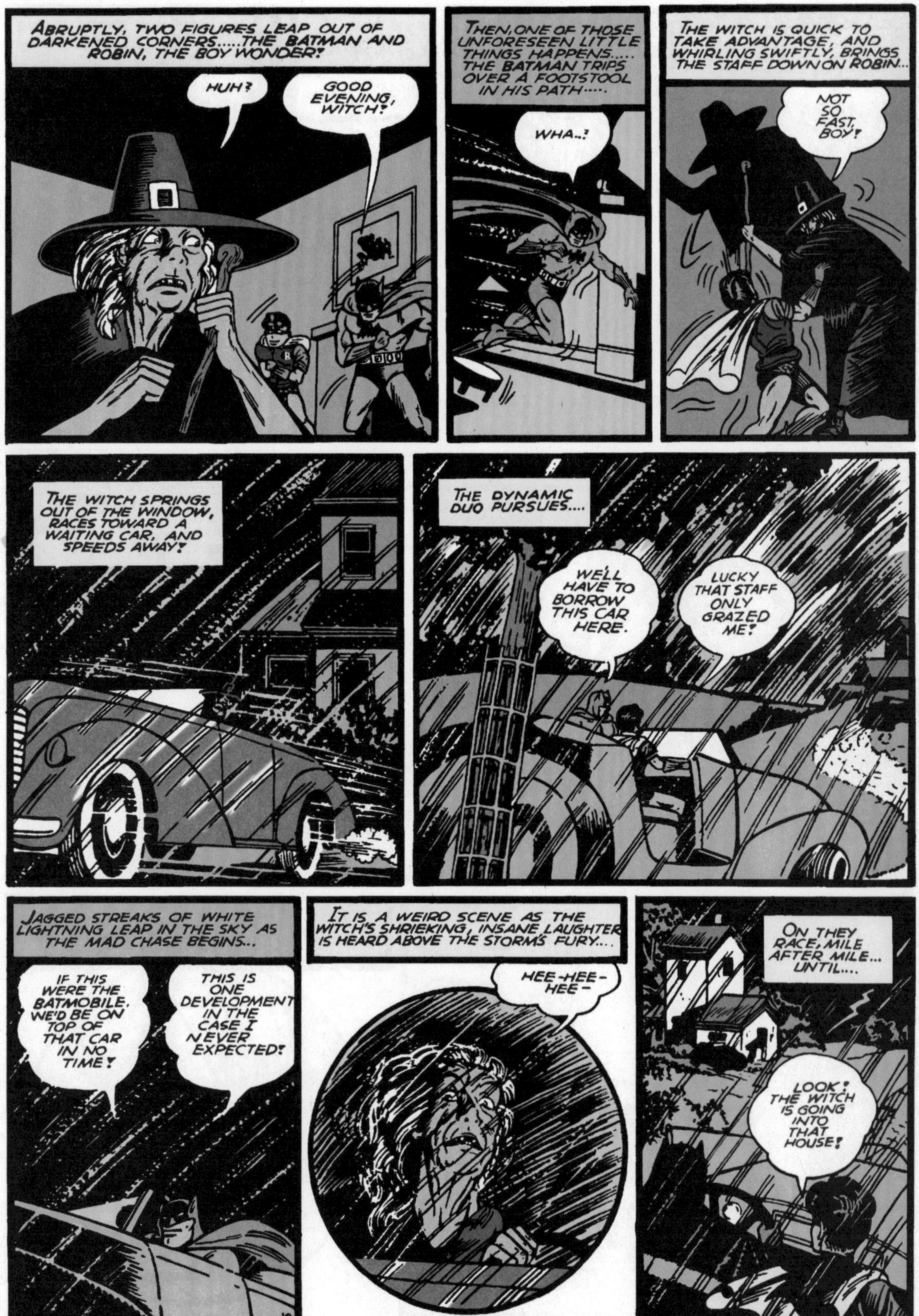
ABRUPTLY, TWO FIGURES LEAP OUT OF DARKENED CORNERS.....THE BATMAN AND ROBIN, THE BOY WONDER!
HUH?
GOOD EVENING, WITCH!
THEN, ONE OF THOSE UNFORESEEN LITTLE THINGS HAPPENS..... THE BATMAN TRIPS OVER A FOOTSTOOL IN HIS PATH.....
WHA..!
THE WITCH IS QUICK TO TAKE ADVANTAGE, AND WHIRLING SWIFTLY, BRINGS THE STAFF DOWN ON ROBIN...
NOT SO FAST, BOY!
THE WITCH SPRINGS OUT OF THE WINDOW, RACES TOWARD A WAITING CAR, AND SPEEDS AWAY!
THE DYNAMIC DUO PURSUES....
WE'LL HAVE TO BORROW THIS CAR HERE.
LUCKY THAT STAFF ONLY GRAZED ME!
JAGGED STREAKS OF WHITE LIGHTNING LEAP IN THE SKY AS THE MAD CHASE BEGINS...
IF THIS WERE THE BATMOBILE, WE'D BE ON TOP OF THAT CAR IN NO TIME!
THIS IS ONE DEVELOPMENT IN THE CASE I NEVER EXPECTED!
10
IT IS A WEIRD SCENE AS THE WITCH'S SHRIEKING, INSANE LAUGHTER IS HEARD ABOVE THE STORM'S FURY...
HEE-HEE-HEE-
ON THEY RACE, MILE AFTER MILE... UNTIL....
LOOK! THE WITCH IS GOING INTO THAT HOUSE!

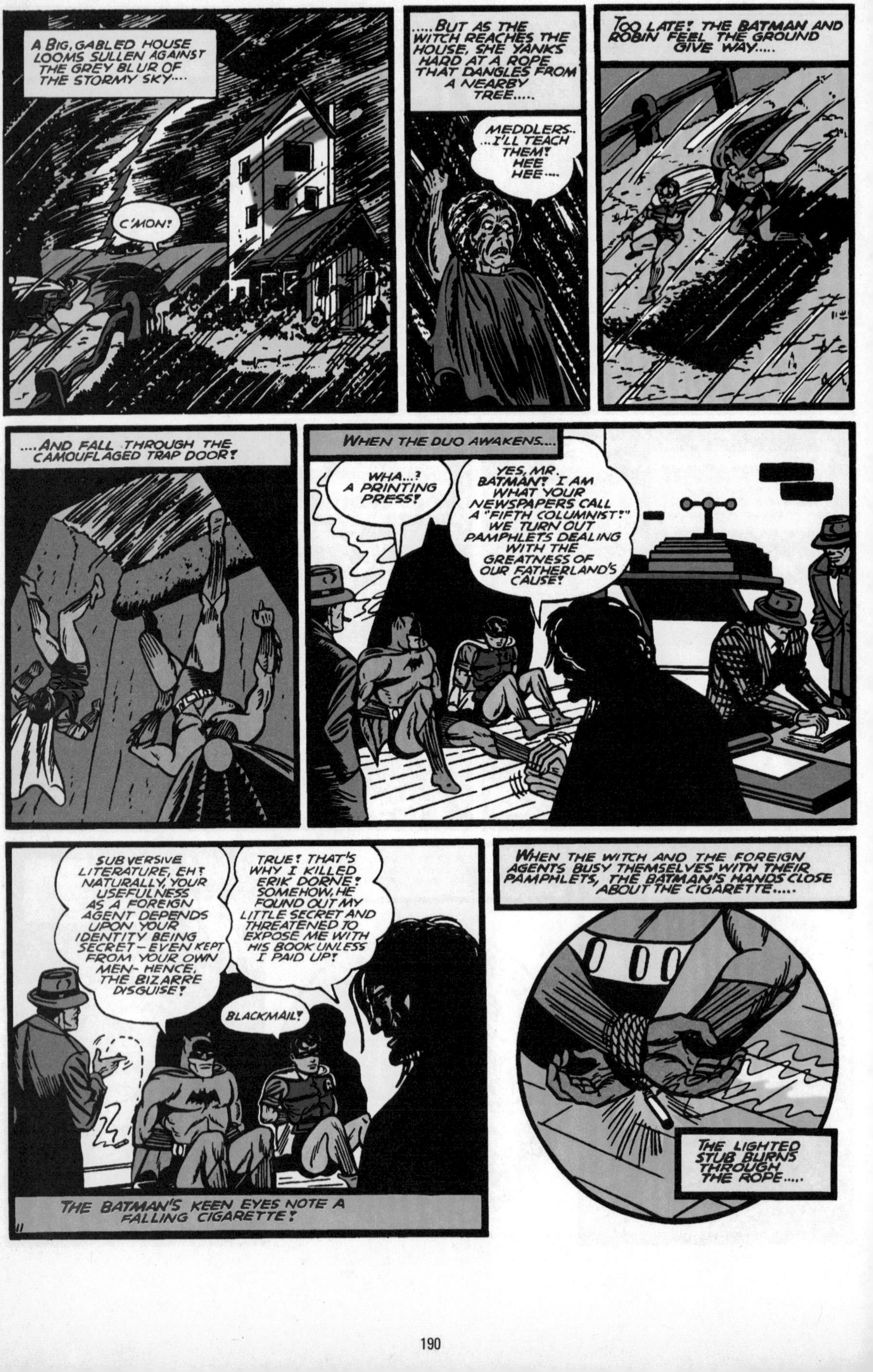
A BIG, GABLED HOUSE LOOMS SULLEN AGAINST THE GREY BLUR OF THE STORMY SKY....
C'MON!
.....BUT AS THE WITCH REACHES THE HOUSE, SHE YANKS HARD AT A ROPE THAT DANGLES FROM A NEARBY TREE.....
MEDDLERS.. ...I'LL TEACH THEM! HEE HEE....
TOO LATE! THE BATMAN AND ROBIN FEEL THE GROUND GIVE WAY.....
....AND FALL THROUGH THE CAMOUFLAGED TRAP DOOR!
WHEN THE DUO AWAKENS....
WHA...? A PRINTING PRESS!
YES, MR. BATMAN! I AM WHAT YOUR NEWSPAPERS CALL A "FIFTH COLUMNIST!" WE TURN OUT PAMPHLETS DEALING WITH THE GREATNESS OF OUR FATHERLAND'S CAUSE!
SUBVERSIVE LITERATURE, EH? NATURALLY, YOUR USEFULNESS AS A FOREIGN AGENT DEPENDS UPON YOUR IDENTITY BEING SECRET – EVEN KEPT FROM YOUR OWN MEN- HENCE, THE BIZARRE DISGUISE!
TRUE! THAT'S WHY I KILLED ERIK DORNE! SOMEHOW, HE FOUND OUT MY LITTLE SECRET AND THREATENED TO EXPOSE ME WITH HIS BOOK UNLESS I PAID UP!
BLACKMAIL!
THE BATMAN'S KEEN EYES NOTE A FALLING CIGARETTE!
WHEN THE WITCH AND THE FOREIGN AGENTS BUSY THEMSELVES WITH THEIR PAMPHLETS, THE BATMAN'S HANDS CLOSE ABOUT THE CIGARETTE.....
THE LIGHTED STUB BURNS THROUGH THE ROPE.....

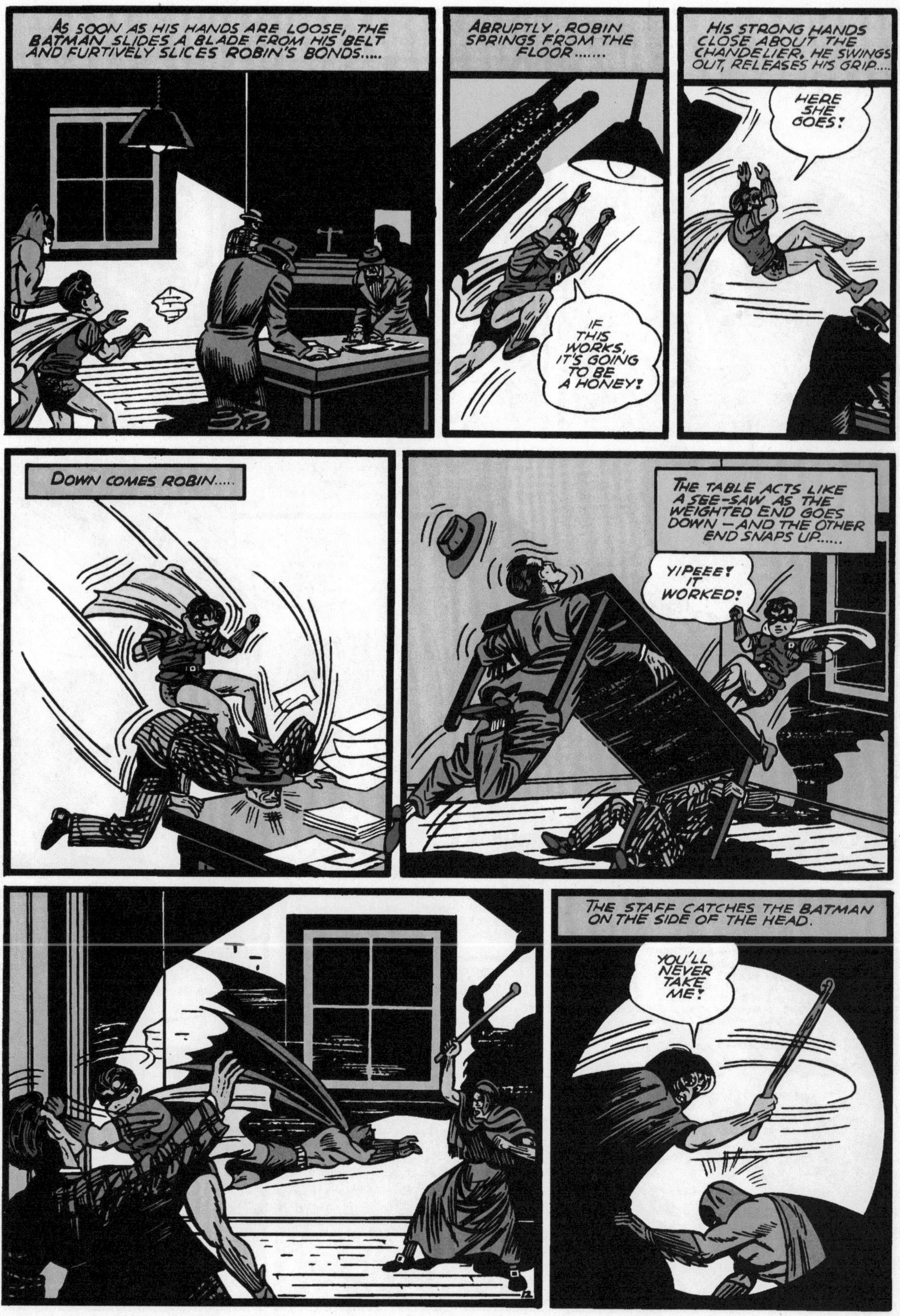
AS SOON AS HIS HANDS ARE LOOSE, THE BATMAN SLIDES A BLADE FROM HIS BELT AND FURTIVELY SLICES ROBIN'S BONDS.....
ABRUPTLY, ROBIN SPRINGS FROM THE FLOOR.......
IF THIS WORKS, IT'S GOING TO BE A HONEY!
HIS STRONG HANDS CLOSE ABOUT THE CHANDELIER. HE SWINGS OUT, RELEASES HIS GRIP.....
HERE SHE GOES!
DOWN COMES ROBIN.....
THE TABLE ACTS LIKE A SEE-SAW AS THE WEIGHTED END GOES DOWN — AND THE OTHER END SNAPS UP......
YIPEEE! IT WORKED!
THE STAFF CATCHES THE BATMAN ON THE SIDE OF THE HEAD.
YOU'LL NEVER TAKE ME!

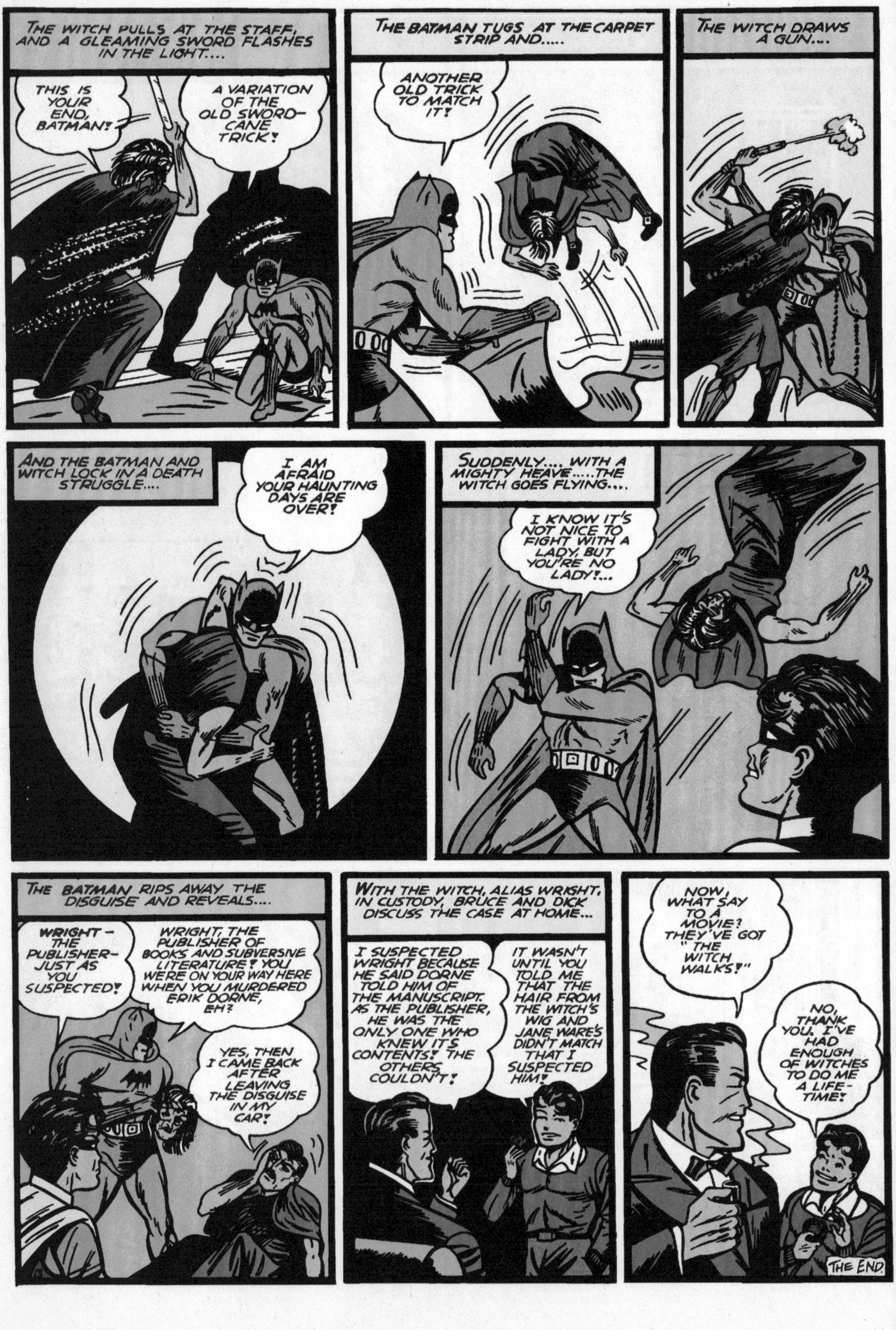
THE WITCH PULLS AT THE STAFF, AND A GLEAMING SWORD FLASHES IN THE LIGHT....
THIS IS YOUR END, BATMAN!
A VARIATION OF THE OLD SWORD-CANE TRICK!
THE BATMAN TUGS AT THE CARPET STRIP AND.....
ANOTHER OLD TRICK TO MATCH IT!
THE WITCH DRAWS A GUN....
AND THE BATMAN AND WITCH LOCK IN A DEATH STRUGGLE....
I AM AFRAID YOUR HAUNTING DAYS ARE OVER!
SUDDENLY.... WITH A MIGHTY HEAVE.....THE WITCH GOES FLYING....
I KNOW IT'S NOT NICE TO FIGHT WITH A LADY, BUT YOU'RE NO LADY!...
THE BATMAN RIPS AWAY THE DISGUISE AND REVEALS....
WRIGHT - THE PUBLISHER - JUST AS YOU SUSPECTED!
WRIGHT, THE PUBLISHER OF BOOKS AND SUBVERSIVE LITERATURE! YOU WERE ON YOUR WAY HERE WHEN YOU MURDERED ERIK DORNE, EH?
YES, THEN I CAME BACK AFTER LEAVING THE DISGUISE IN MY CAR!
WITH THE WITCH, ALIAS WRIGHT, IN CUSTODY, BRUCE AND DICK DISCUSS THE CASE AT HOME...
I SUSPECTED WRIGHT BECAUSE HE SAID DORNE TOLD HIM OF THE MANUSCRIPT. AS THE PUBLISHER, HE WAS THE ONLY ONE WHO KNEW ITS CONTENTS! THE OTHERS COULDN'T!
IT WASN'T UNTIL YOU TOLD ME THAT THE HAIR FROM THE WITCH'S WIG AND JANE WARE'S DIDN'T MATCH THAT I SUSPECTED HIM!
NOW, WHAT SAY TO A MOVIE? THEY'VE GOT "THE WITCH WALKS!"
NO, THANK YOU. I'VE HAD ENOUGH OF WITCHES TO DO ME A LIFE-TIME!
THE END.